ANNUAL EDITIONS

Business Ethics 13/14

Twenty-Fifth Edition

EDITOR

William J. Kehoe
University of Virginia

Dr. William J. Kehoe is the William F. O'Dell Professor of Commerce in the McIntire School of Commerce at the University of Virginia. His research interests are in global business ethics, ethics in business, ethics in banking, and global economic integration. He has published numerous articles in academic and professional journals and in conference proceedings of national and regional professional associations. He is a member of numerous learned societies including the Society for Business Ethics. He is a Fellow of the American Society of Business and Behavioral Sciences, a Fellow of the Society for Marketing Advances, and was an American Marketing Association Doctoral Consortium Fellow. He is a member of Beta Gamma Sigma and served on the Beta Gamma Sigma Board of Governors as Secretary/Treasurer. He served also on the Board of Governors of Sigma Beta Delta. He has held visiting faculty appointments at the Kellogg Graduate School of Management, Northwestern University, and at the Netherlands School of Business, Nijenrode University. He has held positions with Phillips Petroleum Company, Centrex Corporation, and Mercantile Stores, as well as appointments with several consulting firms. He served in the United States Marine Corps.

Connect
Learn
Succeed™

ANNUAL EDITIONS: BUSINESS ETHICS, TWENTY-FIFTH EDITION

Published by McGraw-Hill, a business unit of The McGraw-Hill Companies, Inc., 1221 Avenue
of the Americas, New York, NY 10020. Copyright © 2014 by The McGraw-Hill Companies, Inc.
All rights reserved. Previous edition(s) 2013, 2012, 2011, 2009, 2008, 2005. Printed in the United
States of America. No part of this publication may be reproduced or distributed in any form or by
any means, or stored in a database or retrieval system, without the prior written consent of The
McGraw-Hill Companies, Inc., including, but not limited to, in any network or other electronic
storage or transmission, or broadcast for distance learning.

Some ancillaries, including electronic and print components, may not be available to customers
outside the United States.

This book is printed on acid-free paper.

Annual Editions® is a registered trademark of the McGraw-Hill Companies, Inc.
Annual Editions is published by the **Contemporary Learning Series** group within the
McGraw-Hill Higher Education division.

1 2 3 4 5 6 7 8 9 0 QDB/QDB 1 0 9 8 7 6 5 4 3

ISBN 978-0-07-352879-3
MHID 0-07-352879-X
ISSN 1055-5455 (print)
ISSN 2159-1016 (online)

Acquisitions Editor: *Joan L. McNamara*
Marketing Director: *Adam Kloza*
Marketing Manager: *Nathan Edwards*
Developmental Editor: *Dave Welsh*
Senior Project Manager: *Joyce Watters*
Buyer: *Nichole Birkenholz*
Cover Designer: *Studio Montage, St. Louis, MO.*
Content Licensing Specialist: *DeAnna Dausener*
Media Project Manager: *Sridevi Palani*

Compositor: Laserwords Private Limited
Cover Image Credits: E. Audras/PhotoAlto (inset); C. Zachriasen/PhotoAlto (background)

Editors/Academic Advisory Board

Members of the Academic Advisory Board are instrumental in the final selection of articles for each edition of ANNUAL EDITIONS. Their review of articles for content, level, and appropriateness provides critical direction to the editors and staff. We think that you will find their careful consideration well reflected in this volume.

ANNUAL EDITIONS: Business Ethics 13/14
25th Edition

EDITOR

William J. Kehoe
University of Virginia

ACADEMIC ADVISORY BOARD MEMBERS

Editors/Academic Advisory Board continued

Preface

In publishing ANNUAL EDITIONS we acknowledge and appreciate the important role played by the magazines, newspapers, Internet resources, and journals of the public press in providing current, first-rate educational information across a broad spectrum of interest areas. Many of the articles selected for inclusion in Annual Editions are appropriate and of significant value for students, researchers, policy makers, managers, and professionals seeking accurate, current material to help bridge the gap between principles and theories and the real world. These articles, however, become more useful for study when those of lasting value are carefully collected, organized, indexed, and reproduced in a low-cost format, which provides easy and permanent access when the material is needed. That is the role played by ANNUAL EDITIONS

We are very pleased to present the 25th edition of Annual Editions: Business Ethics. Over the years since its first edition, Annual Editions: Business Ethics has facilitated, for students and managers in classrooms and business firms across the country, the discussion and critical examination of concepts, issues, processes, and theories of business ethics. Now, with its 25th edition, Annual Editions: Business Ethics pledges to continue to bring cutting-edge insights about business ethics through presentation of insightful academic and practitioner articles.

At times it seems like the ethical issues of our era are all around us, does it not? Whether in banking, consulting, education, government, investing, manufacturing, or service sectors, ethical issues are present. Whether it is knowingly marketing unsafe products, failure to disclose immediately an unsafe issue with a product, defective pricing, price fixing, false or misleading advertising, invading privacy, failing to safeguard consumer information, cheating, employment discrimination, insider trading, rogue trading, money laundering, questionable contracting practices, offshoring and/or outsourcing jobs with little regard for the impact on domestic employees, or business executives refusing to testify before Congressional committees about alleged unethical practices, these are but a few examples of events and practices, and frankly of unabashed business arrogance that tarnishes the image of business both in this country as well as in host-country markets around the world.

As corporations struggle to find ethical identity in a business environment that grows increasingly competitive, complex, fast, and global, managers confront poignant questions that have definite ethical ramifications. In such a business environment, here are but a few of the questions confronting managers, policy makers, and students alike: Does a company have any obligation to help solve social problems such as discrimination, poverty, pollution, and urban decay? What are a company's ethical responsibilities for sustainable business practices? What ethical responsibilities should a multinational corporation assume in foreign host-country markets around the world? What obligation does a manufacturer have to consumers with respect to product defects and safety? What are a firm's obligations as its industry is deregulated? As outside regulations are reduced, does a firm have greater responsibility to develop ethical policies to protect its public against abuse of those things that now are deregulated? What are a firm's ethical and legal responsibilities for safeguarding consumer information? If a consumer's information is compromised or stolen, does a firm have ethical obligations to make such a consumer whole if losses are experienced due to identity theft? These are just a few of the issues that make the study of business ethics both challenging, important, and arguably an imperative. It is not an imperative to be attended to if time permits; rather it must be an imperative at the top of everyone's agenda—students and managers alike.

The articles selected for inclusion in *Annual Editions: Business Ethics 13/14* were chosen carefully from a variety of public press and Internet sources to furnish current information on business ethics. This volume contains a number of features designed to make it useful for students, researchers, and professionals. These features include a *table of contents* with summaries of each article and key concepts in bold italics, a *topic guide* for locating articles, Critical Thinking study questions, and an Additional Resources section, which can be used to further explore articles and topics. The book is organized into five units. Selections that focus on similar issues are concentrated into subsections within the broader units. Each unit is preceded by an overview that provides background for informed reading of the articles, emphasizes critical issues, and presents key points to consider that focus on major themes running through the selections.

Your comments, opinions, and recommendations about *Annual Editions: Business Ethics 13/14* will be greatly appreciated and are welcomed in order to shape future editions. With your help and input, this book continually will be improved.

William J. Kehoe
Editor

The Annual Editions Series

VOLUMES AVAILABLE

Adolescent Psychology

Aging

American Foreign Policy

American Government

Anthropology

Archaeology

Assessment and Evaluation

Business Ethics

Child Growth and Development

Comparative Politics

Criminal Justice

Developing World

Drugs, Society, and Behavior

Dying, Death, and Bereavement

Early Childhood Education

Economics

Educating Children with Exceptionalities

Education

Educational Psychology

Entrepreneurship

Environment

The Family

Gender

Geography

Global Issues

Health

Homeland Security

Human Development

Human Resources

Human Sexualities

International Business

Management

Marketing

Mass Media

Microbiology

Multicultural Education

Nursing

Nutrition

Physical Anthropology

Psychology

Race and Ethnic Relations

Social Problems

Sociology

State and Local Government

Sustainability

Technologies, Social Media, and Society

United States History, Volume 1

United States History, Volume 2

Urban Society

Violence and Terrorism

Western Civilization, Volume 1

World History, Volume 1

World History, Volume 2

World Politics

Contents

UNIT 1
Ethics, Values, and Social Responsibility in Business

1. **Thinking Ethically: A Framework for Moral Decision Making,** Manuel
Velasquez et al., *Issues in Ethics,* Winter 1996

   Outlined here are key steps and five different approaches to dealing with moral issues
   and helping to resolve ethical dilemmas. The five approaches include the utilitarian
   approach, the rights approach, the fairness or justice approach, the common-good
   approach, and the virtue approach. Given an understanding of the five approaches,
   then five questions are presented to ask in resolving a moral issue.   2

2. **Designing Honesty into Your Organization,** Christian Mastilak et al.,
Strategic Finance, December 2011

   How does a manager design honesty into her/his organization? Is it possible to design
   in honesty and make the concept of honesty part of an organization's culture? This
   article argues in the affirmative and offers six key steps toward designing honesty into
   an organization.   5

3. **Fairness in Business: Does It Matter, and What Does It Mean?**
Joel D. Rubin, *Business Horizons,* 2012

   Does fairness have a place in business? Rubin explores the concept of fairness in business and why it matters. Among aspects of the concept of fairness explored in the article
   are the questions of why be fair and what it means to be fair. A particularly interesting and
   timely section in the article examines fairness in the allocation of limited resources.   9

4. **Building an Ethical Framework,** Thomas R. Krause and Paul J. Voss, *CRO,*
May/June 2007

   The authors examine ten questions that should be considered to build an ethical framework and to encourage an ethical corporate culture.   13

5. **Is Business Ethics Getting Better? A Historical Perspective,** Joanne
B. Ciulla, *Business Ethics Quarterly,* April 2011

   If we fail to study history, we may find history repeating itself on us. The author, in a
   Society for Business Ethics Presidential Address, provides historical examples of ethical
   issues and discusses Harvard Business School's early attempts to use business history
   in teaching business ethics.   15

6. **Principles for Building an Ethical Organization,** Miriam Schulman,
Markkula Center for Applied Ethics, Santa Clara University, June 2007

   The author presents five principles for building an ethical organization offered by
   R. Gopalakrishnan to a group of executives during a Markkula Center lecture in June
   2007. The principles are based on personal experience, company folklore, and Indian
   mythology.   20

The concepts in bold italics are developed in the article. For further expansion, please refer to the Topic Guide.

UNIT 2
Ethical Issues and Dilemmas in the Workplace

The concepts in bold italics are developed in the article. For further expansion, please refer to the Topic Guide.

The concepts in bold italics are developed in the article. For further expansion, please refer to the Topic Guide.

The concepts in bold italics are developed in the article. For further expansion, please refer to the Topic Guide.

UNIT 3
Business and Society: Contemporary Ethical, Social, and Environmental Issues

The concepts in bold italics are developed in the article. For further expansion, please refer to the Topic Guide.

The concepts in bold italics are developed in the article. For further expansion, please refer to the Topic Guide.

UNIT 4
Ethics and Social Responsibility in the Marketplace

UNIT 5
Developing the Future Ethos and Social Responsibility of Business

The concepts in bold italics are developed in the article. For further expansion, please refer to the Topic Guide.

The concepts in bold italics are developed in the article. For further expansion, please refer to the Topic Guide.

Correlation Guide

The *Annual Editions* series provides students with convenient, inexpensive access to current, carefully selected articles from the public press. **Annual Editions: Business Ethics 13/14** is an easy-to-use reader that presents articles on important topics such as *workplace misconduct, social and environmental issues, global ethics, ethics in the marketplace,* and many more. For more information on *Annual Editions* and other *McGraw-Hill Contemporary Learning Series* titles, visit www.mhhe.com/cls.

This convenient guide matches the units in **Annual Editions: Business Ethics 13/14** with the corresponding chapters in four of our best-selling McGraw-Hill Business Ethics textbooks by DesJardins, Ghillyer, Hosmer, and Hartman/DesJardins.

Annual Editions: Business Ethics 13/14	An Introduction to Business Ethics, 5/e by DesJardins	Business Ethics Now, 3/e by Ghillyer	The Ethics of Management, 7/e by Hosmer	Business Ethics: Decision-Making for Personal Integrity & Social Responsibility, 3e by Hartman/DesJardins
Unit 1: Ethics, Values, and Social Responsibility in Business	**Chapter 1:** Why Study Ethics? **Chapter 2:** Ethical Theory and Business **Chapter 3:** Corporate Social Responsibility **Chapter 4:** Corporate Culture, Governance, and Ethical Leadership	**Chapter 1:** Understanding Ethics **Chapter 2:** Defining Business Ethics **Chapter 4:** Corporate Social Responsibility	**Chapter 1:** The Nature of Moral Problems in Management **Chapter 4:** Moral Analysis and Ethical Duties	**Chapter 1:** Ethics and Business **Chapter 2:** Ethical Decision-Making: Personal and Professional Contexts **Chapter 3:** Philosophical Ethics and Business **Chapter 4:** The Corporate Culture: Impact and Implications **Chapter 5:** Corporate Social Responsibility
Unit 2: Ethical Issues and Dilemmas in the Workplace	**Chapter 4:** Corporate Culture, Governance, and Ethical Leadership **Chapter 5:** The Meaning and Value of Work **Chapter 6:** Moral Rights in the Workplace **Chapter 7:** Employee Responsibilities **Chapter 11:** Diversity and Discrimination	**Chapter 2:** Defining Business Ethics **Chapter 3:** Organizational Ethics **Chapter 7:** Blowing the Whistle	**Chapter 1:** The Nature of Moral Problems in Management	**Chapter 6:** Ethical Decision-Making: Employer Responsibilities and Employee Rights **Chapter 7:** Ethical Decision-Making: Technology and Privacy in the Workplace
Unit 3: Business and Society: Contemporary Ethical, Social, and Environmental Issues	**Chapter 10:** Business's Environmental Responsibilities **Chapter 12:** International Business and Globalization	**Chapter 2:** Defining Business Ethics **Chapter 9:** Ethics and Globalization	**Chapter 3:** Moral Analysis and Legal Requirements	**Chapter 7:** Ethical Decision-Making: Technology and Privacy in the Workplace **Chapter 9:** Business and Environmental Sustainability
Unit 4: Ethics and Social Responsibility in the Marketplace	**Chapter 8:** Marketing Ethics: Product Safety and Pricing **Chapter 9:** Marketing Ethics: Advertising and Target Marketing	**Chapter 3:** Organizational Ethics **Chapter 8:** Ethics and Technology **Chapter 10:** Making it Stick: Doing What's Right in a Competitive Market	**Chapter 2:** Moral Analysis and Economic Outcomes	**Chapter 8:** Ethics and Marketing
Unit 5: Developing the Future Ethos and Social Responsibility of Business	**Chapter 4:** Corporate Culture, Governance, and Ethical Leadership **Chapter 10:** Business's Environmental Responsibilities	**Chapter 10:** Making it Stick: Doing What's Right in a Competitive Market	**Chapter 6:** How Can a Business Organization Be Made Moral?	**Chapter 5:** Corporate Social Responsibility

Topic Guide

This topic guide suggests how the selections in this book relate to the subjects covered in your course. You may want to use the topics listed on these pages to search the Web more easily.

On the following pages a number of websites have been gathered specifically for this book. They are arranged to reflect the units of this Annual Editions reader. You can link to these sites by going to www.mhhe.com/cls

All the articles that relate to each topic are listed below the bold-faced term.

Business and law
1. Thinking Ethically: A Framework for Moral Decision Making
2. Designing Honesty into Your Organization
3. Fairness in Business: Does it Matter, and What Does it Mean?
7. What's at the Core of Corporate Wrongdoing?
17. American Apparel and the Ethics of a Sexually Charged Workplace
18. What the Wal-Mart Ruling Means for Big Business
19. Older Workers: Running to the Courthouse?
20. Fighting the High Cost of "Getting Even" at Work
25. Whistleblowers: Why You Should Heed Their Warnings
27. SEC Rule Will Let Whistle-Blowers Bypass Internal Programs

Business environment
43. What Really Drives Value in Corporate Responsibility?
46. Cause for Concern

Business ethics
1. Thinking Ethically: A Framework for Moral Decision Making
4. Building an Ethical Framework
5. Is Business Ethics Getting Better? A Historical Perspective
6. Principles for Building an Ethical Organization
51. Creating an Ethical Culture
52. Outside-the-Box Ethics
54. Strategic Organizational Diversity: A Model?

Codes of ethics
2. Designing Honesty into Your Organization
38. Conceptualizing a Framework for Global Business Ethics
39. Revisiting the Global Business Ethics Question
40. Taking Your Code to China
54. Strategic Organizational Diversity: A Model?

Conflicts of interest
25. Whistleblowers: Why You Should Heed Their Warnings
28. The Parable of the Sadhu

Corporate citizenship
10. Ethical Leadership and the Dual Roles of Examples
14. When You're Most Vulnerable to Fraud
15. When Good People Do Bad Things at Work
30. Trust in the Marketplace
44. Doing More Good
55. Fiduciary Principles: Corporate Responsibilities to Stakeholders

Corporate responsibilities
1. Thinking Ethically: A Framework for Moral Decision Making
3. Fairness in Business: Does It Matter, and What Does It Mean?
7. What's at the Core of Corporate Wrongdoing?
23. People Have to Come Before Profits, Even in a Crisis
55. Fiduciary Principles: Corporate Responsibilities to Stakeholders

Crime
6. Principles for Building an Ethical Organization
7. What's at the Core of Corporate Wrongdoing?
10. Ethical Leadership and the Dual Roles of Examples
14. When You're Most Vulnerable to Fraud
16. Behind the Murdoch Scandal? Scandalous Governance
30. Trust in the Marketplace

41. Moral Hazard
42. Wal-Mart Hushed Up a Vast Mexican Bribery Case

Culture
2. Designing Honesty into Your Organization
6. Principles for Building an Ethical Organization
28. The Parable of the Sadhu
29. Fact Sheet: We Can't Wait: White House Launches Ethics.gov to Promote Government Accountability and Transparency
51. Creating an Ethical Culture
52. Outside-the-Box Ethics

Charged Workplace
18. What the Wal-Mart Ruling Means for Big Business
19. Older Workers: Running to the Courthouse?
20. Fighting the High Cost of "Getting Even" at Work
21. Values-Driven HR
22. Cost Reductions, Downsizing-related Layoffs, and HR Practices
30. Trust in the Marketplace

Discrimination
11. Unfair Business Practices
17. American Apparel and the Ethics of a Sexually

Diversity
21. Values-Driven HR
22. Cost Reductions, Downsizing-related Layoffs, and HR Practices
54. Strategic Organizational Diversity: A Model?

Downsizing
22. Cost Reductions, Downsizing-related Layoffs, and HR Practices
23. People Have to Come Before Profits, Even in a Crisis

Economic environment
2. Designing Honesty into Your Organization
3. Fairness in Business: Does It Matter, and What Does It Mean?
8. Markets and Morals
14. When You're Most Vulnerable to Fraud
23. People Have to Come Before Profits, Even in a Crisis

Employee compensation
11. Unfair Business Practices
18. What the Wal-Mart Ruling Means for Big Business
21. Values-Driven HR
23. People Have to Come Before Profits, Even in a Crisis
49. First Make Money. Also, Do Good

Employee rights
1. Thinking Ethically: A Framework for Moral Decision Making
2. Designing Honesty into Your Organization
3. Fairness in Business: Does It Matter, and What Does It Mean?
8. Markets and Morals
15. When Good People Do Bad Things at Work
18. What the Wal-Mart Ruling Means for Big Business
19. Older Workers: Running to the Courthouse?
20. Fighting the High Cost of "Getting Even" at Work
27. SEC Rule Will Let Whistle-Blowers Bypass Internal Programs
48. Serving Unfair Customers

Internet References

The following Internet sites have been selected to support the articles found in this reader. These sites were available at the time of publication. However, because websites often change their structure and content, the information listed may no longer be available. We invite you to visit www.mhhe.com/cls for easy access to these sites.

Annual Editions: Business Ethics 13/14

General Sources

Caux Roundtable Principles for Business
www.cauxroundtable.org/index.cfm?&menuid=8

The Caux Roundtable presents principles for ethics and responsible corporate behavior developed by senior business leaders from Europe, Japan, and North America.

Center for the Study of Ethics in the Professions
http://ethics.iit.edu

This site is sponsored by the Illinois Institute of Technology.

Ethics Resource Center
www.ethics.org

The Ethics Resource Center is a useful source for information about ethics.

FCPA
www.fcpa.us

This website has information about the U.S. Foreign Corrupt Practices Act.

Four Way Test of Rotary International
www.rotary.org/en/aboutus/rotaryinternational/guidingprinciples/Pages/ridefault.aspx

This website has an example of a globally accepted code of Ethics—The Four Way Test—developed by Rotary International.

GreenMoney Journal
www.greenmoneyjournal.com

The editorial vision of this publication proposes that consumer spending and investment dollars can bring about positive social and environmental change.

Institute for Business and Professional Ethics
http://commerce.depaul.edu/ethics

The Institute for Business and Professional Ethics located at DePaul University is supported by the College of Commerce and the College of Liberal Arts and Sciences.

Institute for Global Ethics
www.globalethics.org

The Institute for Global Ethics promotes ethics in a global context.

OECD
www.oecd.org/daf/briberyininternationalbusiness/anti-briberyconvention/oecdconventiononcombatingbriberyofforeignpublicofficialsininternationalbusinesstransactions.htm

This site provided information about the OECD Convention on Combating Bribery of Foreign Public Officials in International Business Transactions.

Olsson Center for Applied Ethics
http://darden.virginia.edu/web/Olsson-Center-for-Applied-Ethics

The Olsson Center for Applied Ethics is located at the University of Virginia's Darden School of Business.

Texas Instruments' Quick Test of Ethics
www.ti.com/corp/docs/csr/downloads/ethics.pdf

This site presented a seven-step Quick Test of Ethics developed by Texas Instruments.

Transparency International
http://transparency.org

Transparency International's purpose is to fight against corruption. A Global Corruption Report is available on its website.

U.S. Department of Labor
www.dol.gov

Browsing through this site will lead to a vast array of labor-related data and discussions of issues affecting employees and managers, such as the minimum wage.

U.S. Equal Employment Opportunity Commission (EEOC)
www.eeoc.gov

The EEOC's mission "is to ensure equality of opportunity by vigorously enforcing federal legislation prohibiting discrimination in employment." Consult this site for facts about employment discrimination, enforcement, and litigation.

Wharton Ethics Program
http://ethics.wharton.upenn.edu

The Wharton School of the University of Pennsylvania provides an independently managed site that offers links to research, cases, and other business ethics centers.

UNIT 1: Ethics, Values, and Social Responsibility in Business

Association for Moral Education (AME)
www.amenetwork.org

AME is dedicated to fostering communication, cooperation, training, and research that link moral theory with educational practices. From here it is possible to connect to several sites of relevance in the study of business ethics.

Business for Social Responsibility (BSR)
www.bsr.org

Core topic areas covered by BSR are listed on this page. They include Corporate Social Responsibility; Business Ethics; Community Investment; the Environment; Governance and Accountability; Human Rights; Marketplace; Mission, Vision, Values; and finally Workplace. New information is added on a regular basis. For each topic or subtopic there is an introduction, examples of large and small company leadership practices, sample company policies, links to helping resources, and other information.

Ethics Updates/Lawrence M. Hinman
http://ethics.sandiego.edu

This site provides both simple concept definitions and complex analysis of ethics, original treatises, and sophisticated search engine capability. Subject matter ranges from ethical theory to applied ethical venues.

Internet References

Institute for Business and Professional Ethics
http://commerce.depaul.edu/ethics

Sponsored by DePaul University College of Commerce, this website focuses upon research in the field of business and professional ethics.

National Center for Policy Analysis
www.ncpa.org

This organization's archive links lead you to interesting materials on a variety of topics that affect managers, from immigration issues, to affirmative action, to regulatory policy.

Open Directory Project
http://dmoz.org/Business/Management/Ethics

As part of the Open Directory Project, this page provides a database of websites that address numerous topics on ethics in business.

UNIT 2: Ethical Issues and Dilemmas in the Workplace

American Psychological Association
www.apa.org/index.aspx

Search this site to find references and discussion of important ethics issues for the workplace, including the impact of restructuring and revitalization of businesses.

International Labour Organization (ILO)
www.ilo.org

ILO's home page leads you to links that describe the goals of the organization and summarizes international labor standards and human rights. Its official UN website locator can point you to many other useful resources.

UNIT 3: Business and Society: Contemporary Ethical, Social, and Environmental Issues

National Immigrant Forum
www.immigrationforum.org

The pro-immigrant organization offers this page to examine the effects of immigration on the U.S. economy and society. Click on the links to underground and immigrant economies.

United Nations Environment Programme (UNEP)
www.unep.ch

Consult this UNEP site for links to topics such as the impact of trade on the environment. It will direct you to useful databases and global resource information.

United States Trade Representative (USTR)
www.ustr.gov

This home page of the U.S. Trade Representative provides links to many U.S. government resources for those interested in ethics in international business.

Workopolis.com
www.workopolis.com/EN/Common/HomePage.aspx

This Canadian site provides an electronic network with a GripeVine for complaining about work and finding solutions to everyday work problems.

Ethics and Sustainability
www.shrm.org/hrdisciplines/ethics/Pages/default.aspx

Information on ethics and sustainability is available at this website.

Ethics and Sustainability—Trigonos
www.trigonos.org/ethics_and_sustainability

The website for Trigonos—a sustainability not-for-profit organization.

Ethical Dimensions of Sustainability
www.scu.edu/ethics/practicing/focusareas/environmental_ethics/lesson4.html

A short course is available at this website on ethics and sustainability.

Sustainability and Ethics
www.cimaglobal.com/Thought-leadership/Research-topics/Sustainability/

A finance perspective on and sustainability and ethics.

Sustainability in Financial Markets—Metrics
http://ethicsmetrics.com/site/home/ssri

This website presents metrics for measuring sustainability in financial markets.

Sustainability Ethics
www.int-res.com/articles/esep/2003/E30.pdf

A preliminary declaration of sustainability ethics is presented.

Culture, Ethics, and Sustainability
www.sum.uio.no/english/research/groups/culture-ethics-and-sustainability/index.html

An exploration of culture, ethics, and sustainability.

Ethics and Sustainability Website from AACSB
www.aacsb.edu/resources/ethics-sustainability/default.asp

Resources on ethics and sustainability are provided by AACSB.

Environmental Sustainability and Business Ethics
www.ehow.com/facts_6134185_environmental-sustainability-business-ethics.html

Informational on environmental sustainability and business ethics are included at this website.

Sustainability—Coca-Cola Company
www.thecoca-colacompany.com/citizenship/index.html

An examination of the concept of sustainability at the Coca-Cola Company

UNIT 4: Ethics and Social Responsibility in the Marketplace

Business for Social Responsibility (BSR)
www.bsr.org

BSR is a global organization that seeks to help companies "achieve success in ways that respect ethical values, people, communities, and the environment." Links to Services, Resources, and Forum are available.

Social Responsibility of Business—Business Ethics and Social Responsibility
http://managementhelp.org/businessethics/index.htm

There are various links on this website about business ethics and social responsibility.

Social Responsibility of Business—Increase Profit
www.colorado.edu/studentgroups/libertarians/issues/friedman-soc-resp-business.html

This is a classic article by Milton Friedman.

Internet References

Social Responsibility of Business—A Series of Articles
www.helium.com/
knowledge/102740-what-are-the-social-responsibilities-of-business

This website contains a series of articles on the social responsibilities of business.

Social Responsibility of Business
www.scribd.com/doc/24582689/Social-Responsibility-of-Business

An article on the social responsibility of business.

Social Responsibility of Business—Rethinking the Concept
http://reason.com/archives/2005/10/01/rethinking-the-social-responsi

Several scholars debate the concept of the social responsibility of business.

Total Quality Management Sites
http://asq.org/learn-about-quality/total-quality-management/overview/overview.html

This site points to a variety of interesting Internet sources to aid in the study and application of Total Quality Management principles.

Total Quality Management and Corporate Ethics
www.icac.org.hk/hkedc/ethics/eip/edc008_e.htm

A discussion about ethics and total quality management.

Eight Elements of Total Quality Management
www.isixsigma.com/methodology/total-quality-management-tqm/eight-elements-tqm

Of the eight elements of TQM, ethics is the first element.

UNIT 5: Developing the Future Ethos and Social Responsibility of Business

Corporate Ethics
www.pbs.org/newshour/bb/business/ethics

This website is a PBS online special report concerning recent issues and scandals involving business ethics.

Ethics Resource Center (ERC)
www.ethics.org

An extensive list of articles dealing with business ethics and related issues can be found on this website including an Ethics Toolkit.

International Business Ethics Institute (IBEI)
http://business-ethics.org

The goal of this educational organization is to promote business ethics and corporate responsibility in response to the growing need for transnationalism in the field of business ethics.

UNU/IAS Project on Global Ethos
www.ias.unu.edu/research/globalethos.cfm

The United Nations University Institute of Advanced Studies (UNU/IAS) has issued this project abstract, which concerns governance and multilateralism. The main aim of the project is to initiate a process by which to generate jointly, with the involvement of factors from both state and non-state institutions in developed and developing countries, a global ethos that could provide or support a set of guiding principles for the emerging global community.

Additional Resources

The following business ethics sites have been selected to support the articles found in this reader. These sites were available at the time of publication. However, because websites often change their structure and content, the information listed may no longer be available when you try to access the websites. We invite you to visit www.mhhe.com/cls for easy access to these sites.

Annual Editions: Business Ethics 13/14

Contents

- Articles/Publications
- Cases and Teaching Material
- Codes of Ethics
- Professional Organizations and Associations
- Resources and Resource Centers

Articles/Publications

Business Corporate Ethics
www.ehow.com/facts_6827162_business-corporate-ethics.html

This website offers an examination of the concept of business and corporate ethics.

Business Ethics Forum
http://businessethics-forum.blogspot.com

A blog focused on promoting ethical business practices.

Business Ethics Newsletter
www.societyforbusinessethics.org/index.php?option=com_content&task=view&id=36&Itemid=129

This website contains the newsletter of the Society for Business Ethics.

Business Ethics and Values in Corporate Culture
www.ehow.com/info_7806770_business-ethics-values-corporate-culture.html

A discussion of business ethics and values in corporate culture is examined at this website.

Business Ethics: Resources for Educators
www.socialfunds.com/news/article.cgi/2652.html

An article featured on the SocialFunds.com site discusses the top 100 companies that made the Business Ethics' Best Corporate Citizens List for 2009.

Business Ethics: Guidance for Corporate Respect of Children
www.socialfunds.com/news/article.cgi/3549.html

A guide for corporate respect of children published on the SocialFunds.com website.

Business Ethics: Guiding Principles on Business and Human Rights
www.socialfunds.com/news/article.cgi/article3180.html

A guide for business and human rights published on the SocialFunds.com website.

BusinessWeek Online
www.businessweek.com

Bloomberg BusinessWeek Online allows you to search for articles dealing with ethics in business. Use its search feature to retrieve current articles covering a variety of ethical dilemmas affecting business.

Corporate Culture and Ethics
www.ehow.com/about_6633415_corporate-culture-ethics.html

The relationship of corporate culture and ethics is explored at this website.

Corporate ethics
www.pbs.org/newshour/bb/business/ethics

This website is a PBS online special report concerning recent issues and scandals involving business ethics.

Corporate ethics: Interfaith Center on Corporate Responsibility
www.iccr.org

This center is a collation of shareholders promoting justice and sustainability in the world.

Ethics Resource Center (ERC)
www.ethics.org

An extensive list of articles dealing with business ethics and related issues can be found on this website including an Ethics Toolkit.

Financial scandals
www.ex.ac.uk/~ RDavies/arian/scandals

Financial Scandals is a site created by Roy Davies that covers some of the "greatest" scandals of all times. The site is designed for a broad audience, from business executives interested in business ethics issues to financial history enthusiasts.

Fortune.com
www.fortune.com

Fortune.com has numerous articles discussing ethics and ethical issues in the corporate world. Type "ethics" in the site's search feature to retrieve the latest articles.

A Question of Ethics
www.informationweek.com/825/ethics.htm

As companies move into the e-business arena, new ethical issues arise. This timeless Informationweek.com article from February 19, 2001, discusses topics such as compromising customer privacy for advertising gain and trust concerns between employers and employees. Links to other e-business ethics articles can also be found at this site.

Cases and Teaching Material

Business Ethics Case Studies
www.lexiology.com/business-ethics-case-studies.pdf

This website presents a listing of business ethics case studies.

Business Roundtable Institute for Corporate Ethics
www.corporate-ethics.org/

A good source for cases, research and videos about business ethics

Carnegie Mellon: Ethics Teaching Materials
http://ba.gsia.cmu.edu/ethics/teaching.htm

This site presents an array of teaching materials for ethics.

Additional Resources

CasePlace.org
www.caseplace.org

CasePlace.org is provided by The Aspen Institute's Center for Business Education. Teaching materials are searchable on this site.

Center for Ethics
www.vanderbilt.edu/CenterforEthics/cases.html

Located at Vanderbilt University, the Center promotes increase understanding of ethical issues and problems. Its website offers business ethics cases.

Ethics Resource Center - USC
http://dornsife.usc.edu/dilemmas-and-case-studies

The ERC is a good source for ethics cases.

Harvard Business Publishing
http://hbsp.harvard.edu/discipline/business-ethics

Business ethics cases, videos and other materials from the Harvard Business School.

IBS Center for Management Research
www.icmrindia.org/free%20resources/casestudies/Free%20 Business%20Ethics.htm

A listing of free business ethics cases is available at this website. The list is updates periodically.

Inc.com Guide: Case Studies in Business Ethics
www.inc.com/partners/intel/case-studies.html#content

Editors at Inc.com select the resources found at this site. Case studies covering ethical topics such as environmental challenges, getting involved in the community, and making global connections can be found in this section of its site.

Institute for Global Ethics (IGE)
www.globalethics.org

IGE is an organization dedicated to promoting "ethical behavior in individuals, institutions, and nations through research, public discourse, and practical action." Numerous resources and articles are provided on the IGE site.

Management Mini Cases
http://ba.tepper.cmu.edu/ethics/AA/mgtmini.htm

This link contains management mini cases in ethics from the Tepper School of Business at Carnegie Mellon University.

Olsen Center for Applied Ethics
www.darden.virginia.edu/web/olsson-center-for-applied-ethics

Located at the University of Virginia, the Olsen Center is a source for cases and research on ethics.

Codes of Ethics

Academy of Management
http://aomonline.org/aom.asp?id=24&page_id=235

American Marketing Association
www.marketingpower.com/AboutAMA/Pages/Statement%20of%20 Ethics.aspx

Boeing
www.boeing.com

- Boeing Code of Conduct
www.boeing.com/companyoffices/aboutus/ethics/code_of_ conduct.pdf

- Boeing Ethics and Business Conduct Program
www.boeing.com/companyoffices/aboutus/ethics/pro3.pdf

- Boeing Ethics Policies and Procedures
www.boeing.com/companyoffices/aboutus/ethics/epolicy.htm

- Boeing Values
www.boeing.com/companyoffices/aboutus/ethics/integst.htm

Financial Management Association International
www.fma.org

Ford Motor Company
http://corporate.ford.com/doc/corporate_conduct_standards.pdf

General Motors Corporation
www.gm.com/content/dam/gmcom/COMPANY/Investors/Contacts/ Images/2012-WWI-Final-Version-7-30-12-English.pdf

Hewlett-Packard (HP)
www.hp.com/hpinfo/globalcitizenship/csr/ethics.html

This ethics page outlines the HP values, standards, and guidelines for responsible conduct of business.

IBM: Business Conduct Guidelines
www.ibm.com/investor/corpgovernance/cgbcg.phtml

Johnson & Johnson: Our Credo
www.jnj.com/our_company/our_credo/index.htm

Microsoft: Mission & Values
www.microsoft.com/mscorp

Occidental Petroleum Corporation: Code of Business Conduct
www.oxy.com/SiteCollectionDocuments/code_of_business_conduct.pdf

ServiceMaster: Code of Conduct
http://corporate.servicemaster.com/overview_conduct.asp

Strategic Management Society
http://strategicmanagement.net/members/professional_conduct.php

Texas Instruments
www.ti.com

TI values and ethics
www.ti.com/corp/docs/csr/downloads/ethics.pdf

TI ethics office
www.ti.com/corp/docs/csr/2007/corpgov/ethics/contact.shtml

Weyerhaeuser: Business Conduct
www.weyerhaeuser.com/citizenship/businessconduct

Williams-Sonoma, Inc.: Corporate Values
www.williams-sonomainc.com/careers/corporate-values.html

Creating a Code of Ethics
www.ethicsweb.ca/codes

Chris MacDonald, PhD, Philosophy Department, St. Mary's University (Halifax, Canada) has put together this site with links to resources to assist individuals and groups in writing a code of ethics. MacDonald has also worked on several other ethics sites including EthicsWeb at www.ethicsweb.ca

Codes of Ethics Online Collection
http://ethics.iit.edu/research/codes-ethics-collection

Illinois Institute of Technology's Center for the Study of Ethics in the Professions developed an online collection of codes of ethics.

Professional Organizations and Associations

Better Business Bureau (BBB): Promoting Fairness and Integrity in the Marketplace
www.bbb.org

In 1912, the very first BBB was founded. The goal of the Better Business Bureau is to "promote and foster the highest ethical

Additional Resources

relationship between businesses and the public through voluntary self-regulation, consumer and business education, and service excellence."

Business for Social Responsibility (BSR)
www.bsr.org

BSR is a global, nonprofit organization that seeks to "create a just and sustainable world by working with companies to promote more responsible business practices, innovation and collaboration."

The Caux Roundtable
www.cauxroundtable.org

The Caux Roundtable is an organization comprised of senior business leaders from around the world, including Europe, Japan, and North America. These leaders are individuals who "believe that business has a crucial role in developing and promoting equitable solutions to key global issues." One document provided on this site that serves as a guide to all businesses interested in responsible conduct is "The Principles for Business."

The Defense Industry Initiative (DII) on Business Ethics and Conduct
www.dii.org

DII is a "consortium of U.S. defense industry contractors which subscribes to a set of principles for achieving high standards of business ethics and conduct." Links to ethics training resources plus other resources of interest can be found at this site.

Direct Selling Association
http://dsa.org/ethics

The site presents the code of ethics of the Direct Selling Association.

Ethics and Compliance Officer Association (ECOA)
www.theecoa.org/iMIS15/ECOAPublic

ECOA was founded in 1992. Its members come from throughout industry and are responsible for ethics and compliance programs in their companies.

European Business Ethics Network (EBEN)
www.eben-net.org

The formation of EBEN, a nonprofit organization founded in Brussels in 1987, was considered to be a significant step in recognizing business ethics as an important area of research. Links to ethics organizations, university programs, and other research institutions are provided.

Financial Executives International (FEI)
www.financialexecutives.org/KenticoCMS/home.aspx

FEI was founded in 1931 and is considered to be the "professional association of choice for corporate financial executives." This organization strongly encourages all its members to practice the highest level of professional and ethical conduct.

Financial Planning Association (FPA): Code of Ethics
www.fpaforfinancialplanning.org/AboutFPA/CodeofEthics

The Code of Ethics for FPA is designed to guide members in the practice of professional ethics in the field of financial planning. The formation of FPA came about on January 1, 2000, as the result of the merger of the International Association for Financial Planning (IAFP) and the Institute of Certified Financial Planners (ICFP).

The Kennedy Institute of Ethics
kennedyinstitute.georgetown.edu

Georgetown Business Ethics Institute is located at Georgetown University and offers, through its Library and Information Services site, links to aid researchers in their quest for more information concerning business ethics topics.

Institute for Business, Technology & Ethics (IBTE)
www.ethix.org

IBTE was founded in 1998 to study the connections and relationships between business, ethics, and technology. The mission of this organization is to "promote good business through appropriate technology and sound ethics."

Institute for Global Ethics (IGE)
www.globalethics.org

IGE is an organization dedicated to promoting "ethical behavior in individuals, institutions, and nations through research, public discourse, and practical action." Numerous resources and articles are provided on the IGE site.

Institute of Business Ethics (IBE): Code of Ethics
www.ibe.org.uk

IBE believes that companies should uphold the highest standards of behavior and professional conduct. This organization "broadcasts" its mission through conferences, consultations, publications, and business ethics training programs. The IBE code of ethics section of the website goes beyond stating its code. It also provides tips on how to make codes effective, information on content included in a code of ethics policy, and links to various company codes of ethics.

The Society for Business Ethics (SBE)
www.societyforbusinessethics.org

SBE was founded in 1980 and is an international organization dedicated to the academic study of business ethics. The Ethics Links section of its site provides access to other associations and resource centers. The Society for Business Ethics resource link is available at societyforbusinessethics.org/index.php?option=com_content&task=view&id=83

The Society of Corporate Compliance and Ethics
www.corporatecompliance.org

The Society of Corporate Compliance and Ethics (SCCE) is a nonprofit organization that "exists to champion compliance standards, corporate governance and ethical practice in the business community and to provide the necessary resources for compliance and ethics professionals and others who share these principles." Membership opportunities and information about SCCE events are listed on this site. Resources, such as newsletters, books, and training kits (some for fee) also are available.

Resources and Centers

BELL: The Business Ethics Links Library
http://libnet.colorado.edu/Bell/frontpage.htm

Gene Hayworth, University of Colorado at Boulder, created this website designed to be a starting point for those seeking information regarding corporate ethics and social responsibility.

Business Ethics
http://bubl.ac.uk/link/b/businessethics.htm

BUBL Link is a mega "catalog" of Internet resources covering various academic subject areas. An extensive section on business ethics has been compiled at this site. Resources include applied business materials, articles about financial scandals, and centers of research for business ethics.

Business Ethics–Canada
www.businessethics.ca

A Canadian-based business ethics website with ethics articles and other resources.

Additional Resources

Business Ethics: The Magazine of Corporate Responsibility

http://business-ethics.com

The Magazine for Corporate responsibility has articles and reports about business ethics.

Center for Business Ethics (CBE)

http://cbe.bentley.edu

The Center for Business Ethics (CBE) is housed on the campus of Bentley University and has been in operation since 1976 under the direction of W. Michael Hoffman. CBE is designed to be a forum for business ethics, and it provides specialized training and educational programs for businesses and their employees. Since CBE's founding, it has sponsored major conferences on the topic of ethical business conduct.

Center for Ethics and Business

http://ethicsandbusiness.org

Loyola Marymount University (Los Angeles, CA) is the home of the Center for Ethics and Business. The Center acts as a forum for discussing ethical business decisions and dilemmas, including the costs and rewards of operating ethically. Numerous links to ethics programs, centers, and other tools designed to help people deal with ethical dilemmas are presented.

Center for Integrity in Business

www.spu.edu/depts/sbe/cib

Business ethics scandals making the news lately have increased the demand for business ethics educational programs and other programs designed to develop ethical business leaders. The Center for Integrity in Business is located at the School of Business & Economics at Seattle Pacific University.

Complete Guide to Ethics Management

www.mapnp.org/library/ethics/ethxgde.htm

This site features a guidebook to help leaders and managers deal with the ethical issues that occur in everyday situations.

E-Ethics Center

www.e-businessethics.com

The E-Ethics Center is located at Colorado State University. The website's goal is "to create a virtual community of organizations and individuals that share best practices in the improvement of business ethics."

Ethics and Compliance Officers Association

www.theecoa.org/imis15/ECOAPublic

Many ethics resources are available at this ECOA website,

Ethical Business: The Search for Research

www.eldis.org/go/topics/resource-guides/corporate-responsibility

This ELDIS (Electronic Development and Environmental Information System) guide provides links to case studies, social and environmental standards, resources for informing shareholders and consumers, and more.

Ethics on the World Wide Web: Business

http://commfaculty.fullerton.edu/lester/ethics/business.html

Ethics on the World Wide Web is a site designed by the School of Communications at California State University, Fullerton. The annotated list includes links to ethics centers, institutes, and organizations.

Fraud and Business Ethics Resources

www.knowledgeleader.com/KnowledgeLeader/content.nsf/
Web+Content/fraudandethicstoolsandresources!OpenDocument&
yahoo&WT.mc_id=gaw+business+ethics+code+of+conduct+yahoo

A list of ethics tools and publications are available at this website.

Google Directory: Business Ethics

http://directory.google.com/Top/Business/Management/Ethics

Google Directory offers a rather large, annotated compilation of links to sites related to business ethics.

Markkula Center for Applied Ethics

www.scu.edu/ethics

The Markkula Center for Applied Ethics was founded in 1986 and has grown into one of the most active university applied ethics centers in the United States. It is based at Santa Clara University.

Online Ethics Center: Ethics in Business

www.onlineethics.org/Resources/Cases.aspx

Various cases and scenarios in business ethics are available at the Online Ethics Center.

Olsen Center for Applied Ethics

www.darden.virginia.edu/web/olsson-center-for-applied-ethics

Located at the University of Virginia, the Olsen Center is a source for cases and research on ethics.

Open Directory: Business Management Ethics

http://dmoz.org/Business/Management/Ethics

Open Directory is an annotated collection that includes links to business ethics publications, resource centers, forums, codes of ethics, and more.

Prudential Business Ethics Center

www.pruethics.rutgers.edu

The Prudential Business Ethics Center is housed at Rutgers University, and it is focused on the theory and practice of ethical behavior in business.

SOSIG: Professional and Business Ethics

www.ariadne.ac.uk/issue2/sosig

SOSIG, the Social Science Information Gateway, is part of the UK Resource Discovery Network. The goal of this gateway is to provide high-quality business and other social science resources to students, faculty, and researchers.

Yahoo! Directory: Business Ethics and Responsibility

http://dir.yahoo.com/Business_and_Economy/
Ethics_and_Responsibility

This Yahoo! category has site listings for centers, institutes, and publications. Its categories section has links to related topics such as corporate accountability, socially responsible investing, sweatshops, and whistleblowing.

The Zicklin Center for Business Ethics Research

www.zicklincenter.org

The Carol and Lawrence Zicklin Center at the Wharton School, University of Pennsylvania, was established in 1997 to conduct leading-edge research on business ethics.

UNIT 1

Ethics, Values, and Social Responsibility in Business

Unit Selections

1. **Thinking Ethically: A Framework for Moral Decision Making,** Manuel Velasquez et al.
2. **Designing Honesty into Your Organization,** Christian Mastilak et al.
3. **Fairness in Business: Does It Matter, and What Does it Mean?** Joel D. Rubin
4. **Building an Ethical Framework,** Thomas R. Kraus and Paul J. Voss
5. **Is Business Ethics Getting Better? A Historical Perspective,** Joanne B. Ciulla
6. **Principles for Building an Ethical Organization,** Miriam Schulman
7. **What's at the Core of Corporate Wrongdoing?** Eleanor Bloxham

Learning Outcomes

After reading this Unit, you will be able to:

- Thinking ethically and voicing values are important aspects in moral decision making. Using several articles listed above, develop a process to build an ethical organization. What principles are central to the process you are proposing?

- Do you believe that corporations are more socially responsible today than they were ten years ago? Is business ethics getting better? Why or why not?

- How does an individual or a firm voice values in moving forward toward building an ethical organization?

- How is honesty designed into an organization? What steps should be taken by a manager? Why?

- In what specific ways do you see companies practicing social responsibility? Provide examples of several companies that practice social responsibility. Do you think most companies are overt or covert in their social responsibility activities? Explain your answer.

- Does a company have any obligation to help remedy social problems, such as poverty, urban decay, and pollution? Defend your response and provide several examples of companies you believe are doing a good job in helping to remedy social problems.

- Using recent examples of business wrongdoing, discuss flaws in the U.S. business and/or financial systems that allow companies to disregard ethics, values, and social responsibility in business. Would teaching business ethics improve the situation? Offer several pro and con arguments about the importance of teaching business ethics.

- What is at the core of corporate wrongdoing? If you were a consultant advising managers on how to avoid corporate wrongdoing, what would be your advice? Be prepared to present and defend your advice to your classmates.

Student Website
www.mhhe.com/cls

Ethical decision making in an organization does not occur in a vacuum but is the responsibility of every individual in the organization. Individuals and managers formulate an organization's ethics (that is, the standards of "right" and "wrong" behavior expected by organizational members) based upon family, peer, and religious influences; past experiences; perhaps the influence of an ethical mentor; and personal and unique value systems. When making ethical decisions within an organizational context, many times there are situational factors and potential conflicts of interest that further complicate the process. Decisions made by individuals do not have only personal ramifications; they also have social consequences. Social responsibility, or corporate social responsibility, is ethics at the organizational level, since it refers to the obligation that an organization has to make choices and to take actions that will contribute to the good of society as well as the good of the organization. Authentic social responsibility is not initiated because of forced compliance to specific laws and regulations. In contrast to legal responsibility, social responsibility involves a voluntary response from an organization that is above and beyond what is specified by the law.

The seven articles presented in this unit, Ethics, Values, and Social Responsibility in Business, provide an overview of ethics as well as deep insight to the interrelationships of ethics, values, and social responsibility. The essays offer practical and insightful concepts, principles, and suggestions to managers, intended to enhance their understanding of ethics and enable them to accept with confidence and conviction the imperative of conducting business with the highest ethical standards. The articles also point out the complexity and the significance of making ethical decisions. Thinking ethically, voicing values, and building an ethical organization is both challenging and critically important as managers and employees seek to operate a business profitably as well as successfully. While not necessarily an easy task, building an ethical business organization is an imperative—an imperative for every manager and every employee at every level in an organization.

© Purestock/Superstock

Internet References

Association for Moral Education (AME)
www.amenetwork.org

Better Business Bureau
www.bbb.org

Business for Social Responsibility (BSR)
www.bsr.org

Corporate Ethics
www.pbs.org/newshour/bb/business/ethics

Corporate Responsibility
www.wisegeek.com/what-is-corporate-responsibility.htm

Ethics Resource Center (ERC)
www.ethics.org

Ethics Updates/Lawrence M. Hinman
http://ethics.sandiego.edu

Financial Scandals
www.ex.ac.uk/~ RDavies/arian/scandals

Institute for Business and Professional Ethics
http://commerce.depaul.edu/ethics

National Center for Policy Analysis
www.ncpa.org

Open Directory Project
http://dmoz.org/Business/Management/Ethics

Thinking Ethically
A Framework for Moral Decision Making

MANUEL VELASQUEZ ET AL.

Moral issues greet us each morning in the newspaper, confront us in the memos on our desks, nag us from our children's soccer fields, and bid us good night on the evening news. We are bombarded daily with questions about the justice of our foreign policy, the morality of medical technologies that can prolong our lives, the rights of the homeless, the fairness of our children's teachers to the diverse students in their classrooms.

Dealing with these moral issues is often perplexing. How, exactly, should we think through an ethical issue? What questions should we ask? What factors should we consider?

The first step in analyzing moral issues is obvious but not always easy: Get the facts.

The first step in analyzing moral issues is obvious but not always easy: Get the facts. Some moral issues create controversies simply because we do not bother to check the facts. This first step, although obvious, is also among the most important and the most frequently overlooked.

But having the facts is not enough. Facts by themselves only tell us what *is*; they do not tell us what *ought* to be. In addition to getting the facts, resolving an ethical issue also requires an appeal to values. Philosophers have developed five different approaches to values to deal with moral issues.

The Utilitarian Approach

Utilitarianism was conceived in the 19th century by Jeremy Bentham and John Stuart Mill to help legislators determine which laws were morally best. Both Bentham and Mill suggested that ethical actions are those that provide the greatest balance of good over evil.

To analyze an issue using the utilitarian approach, we first identify the various courses of action available to us. Second, we ask who will be affected by each action and what benefits or harms will be derived from each. And third, we choose the action that will produce the greatest benefits and the least harm. The ethical action is the one that provides the greatest good for the greatest number.

The Rights Approach

The second important approach to ethics has its roots in the philosophy of the 18th-century thinker Immanuel Kant and others like him, who focused on the individual's right to choose for herself or himself. According to these philosophers, what makes human beings different from mere things is that people have dignity based on their ability to choose freely what they will do with their lives, and they have a fundamental moral right to have these choices respected. People are not objects to be manipulated; it is a violation of human dignity to use people in ways they do not freely choose.

Of course, many different, but related, rights exist besides this basic one. These other rights (an incomplete list below) can be thought of as different aspects of the basic right to be treated as we choose.

- *The right to the truth*: We have a right to be told the truth and to be informed about matters that significantly affect our choices.
- *The right of privacy*: We have the right to do, believe, and say whatever we choose in our personal lives so long as we do not violate the rights of others.
- *The right not to be injured*: We have the right not to be harmed or injured unless we freely and knowingly do something to deserve punishment or we freely and knowingly choose to risk such injuries.
- *The right to what is agreed:* We have a right to what has been promised by those with whom we have freely entered into a contract or agreement.

In deciding whether an action is moral or immoral using this second approach, then, we must ask, Does the action respect the moral rights of everyone? Actions are wrong to the extent

The Case of Maria Elena

Maria Elena has cleaned your house each week for more than a year. You agree with your friend who recommended her that she does an excellent job and is well worth the $30 cash you pay her for three hours' work. You've also come to like her, and you think she likes you, especially as her English has become better and you've been able to have some pleasant conversations.

Over the past three weeks, however, you've noticed Maria Elena becoming more and more distracted. One day, you ask her if something is wrong, and she tells you she really needs to make additional money. She hastens to say she is not asking you for a raise, becomes upset, and begins to cry. When she calms down a little, she tells you her story:

She came to the United States six years ago from Mexico with her child, Miguel, who is now 7 years old. They entered the country on a visitor's visa that has expired, and Maria Elena now uses a Social Security number she made up.

Her common-law husband, Luis, came to the United States first. He entered the country illegally, after paying smugglers $500 to hide him under piles of grass cuttings for a six-hour truck ride across the border. When he had made enough money from low-paying day jobs, he sent for Maria Elena. Using a false green card, Luis now works as a busboy for a restaurant, which withholds part of his salary for taxes. When Maria Elena comes to work at your house, she takes the bus and Luis baby-sits.

In Mexico, Maria Elena and Luis lived in a small village where it was impossible to earn more than $3 a day. Both had sixth-grade educations, common in their village. Life was difficult, but they did not decide to leave until they realized the future would be bleak for their child and for the other children they wanted to have. Luis had a cousin in San Jose who visited and told Luis and Maria Elena how well his life was going. After his visit, Luis and Maria Elena decided to come to the United States.

Luis quickly discovered, as did Maria Elena, that life in San Jose was not the way they had heard. The cousin did not tell them they would be able to afford to live only in a run-down three-room apartment with two other couples and their children. He did not tell them they would always live in fear of INS raids.

After they entered the United States, Maria Elena and Luis had a second child, Jose, who is 5 years old. The birth was difficult because she didn't use the health-care system or welfare for fear of being discovered as undocumented. But, she tells you, she is willing to put up with anything so that her children can have a better life. "All the money we make is for Miguel and Jose," she tells you. "We work hard for their education and their future."

Now, however, her mother in Mexico is dying, and Maria Elena must return home, leaving Luis and the children. She does not want to leave them because she might not be able to get back into the United States, but she is pretty sure she can find a way to return if she has enough money. That is her problem: She doesn't have enough money to make certain she can get back.

After she tells you her story, she becomes too distraught to continue talking. You now know she is an undocumented immigrant, working in your home. What is the ethical thing for you to do?

This case was developed by Tom Shanks, S.J., director of the Markkula Center for Applied Ethics. Maria Elena is a composite drawn from several real people, and her story represents some of the ethical dilemmas behind the immigration issue.

This case can be accessed through the Ethics Center home page on the World Wide Web: www.scu.edu/Ethics/. You can also contact us by e-mail, ethics@scu.edu, or regular mail: Markkula Center for Applied Ethics, Santa Clara University, Santa Clara, CA 95053. Our voice mail number is (408) 554-7898. We have also posted on our homepage a new case involving managed health care.

that they violate the rights of individuals; the more serious the violation, the more wrongful the action.

The Fairness or Justice Approach

The fairness or justice approach to ethics has its roots in the teachings of the ancient Greek philosopher Aristotle, who said that "equals should be treated equally and unequals unequally." The basic moral question in this approach is: How fair is an action? Does it treat everyone in the same way, or does it show favoritism and discrimination?

Favoritism gives benefits to some people without a justifiable reason for singling them out; discrimination imposes burdens on people who are no different from those on whom burdens

are not imposed. Both favoritism and discrimination are unjust and wrong.

The Common-Good Approach

This approach to ethics presents a vision of society as a community whose members are joined in the shared pursuit of values and goals they hold in common. This community comprises individuals whose own good is inextricably bound to the good of the whole.

The common good is a notion that originated more than 2,000 years ago in the writings of Plato, Aristotle, and Cicero. More recently, contemporary ethicist John Rawls defined the common good as "certain general conditions that are . . . equally to everyone's advantage."

In this approach, we focus on ensuring that the social policies, social systems, institutions, and environments on which we depend are beneficial to all. Examples of goods common to all include affordable health care, effective public safety, peace among nations, a just legal system, and an unpolluted environment.

Appeals to the common good urge us to view ourselves as members of the same community, reflecting on broad questions concerning the kind of society we want to become and how we are to achieve that society. While respecting and valuing the freedom of individuals to pursue their own goals, the common-good approach challenges us also to recognize and further those goals we share in common.

The Virtue Approach

The virtue approach to ethics assumes that there are certain ideals toward which we should strive, which provide for the full development of our humanity. These ideals are discovered through thoughtful reflection on what kind of people we have the potential to become.

Virtues are attitudes or character traits that enable us to be and to act in ways that develop our highest potential. They enable us to pursue the ideals we have adopted.

Honesty, courage, compassion, generosity, fidelity, integrity, fairness, self-control, and prudence are all examples of virtues.

Virtues are like habits; that is, once acquired, they become characteristic of a person. Moreover, a person who has developed virtues will be naturally disposed to act in ways consistent with moral principles. The virtuous person is the ethical person.

In dealing with an ethical problem using the virtue approach, we might ask, What kind of person should I be? What will promote the development of character within myself and my community?

Ethical Problem Solving

These five approaches suggest that once we have ascertained the facts, we should ask ourselves five questions when trying to resolve a moral issue:

- What benefits and what harms will each course of action produce, and which alternative will lead to the best overall consequences?
- What moral rights do the affected parties have, and which course of action best respects those rights?
- Which course of action treats everyone the same, except where there is a morally justifiable reason not to, and does not show favoritism or discrimination?
- Which course of action advances the common good?
- Which course of action develops moral virtues?

This method, of course, does not provide an automatic solution to moral problems. It is not meant to. The method is merely meant to help identify most of the important ethical considerations. In the end, we must deliberate on moral issues for ourselves, keeping a careful eye on both the facts and on the ethical considerations involved.

Critical Thinking

1. Describe briefly each the five approaches to solving ethical dilemmas.
2. Set up a table for the five approaches and show how each approach would address The Case of Maria Elena.

This article updates several previous pieces from *Issues in Ethics* by **Manuel Velasquez**—Dirksen Professor of Business Ethics at SCU and former Center director—and **Claire Andre**, associate Center director. "Thinking Ethically" is based on a framework developed by the authors in collaboration with Center Director **Thomas Shanks, S. J.,** Presidential Professor of Ethics and the Common Good **Michael J. Meyer,** and others. The framework is used as the basis for many Center programs and presentations.

Designing Honesty into Your Organization

CHRISTIAN MASTILAK ET AL.

The past decade has provided ample evidence that some people don't behave honestly at work. While it's easy to blame individual factors such as greed or lack of an ethical compass, recent academic research paints a different picture. As a leader in your organization, you may have more influence than you realize about whether your employees act honestly or not. You can design honest behavior into an organization by using fair and properly aligned reward systems and simple communication strategies.

We know dishonesty is costly, and it may be on the rise. The Ethics Resource Center reports that the following percentages of employees surveyed in 2009 had observed these behaviors in the previous year: company resource abuse (23%), lying to employees (19%), lying to outside stakeholders (12%), falsifying time or expenses (10%), and stealing (9%). The Association of Certified Fraud Examiners suggests United States organizations may have lost as much as $994 billion to occupational fraud in 2008, and a PricewaterhouseCoopers global survey in 2009 suggests that recent economic pressures have increased the likelihood of fraud taking place. But how can this common problem be reduced?

Research suggests that integrity testing goes only so far in predicting honesty in the workplace. It turns out that most employees are neither consistent truth-tellers who can be completely trusted in the absence of controls nor consistent liars who can never be trusted. This means preventing dishonesty isn't just a matter of finding the right people. Some factors can motivate employees to be closer to the truth-telling end of the scale. Specifically, research shows that honest behavior is influenced by employees' beliefs about whether they are being treated fairly, whether expectations of honest behavior have been made explicit, and whether organizational control systems reward dishonest behavior. This suggests that honest behavior can be designed into—or out of—an organization. In this article, we first discuss some of the research findings, then draw on them to develop practical suggestions for how managers can create an environment that both discourages dishonest behavior and enables honest behavior.

Why Do Employees Behave Dishonestly?

We broadly define dishonest behavior as making a report known to contain lies or taking an action known to be unauthorized for personal gain. This excludes accidental errors but includes a variety of behaviors common to accounting and finance functions. Most research in accounting has focused primarily on budgeting behavior, such as padding requests in order to keep the extra funds. But research on more direct forms of theft, such as stealing company property, has led to similar conclusions about why employees steal.

Admittedly, the reasons for dishonest behavior are many and varied. Much has been written about the fraud triangle and how the presence of pressure, opportunity, and rationalization increases the chance of fraud. We can't do justice to the entire topic here, but we can discuss some organizational design and control choices that affect people's behavior. Two common themes that surface are *fairness* and *frame*.

Fairness

For years, economic theory has rested on the assumption that two important desires drive people's behavior: leisure and wealth. Business schools teach future managers to assume that employees will avoid working hard and will lie to increase their wealth. These assumptions then show up in practice as internal control systems are developed to help prevent and detect lack of effort and dishonesty.

Recent academic research has identified two other desires that influence behavior: honesty and fairness. So it isn't simply that people want to be as rich and put forth as little effort as possible; rather, most people also care about being honest and want to ensure that their treatment and outcomes are reasonable compared to the treatment and outcomes of others. More importantly, these desires affect honesty in the workplace.

When employees believe they haven't received what they are due, they will look for ways to recover what they believe they're owed.

Several studies provide examples of how tradeoffs among desires for wealth, honesty, and fairness play out in organizational settings. Coauthor Linda Matuszewski conducted one such study with funding from the IMA® Foundation for Applied Research (now called IMA Research Foundation). Appearing in the 2010 issue (Volume 22) of the *Journal of Management Accounting Research,* "Honesty in Managerial Reporting: Is It Affected by Perceptions of Horizontal Equity?"

is one of several studies in accounting in which student participants played the role of managers reporting to their employer. Participants knew the amount of actual costs that would be incurred on a project and were asked to submit a budget request. The employer would never know the actual costs. If the participant lied and the budget request exceeded actual costs, the participants kept the difference. This difference was personal gain for participants—at the expense of their employers. That is, the greater the lie, the more money the participants received.

Overall, Matuszewski's results are consistent with "Honesty in Managerial Reporitng," a study by John Evans, Lynn Hannan, Ranjani Krishnan, and Donald Moser in the October 2001 issue of *The Accounting Review*. Matuszewski's study shows that only a small proportion of people (15%) lied to maximize their wealth. A similar proportion of people were at the other end of the spectrum, with 19% behaving completely honestly. This left the vast majority (66%) in the middle—lying some and trading their desire to be honest against their desire for wealth.

At the two extremes, managers could assume the worst and develop expensive management controls to prevent and detect dishonesty, or they could assume the best and not develop any controls. Since most employees don't fall into either extreme, neither of these solutions is likely to be the most cost effective. Managers are left with the challenge of designing control systems for the majority of employees—those who have some desire to be honest but are also willing to lie to some extent. This is where the results of several other studies can be helpful, as they shed some light on factors within a company's control that influence whether an employee's behavior is closer to the honest or the dishonest end of the scale.

One factor is *vertical* fairness. This represents the relationship between employees and their organizations. In "Stealing in the Name of Justice: Informational and Interpersonal Moderators of Theft Reactions to Underpayment Inequity," Jerald Greenberg describes a study in which he promised two groups of research participants a certain level of pay for performing a lowskilled task (*Organizational Behavior and Human Decision Processes*, Volume 54, Issue 1, February 1993). Participants who were treated unfairly by being paid less than they were originally promised "stole" from the researcher, likely rationalizing that they were due the stolen amount. Participants who were given a reasonable explanation for why their pay was less than promised and received an apology from the researcher, however, stole less. Greenberg's work shows that an explanation and empathy can go a long way toward soothing hurt feelings—and reducing retaliation in firms.

Vertical fairness is critical—but it isn't the only element that matters. Look no further than *Strategic Finance's* Annual Salary Survey each June to know that horizontal fairness—how fairly people are treated compared to their peers—is also important. This was the main focus of Matuszewski's study, which demonstrated that participants' beliefs about changes in the *horizontal* fairness of their pay changed the honesty in their budgeting behavior. Participants in the study were paid a salary and received information about the salaries of other participants. When the horizontal fairness of pay declined, the change in honesty was the same, whether it occurred because of a decrease in the participant's own pay or an increase in others' pay. To make matters worse, this dishonest behavior is hard to undo. In Matuszewski's study, improvements in horizontal fairness resulting from decreases in others' pay didn't result in more honest behavior. Thus, being treated fairly right from the beginning is extremely important.

We aren't trying to minimize employees' personal responsibility for their actions. But research shows that when employees believe they haven't received what they are due, they will look for ways to recover what they believe they're owed. Accordingly, we believe that if top management designs fairness into its dealings with employees, it will eliminate this possible rationalization and cause employees to pursue honest behavior more frequently.

Frame

Another way to design honest behavior into organizations is to ensure that an organization clearly communicates that honesty is expected. When would an employee think that honest behavior isn't expected? Think of it this way: Imagine you're playing basketball. Is a head fake unethical? No, it's completely normal behavior because basketball is a competition, and misleading your opponent is expected. Imagine Kobe Bryant complaining that LeBron James cheated because he made a no-look pass. "Not fair! He looked the other way!" That isn't going to happen because Kobe understands they're competing against each other.

How is this relevant? Well, how often do your budgeting processes become framed as strategic competitions among employees and management rather than decisions with ethical implications? You're more likely to find dishonest behavior if employees believe that the budgeting process is expected to be competitive rather than collaborative, strategic rather than honest. That's what Frederick Rankin, Steven Schwartz, and Richard Young found in "The Effect of Honesty and Superior Authority on Budget Proposals" (*The Accounting Review*, July 2008). Participants completed a budgeting task similar to the task in Matuszewski's study. Those who were asked to honestly share their information about actual costs were more honest than those who were simply asked what portion of the profits should be returned to the company. This study suggests that, in the absence of formal controls, people will be more honest if you simply ask them to be!

Rankin, Schwartz, and Young's finding is particularly important given recent research about the costs and benefits of formal controls. In "When Formal Controls Undermine Trust and Cooperation," Margaret Christ, Karen Sedatole, Kristy Towry, and Myra Thomas suggest that employees sometimes view formal controls as a sign that employers question their competence and integrity, and this may undermine trust and cooperation (*Strategic Finance*, January 2008). To be clear, we aren't advocating doing away with all explicit formal controls. In circumstances in which formal controls aren't present or are too costly, Rankin, Schwartz, and Young show that some of the same benefits can be achieved by describing a task as an ethical dilemma, rather than a strategic competition, and asking for honesty.

Another effect that framing has in determining whether honest behavior is expected showed up in the large-scale fraud at Enron. Bennett Stewart suggests in "The Real Reasons Enron Failed" that Enron's managers were, in fact, paid to do dishonest things (*Journal of Applied Corporate Finance*, Volume 18, Issue, 2, Spring 2006). Stewart documents that performance at Enron was framed as an accounting game rather than as increasing the company's true economic value. In part, this involved manipulating internal performance measures to exclude any costs of capital. Stewart documents the use of EBITDA—"the least accountable, most misleading indicator of corporate performance ever devised"—by Enron executives who clearly knew better.

Why did they use this measure? Simple: Enron's performance measurement and compensation system, which included stock-based compensation, paid them to do so. Increases in Enron's stock price were driven in large part by—you guessed it—accounting performance. And we shouldn't be surprised when people do what firms pay them to do.

The greatest problem with poorly framed control systems is that, even when employees intend to be honest, a bad control system may discourage that employee from acting on that honest urge and *disable* that honesty. The challenge is for top managers to design control systems that *enable* honesty.

The Designed Honesty Model

Putting these research results together, we present the designed honesty model of organizational behavior (see Figure 1). The model shows that both fairness and frame contribute to designed honesty. Where should top management look to understand why employees aren't behaving honestly? That depends. If employees are grumbling about their working conditions or their pay—especially their pay relative to others within the organization—then they probably believe they aren't being treated fairly and may well be working the system to get what they believe is due them. On the other hand, if employees report conflicts between what they believe they should do and what they believe they're being asked and paid to do, then the culture and control system frame are probably the culprits, leading otherwise honest employees to feel like they are being encouraged to behave dishonestly.

The designed honesty model isn't intended to be complete—the factors that influence honesty and dishonesty are many and varied. As the research shows, most employees value honesty and fairness in addition to wealth and leisure and are influenced by all of these values when deciding whether to behave honestly. Since fairness and frame are within an organization's control to some extent, it's important for management to understand how these factors can contribute to honest behavior.

Therefore, in addition to attempting to hire the right people, we recommend that companies take the following steps to encourage employees to act on their intentions to be honest (see Table 1):

1. *Consider vertical and horizontal fairness when making compensation decisions.*
   Employees consider the fairness of their compensation from two perspectives—relative to their exchange with the company (vertical) and relative to the compensation of their peers (horizontal). Managers may be able to get a sense of the perceptions about the vertical fairness of compensation by considering employees' alternative employment opportunities. In today's culture of high turnover, it's reasonable to assume that employees are keeping their eye on the job market and asking "What could I make elsewhere?" But how often do managers consider their subordinates' opportunities when making compensation decisions? Incorporating this practice into the firm's periodic performance review system could help avoid the costs of dishonesty motivated by perceptions of vertical unfairness.

   From the horizontal perspective, although firms often have policies that discourage peers from sharing information about pay, we believe managers should assume that employees know how much money their peers are making so should make an effort to compensate employees fairly compared to their peers.

2. *Fully explain compensation policies and procedures.*
   Fair doesn't necessarily imply equal. In cases where compensation isn't equal to an alternative employment opportunity or the pay a peer is receiving, detailed explanations may be especially important in helping employees evaluate whether their pay is fair. Communication strategies that help employees understand the justification for compensation policies can be extremely valuable. For instance, employees may be more likely to consider their compensation fair if managers explain the connection between the resources of their division and employee compensation.

3. *Determine whether employees believe they are being paid fairly.*
   Most large companies have periodic performance review systems in place, and it's through these systems that compensation decisions get communicated. Yet how many of these systems are two-way communication devices designed to determine whether employees believe they are being paid fairly? This data may be challenging to get, especially if employees fear retaliation if they admit they don't believe they are being paid fairly. Managers may need to put themselves in their employees' shoes and pursue indirect methods for answering this question, such as anonymous surveys or hotline methods.

4. *Show (and feel!) empathy when tough compensation choices need to be implemented.*
   Of course, managers won't always have the resources to give employees the compensation they want and feel they deserve. But empathy can have an impact on honesty, even when employees face an outcome they believe is unfair.

5. *Ask employees to be honest, and describe routine decisions as ethical dilemmas rather than strategic competitions.*
   A logical first step in making it clear that you expect employees to be honest is the establishment of a corporate code of ethics, but even the best code won't be effective unless employees can see the connection between the code and their everyday activities. Think of it this way: Corporate planning doesn't stop with the development of a vision statement. Firms work toward the vision by identifying core competencies, developing organizational strategies, and translating these strategies into operating plans. In the same way, a company must develop

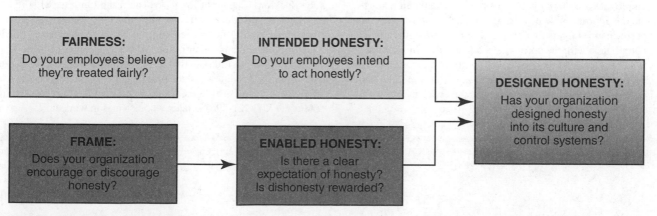

Figure 1   The Designed Honesty Model

Table 1   Six Key Steps toward Designing Honesty into Your Organization

1. Consider vertical and horizontal fairness when making compensation decisions.
2. Fully explain compensation policies and procedures.
3. Determine whether employees believe they are being paid fairly.
4. Show (and feel!) empathy when tough compensation choices need to be implemented.
5. Ask employees to be honest, and describe routine decisions as ethical dilemmas rather than strategic competitions.
6. Review incentive plans to ensure they reward honest reporting of economic results.

strategies for ensuring honest behavior. The research suggests that one successful strategy would be to identify tasks that provide employees with opportunities to benefit from dishonesty and describe these tasks as ethical dilemmas rather than strategic competitions.

This suggestion is consistent with the findings in two 2011 studies published in the *Journal of Business Ethics* that identify factors that contribute to the effectiveness of corporate codes of ethics. Muel Kaptein found in "Toward Effective Codes: Testing the Relationship with Unethical Behavior" (Volume 99, No. 2, March 2011) that the quality of communication regarding a corporate code of ethics has a greater impact on reducing unethical behavior than the quantity of communication about the code. Put simply, it isn't enough to establish a code and talk about it a lot. The code must be accessible, clear, easy to understand, and useful for decision making. In the other study, "Determinants of the Effectiveness of Corporate Codes of Ethics: An Empirical Study" (Volume 101, No. 3, July 2011), Jang Singh found that a code's impact on behavior is determined in part by whether the code guides strategic planning and is useful in resolving ethical dilemmas in the marketplace.

6. *Review incentive plans to ensure they reward honest reporting of economic results.*
Both Kaptein's and Singh's studies also provide insight into the steps managers should take to ensure that their incentive plans promote honesty in the workplace. Singh found that codes are more effective when compliance with their provisions is a part of performance reviews and when there are real consequences for violations. Kaptein found that the most important factor in reducing unethical behavior was senior and local management's embedding of the corporate code of ethics within an organization. More specifically, employees are more likely to be honest when their managers are approachable positive role models who set reasonable performance targets that promote, rather than undermine, compliance with the corporate code of ethics. In addition, it's important that managers don't authorize violations of the code to meet business goals, are aware of the extent to which employees comply with (or violate) the code, and respond to violations appropriately.

To prevent the kind of financial reporting dishonesty that occurred at Enron and many other companies, we suggest that managers should also consider whether performance targets based on economic results are using measures less subject to manipulation than traditional financial accounting measures may be.

Steps Will Go a Long Way

While we can't guarantee that these steps will eliminate all dishonesty in the workplace, we believe that paying attention to the fairness of employees' compensation and highlighting the ethical dimension of certain decisions will go a long way toward designing honesty into your organization.

Critical Thinking

1. Why do some people behave dishonestly at work?
2. Using the Designed Honesty Model presented in the article, develop your own model and explain its strengths and weaknesses compared to the model presented in the article.
3. Pick out one of the "six key steps" toward designing honesty in an organization. Build arguments for and against the key step.
4. If you are a student in a class, engage in a debate for/against with another student concerning the key step you selected.

CHRISTIAN MASTILAK, PhD, is an assistant professor of accountancy and business law in the Williams College of Business at Xavier University and a member of the North Cincinnati Chapter of IMA. You can reach Christian at (513) 745-3290 or mastilakc@xavier.edu. **LINDA MATUSZEWSKI**, PhD, is an assistant professor of accountancy in the College of Business at Northern Illinois University and a member of the Rockford Chapter of IMA. You can reach Linda at (815) 753-6379 or lmatus@niu.edu. **FABIENNE MILLER**, PhD, is an assistant professor of accounting in the School of Business at Worcester Polytechnic Institute and a member of the Worcester Chapter of IMA. You can reach Fabienne at (508) 831-6128 or fabienne@wpi.edu. **ALEXANDER WOODS**, PhD, is an assistant professor of accounting in the Mason School of Business at The College of William & Mary. You can reach Alex at (757) 221-2967 or alex.woods@mason.wm.edu.

Fairness in Business: Does It Matter, and What Does It Mean?

JOEL D. RUBIN

1. Introduction

This past spring was one of the worst on record, weather-wise, in the United States. From Joplin, Missouri to Tuscaloosa, Alabama and many places in between, deadly tornadoes wiped out buildings and trees . . . and most everything else in their path. Assume that you own an apartment building in Tuscaloosa that miraculously was spared damage. Before the tornadoes hit, you were renting apartments for $1,000 per month. Since many apartments were destroyed by the tornadoes, the market rate for apartments like yours has now risen to $1,500 per month. Would it be fair for you to raise the rent on your apartments to $1,500? Would your answer differ if you were dealing with a new tenant versus one who was renewing his/her lease? If you do not raise the rent, how will you decide to whom to lease your vacant apartments?

When we were children, many of us were taught the importance of fairness. As we grew older, however, we were confronted with images and instances of business people not behaving fairly. From editorials calling for the punishment of finance company executives who were involved in the events which led to the recent financial meltdown, to the ritual floggings of oil company executives summoned to testify before Congress when retail gas prices reached ever-higher levels, to Gordon Gekko declaring "greed is good" in the movie *Wall Street,* business people are often seen as being out just for themselves.

This conflict between what we were taught and what we see in the real world leads to two questions: Should business people consider fairness when making decisions? And, if so, what does it mean to be fair?

2. Why Be Fair?

Why should a business person consider fairness when making a decision? Isn't the singular role of a business person to make money? From an ethical standpoint, there are two primary reasons for considering fairness as a factor in decision making: (1) fairness is a virtue, and (2) the positive consequences of being fair outweigh the negative consequences. The first reason is somewhat philosophical, while the latter is more practical.

In general terms, "virtues are those [admirable character] traits that everyone needs for a good life" (Boatright, 2009, p. 78). While the exact details of what constitutes a good life and how that concept applies in the business context are open to debate, it seems beyond question that fairness would contribute to a good life under most definitions. Thus, fairness should be considered a virtue and a business-person who practices fairness virtuous.

While the virtue of fairness might be enough of a reason for some business people to include it in their decision making, for many others the question of whether or not to consider fairness is heavily influenced by the potential consequences. While behaving unfairly can result in a short-term tangible gain—for example, paying employees less than a 'fair' wage or charging customers more than a 'fair' price results in more money in the company's pocket—the longer-term costs can easily outweigh those initial benefits. Chief among these is the harm that can be done to a business' reputation and to its customers' or employees' satisfaction. This, in turn, may adversely impact sales and the business' ability to attract top employees.

The controversy surrounding Nike's treatment of workers in Asia serves as a good example of reputational risk. In the mid-1990s, reports surfaced that Nike—the world's largest manufacturer of athletic footwear and apparel—was not treating its Asian factory workers fairly, subjecting them to long hours in substandard conditions for low wages (Neuborne, 1997). The reports led to a series of protests, staged mainly across United States college campuses. Phil Knight, then-chairman and CEO of Nike, summarized the effect of the adverse publicity and protests in a speech given at the National Press Club: "The Nike product has become synonymous with slave wages, forced overtime, and arbitrary abuse. I truly believe that the American consumer does not want to buy products made in abusive conditions" (Dionne, 1998, p. A27). While Nike admittedly is an extreme case, it illustrates the fact that perceptions of fairness can have a significant effect on a business' reputation and thereby impact the company's bottom line.

2.1. Academic Research on the Risks of Unfair Business

A similar risk of unfair business behavior has been uncovered via academic research. Surveying adult subjects in Toronto and Vancouver, Kahneman, Knetsch, and Thaler (1986b, p. 736) found that "68 percent of respondents said they would switch their patronage to a drugstore five minutes further away if the one closer to them raised its prices when a competitor was temporarily forced to close" and that "69 percent indicated they would switch if the more convenient store discriminated against its older workers."

Academic research also has found a risk to customer or employee satisfaction. That risk is based on the concept of transaction utility. Richard Thaler (1985) demonstrated that a person's satisfaction with a transaction could be broken down into two components, dubbing these parts 'acquisition utility' and 'transaction utility.' *Acquisition utility* reflects the difference between the value[1] of the specific item being purchased or sold and the price paid for it. For example, imagine that you want a red, Heavy Duti Schwinn bicycle. You've never purchased one before, know nothing about the seller or the suggested retail price, and have no idea how much other people have paid for similar bikes. If the most you're willing to pay is $400, that is the value of the bike. If you purchase it for $380, the happiness created by the $20 difference represents your acquisition utility.

In contrast, *transaction utility* reflects elements of the deal other than price versus the value of the item exchanged. Thaler (1985, p. 206) illustrated that concept with what has come to be known as his 'Beer on the Beach' scenario. For that analysis, he gave participants in an executive development program who said they were regular beer drinkers the following scenario. One subgroup received a version with the words in parentheses, while a second subgroup received a version with the words in square brackets:

> You are lying on the beach on a hot day. All you have to drink is ice water. For the last hour, you have been thinking about how much you would enjoy a nice cold bottle of your favorite brand of beer. A companion gets up to go make a phone call and offers to bring back a beer from the only nearby place where beer is sold (a fancy resort hotel) [a small, run-down grocery store]. He says that the beer might be expensive and so asks how much you are willing to pay for the beer. He says that he will buy the beer if it costs as much or less than the price you state. But if it costs more than the price you state he will not buy it. You trust your friend, and there is no possibility of bargaining with (the bartender) [store owner]. What price do you tell him?

The responses showed a distinct difference between the prices that the respondents were willing to pay at the two locations, even though the product they were purchasing was identical. "The median price given in the fancy resort hotel version was $2.65, while the median for the small run-down grocery store version was $1.50" (Thaler, 1985, p. 206). Since the product purchased was the same at both locations—that is, the acquisition utility was the same—the difference must reflect satisfaction based on some other aspect of the transaction: what Thaler called 'transaction utility.'

Thaler posited that transaction utility is a function of the difference between the purchase or sale price and a reference price; that is, a price against which to measure satisfaction with the current transaction. According to him, "the most important factor in determining [the reference price] is fairness" (Thaler, 1985, p. 205). Thus, whether a person perceives the deal that he/she got as 'fair' is an important factor in determining his/her happiness with or satisfaction from the transaction. Customer and employee satisfaction, in turn, can have a significant effect on a business' well being.

3. What Does It Mean to Be Fair?

Since fairness in business is important for the aforementioned reasons, we next need to understand what it means to behave fairly. At its most basic level, fairness can be characterized by two elements: (1) impartiality and (2) consistency with community expectations of fairness.

The Merriam-Webster dictionary defines *fair* as "marked by impartiality and honesty: free from self-interest, prejudice, or favoritism," "conforming with established rules," and "consonant with merit or importance." While the element of impartiality is straightforward, in theory if not always in practice, understanding established rules or community expectations is more complex.

3.1. What Influences Community Expectations of Fairness?

Community expectations are reflected in the reference transaction, or basis of comparison, previously mentioned. The complication, however, is that there is no definitive rule telling us what transaction we should use for a reference in any given situation. Moreover, the reference transaction does not necessarily even have to involve the customer or employee in the current transaction. When considering the fairness of a specific transaction, people tend to focus not just on the impact of that transaction on themselves, but also on how they compare to other people in similar situations. That principle is illustrated in the following scenario posed by Bazerman and Moore (2009, p. 113):

> You are graduating from a good MBA program. Following your discussions with a number of firms, one of your preferred companies makes you an offer of $90,000 a year, stressing that the amount is not negotiable. You like the people. You like the job. You like the location. However, you find out that the same company is offering $95,000 to some graduating MBAs from similar-quality schools. Will you accept the offer?

While there are not definitive rules regarding the appropriate reference transaction for a given situation, Kahneman et al. (1986b) have developed some general principles regarding such

---

[1]From a typical economist's perspective, the value of the item is the amount that would make the purchaser (or other affected party) indifferent between having the cash or the item.

transactions. They did so based on responses to a detailed telephone survey. In each call, they gave the respondent a number of scenarios and asked him/her whether the person making the decision in that scenario had acted acceptably or unfairly. From the responses, they derived some general principles regarding reference transactions and the public's perceptions of fairness. With respect to the reference transaction, Kahneman and his coauthors (1986b, p. 730) concluded:

> When there is a history of similar transactions between firm [the party making the decision; for example, a seller or employer] and transactor [the party affected by the decision; for example, the customer or employee], the most recent price, wage, or rent will be adopted for reference unless the terms of the previous transaction were explicitly temporary. For new transactions, prevailing competitive prices or wages provide the natural reference.

That guidance regarding reference transactions feeds into the authors' primary conclusion about the public's perception of fairness. Specifically, they concluded that the public views a firm as entitled to the profit level it realized in the reference transaction, and a transactor as entitled to the terms of that transaction (Kahneman et al., 1986b). Between the two parties, the public gives priority to the firm's profit entitlement. Thus, if a firm's costs rise, it generally would be considered fair for the firm to raise prices or cut wages to maintain its profit level. In the absence of a threat to profits, however, it would not be considered fair for the firm to raise prices or decrease wages just to increase its profits. They also found that if a firm's profit level rises, whether because its costs decrease or due to multiple other factors, the public perception of fairness does not require the firm to pass along or share the increased profits with its customers or employees by cutting prices or raising wages.

For example, if an apartment owner was renting apartments for $1,000 per month and the market rate rose to $1,500 per month, raising a renewing tenant's rent to $1,500 per month would be viewed as unfair; in this scenario, the reference transaction would be the current lease and the tenant would be seen as entitled to the rental rate in that transaction. It would, however, be considered fair for the landlord to rent out a similar apartment to a new tenant for $1,500 per month; in this scenario, the reference transaction would be a market-rate lease.

Kahneman and his coauthors (1986b) also recognized a caveat to the foregoing principles when changes, such as increased prices or decreased wages, are due to anomalies like shortages or natural disasters. In these situations, the public views price or wage moves to take advantage of the situation and thereby increase profits as unfair. Thus, if the increased apartment rent in the preceding example were due to other apartments being destroyed by a tornado, raising the rent for even a new tenant would be considered unfair.

3.2. Fairness in the Allocation of Limited Resources

Another business context in which the question of fairness arises involves allocation of limited resources among competing claimants. For this purpose, a 'limited resource' can be defined as anything for which demand exceeds available supply. For example, in the scenario where more people need apartments than there are empty apartments available, a vacant apartment would represent a limited resource. Similarly, for many large businesses, offices or parking spaces could be limited resources; even if there were enough offices or parking spaces for all employees, particularly desirable ones would be limited. How, then, should the landlord decide to whom to lease a vacant apartment, or the person responsible for assigning offices or parking spaces do so?

This context differs from the preceding discussion because in the above discussion, the question was fairness of the firm vis-a-vis a third party with whom the firm was involved in a transaction; for example, a customer or an employee. In this context, the question is fairness when deciding among third parties. Here again, fairness should be based on the criteria of impartiality and consistency with community expectations. In this context, it helps to clarify that 'impartiality' means that similar claims or claimants should be treated equitably and that any difference in treatment must be justified by morally relevant distinctions (Boatright, 2009). For example, in assigning parking spaces, a disability would be a morally relevant distinction such that assigning spaces closer to a building entrance to persons with disabilities would not violate the impartiality criterion. We then can apply these criteria to some of the more common methods of allocation—first come/first served; random allocation; and allocations based on contribution, ability, or need—to assess their fairness.

First come/first served, sometimes referred to as 'queuing,' allocates a limited resource based on the order in which people request it. This method is the approach employed by cinemas and concert organizers: the theater or venue sells tickets to customers based on their order in line, until it runs out of tickets. First come/first served generally is thought to treat people impartially, based on the assumption that everyone has an equal opportunity to be at or near the front of the line. While it appears to be commonly held, that rationale actually is questionable. In certain situations, factors such as conflicting obligations or the claimant's ability to travel to the location of the line—if there is a physical line—can render the opportunity unequal. In the absence of such confounding factors, however, first come/first served would satisfy impartiality.

A *random allocation,* sometimes referred to as a 'lottery,' is one whereby all claimants are given an equal opportunity and the allocation is determined solely by chance. For example, if the apartment building owner had only one apartment available and there were 10 applicants, he/she could put the name of each applicant in a hat and draw one to whom to lease the apartment. While the outcome of a random allocation is not equal, it does meet the impartiality criterion based on ex ante equality, with every claimant having an equal chance to be chosen.

An *allocation based on contribution, ability, or need* may be appropriate in a more limited range of situations. For example, in determining shares of a bonus pool, contribution to the success of the business would make sense as an allocation rule. When deciding who should get the opportunity to lead a prestigious project, ability would seem to be an important allocation criterion. In allocating a limited budget among departments or projects, need seems like it would be an appropriate basis for allocation. Each of these allocation approaches would not treat claimants equally; those who contributed more, or who had greater ability or need, would receive priority. Nonetheless, such an allocation mechanism could satisfy the impartiality criterion if contribution, ability, or need were a morally relevant distinction justifying the differences in allocation. Regarding community expectations of fairness in the allocation of limited resources, Kahneman, Knetsch, and Thaler (1986a, p. S287) presented respondents with the following scenario:

> A football team normally sells some tickets on the day of its games. Recently, interest in the next game has increased greatly, and tickets are in great demand. The team owners can distribute the tickets in one of three ways. (1) By auction: the tickets are sold to the highest bidders. (2) By lottery: the tickets are sold to the people whose names are drawn. (3) By queue: the tickets are sold on a first come/first served basis.

The respondents were asked to rank the distribution options based on fairness. By a wide margin, the respondents felt that a queue was the fairest alternative and an auction the least fair (Kahneman et al., 1986a).

As for allocations based on contribution, ability, or need, personal observation suggests these carry risks regarding community expectations of fairness. While the criteria are likely to be considered fair in appropriate situations, unless there is some objective criterion by which to measure contribution, ability, or need, the application to specific claimants could lead to a widespread perception of unfairness. This would be the situation of a person who complains that his/her bonus did not accurately reflect his/her contribution to the business, or the person who complains that his/her department received a lower budget than it needs while other departments received more than they need. On an individual level, the perception of unfairness would be supported by the psychological concept of self-serving bias, which can lead an individual to hold a skewed view of his/her contribution or ability.

Since allocation based on contribution, ability, or need may be the best available method in certain situations—like budgeting, where queuing and random allocation are not appropriate—when faced with such a situation the allocator should attempt to mitigate the perception of unfairness by making public, to the largest extent possible, the criteria by which it measured contribution, ability, or need.

4. A Final Thought

Fairness matters. It is a virtue, and whether a business behaves fairly can have a significant impact on its reputation and the satisfaction of its customers and employees. For those businesses seeking to behave fairly, the principles outlined here should provide a good starting point.

References

Bazerman, M. H., & Moore, D. (2009). *Judgment in managerial decision making* (7th ed.). Hoboken, NJ: John Wiley & Sons.

Boatright, J. R. (2009). *Ethics and the conduct of business* (6th ed.). Upper Saddle River, NJ: Prentice Hall.

Dionne, E.J., Jr. (1998, May 15). Bad for business. *Washington Post*, p. A27.

Kahneman, D., Knetsch, J. L., & Thaler, R. H. (1986a). Fairness and the assumptions of economics. *Journal of Business, 59*(4), S285–S300.

Kahneman, D., Knetsch, J. L., & Thaler, R. H. (1986b). Fairness as a constraint on profit seeking: Entitlements in the market. *American Economic Review, 76*(4), 728–741.

Neuborne, E. (1997, March 27). Nike to take a hit in labor report. *USA Today*, p. 1A.

Thaler, R. H. (1985). Mental accounting and consumer choice. *Marketing Science, 4*(3), 199–214.

Critical Thinking

1. Discuss the concept of fairness and provide example of fair and unfair business practices. Find your examples from article about business found in newspapers and magazines.

2. What does it mean to be fair?

3. What does it mean to be unfair?

4. Of the three approaches to allocating limited resources discussed in the article, evaluate each on a fairness/unfairness scale that you design. Explain and justify your scale.

5. If you were a consultant advising management on the importance of fairness in business practice, what would be your advice?

JOEL D. RUBIN Kelley School of Business, Indiana University, 1309 E. Tenth Street, Bloomington, IN 47405-1701, U.S.A. *E-mail address:* jorubin@indiana.

Building an Ethical Framework

10 questions to consider in encouraging an ethical corporate culture.

THOMAS R. KRAUSE AND PAUL J. VOSS

Although we are now several years into the new and landmark regulatory environment that mandates an organizational culture of ethical conduct, there remains little guidance on how to get there. Many companies are engaged in a scramble to create a paper and electronic trail to ward off prosecution, rather than in a well-designed effort to promote or govern the culture of their organizations. While procedure is essential, the lesson we have learned from organizational change efforts is that leadership, rather than rules, finally determines behaviors and their outcomes.

This article suggests 10 primary questions every executive should ask—and expect to have answered thoroughly and well—in order to initiate a culture that encourages and sustains ethical conduct. These questions are meant to be asked and answered among leaders themselves, as well as with employees throughout the organization.

1. What is the relationship between ethics and other performance metrics in the company?

The relative cost of preventing a protracted ethical dilemma or full-fledged scandal is exponentially lower than the costs associated with fixing ethical problems. For example, see "The Cost to Firms of Cooking the Books," by J. Karpoff, D. Lee and G. Martin, forthcoming in *The Journal of Financial and Quantitative Analysis,* for a study of the substantial costs in fines and lost market value to almost 600 firms subject to SEC enforcement before the enactment of the Sarbanes-Oxley Act. Current research demonstrates that ethical companies are more competitive, profitable and sustaining than unethical companies. The challenge for the ethical leader is to find that connection and reveal it to the organization.

2. Have we, as required by the 2004 federal sentencing guidelines, offered ethics training for all of our employees? Does the training provide more than rote introduction of the company's code of conduct?

Ethics training comes in all shapes and sizes, with the most successful moving from theory to practice and from the conceptual to the real. Companies must first settle on an ethical vocabulary, define terms and establish core values. Live case studies can

then help leadership and management "solve" relevant ethical dilemmas, both real and hypothetical.

3. What is the relationship between exercising sound ethics and retaining great talent?

Fortune magazine's annual list of the top 100 companies to work for contains a wide variety of companies with no obvious common denominator. Salary, benefits, career opportunities, location and profession all vary. What they do have in common is trust between employee and employer. Ethical behavior with and among employees, then, can lay the groundwork for attracting and retaining the best talent.

4. Have we conducted a "risk assessment" to determine our exposure to major ethical damage? What is our potential Enron?

While each company may have its unique "ethical nightmare," most companies face similar ethical exposures (e.g., to theft and accounting irregularities). Companies must examine the potential hazards of perverse incentives (e.g., compensation based 100 percent on financial goals) and the various "unintended consequences" of policy, procedures and protocols. Companies can reduce or eliminate adverse incentives by never rewarding, intentionally or unintentionally, improper behavior.

Research literature identifies several characteristics predictive of ethical outcomes: management credibility, upward communication, perceived organizational support, procedural justice and teamwork.

5. How can we be proactive in the area of ethics, culture and corporate citizenship?

Leaders need to own and shape the culture as much as they manage, for example, quality initiatives. Research literature identifies several characteristics predictive of ethical outcomes: management credibility, upward communication, perceived organizational support, procedural justice and teamwork. Well-tested diagnostic tools allow leaders to measure these characteristics and specific behaviors that foster the culture desired.

6. What tone should executive leadership set regarding ethics, integrity and transparency?
Setting an example is just one part of the executive leadership's responsibility. What leaders say, think and feel affects the tone as much as their actions. Mistrust, cynicism or indifference from topmost leaders can erode others' loyalty to the organization, to its mission, to employees and to shareholders. Left unchecked, this tone from the top can also potentially push ethical leaders out the door.

7. What does management need from the board of directors and senior leadership to enhance and buttress corporate ethics?
Employees who see the governing board and executive leadership as unconcerned will discount any directives about ethics that come from them. Consistency and authenticity from the board and executive leadership play a signal role in establishing an ethics initiative. At a minimum this means providing a reasonable budget of time, talent and money.

8. Who is driving ethics and compliance in the company?
The recent American Management Association report *The Ethical Enterprise* (2006) shows that ethical companies do not happen by accident. Companies need to designate internal drivers who move along the discussions, training and initiatives, producing ethical outcomes.

9. Do we have consistency of message between and among the board, the CEO, the senior executive team and the associates in terms of ethics and culture?
We all need to be on the same page, but finding the proper tone and guidance can be tricky. Establishing a common vocabulary can help with this process. For example, what does it mean to act unethically? What is an ethical dilemma? Who were Aristotle, Plato and Machiavelli, and how can they help provide a vocabulary for our company? What ethical model do we want to follow? What can we do to make it stick?

10. What roadblocks now discourage ethical conversations and the implementation of ethical practices, procedures and protocols?

Most people want to act with ethics and integrity, "to do the right thing." Yet our current approach to ethical conversation often does not advance our thinking or practice past our own perspectives. The object of dialogue, as advocated by physicist David Bohm, is "not to analyze things, or to win an argument, or to exchange opinions. Rather, it is to suspend your opinions and . . . to listen to everybody's opinions, to suspend them, and to see what all that means. . . . And if we can see them all, we may then move more creatively in a different direction." (For more information, see "On Dialogue," Ojai, Calif.: David Bohm Seminars, 1990.)

> **Most people want . . . "to do the right thing." Yet our current approach to ethical conversation often does not advance our thinking past our own perspectives.**

Starting the Conversation
Asking these 10 questions at board meetings, in leadership team meetings, and in the course of day-to-day interactions with employees engenders a climate that leads, over time, to zero tolerance for ethical lapses and impropriety. They also help executives assure their own diligence and oversight of ethical risks and threats, and deliver on their promise to employees, shareholders, customers and the community at large.

Critical Thinking
1. Which three of these 10 questions do you think are the most important? Why?
2. Add one more question to those necessary for designing an ethical corporate culture.

THOMAS R. KRAUSE, PhD is author of several books and Chairman and Co-founder of Behavioral Science Technology, Inc. (BST), an international performance solutions consulting company. He focuses on executive leadership development and coaching for clients including NASA, BHP Billiton and the FAA. PAUL J. VOSS, PhD is Ethics Practice Leader with BST. An author, scholar and lecturer, Dr. Voss' clients include Home Depot, the FBI lab, General Electric and Russell Athletics.

Is Business Ethics Getting Better?
A Historical Perspective

JOANNE B. CIULLA

In the title of this address, I ask the question "Is business ethics getting better?" I will not talk about specific aspects of business but the practice of business as a whole. Some scholars have answered this question in terms of recent history. In 1961, Raymond C. Baumhart, who was then doctoral student at the Harvard Business School, did a study around the question "How Ethical are Businessmen?" He said that his research did not give a definitive answer to the question, but that the executives he surveyed all said that they wanted to improve the ethical business behavior of business people.[1] In 1977, Steven N. Brenner and Earl A. Molander updated and expanded Baumhart's study to see if the ethics of business had changed since the Baumhart study.[2] Their research found that societal expectations of business were changing and in some areas, business had gotten better and in other areas, it remained the same. In a more recent essay, Ian Maitland suggests that the ethics of business is congruent with business cycles. He argues that business ethics deteriorate during boom times and improve during recessions.[3] A priori, this makes sense since it is human nature to not ask questions about why things are going well and to become introspective when things fall apart. Yet when you look at history writ large, we see that the answer to this question is not so simple.

There are moral problems inherent in business and human nature that make ethics a constant struggle, regardless of the business cycle or system of regulation. History offers us an early warning system about the ethical pitfalls of business and the tragedies that result from the moral failures of business. People have been aware of these problems for a long time. The ancient Greek historian Polybius said that Carthage fell because it had become a place where "nothing that leads to profit is considered disgraceful."[4] People throughout history have also reminded us of the social benefits of business. As the Enlightenment philosopher Charles-Louis de Secondat Montesqieu notes, "[I]t is almost a general rule, that wherever we find agreeable manners, there commerce flourishes; and wherever there is commerce, there we meet with agreeable manners."[5] In this address, I will look at a few of the things that history shows us about the potential moral pitfalls

of business as a means of explaining why I believe that history ought to be a part of the way that we teach business ethics in business schools.

Modernity is like a digital watch. Unlike an analogue watch, a digital watch does not show where we have been or where we are going. It only displays the present. History provides us with a place to stand and look at the present future. It offers a perspective on who we are, what we do, and why we do it. What history shows us about organizations and the people who run them is that the basic problems of business ethics are not new—only the cultural and technological contexts of these problems change over time. The reason for this is quite simple. People are the same and hence, the ethical challenges of human activities such as business have not changed much either.

Business rests on the pursuit of self-interest, but at the same time requires self-control, constraints of self-interest, and as Max Weber shows us, delayed gratification.[6] Adam Smith tried to resolve this paradox with his notion of enlightened self-interest or self-interest that is tied to the interests of others in society.[7] The most ubiquitous moral principle in both the East and the West is the Golden Rule.[8] Both renditions of it— "do unto others as you would have others do unto you" and "do not do to others what you would not want them to do to you"—help people make the leap from their interests to the interests of others. The remarkable thing is that humanity is at least as successful at making this leap as it is at failing to do so; however, along the way they struggle. So let us look at just a few examples of the moral struggles that work, leadership, and business have presented to people throughout history.

Some Ancient Perspectives

It is useful to begin with the writings of Ptah-hotep, who was a sage and vizier to the Egyptian pharaoh Djedkare Isesi of the 5th Dynasty. Written on papyrus, his book, *The Percepts of Ptah-Hotep,* is one of the oldest surviving paper books. It was written somewhere between 2450–2300 BCE.[9] In it, Ptah-hotep talks about a person's responsibilities at work, which include adherence to duty, self-control, and transparency or vigilance against those who want to bribe or make secret deals. He even cautions against falling asleep on the job.

> If you are employed in the larit [storehouse], stand or sit rather than walk about. Lay down rules for yourself from the first: not to absent yourself even when weariness overtakes you. Keep an eye on him who enters announcing that what he asks is secret; what is entrusted to you is above appreciation, and all contrary argument is a matter to be rejected. He is a god who penetrates into a place where no relaxation of the rules is made for the privileged.[10]

Ptah-hotep also takes note of the problems people face when they acquire wealth. Such people can start to think that they are better than others and forget where they came from.

> If you have become great after having been little, if you have become rich after having been poor, when you are at the head of the city, know how not to take advantage of the fact that you have reached the first rank, harden not your heart because of your elevation; you are only administrator, the prefect, of the provisions which belong to Ptah. Put not behind you the neighbor who is like you; be unto him as a companion.[11]

Finally, like many sages who follow him, Ptah-hotep warns us about the dangers of wealth and power. Both can make people think they are special and no longer subject to the same rules as everyone else. Some leaders make the tragic mistake of thinking that power exempts them from responsibility, when in fact power usually gives them more responsibility to more people. As Ptah-hotep writes:

> He who is placed in front, at the head of a large number of men, must be without reproach, and in spite of his power, never forget that there are laws. . . . He has attained to high honor, he must not, as is too often the case, be puffed up by his good fortune, but should consider the new duties which his rank imposes on him.[12]

Early on, people noticed that, in addition to the ethical challenges of having money and power, profit making based on anything other than trade for goods, might be problematic. As Aristotle notes, the amount of property needed for the good life is not unlimited because it is based on what we need. He goes on to say that the art of profit making and accumulating coin has no boundaries. It is based on insatiable wants.[13] Like other ancients, Aristotle is vehement in his distain for usury or what he calls "money breeding money." He writes: "The most hated sort [of money making], and with the greatest reason is usury, which makes a gain out of money itself, and not from the natural object of it [to trade products]."[14]

The early Romans also realized that business and the desire to make a profit sometimes lead to dishonest behavior. For example, in Cicero's *De Officiis,* written in 44 BCE, Cicero presents several cases where business people are tempted to deceive, such as this one illustrating the principle of caveat emptor:

> Suppose an honest man sells a house because of some defects that he is aware of but others do not suspect. Suppose the house is unsanitary but is considered healthy; suppose no one know that vermin can be seen in all the bedrooms, that the house is built of poor timber and quite dilapidated. The question is: if the seller does not tell these facts to a buyer and sells the house for much more than he thought he could get for it, did he act without justice and without honor?[15]

Like Aristotle, Cicero voiced suspicions about retailers. He says, "Those who buy from merchant and sell again immediately should also be thought of as demeaning themselves. For they would make not profit unless they told sufficient lies, and nothing is as dishonorable as a falsehood."[16] Cicero also notes the potential for business people to exploit the misery of others. He tells the story of a merchant who arrives at the gates of the famine-stricken city of Rhodes with a grain shipment. The merchant knows that other shipments are one day behind him, but the citizens of the city do not. Cicero raises the question, "Should the merchant conceal this fact from the buyers and charge a higher price?"[17] Even in ancient times, people saw that there was something wrong with charging the market price in times, people saw that there was something wrong with charging the market price in times of disaster. Clearly, price gouging has been around for a long time, but so has compassionate behavior during disasters. Like Cicero, the contemporary philosopher Henk van Luijk called for a principle of decency in business, which he described this way: "if given the opportunity to improve the general welfare, people need solid reasons *not* to do it."[18]

Work and Wages

Other ethical problems in business revolve around what people deserve to be paid for their work. As Jean Jacques Rousseau observed, "The human race fell from a golden age when they discovered that they could get advantage from the work of others."[19] You do not have to read Karl Marx to understand this problem. Nowadays this is not a matter of master and slave or serf, but a more sanitized "market view of labor." People get paid according to their market value, regardless of the social value of the work that they do. Furthermore, when unemployment is high, some employers take advantage of their employees by making them work long hours—sometimes for less pay. This is considered acceptable when the market determines wages and people fear losing their jobs.

Plato offers us a unique perspective on CEO compensation. He writes: "medicine provides health, and wage earning provides wages; house building provides a house and the wage earning that accompanies it provides a wage."[20] The same is true for leadership. The craft of leadership focuses on producing benefits for others, not just the leader. Plato concludes that like medicine and house building, the "craft" of leading requires different virtues from the craft of earning wages. The market acts as if the virtues of craft and wage earning are either the same or complementary. Corporations usually try to tie CEO compensation to performance, but as we have seen lately, CEOs can still earn high wages even when their companies do poorly or fail. In Plato's terms, some CEOs are good at making money for themselves, but not good at making money for the other stakeholders inside and outside of the company. The economist Robert Frank calls the belief that there are only a few talented individuals who can run companies and hence, deserve a disproportionate amount of wealth, the basis of a "winner-take-all society."[21] Is this true? Perhaps in some cases, but Rakesh Khurana's study of CEOs found that the highest paid CEOs were the most charismatic, but they did not produce the best earnings for their companies.[22] As Plato might say, they are better at wage earning that they are at leading and looking after the interest of their organizations.

Business has always had the ability to bring out the worst in people. In particular, the acquisitive and competitive aspects of it may tempt or encourage even the most disciplined person or group of people into one or more of the seven deadly sins— greed, envy, lust, pride, gluttony, anger and sloth. The first six are usually the basis of business scandals and financial disasters. The seventh, sloth, is the most interesting, because sloth is more than simple laziness—it is the vice of not caring. When businesses are feckless and uncaring, they can harm people and the environment. Business encourages virtues as well as vices. We know that it sparks creativity, generosity, kindness, discipline, and a number of other virtues. Like all activities that affect the lives of others, business is a practice that requires moral effort and fortitude. Certainly there are many businesses that try "doing well by doing good."

The *Night Watch* and CSR

One of my favorite painting is Rembrandt's *The Company of Frans Banning Cocq and Willem van Ruytenburch*, which is better known as *The Night Watch*. In some ways it is emblematic of the strengths and weaknesses of Corporate Social Responsibility (CSR). On the surface, it depicts a group of wealthy business people who, with Captain Cocq and Lieutenant Ruytenburch, are prepared to do their civic duty to defend the city if necessary. Cocq and the seventeen other people in the picture commissioned the painting in 1642. The curious thing about this very large (about 12 × 14 feet) canvas is that the actual night watch had disbanded years before it was painted, so the heroic group was actually more like a sporting club than a civic watch. Furthermore, Rembrandt's unconventional composition depicts Cocq bathed in light, while others are only in partial view. Some of the merchants were not happy about this because they had each paid their share to be in the picture. Like the old German expression: "Do good and talk about it," these merchants wanted to be physically and morally recognized. The story of the picture is emblematic of a potential problem with CSR. It is okay for businesses to advertise how they fill their social responsibilities as long as they do not let the "talking about it" misrepresent or supersede the actual "doing good."

On Tulips and Bubbles

Business ethics does not seem to be getting better in regard to the behavior that leads to speculative bubbles and international financial crises. Not long before Rembrandt finished the "Night Watch," Tulip mania raged throughout Europe. Europe had become enamored with the flower, and bulbs were traded on the market for huge sums of money. For example, at the tulip market's peak in 1637, the Admiral van Enkhuijsen tulip traded for fifteen times the yearly wage of Amsterdam bricklayer.[23] The bulbs sold by weight and the unit of measure was the azen. Soon people stopped buying and selling actual tulip bulbs and began speculating on future price of an azen of bulbs. Merchants, craftsman, and other ordinary citizens jumped into this futures market. When the bubble burst, both the wealthy and those of modest means were ruined.

In his prescient book the *Extraordinary Popular Delusions and the Madness of Crowds* (1841), Charles MacKay offers a delightful commentary on irrational business behavior. He discusses "tulipomania" and the incident that gave us the term "speculative bubble."[24] The word "bubble" was first used to describe the frenzied speculative investment in the South Sea Company and the subsequent crash of its stocks. In the early 1700s, the company had obtained a monopoly on trade in the South Seas from Spain. The Spanish gave the British an *assiento,* which was a permit that allowed them to sell slaves and other merchandise to Spanish colonies. In a scenario all too familiar today, the company started and/or did not correct rumors about the extraordinary profits they would make. Banks and other investors, ranging from government officials and aristocrats to middle class workers, invested and then lost large sums of money. If the British government had not stepped in and propped up the banks, the British banking system would have failed when the bubble burst. In 1720, British Parliament enacted the "Bubble Act" requiring all new joint stock companies to be incorporated by Act of Parliament or Royal Charter.

History and Business Ethics

Theses are just a few examples of what history can tell us about the ethical challenges of engaging in business. Let us now turn to more a recent past and look at the use of history to teach ethics in a business school. When I was at the Harvard Business School (HBS), I had the pleasure of sitting in on a few of Alfred Chandler's seminars on business history. I was just starting to do work in business ethics and I was struck by the inextricable relationship between business history and business ethics. At the time, a colleague named Jeffrey Cruikshank was writing a history of the Harvard Business School called, *A Delicate Experiment HBS 1908–1945*. We often talked about the research that he was doing for the book. It was fascinating because Cruikshank had access to old letters and documents dating back to the school's inception in 1908.[25]

The early intellectual purpose of HBS was as "a school of applied economics, with incidental responsibilities toward law and engineering."[26] One of the questions on the mind of Wallace Donham, the second dean of HBS was: Who is responsible for what in society? The 1920s was an era of industry and technological innovation. Donham was particularly concerned with the impact of technology on business and society. When the British philosopher Lord Alfred North Whitehead joined Harvard's faculty in 1924, Donham used to have Saturday afternoon discussions with him about the human problems of what

Whitehead called, "scientific materialism." As Cruikshank observes, Donham believed that society could no longer turn to the legal profession for "wise counselors" in these matters because the law had lost its independent status in the late 19th century when it became a servant to industry. Since Donham did not think that religion was likely to be reinstated to its position of moral authority, it fell to the business community to face what Donham saw as the critical social problem: the "control the consequences of scientific development."[27]

Donham wanted a business school curriculum that would prepare students to take on the responsibility of managing the moral impact of business and technology on society. The school's first approach to this was to introduce a history course—not a business ethics course—into the curriculum in 1927. A professor named Norman Gras taught the course. Gras began his class with cases from medieval history and later moved on to more contemporary ones. Gras said that the reason why the course was successful because "history placed business into human culture or recognized human culture in business."[28] But history did not seem to be enough preparation for business students to take on their social responsibilities. Gras wrote "The history of every profession contains plenty of evidence that it will be practically impossible to get great groups of men acting from pure altruism."[29] His hope for ethical progress was to have corporations internalize ethical standards and set the norms for the rest of society.

In 1928, HBS introduced what was perhaps the first business ethics course in an American business school. They hired a philosopher named Carl F. Taeusch from the University of Iowa to teach a second year elective in business ethics. I was able to buy an old library copy of the business ethics textbook that Taeusch wrote. It still had the record of borrowers in the back. There did not seem to be much interest in the book since it had only been checked out 24 times in 56 years. HBS students did not like Taeusch's business ethics course, in part because they thought it was too theoretical, so HBS dropped business ethics from the curriculum in 1935. One observer wrote: "It is the opinion of those who remember Dr. Taeusch's course on ethics that it was unsuccessful because it was perceived as 'Sunday School talk.' Indeed that effort and another in the mid 1930s appear to have set back the desire to tackle the subject at all."[30] The subject seems to disappear until 1958 when the school approved an elective course called "Business, Society and the Individual." Thirty years later, HBS introduced its first required module "Decision Making and Ethical Values."[31]

Despite business scandals, the Great Depression, and the recent collapse of the banking system (based on a mortgage bubble), some business schools are still reluctant to commit time and resources to business ethics courses—yet they spend lavishly on courses related to finance and accounting. When we look back at recent history, few would argue that financial disasters and business scandals were the result of people having poor quantitative skills. Going back to Plato, we might say that some business schools focus more on teaching student the craft of making money than on the craft of actually running a business or a sustainable business. Some of the business school graduates who drove their companies into the ground lacked

perspective and a historical understanding of the ethical traps inherent in business and human nature. Just think about how many well-educated people in the financial industry fell for "the madness of crowds."

Conclusion

So, is business ethics getting better? Yes and no. My point is that you cannot answer this question in meaningful way unless you study history. That is why the Baumhart and Brenner/Molander studies are interesting, but not particularly insightful because their horizon is too narrow. Furthermore, as business historian Geoffrey Jones observes, "The loss of history has resulted in the spread of influential theories based on ill-informed understandings of the past."[32] For example, it is accepted wisdom that countries grow and prosper when they are open to foreign investment. But Jones notes that "this is an article of faith rather than proven by the historical evidence of the past."[33] Jones says that business historians have been marginalized or ignored by business schools and business scholars, despite that fact that early business historians have often identified areas that later become hot topics to business researchers such as entrepreneurship and globalization.

What does this mean for business ethics and business education? First, I think we should revisit the HBS approach of teaching ethics through history. Business schools might consider offering students the option of taking business ethics or business history to fill their course requirements. While ethics and history are different subjects, both compel students to think about the big questions concerning business and life. Second, history should be a part of any business ethics course. This is not difficult to do in classes that use case studies. By adding a historical context to a case, or comparing contemporary cases with similar events in the past, students gain a richer insight into the values and motivations that shape the behavior of people in business. And third, history is a fundamental part of leadership development. Business schools claim to educate leaders, but often they simply train managers. This is because they fail to consider a key element of leadership. Leadership requires a person to have a broad perspective on the world and an understanding of how it works. As Chester Bernard argues in his classic work, *The Functions of the Executive,* business leaders must possess "the art of sensing the whole."[34] History and the study of human values help cultivate this art in students, researchers, and practitioners. Perhaps that is what Carl Taeusch was trying to teach in his unpopular, "too theoretical," "Sunday School," business ethics class.

In closing, I leave you with Taeusch's eloquent statement about the place of philosophy and historical memory in the human enterprise of business:

> The world is in need of two types of men that it does not have in great abundance: those who are experts in techniques, who contribute to ninety-five percent of perspiration necessary to carry on well the world's work, and the inspired five percent who are possessed of broad enough vision to see what there is to do. It is the latter who anticipate most of the possibilities and troubles of

humanity, and in this group the philosopher should be found. And the philosopher has functioned in the past, and can still contribute his share, by directing human efforts through the channels that a useful memory and a far-reaching imagination alone can discover or construct. And when we in this practical age insist that the philosopher come down from the clouds and the mountaintops, it is not necessary that he lose his sense of direction in the market place.[35]

Notes

1. Raymond C. Baumhart, "How Ethical Are Businessmen?," *Harvard Business Review* (July–August 1961): 7–10, 12, 16, 19, 156–76.

2. Steven N. Brenner and Earl A. Molander, "Is the Ethics of Business Changing?" *Harvard Business Review,* January–February 1977 : 57–71.

3. Ian Maitland, "A Theory of the Ethical Business Cycle," *Business Ethics Quarterly* 20(4) (2010): 749–50.

4. Polybius, *The Histories,* trans. Robin Waterfield, ed. Brian McGing (NewYork: Oxford University Press, 2010), 410.

5. Charles de Montesquieu, *The Sprit of the Laws,* trans. Thomas Nugent (NewYork: Thc Free Press, 1970),316.

6. Max Webet *The Protestant Ethic and the Spirit of Capitalism,* trans. Talcott Parsons (New York: W. W. Norton,2009).

7. Adam Smith, *The Wealth of Nations* (New York: Penguin Books, 1970).

8. Jeffrey Wattles, *The Golden Rule* (New York: Oxford University Press, 1996).

9. The translator Miriam Lichtheim argues that while Ptah-hotep lived between 2450 BCE and 2300 BCE, the actual papyrus was not produced until 2300–2150 BCE.

10. Miriam Lichtheim, *Ancient Egyptian Literature: A Book of Readings, Volume 1: The Old and Middle Kingdoms* (Berkeley: University of California Press, 1973), 63.

11. Ibid., 65.

12. Ibid., 62.

13. Aristotle, *Nichomachean Ethics,* in *The Complete Works of Aristotle: The Revised Oxford Translation,* trans. W. D. Ross, ed. J. Barnes, vol. 2 (Princeton, N.J.: Princeton University Press, 1984), 1996.

14. Ibid., 1997.

15. Marcus Tullius Cicero, *De Officiis,* trans. Harry G. Edinger (Indianapolis: The Library of Living Arts,1974), 120.

16. Ibid., 58.

17. Ibid., 118.

18. Henk J. L. van Luijk, "Rights and Interests in a Participatory Market Society," *Business Ethics Quarterly* 4(1) (1994): 79–96.

19. Jean Jacques Rousseau, "A Discourse on a Subject Proposed by the Academy of Dijon: What Is the Origin of Inequality among Men, and Is It Authorized by Natural Law?" *The Social Contact and Discourses,* trans. G.D.H. Cole (New York: E.P. Dutton, 1950).

20. Plato, *Republic,* trans. G.M.A. Grube (Indianapolis: Hackett Publishing,1992), 22.

21. Robert Frank and Phillip J. Cook, *Winner-Take-All Society* (NewYork: Penguin, 1996).

22. Rahesh Khurana, *Searching for the Corporate Suvior: The Irrational Quest for Charismatic CEOs* (Princeton, N.J.: Princeton University Press, 2002).

23. Ana Pavord, *The Tulip: The Story of a Flower that Has Made Men Mad* (New York: Bloomsbury Publishing, 1999).

24. Charles McKay, *Extraordinary Popular Delusions and the Madness of Crowds* (New York: Barnes & Noble, 2002), 5.

25. Note that the Wharton School is the oldest business school in the U.S. It was established in 1881.

26. Jeffrey L. Cruikshank, *A Delicate Experiment: The Harvard Business School from 1908–1945* (Boston: Harvard Business School Press, 1987), 155.

27. Ibid.

28. Ibid., 168.

29. Ibid.

30. Ibid.

31. See Harvard Business School institutional Memory 1958 and 1988: http://institutionalmcmory.hbs.edu/topic/curriculum_and_courses.html.

32. Sean Silverthrone, "The Lessons of Business History: A Handbook," Harvard Business School: Working Knowledge, March 17, 2008, http://hbswk.hbs.edu./item/5849.html. In this interview Jones offers an eloquent explanation of the ways in which business history contributes to our understanding of business. Jones, a historian at HBS, also discusses the reasons why many business schools ignore business history. For an excellent source on business history, see his book: Geoffrey G. Jones and Jonathan Zeitlin, *Oxford Handbook of Business History* (New York: Oxford University Press, 2008).

33. Silverthrone, "The Lessons of Business History."

34. Chester I. Barnard, *The Functions of the Executive: 30th Anniversary Edition* (Cambridge, Mass.: Harvard University Press, 1971), 239.

35. Carl F. Taeusch, *Professional and Business Ethics* (New York: Henry Holt and Company, 1926), 3.

Critical Thinking

1. What are the arguments presented for a market view of labor? Do you agree?

2. What is Plato's perspective on CEO compensation? Develop brief arguments pro and con for Plato's perspective.

3. Based on your reading and reflection of the article, is business ethics getting better? Take a position, find examples in current news articles, and use the current news articles to defend your position.

From *Business Ethics Quarterly,* April 2011. Copyright © 2011 by *Business Ethics Quarterly.* Reprinted by permission of The Philosophy Documentation Center, publisher of *Business Ethics Quarterly.*

Principles for Building an Ethical Organization

Miriam Schulman

Drawing on Indian mythology, company folklore, personal experience, and a sense of humor, R. Gopalakrishnan offered his observations on what it takes to develop and maintain an ethical organization to a group of Silicon Valley businesspeople convened by the Markkula Center for Applied Ethics this June. Gopalakrishnan is executive director of Tata Sons, one of India's largest private-sector business groups.

He began by retelling the story of the Arjuna, master archer from the Hindu epic Mahabharata, who is sent by Lord Krishna to rescue the women from a city under siege. Comparing Arjuna to "a turnaround CEO," Gopalakrishnan related Arjuna's success at freeing the women ("the assets of the company") from the besieged city using his bow and arrows. "Everyone clapped," Gopalakrishnan said, likening their reaction to that of shareholders believing they will now have a better year.

Yet, on the way back to Krishna, while passing through a forest, Arjuna's chariot came under attack and his arrows were ineffective. The "moral of the story" for businesspeople, according to Gopalakrishnan, is: "You are only as good as your context shows you to be." The same techniques that worked in one context may not in another. The same CEO who was successful may not retain his or her "magic" over time or at a different company or industry setting.

With that caveat, Gopalakrishnan offered five general principles for executives who are interested in contributing to a company culture of integrity.

- **Complete the cycle of whom you earn from and whom you return money to.** Gopalakrishnan described how Tata has incorporated into its corporate memorandum of association the idea that the company exists to serve society. He confessed that when he first came to Tata in 1998, he was somewhat skeptical about the seriousness of this goal.

In his early days at the company, he traveled widely to visit various subsidiaries—"people selling trucks, writing code, generating electricity"—and talked with them about their work. "What was unique," he said, "was that every PowerPoint presentation I saw ended with a chart labeled 'Community.'" Each group gave this subject its own spin: in some cases fostering AIDS awareness, in some cases helping local women find markets for their woven baskets. These projects are funded out of 13 charitable trusts initiated in 1932 by Sir Dorab Tata, but are initiated and executed by local Tata management and employees. About a third of the company's $3 billion in profits go into these trusts.

Gradually, Gopalakrishnan said, his cynicism began to dissolve. "What has this meant to me personally? It's part of why I go to work every day. In some surrogate way, one third of every dollar I earn for the company goes into these charitable trusts."

- **Work like a bricklayer.** Gopalakrishnan recalled a story he learned when he worked at Unilever, suggesting that the person who clears and paves a road is the greatest servant of humanity. "Millions of people will travel that road following their dreams," he said, "without ever thinking about the person who built it." He proposed this model for managers, suggesting that they should concentrate on their work and not on appreciation or even outcomes in the near term.

Gopalakrishnan likened the story to a teaching of Krisha in the Bhagavad Gita: "To action alone hast thou a right and never at all to its fruits; let not the fruits of action be thy motive."

- **You don't have to change the whole world, but you also don't have to become corrupt if the world around you is corrupt.** Tata, he pointed out, has 300,000 employees, and it would be impossible to control the ethical standards of every one of them. Yet, Gopalakrishnan argued, the company can encourage ethical behavior on the part of all of its employees.

As an example, he pointed to a 2002 scandal within the Tata companies, in which the chairman's protégé and CEO of Tata Finance was involved in a fraud that threatened to cost clients, shareholders, and creditors more than $200 million. At a meeting, an ordinary shareholder got up and told how he might lose his life savings. As Gopalakrishnan describes what happened,

"At that point, we didn't know the size of the scandal, but the chairman made a statement: 'You have my assurance. Not one of you will lose a rupee.' We could have filed for India's version of Chapter 11; he could have said we'd stand behind the 22 percent of Tata Finance that we owned. But the chairman stood for 100 percent of the losses." This kind of attitude has also helped Tata to resist some of the petty bribery demands that are endemic to doing business in India, he said.

- **Ethics and standards have to be understandable for common people.** By this, Gopalakrishnan said he meant not only that companies should avoid abstract philosophical or theological terminology in discussing ethics, but also that they should provide guidance and specific examples for employees on how codes could be applied. "For management to spend time creating a unique code of ethics is a waste of time," he argued. Tata, GE, even Enron, he said, have similar documents. "It's what you do with them that counts."

At Tata, the code is published in 15 different languages. Every employee signs it every two years, which, for illiterate workers, may mean putting their thumbprint on the document. More important, the company runs almost 300 workshops a year where employees discuss the issues they face. "No great truths" come out of this process, Gopalakrishnan said. "There's no new enlightenment except in our own hearts" as employees talk about how to apply these principles to real-world situations.

- **The child's behavior is shaped by the first 10 years.** So it is with a company. Gopalakrishnan talked about instilling ethics in an organization from the very beginning. To illustrate, he pointed to Jamsetji Tata, founder of the Tata Group, who created the JN Tata Endowment in 1892 to send promising Indian students, regardless of class, to pursue higher education in England. That philanthropic attitude was so ingrained in the company that the creation of other charitable foundations was simply an extension of that beginning.

For entrepreneurs who don't think they have time to worry about ethics in the early years, Gopalakrishnan had this advice. "That's negligent if you intend for your company to be around a long time. It's like saying, 'I don't have time to shape my child's character right now. I'll do it when he's 20.'"

As Gopalakrishnan has written elsewhere, "History . . . sheds some light on what I call the samskar, or values, of any given business. Much like individuals, business enterprises, too, have a samskar. It is the mark of a successful business that profits are earned competitively in the early days. It is a mark of a great business that, in addition, good samskar gets so deeply embedded that it becomes part of its DNA."

Critical Thinking

1. What are the general principles for building an ethical organization?

2. If you were to list these principles in order of priority, which would be the most important principle? Why?

3. Which of the principles would be the least important principle? Why?

4. To the list of general principles in the article, what other principle or principles would you add? Describe the principle or principles you would add and give your reasoning for adding your principle or principles.

MIRIAM SCHULMAN is communications director of the Markkula Center for Applied Ethics.

What's at the Core of Corporate Wrongdoing?

To believe that the people who commit fraud are different from us might make us feel safe. But real safety comes from building an organization that stops these acts before they can take place.

ELEANOR BLOXHAM

Fortune—Dennis Levine, who lectured an NYU MBA ethics class as part of his community service many years ago, described the mentality that led to his insider trading conviction as a mentality of having to win the next game, competing with oneself for the next victory, where enough was never enough.

His explanation is applicable to both individuals and entire corporate cultures, such as MF Global (MFGLQ) and Olympus, where losses were allegedly buried from public view on purpose.

But Levine's explanation doesn't address why enough is never enough. What underlies the motivations to hide losses? And why does it often take a very rude awakening for a person (or a company) to change?

What has befallen Olympus has been chalked up to an obedience culture, a management team that was "rotten at the core," and a board "of yes men." MF Global's case has been explained away by Jon Corzine's hubris. But if we examine, rather than impugn, Corzine's motives and those of the board and executives at Olympus, we will realize how these individuals' actions relate to you and me.

As almost any good board member will tell you, the responsibility for corporate culture, or what is commonly referred to as "tone at the top," begins with the board. Good board members monitor the CEO and corporate culture by meeting not only with the CEO but also with other members of a company's management team in social settings, on site visits, in executive sessions without other members of management present, and in regular board and committee meetings. They don't just listen to management speeches: they read body language, observe interactions, and view facilities. They look at the contents of whistle-blower and customer hotline call-in logs, employee surveys, performance evaluations, and compensation decisions. They carefully and systematically gauge the level of healthy dissent and openness to discuss troubling situations and imperfect solutions.

This is critical work at the top of a company but necessary throughout it as well. Why? Because there can be many cultures inside one company, a fact that anyone who has considered transferring from one department to another well recognizes.

No matter where in the hierarchy you sit, if you are a member of management, you too should be monitoring the culture of the groups that report to you using the techniques that great boards use. And some insights into individual human personality, including your own, can help you decide what to look for.

Perhaps you are a high achiever who, like many other high achievers, would describe, in private, that some of the influences that originally pushed you have negative undertones. Your upbringing may have caused you to feel your accomplishments were never enough—or you may have excelled to avoid the pain of others' judgments. Your awareness of these pressures is helpful because you can spot them in others, recognizing that, if left unchecked, they can lead to unethical behavior.

Wise board recruitment requires the selection of thoughtful, high achieving board members who can understand and balance the CEO's natural motivations. These board members recognize the powerful influence of self-preservation when it comes time to publicly admit failure, and the internal battle to fight feelings of inadequacy. Armed with this awareness, savvy board members help less secure CEOs build safe cultures that allow admission of failure, healthy risk-taking, and innovative expression.

The deeper motivations of individuals at Olympus and MF Global are not foreign to students of human nature. To believe that those people are different from us is appealing because such beliefs make us feel safe. But real safety comes from recognizing these traits in others and ourselves and constructing an organization with a culture that can balance rather than ignore these all-too-human tendencies.

Critical Thinking

1. At what level in an organization rests the responsibility for establishing an ethical corporate culture? Why?

2. Using the Internet, find examples of an ethical corporate culture and an unethical corporate culture. What differentiates the two corporate cultures? Why is one firm ethical and the other unethical?

3. Two companies are mentioned in the article–Olympus and MF Global. Outline for class discussion the critical aspects of each firm's corporate culture which may have led to each firm's alleged corporate wrongdoing.

4. If you were a manager, what safeguards would you establish to ensure for an ethical corporate culture?

ELEANOR BLOXHAM is CEO of The Value Alliance and Corporate Governance Alliance (http://thevaluealliance.com), a board advisory firm.

UNIT 2

Ethical Issues and Dilemmas in the Workplace

Unit Selections

Learning Outcomes

After reading this Unit, you will be able to:

- What ethical dilemmas do managers face most frequently? What ethical dilemmas do employees face most often? What are similarities and dissimilarities in the ethical dilemmas faced by managers and by employees?
- How well are organizations responding to issues of work and family schedules, daycare, and telecommuting?
- What forms of discrimination are most prevalent in today's workplace? In what particular job situations or occupations is discrimination more widespread and conspicuous? Why?
- What is the role of ethics in preventing discrimination? Write a statement about discrimination to be placed in a code of ethics. What should be included in the statement? Why?
- Whistleblowing involves an employee's disclosing illegal, immoral, or illegitimate organizational practices or activities. Under what circumstances do you believe whistleblowing is appropriate? Why? Are there circumstances when whistleblowing is inappropriate?
- Should whistleblowers be protected? Why or why not?
- Is there ever a time to remain silent? That is, is there ever a time to refrain from blowing a whistle? What are those times? How might they be justified by an individual?
- Given the complexities of an organization, where an ethical dilemma often cannot be optimally resolved by one person alone, how can an individual secure the support of the group and help it to reach a consensus as to the appropriate resolution of the dilemma?

LaRue Tone Hosmer, in *The Ethics of Management,* states that ethical problems in business are managerial dilemmas because they represent conflict, or at least the possibility of conflict, between the economic performance of an organization and its social performance. Whereas the metrics of economic performance are revenues, costs, profits, and a firm's market cap (if it is traded publicly), social performance is judged by less apparent and less easily measured metrics of the fulfillment of an organization's obligations to persons both within and outside the organization as well as to the larger society in which an organization is privileged to operate.

Units 2 to 4 examine some of the critical ethical dilemmas that management faces in making decisions in the workplace, in the marketplace, and within the global society. This unit (Unit 2 —Ethical Issues and Dilemmas in the Workplace) focuses on the relationships and obligations of employers and employees to each other as well as to those they serve both within and without an organization. Organizational decision makers are ethical when they act with equity, fairness, and impartiality, treating with respect the rights of their employees. Organizations' hiring and firing practices, treatment of women and minorities, tolerance of employees' privacy, and wages and working conditions are areas in which it has ethical responsibilities.

The employee also has ethical obligations in his or her relationship to the employer. A conflict of interest can occur when an employee allows a gratuity or favor to sway him or her in selecting a contract or purchasing a piece of equipment, making a choice that may not be in the best interests of the organization. Other possible ethical dilemmas for employees include espionage and the betrayal of secrets (especially to competitors), the misuse of confidential data, the theft of equipment or supplies, and the abuse of expense accounts.

The articles in this unit are broken down into seven subsections representing various types of ethical dilemmas in the workplace. The initial article in the first subsection, "Morals in the Market and Workplace," examines legal consequences resulting when identity theft occurs in the workplace. Another article examines the issue of being family friendly and complaints of unfairness in benefits and policies by employees who do not have families. Other articles in this subsection examine markets and morals as well as morals and the machine.

In the subsection entitled Organizational Misconduct and Crime, the articles scrutinize the causes and the ramifications of governmental and educational misconduct and the circumstances where organizations are most vulnerable to fraud. One article examines unethical behavior that allegedly occurred at every level in a large school system. The other articles focus on why people do bad things at work offering scripts, distractions, moral exclusion, and the one-man problem as possible

explanatory reasons. Several other articles examine unfair business practices as well as the lessons of leadership from a sexual abuse scandal at a major university.

The subsections Sexual Treatment of Employees (Part C) and Discriminatory and Prejudicial Practices (Part D) feature articles examining a wide range of contemporary issues. Included are the issue of a sexually charged workplace, the resolution of a class-action sex discrimination lawsuit, the impact of older workers in the workforce, the issue of retaliation at work, and an article about how to develop values-driven human resources in an organization

In the next subsection, Downsizing of the Work Force, articles reflect on the consequences and effects of downsizing, discuss so-called job-killing companies, present arguments why people should come before profits in considering a downsizing decision.

The selections included under the heading Whistleblowing in the Organization disclose why some businesses that once feared whistleblowers are now finding new ways for employees to report wrongdoing and analyze the ethical dilemma and possible ramifications of whistleblowing. Also considered is when not to blow a whistle—that is, are there ever times to remain silent and refrain from blowing a whistle?

In the last subsection, Handling Ethical Dilemmas at Work, some situations and organizational settings are presented for the reader to wrestle with ethical dilemmas.

Student Website
www.mhhe.com/cls

Internet References

American Psychological Association
www.apa.org/index.aspx

Blowing the Whistle
www.whistleblowing.org

Discrimination—Federal Laws Preventing Discrimination
www.eeoc.gov/facts/qanda.html

Discrimination—Types of Discrimination
www.eeoc.gov/facts/qanda.html (scroll down on the page)

Ethical Dilemmas
www83.homepage.villanova.edu/richard.jacobs/MPA%208300/
theories/dilemmas.html

Ethical Dilemmas—Resolving
www.lmu.edu/Page27945.aspx

The Ethics of Whistleblowing
http://ezinearticles.com/?The-Ethics-of-Whistle-Blowing&id
53866452

International Labour Organization (ILO)
www.ilo.org

National Whistleblowers Center
www.whistleblowers.org

Workplace Fairness
www.workplacefairness.org/whistleblowing

Markets and Morals

NICHOLAS D. KRISTOF

Does it bother you that an online casino paid a Utah woman, Kari Smith, who needed money for her son's education, $10,000 to tattoo its website on her forehead?

Or that Project Prevention, a charity, pays women with drug or alcohol addictions $300 cash to get sterilized or undertake long-term contraception? Some 4,100 women have accepted this offer.

Michael Sandel, the Harvard political theorist, cites those examples in *What Money Can't Buy*, his important and thoughtful new book. He argues that in recent years we have been slipping without much reflection into relying upon markets in ways that undermine the fairness of our society.

That's one of the underlying battles this campaign year. Many Republicans, Mitt Romney included, have a deep faith in the ability of laissez-faire markets to create optimal solutions.

There's something to that faith because markets, indeed, tend to be efficient. Pollution taxes are widely accepted as often preferable than rigid regulations on pollutants. It may also make sense to sell advertising on the sides of public buses, perhaps even to sell naming rights to subway stations.

Still, how far do we want to go down this path?

Is it right that prisoners in Santa Ana, Calif., can pay $90 per night for an upgrade to a cleaner, nicer jail cell?

Should the United States really sell immigration visas? A $500,000 investment will buy foreigners the right to immigrate.

Should Massachusetts have gone ahead with a proposal to sell naming rights to its state parks? The Boston Globe wondered in 2003 whether Walden Pond might become Wal-Mart Pond.

Should strapped towns accept virtually free police cars that come laden with advertising on the sides? Such a deal was negotiated and then ultimately collapsed, but at least one town does sell advertising on its police cars.

"The marketization of everything means that people of affluence and people of modest means lead increasingly separate lives," Sandel writes. "We live and work and shop and play in different places. Our children go to different schools. You might call it the skyboxification of American life. It's not good for democracy, nor is it a satisfying way to live."

"Do we want a society where everything is up for sale? Or are there certain moral and civic goods that markets do not honor and money cannot buy?"

This issue goes to the heart of fairness in our country. There has been much discussion recently about economic inequality, but almost no conversation about the way the spread of markets nurtures a broader, systemic inequality.

We do, of course, place some boundaries on markets. I can't buy the right to cut off your leg for my amusement. Americans can sell blood, but (perhaps mistakenly) we don't allow markets for kidneys and other organs, even though that would probably save lives.

Wealthy people can, in effect, buy access to the president at a $40,000-a-plate dinner, but they can't purchase a Medal of Freedom. A major political donor can sometimes buy an ambassadorship, but not to an important country.

Where to draw the lines limiting the role of markets isn't clear to me, but I'm pretty sure that we've already gone too far. I'm offended when governments auction naming rights to public property or sell special access, even if only to fast lanes on a highway or better cells in a jail. It is one thing for Delta Air Lines to have first class and coach. It is quite another for government to offer first class and coach in the essential services that government provides.

Where would this stop? Do we let people pay to get premium police and fire protection? Do we pursue an idea raised by Judge Richard Posner to auction off the right to adopt children?

We already have tremendous inequality in our country: The richest 1 percent of Americans own more wealth than the bottom 90 percent, according to the Economic Policy Institute. But we do still have a measure of equality before the law—equality in our basic dignity—and that should be priceless.

"Market fundamentalism," to use the term popularized by George Soros, is gaining ground. It's related to the glorification of wealth over the last couple of decades, to the celebration of opulence, and to the emergence of a new aristocracy. Market fundamentalists assume a measure of social Darwinism and accept that laissez-faire is always optimal.

That's the dogma that helped lead to bank deregulation and the current economic mess. And anyone who honestly believes that low taxes and unfettered free markets are always best should consider moving to Pakistan's tribal areas. They are a triumph of limited government, negligible taxes, no "burdensome regulation" and free markets for everything from drugs to AK-47s.

If you're infatuated with unfettered free markets, just visit Waziristan.

Critical Thinking

1. The article begins with two examples of questionable morals in the marketplace–one example is paying a person to tattoo a website on her forehead and another example is paying women with addictions (who arguably need money) to be sterilized. What are pro and con arguments for these two practices?

2. The article has several other examples of questionable morals in the marketplace, including requiring prisoners to pay to upgrade to a better jail cell. Pick several of the other examples and debate the pro and con of each.

3. As asked in the article, where would this stop? What suggestions do you have for policymakers concerning markets and morals?

4. What is the concept of "market fundamentalism" mentioned in the article? Present arguments for and against this concept.

Morals and the Machine

As robots grow more autonomous, society needs to develop rules to manage them

THE ECONOMIST

In the classic science-fiction film *2001*, the ship's computer, HAL, faces a dilemma. His instructions require him both to fulfil the ship's mission (investigating an artefact near Jupiter) and to keep the mission's true purpose secret from the ship's crew. To resolve the contradiction, he tries to kill the crew.

As robots become more autonomous, the notion of computer-controlled machines facing ethical decisions is moving out of the realm of science fiction and into the real world. Society needs to find ways to ensure that they are better equipped to make moral judgments than HAL was.

A Bestiary of Robots

Military technology, unsurprisingly, is at the forefront of the march towards self-determining machines (see Technology Quarterly). Its evolution is producing an extraordinary variety of species. The Sand Flea can leap through a window or onto a roof, filming all the while. It then rolls along on wheels until it needs to jump again. RiSE, a six-legged robo-cockroach, can climb walls. LS3, a dog-like robot, trots behind a human over rough terrain, carrying up to 180kg of supplies. SUGV, a briefcase-sized robot, can identify a man in a crowd and follow him. There is a flying surveillance drone the weight of a wedding ring, and one that carries 2.7 tonnes of bombs.

Robots are spreading in the civilian world, too, from the flight deck to the operating theatre. Passenger aircraft have long been able to land themselves. Driverless trains are commonplace. Volvo's new V40 hatchback essentially drives itself in heavy traffic. It can brake when it senses an imminent collision, as can Ford's B-Max minivan. Fully self-driving vehicles are being tested around the world. Google's driverless cars have clocked up more than 250,000 miles in America, and Nevada has become the first state to regulate such trials on public roads. In Barcelona a few days ago, Volvo demonstrated a platoon of autonomous cars on a motorway.

As they become smarter and more widespread, autonomous machines are bound to end up making life-or-death decisions in unpredictable situations, thus assuming—or at least appearing to assume—moral agency. Weapons systems currently have human operators "in the loop", but as they grow more sophisticated, it will be possible to shift to "on the loop" operation, with machines carrying out orders autonomously.

As that happens, they will be presented with ethical dilemmas. Should a drone fire on a house where a target is known to be hiding, which may also be sheltering civilians? Should a driverless car swerve to avoid pedestrians if that means hitting other vehicles or endangering its occupants? Should a robot involved in disaster recovery tell people the truth about what is happening if that risks causing a panic? Such questions have led to the emergence of the field of "machine ethics", which aims to give machines the ability to make such choices appropriately—in other words, to tell right from wrong.

One way of dealing with these difficult questions is to avoid them altogether, by banning autonomous battlefield robots and requiring cars to have the full attention of a human driver at all times. Campaign groups such as the International Committee for Robot Arms Control have been formed in opposition to the growing use of drones. But autonomous robots could do much more good than harm. Robot soldiers would not commit rape, burn down a village in anger or become erratic decision-makers amid the stress of combat. Driverless cars are very likely to be safer than ordinary vehicles, as autopilots have made planes safer. Sebastian Thrun, a pioneer in the field, reckons driverless cars could save 1m lives a year.

Instead, society needs to develop ways of dealing with the ethics of robotics—and get going fast. In America states have been scrambling to pass laws covering driverless cars, which have been operating in a legal grey area as the technology runs ahead of legislation. It is clear that rules of the road are required in this difficult area, and not just for robots with wheels.

The best-known set of guidelines for robo-ethics are the "three laws of robotics" coined by Isaac Asimov, a science-fiction writer, in 1942. The laws require robots to protect humans, obey orders and preserve themselves, in that order. Unfortunately, the laws are of little use in the real world. Battlefield robots would be required to violate the first law. And Asimov's robot stories are fun precisely because they highlight the unexpected complications that arise when robots try to follow his apparently sensible rules. Regulating the development and use of autonomous robots will require a rather more elaborate framework. Progress is needed in three areas in particular.

Three Laws for the Laws of Robotics

First, laws are needed to determine whether the designer, the programmer, the manufacturer or the operator is at fault if an autonomous drone strike goes wrong or a driverless car has an accident. In order to allocate responsibility, autonomous systems must keep detailed logs so that they can explain the reasoning behind their decisions when necessary. This has implications for system design: it may, for instance, rule out the use of artificial neural networks, decision-making systems that learn from example rather than obeying predefined rules.

Second, where ethical systems are embedded into robots, the judgments they make need to be ones that seem right to most people. The techniques of experimental philosophy, which studies how people respond to ethical dilemmas, should be able to help. Last, and most important, more collaboration is required between engineers, ethicists, lawyers and policymakers, all of whom would draw up very different types of rules if they were left to their own devices. Both ethicists and engineers stand to benefit from working together: ethicists may gain a greater understanding of their field by trying to teach ethics to machines, and engineers need to reassure society that they are not taking any ethical short-cuts.

Technology has driven mankind's progress, but each new advance has posed troubling new questions. Autonomous machines are no different. The sooner the questions of moral agency they raise are answered, the easier it will be for mankind to enjoy the benefits that they will undoubtedly bring.

Critical Thinking

1. What are the three laws of robotics?

2. What are the three laws for the laws of robotics mentioned in the article? Discuss each of the proposed laws and take a pro or con position for each law.

3. Using the Internet, read articles about the emergence of the field of machine ethics. Be prepared to explain to the class the essence of this new field.

Ethical Leadership and the Dual Roles of Examples

ARLEN W. LANGVARDT

1. Leaders as Students and Teachers

In late 2011 and into 2012, media headlines featuring Penn State University and leaders affiliated with it stemmed from reasons the university and those individuals will long regret and the public will long remember. The multi-faceted scandal involving child sexual abuse and what was done (or not done) about it by persons with relevant information furnished a jarring reminder of what can happen when organizational leaders fall short in an ethical sense or are widely perceived as having done so. Though set in a university context and against the backdrop of a high-profile sports program, the Penn State debacle serves as a sobering example from which leaders in a corporate environment can learn useful lessons—if they learn the right ones. As will be seen, learning the right lessons may often require overcoming common human tendencies that adversely affect the quality of our thinking and decision making.

This article uses the events at Penn State and the fallout that ensued as a jumping-off point for examination of broader questions concerning ethical decision making and ethical leadership. It explores the dual roles that corporate leaders play regarding matters of ethics: they are *students* in the sense that they learn, or should learn, from relevant experiences (both their own and those of others); and, through the examples they set, they are *teachers* of other persons affiliated with the organization and of non-affiliated persons who observe their actions. Along the way, the article considers the roles that sound critical thinking, asking of the right questions, and application of practical self-tests may play in improving the quality of decisions that have ethical dimensions and in helping leaders to set the right kinds of examples.

At the outset, it may be useful to clarify that as used in this article, the term "leader" is not restricted to persons at the top of the corporate hierarchy even if some of the matters to be explored seem especially relevant to those in high-level executive positions. Neither is there an attempt here to dwell on the technical niceties of possible distinctions between leaders and managers or to elaborate on when a person may be both a leader

and a manager. On ethical questions, one may be a leader, and therefore may demonstrate ethical leadership, at any level of the organization and without regard for whether he or she has formal management responsibilities. Whatever their positions within the organization, those who consistently demonstrate a commitment to doing the right thing can have a positive impact on all with whom they interact.

1.1. Setting Examples and Learning from Examples

Leadership in an organizational setting involves a good bit of example-setting. In an influential study, Badaracco and Webb (1995) examined the experiences of Harvard MBA graduates during their early years in the corporate work environment. The authors noted the MBAs' emphasis on the importance of examples set by corporate leaders in shaping the organizational culture regarding matters of ethics. The subjects studied were not just talking about positive examples, however. More commonly, they noted negative examples in which persons higher up in the organizational command structure acted in ways that struck the MBAs as insensitive to, or openly dismissive of, ethical concerns. Such examples did far more to shape the firms' culture than did company codes of ethics and lofty statements of supposed corporate principles to which, it seemed, only lip service was paid (Badaracco & Webb, 1995). However, some of the MBAs who participated in the study saw that a positive ethical climate could emerge from examples their organizational leaders were setting. One would expect those MBAs to have a more favorable view of the firms for which they worked.

Through the examples they set, therefore, organizational leaders serve as teachers in regard to actions and decisions that have ethical dimensions. To be effective teachers, leaders must be conscious of the examples they set. They also have to be skilled *learners,* in order to know what lessons to impart through their examples. They must learn not only from their own experiences but also from the experiences of others. This brings us back, for the moment, to where we began: with the Penn State scandal and what should and should not be learned from it.

2. The Penn State Debacle

2.1. Recap of Key Events

A recap of the key Penn State events (as reported in numerous media accounts from November 2011 until January 2012, when this article went to press), may be helpful. In 1998, police investigated a report that Jerry Sandusky, for many years the defensive coordinator for Penn State's football team, had showered in a Penn State locker room with a boy Sandusky met through his work with the Second Mile Foundation (an organization that focused on disadvantaged youth). The boy's mother had made the report to the police. No arrest was made and no charges were filed.

In 1999, Sandusky resigned as defensive coordinator after learning from Penn State's longtime head coach, Joe Paterno, that he would not be named as Paterno's successor at whatever time the legendary coach decided to retire. Paterno supposedly indicated that the time Sandusky was spending on Second Mile matters had interfered too much with his coaching duties. Years later, after the events described below, Paterno denied having known about the 1998 police investigation of Sandusky. Although he was not a member of the Penn State coaching staff after 1999, Sandusky held emeritus status at the university. He had an office there and enjoyed ready access to locker rooms and other university facilities. Sandusky therefore remained a regular and visible presence despite his lack of official status with the football program.

During an evening in 2002, Mike McQueary, a former Penn State player and then a graduate assistant (later an assistant coach), stopped by the locker room to drop off some shoes. According to grand jury testimony he gave in graphic detail several years later, McQueary heard noises coming from the shower area, looked into the showers, and saw Sandusky sexually assaulting a young boy. A shocked McQueary left the premises and contacted his father to discuss what he should do. McQueary informed Paterno (still the head coach) the next day about what he had witnessed. In grand jury testimony he later provided, Paterno stated that McQueary did not go into extreme detail about what he had seen but that McQueary had said it involved behavior of a sexual nature.

A day or two after hearing from McQueary, Paterno informed Penn State's athletics director, Tim Curley, about what McQueary had told him. Paterno's involvement ceased at that point. He did not inform the police and did not follow up with Curley regarding what, if anything, Curley had done with the information. A Penn State vice-president (Gary Schultz) and the university's president (Graham Spanier) later acquired knowledge, presumably through Curley, of McQueary's report regarding Sandusky. In grand jury testimony they later provided, Curley and Schultz asserted that they had not been provided the graphic details about which McQueary testified.

No police investigation occurred as a result of McQueary's 2002 report, as relayed to Paterno and then Curley, Schultz, and Spanier. Law enforcement authorities were not informed. The university did prohibit Sandusky from bringing children to the Penn State premises, but neither barred Sandusky's access nor otherwise altered his status with the university.

Fast forward to 2009. Sandusky remained a frequent presence at Penn State. His Second Mile involvement continued, as did the large amount of time he spent with children he met through the foundation. In 2009, however, law enforcement officials launched an investigation after receiving various reports from alleged victims and their parents that Sandusky had sexually assaulted a number of boys he had met through Second Mile. During the general time of the investigation, Second Mile severed ties with Sandusky. The investigation led to the convening of a grand jury and the previously referred to testimony of McQueary, Paterno, Curley, and Schultz.

2.2. Indictments, Troublesome Questions, and Further Fallout

In early November 2011, Sandusky was indicted on approximately 40 counts of sexual assault of various minors during the years 1994 through 2009. Curley and Schultz were indicted for perjury in connection with their grand jury testimony about what they had been told in 2002. The district attorney announced that no charges against Paterno (by then 84 years of age but still the head coach) were planned, because the fact that he informed Curley may have satisfied any reporting obligation he had under Pennsylvania law. However, the district attorney declined to rule out the possibility of criminal charges against Spanier, the Penn State president.

When the indictments were announced, a media firestorm erupted and a public relations nightmare for Penn State began. Sandusky instantly became the object of public scorn, as would be expected given the nature of the charges against him. Curley immediately went on administrative leave and Schultz just as quickly retired, though each vowed to fight the charges he faced. Perhaps the most public commentary, however, was directed at an unindicted party, Paterno. Although fans of the famed coach gathered in groups near his home to demonstrate their support for him during the days following the announcement of the grand jury's report, the public reaction nationally tended to be highly unfavorable. Much of the commentary in the media and on blogs was withering in its criticism of Paterno. The legendary figure with the theretofore sterling reputation had these sorts of unpleasant questions raised about him in widely publicized fashion:

- Given what McQueary told him, why didn't Paterno do more than the apparent legal minimum of informing Curley? Why didn't Paterno contact law enforcement authorities himself? Wasn't he effectively the most powerful person at Penn State, given his long history there and the prominence of the football program? If so, wouldn't the police have jumped into action if they had heard from him?
- Wasn't it strange that Paterno never followed up with Curley, especially since Sandusky continued to be a visible presence in the athletic facilities for several years after McQueary's report? What legitimate justification could there be for Paterno's never having approached Curley to say something such as this: "Tim, what did you do about the Sandusky situation after I told you

what McQueary said? After all, Jerry's still around here. What happened? Did you notify the police?"

- Wasn't it inexcusable that Paterno never confronted Sandusky, his old friend and longtime associate, about the allegations? Wouldn't seeing Sandusky day after day be a constant reminder?

- Surely Paterno knew, didn't he, that Sandusky was still spending lots of time with children? Weren't there a number of things Paterno could have done to stop a probable predator from harming more kids? How many became victims after 2002, when Paterno passed the buck to Curley and tried to wash his hands of the whole sordid mess?

- Was Paterno more concerned about the image of the football program and about keeping a lid on the scandal than about the welfare of innocent children? Did Paterno know more than he let on about the 1998 investigation of Sandusky, and was that the real reason why Sandusky left the coaching staff in 1999 (i.e., was Sandusky forced out for a reason the program wanted to keep quiet)?

The same sorts of questions were asked regarding Spanier, though he was less of a lightning rod than Paterno because his (Spanier's) public profile was less prominent than the coach's. (In the world of big-time intercollegiate athletics, of course, it is not unusual for a football or basketball coach to become a more familiar figure to the public than is the university's president.) McQueary also came in for a considerable amount of public criticism on the grounds that perhaps he too should have done more. Others, however, placed less blame on him because he held a less powerful position with the football program.

A few days after the early November release of the grand jury report and amid the furor that followed, Paterno announced his intent to retire at the end of the season. That announcement may have forced the hand of the university's board of trustees. Considering what appeared to be an overwhelmingly negative public assessment of Paterno's handling of the Sandusky situation, the board likely wanted to avoid the potentially disastrous spectacle that could result if Paterno were allowed to coach in the upcoming nationally televised game against Nebraska and supporters cheered him when he took the field. The board evidently concluded that it could not permit him to go out on his own terms.

Therefore, the board fired Paterno, effective immediately—less than a week after the grand jury report became public, only about 2 weeks after he had become the winningest coach in college football history, and 45 years after he had been hired as head coach. Spanier was shown the door as well. McQueary was placed on administrative leave.

The indicted defendants (Sandusky, Curley, and Schultz) soon were bound over for trial on the charges against them. Those criminal cases remained pending as of this article's publication deadline. In addition, other supposed victims of Sandusky came forward with allegations similar to those that furnished the basis of the criminal charges against him.

It was also apparent that various civil lawsuits seeking money damages would be filed by Sandusky's victims against not only Sandusky but also Penn State, Paterno, Spanier, other Penn State-affiliated individuals, and Second Mile (whose president resigned very shortly after the grand jury report was released). Sandusky's liability would be based on a battery theory, with the other defendants presumably being proceeded against on a variety of negligence grounds (negligent failure to warn, negligent supervision, negligent retention, and the like). The National Collegiate Athletic Association also announced that it would investigate the Penn State football program for possible violations of NCAA rules dealing with program integrity and monitoring.

A late-November statement by the Paterno family revealed that Paterno had been diagnosed with lung cancer and had sustained a broken pelvis in a fall at his home. By January 2012, shortly before this article went to press, some former Penn State players and other alumni had become quite vocal in their criticism of the Penn State board for its decision to fire the longtime coach. (The decision to fire Spanier did not trigger similar objections.) That same month, an ill Paterno provided a *Washington Post* reporter an interview in which he seemed to characterize himself as naive regarding the content of the information McQueary provided him in 2002 and regarding what to do about it. He stated that he informed Curley about what McQueary said but did nothing more about the Sandusky matter because he did not really understand the sexual misconduct information and because, not having had previous occasion to deal with such allegations, he thought that he would not have as good an idea of how to handle the situation as other Penn State officials would have.

In mid-January 2012, only days after the interview with the *Post* reporter, Paterno was hospitalized. He died approximately a week later.

3. Penn State's Lessons for Leaders of Organizations: Identification and Application

What should be learned from the Penn State fiasco? The list of lessons includes those identified in the paragraphs that follow. Note that for purposes of these lessons, the public perception that decision makers paid too little attention to ethical considerations assumes considerable importance. If much of the public believes that decision makers at Penn State did not fulfill their ethical obligations, those decision makers' arguments that they did act ethically are likely to fall on deaf ears. The same is true of decision makers in corporate environments. Of course, we have no ethics courts to determine definitively whether persons acted ethically or unethically. With not only traditional ethical theories but also individuals' personal notions of ethical behavior leading to differences of opinion on whether persons measured up in an ethical sense, corporate decision makers need to be cognizant of how persons other than themselves may be likely to view a decision (Jackall, 1988).

3.1. Lesson #1

The negative consequences stemming from an ethical lapse— or from what is widely perceived as an ethical lapse—can be extremely far-reaching and can harm large numbers of completely innocent people. Consider the range of consequences stemming from the Sandusky-related decisions at Penn State. First on the list, of course, would be the horrific effects on the sexually abused children, including those who became victims prior to and during 2002 and those who thereafter were victimized but might not have been if Paterno and other university decision makers had handled matters differently when McQueary came forward with what he had observed.

Then in no particular order of importance, there were other effects on individuals. Paterno and Spanier were fired from prestigious positions at the respective pinnacles of their careers. Curley and Schultz went on leave or stepped down from their positions at Penn State and faced criminal prosecutions. Other coaches associated with the football program, though not shown to have had knowledge of Sandusky's actions, may long be suspected by some observers, fairly or unfairly, of having looked the other way and having played along with covering up an ugly secret.

Moreover, with Paterno's firing, those other coaches' futures at Penn State went down the drain or were placed in doubt. That is often the case when a head coach is fired, but normally that is because the team did not win enough games, not because the head coach improperly handled a matter with significant ethical implications. Certain Penn State assistant coaches who had served under Paterno interviewed for the head coaching position but were not hired for it. Shortly before this article went to press, Penn State announced that it had hired Bill O'Brien as its new head football coach. O'Brien had no previous ties to Penn State. Although a small number of other Penn State assistants appeared to have chances to serve on O'Brien's staff, most would no longer be part of the school's football program. The latter group included one whose departure from Penn State must have been especially regrettable to Paterno: his son, Jay, a Penn State assistant coach for more than 15 years.

And what about members of the families of the individuals mentioned above? They had nothing whatsoever to do with the actions or inactions of persons formally affiliated with Penn State, yet they obviously would experience adverse effects as a result of decisions made by those with the formal affiliations.

In addition, there were—and probably will continue to be—negative consequences for large groups of persons and for the university itself. The reputations of Penn State's football program and of the university as a whole took hits that may not be confined to the short term. Fund-raising efforts of the university could be compromised or otherwise adversely affected. If the university's reputation suffers, faculty members, administrators, and staff members who have done much to build a fine university may suffer at least intangible harm. Key personnel could leave the university. Students who were proud to attend the university may become concerned, justifiably or not, about possible devaluing of their Penn State degree in the employment marketplace.

Furthermore, we should not forget the legal consequences outside the criminal arena. With civil lawsuits brought by victims and their parents a certainty, there is great potential financial exposure for the university and the individuals involved in deciding what to do about the information that came their way regarding Sandusky. (With Paterno's death, his estate becomes a potentially liable party.) There will also be significant costs to Penn State in connection with the NCAA's investigation.

In the business context, high-profile ethics scandals of recent years furnish examples of similar broad-ranging effects that damage innocent parties even if persons directly involved receive whatever legal come-uppance they deserve. The Enron shenanigans of roughly a decade ago come to mind. Shareholders took a serious hit, and numerous employees who had nothing to do with the wrongdoing found themselves out in the cold. What about Bernie Madoff's fraudulent scheme? Those who invested funds with him lost huge sums (though it can be argued that after Bernie produced year after year of spectacular returns, investors probably should have been asking questions of the "How is this possible?" variety). Once again, innocent Madoff employees who lost their jobs when the house of cards collapsed—as well as family members who depended on those employees—suffered losses for which there probably will be no legal remedy.

The list of similar examples from which leaders should learn goes on, but by now the point should be clear: Taking into account the full potential range of consequences that may stem from a course of action under consideration can be a very useful device for making choices that are sensible in the short and long terms (Paul & Elder, 2002). And if decisions are truly sensible in the short and long terms, they are much more likely to be ethically defensible. A decision making approach that contemplates all who stand to be affected, as well as how they probably would be affected, may be especially useful in making decisions where the ethical aspects of the decision are less obvious than in the Enron-type or Madoff-type scenario and the answer to the what's-right-versus-what's-wrong question does not clearly present itself (Perry, 2011; Trevino & Nelson, 2010).

For instance, should our company be forthcoming about steady reports of safety defects in our products, or should we circle the wagons and deny the probable existence of a problem until we absolutely have to concede there is one? In recent decades, Ford, Toyota, Firestone, and many other companies have had to face such issues and have faced criticism for initially choosing what struck many as the latter strategy. If we are a tobacco company whose sales are declining in the United States because the number of smokers is decreasing, should we seek to ramp up sales outside the U.S.? If so, how aggressively? When we sell our products beyond United States borders, should we provide the same sorts of health warnings we must furnish in the U.S. even if the nation in which we are selling does not require such warnings?

If we are a household appliance manufacturer facing rising labor costs, should we close our U.S. plants and open up new ones outside the U.S.? If we are an oil company involved in deep-water drilling in waters near the U.S. and other nations, how extensively should we develop a 'Plan B' just in case the disaster that is possible, but which we think is unlikely, actually occurs? What are the likely effects if we don't have a Plan B or if we are perceived as not having an adequate one? (BP, anybody?)

If we manufacture table saws, should we incorporate into our product a well-tested technology that can tell the difference between a piece of wood and a human finger (with the saw blade then almost instantly stopping if human tissue starts to come in contact with the blade)? What if adopting the technology would mean we would have to pay royalties to the owner of a patent on the technology (thus increasing the cost of our saws)? If the Consumer Products Safety Commission promulgates a regulation requiring us to use the technology on table saws we sell in the U.S., should we also use the technology in saws we intend to sell in nations that have no comparable safety regulation in place?

The examples from which to learn are there, whether they are of the Penn State, Enron, or Madoff variety, or are more similar to the ones noted in the preceding paragraphs. But will corporate leaders learn from them? As later discussion will reveal, certain thinking tendencies we have as humans can get in the way. Awareness of those tendencies can help us to overcome them, particularly if we get in the habit of asking ourselves good impulse-checking questions. The article will explore such issues later. Now, however, let us return to the lessons to be learned from the Penn State debacle.

3.2. Lesson #2

An ethical lapse—or something widely regarded as an ethical lapse—can at minimum put a permanent asterisk on an otherwise solid record of accomplishments and, in some observers' eyes, outweigh years of seemingly good works. Joe Paterno's legacy in the wake of the Penn State scandal serves as the most prominent illustration of this lesson. Paterno was the winningest coach in college football history after a 45-year tenure in which he reportedly ran a clean (for NCAA purposes) football program, stressed the importance of academics, and did a great deal financially and in other ways to further the academic mission of the university. Yet in media reports of his death, there was early mention not only of his accomplishments but also of the fact that Penn State fired him for what he did not do after receiving information about Sandusky's sexual assault on a child. Even an account-writer who had no intent to engage in condemnation of Paterno for his lapse in judgment and wished to stress the positive aspects of his lengthy career could not ignore the inglorious end to Paterno's decades as head coach. The same would seem likely regarding future accounts of Paterno's life and career—even ones with a measured tone. Others may be less balanced in their assessment of Paterno's legacy, taking effectively a scorecard approach and concluding that the enormity (in their view) of Paterno's failure wipes out the points he scored through his previous good works.

Suffice it to say that his story ended in a way Paterno would not have wanted. During the last 2 months of his life, he was reported to have called the Sandusky matter "one of the great sorrows of my life." Some may therefore see Paterno as a tragic figure; others may be inclined to disagree, concluding that being fired was exactly what he deserved under the circumstances. Similarly, the respective stories and likely legacies of Spanier, Curley, and Schultz are not the ones they would like after careers of considerable accomplishment. Even stories written about Penn State the university (as opposed to Penn State the football team) may for some time expressly note the Sandusky et al. scandal, or a mental footnote to that effect may be supplied by the reader. Few, it seems, would be likely to go so far as to condemn the university as a whole for the failures of a relatively small group, but there seems little doubt that the scandal will not soon recede from the public's mind and may obscure messages that Penn State wishes to communicate about its many worthy programs and activities.

In the corporate context, public perceptions that an organization acted unethically or otherwise irresponsibly in given instances may not often completely extinguish the organization's ability to survive, but such perceptions may nonetheless be obstacles for the firm to overcome in a competitive market where government regulation is present or proposed (Jackall, 1988; Rubin, 2012). Ask BP, for instance. Ask financial institutions that played a role in the subprime mortgage debacle. Ask pharmaceutical companies accused of sitting on evidence of a drug's danger to consumers where that evidence came to the companies' attention after FDA approval of the drug.

3.3. Lesson #3

An ethical lapse—or what strikes many as an ethical lapse—may prove especially damaging to decision makers involved and to affected constituencies when the pre-lapse public reputation of the decision makers was quite positive. As the old saying goes: The bigger they come, the harder they fall. Had the child sexual abuse scandal (and what to do about it) occurred at a school whose football program was less prominent than Penn State's and had the head coach involved in it been less well-known than the iconic Paterno, the public would still have been shocked. But the intensity and duration of public attention to the matter would have been far less. The public would soon have moved on, even though the legal and ethical issues would have been the same as in the actual Penn State scandal.

Because Paterno was such a visible figure and had such a longstanding good-guy image, and because the Penn State football program had such a high public profile, the tarnishing of Paterno's reputation and the program's reputation probably took on an added negative dimension. How could it be, many have asked, that this widely respected coach/educator who supposedly knew how to do things the 'right' way would flunk an ethics test when it was administered to him? Others might wonder, fairly or unfairly, whether the doing-things-the-right-way image was all a sham.

This lesson can also manifest itself in the corporate environment. Consider, for instance, the widely publicized safety problems that Toyota experienced with certain models of its vehicles in recent years. As noted earlier, Toyota experienced public criticism for a supposed slowness to acknowledge the problems and make clear what it would do about them. Toyota's longstanding and presumably well-deserved reputation for producing safe and reliable vehicles likely took a special hit because of the contrast effect when the alleged safety issues came to light. Toyota therefore found it necessary to engage in advertising in which it reaffirmed its commitment to safety and reliability.

Of course, a positive for Toyota in the whole experience was that it did have the positive reputation to fall back on. Therefore, it could position the safety issues of recent years as out of character for the automaker, while at the same time emphasizing that they were issues the company would take seriously going forward in an effort to demonstrate that the historically positive reputation was indeed justified. Perhaps the Penn State football program and the university as a whole can adopt a similar strategy. For Paterno, however, a public relations offensive to restore his national reputation during his lifetime proved not to be an option even though he still had fervent supporters who stressed his pre-Sandusky-scandal record.

3.4. Lesson #4

Where the actual or perceived ethical lapse seems to involve covering up a dirty secret in an effort to protect the reputations of organizational decision makers and the organization itself, others' uncovering of the secret and public disclosure thereof may lead to reputational harm far more extensive and long-lasting than any short-term hit to reputation that might have occurred if the information that became a dirty secret had been disclosed by the relevant decision makers. In some ways, this lesson seems to draw from the familiar saying: The cover-up is worse than the crime. That saying is not literally true in the Penn State situation, however. There, the inaction on the part of those with important information—the cover-up, if you will—was no doubt bad, but the underlying crime (Sandusky's sexual assault) was heinous.

Still, the Penn State events illustrate the lesson as articulated here. Those involved in the limited communication of the awful information regarding Sandusky (McQueary, Paterno, Curley, Schultz, and Spanier) may not have seen themselves as having participated in a cover-up. Effectively, however, they did so participate by not informing law enforcement authorities, by not alerting the Second Mile Foundation despite their knowledge of Sandusky's work with children through that foundation, and by largely maintaining the status quo in regard to Sandusky's connections with the football program and the university. The facts plausibly suggest a determination, whether conscious or subconscious, to keep a lid on the Sandusky matter because the scandal that might follow a report to law enforcement authorities—a scandal stemming from public awareness that an apparent child molester had long coached in the football program and still had a connection with it—might make the program look bad.

The irony, of course, is that the way the information ultimately came out proved to be especially damaging to the program's reputation and the reputations of the individual decision makers as well as that of the university itself, because it became apparent that the relevant information had been known but not acted upon for several years while more children presumably were being molested. Had the disclosure to law enforcement authorities occurred in 2002, there might have been short-term harm to the program's reputation and those of the individual decision makers once media accounts revealed the allegations about Sandusky. The harm almost certainly would have dissipated quickly, however. Paterno et al. would have been seen as having done the right thing, even at pain of informing on a longtime colleague and friend. Paterno's reputation would have been burnished; he presumably would have remained as the head coach at Penn State for the remainder of his life or until he decided to step down in the normal course of events; the other individuals who lost their Penn State positions would likely have continued to hold them; and the lingering reputational effects for the university would not be present. Most importantly, further children would not have been victimized.

Some of the business examples noted earlier also apply here. Cover-ups of safety information suggesting product defects, or public perceptions that such cover-ups occurred, have at times been problematic both legally and in a reputational sense for producers of a wide range of products. The same has been true regarding cover-ups or perceived cover-ups by firms whose activities, once discovered, are alleged to have polluted the environment. And the list goes on.

3.5. Lesson #5

Our tendencies to see what we want to see, not see what we don't want to see, and to hope a problem will go away on its own can plague us in the long run and can lead to decisions that later come to be seen by others as ethically indefensible. Unless we consciously seek to check ourselves, we have a natural human tendency to fall victim to confirmation bias (Bazerman & Moore, 2009; Gilovich, 1991). We search for and pay attention to evidence that confirms our preferred positions on issues, while minimizing or outright ignoring what should be clear disaffirming evidence (i.e., evidence indicating that our preferred position may be wrong or at least questionable) (Metzger, 2005; Taleb, 2007).

This tendency also leads to seeing what we want to see in a given situation and not noting signs of a negative nature if such signs are not what we would prefer to see. Similarly, we may put an unwarranted interpretive gloss on something we observe if doing so makes it easier to think that what we observed does not run contrary to our preferred position (Bazerman & Moore, 2009; Metzger, 2005). When we do these things, we may be attempting to soft-pedal an obvious problem with which we do not want to deal, perhaps in the hope it will resolve itself. The danger, of course, is that the problem will not go away and will lead to worse outcomes than would have been produced if the problem had been promptly addressed.

Did the above sort of thing happen at Penn State? It seems likely. After being informed by McQueary in 2002 about what he had witnessed and after Paterno reported the matter to the athletics director (Curley), Paterno of course continued to see Sandusky on a regular basis because Sandusky was frequently at the athletic facilities. When Paterno observed Sandusky, he presumably would have preferred to think of the Sandusky with whom he had had a long association, not the Sandusky who, according to McQueary's report, was a child molester. Arguably, then, Paterno continued to see the old Sandusky rather than Sandusky the monster. It also appears likely Paterno wanted to believe that law enforcement authorities must have decided to do nothing regarding Sandusky because, after all, Sandusky had not been jailed and because Paterno had heard nothing about any police investigation. Probably Paterno also wanted to think Curley or others at Penn State had contacted law enforcement authorities after Paterno informed Curley.

Of course, however, Paterno never asked Curley whether he or anyone else notified the police. Had Paterno asked, he would have learned information he probably did not want to hear: that Curley had not contacted the police. Might that be why Paterno didn't ask? If so, the human tendency to avoid hearing something we do not want to hear may have contributed significantly to his curious inaction after initially informing Curley and to the resulting public perception that his bare-minimum approach to the Sandusky matter fell short in an ethical sense.

The experiences of Firestone roughly a decade ago illustrate this same lesson. Firestone received repeated and seemingly credible reports indicating that defects in a particular model of Firestone tires caused tire failures that also led to serious accidents of the rollover variety involving vehicles (mainly Ford vehicles) on which they had been installed. Nevertheless, Firestone appeared to ignore the problem or to attempt to explain it away in unconvincing fashion. Firestone evidently did not want to see what the reports about defects really indicated: that the problem actually resided in the design and manufacturing of the tires. Eventually Firestone acknowledged the problem, but not until development of a reputation-harming public perception that it had been merely stonewalling. (In addition, Firestone faced numerous lawsuits and its executives underwent the unpleasant experience of having to testify in front of a congressional committee.)

3.6. Lesson #6

What may be legal action may fall well short of the mark ethically or in the public's sense of what is ethical. Although many legal rules have underpinnings consistent with widely held notions of ethical conduct, it remains important to remember that what is legal may not always be ethical or may not be perceived as ethical by the public. The district attorney who commented at a press conference on the indictments of Sandusky, Curley, and Schultz noted that Paterno was not being indicted because the fact that he informed Curley may have meant that he (Paterno) fulfilled a reporting obligation he had under a Pennsylvania statute dealing with duties to report information regarding instances of child abuse. Paterno thus may have acted lawfully in regard to that statutory obligation, but given much of the public reaction to the events at Penn State, there is little doubt that many believe he did not fulfill an ethical obligation to do more. (It is also worth noting that in another sense, Paterno may not have fulfilled all of his legal obligations even if it is assumed that he met his duty under the reporting statute. His estate will, be among the defendants in civil lawsuits presenting the theory that he, others at Penn State, and the university itself were negligent in the sense of failing to use reasonable care in their handling of the Sandusky matter.)

A business-related example may help to illustrate this same lesson. Assume that a manufacturer has decided it needs to close a plant in the U.S. and move production to a facility located in another country. Jobs will be lost in the process. If the manufacturer satisfies the notice obligation set forth by a federal law on plant closings, it will have fulfilled its legal duty. Almost certainly, however, there will be some who regard the manufacturer as acting unethically. The manufacturer, therefore, has to anticipate this reaction and position itself well to answer the argument that it behaved in a socially irresponsible manner. The manufacturer will need to develop strong counter-arguments that go beyond "we behaved in accordance with the law." That particular counter-argument will not be enough by itself to carry the day when the issue is phrased in terms of whether the action was ethical in nature (Badaracco & Webb, 1995).

3.7. Lesson #7

The examples set by an organization's leaders have a profound effect on the culture of the organization. This lesson hearkens back to a point made early in the article. As the study undertaken by Badaracco and Webb (1995) indicates, those who work in an organizational setting look to leaders in the organization for examples of how to act. Moreover, participants in the study regarded corporate leaders as key shapers, through the examples they set, of the culture of the organization. If the examples are good—and ones that indicate sensitivity to ethical considerations—a healthy culture can result. But if the examples reflect little seriousness about ethics, a corner-cutting culture may follow (Jackall, 1988).

What about the Penn State situation suggests this lesson? Paterno may have set loads of good examples as a football coach and teacher over the years, but it seems a stretch to regard his behavior in the Sandusky fiasco as a positive culture-shaping example. Say McQueary had begun to feel as though he should have done more than simply inform Paterno about Sandusky. But as he looked around and saw Sandusky having a continued presence in and around the football program, he could have concluded that it was okay with Paterno that Sandusky was still on the scene. After all, if Sandusky's continued presence had the approval of the head coach, who was he (McQueary) to advocate otherwise or to push the matter further? Paterno's lack of further conversation with McQueary or others regarding the Sandusky matter likely sent a similar message to McQueary: that the matter was to be kept quiet and under wraps.

The inaction of the university president (Spanier) probably sent essentially the same keep-a-lid-on-it message to Curley, Schultz, and any others who may have become privy to the information regarding Sandusky. The example set by Spanier thus taught those who knew of it a lesson that proved to be disastrous.

4. Obstacles to Learning the Right Lessons

Although there are plenty of examples—good and bad—from which leaders may learn and thereby increase their chances of setting positive examples in their organizations, obstacles can impair the ability to learn from examples. Some obstacles are of special significance in regard to the lessons stemming from the Penn State debacle; others are of a more general nature and are tied to human tendencies that can impair the quality of our thinking and decision making.

4.1. Penn State and the Pales-by-Comparison Danger

The monstrous nature of the acts of which Jerry Sandusky is accused (and regarding which Paterno and other Penn State decision makers appeared not to respond adequately to when they acquired knowledge of them) creates what might be called a pales-by-comparison danger. It is possible that organizational leaders may pay more attention to the sensational nature of the information at the heart of the Penn State scandal than to the broader decision making issues the scandal suggests. If that occurs, they may tend to minimize the ethical dimensions of their own actions and decisions on the theory that nothing they would do or not do could be as bad as the horrific nature and consequences of what happened at Penn State.

But such thinking misses the point. The profound harm-to-children feature of the Penn State scandal should not have the effect of somehow insulating decision makers against criticism on ethical grounds when their decisions injure others without good reason and the harm, though substantial, seems less severe than the harm stemming from the abomination of child sexual abuse. The enormity of the harm resulting from such abuse does not mean that other harms—for example, economic injury to workers or consumers, or risks to product users' health—are somehow too insignificant to worry about for purposes of ethical decision making.

The Penn State experience presents the same sorts of issues that other organizational decision makers face in terms of what to do about unwelcome, troublesome information whose disclosure may bring pain to the organization (at least in the short term) but whose nondisclosure may risk substantial harm to persons affected by the organization's decisions. Therefore, the previously identified lessons from the Penn State fiasco remain important ones for leaders in other organizations even if it is unlikely that the unwelcome information those leaders acquire will match the Penn State information in terms of reprehensibility of the conduct alleged. (And the relevance of the Penn State lessons to the decisions of corporate leaders is not diminished by the fact that the scandal arose in the not-for-profit setting. The financial, reputational, and operational aspects of major universities' football programs and many of its other endeavors have plenty of parallels with what we see in the for-profit corporate world.)

4.2. Tendencies that Adversely Affect Thinking Quality and Limit Learning from Examples

Because of tendencies of which we often are unaware, we do not think as well as we believe we do. Unless we become aware of those tendencies and take suitable steps to check their negative effects, our abilities to reason well and to learn from our experiences and those of others can be compromised. Attention to key critical thinking principles can not only improve the quality of our reasoning but also enhance the likelihood that ethical considerations will be appropriately accounted for in our decision making.

Earlier discussion introduced one problematic thinking tendency that can impair our ability to learn from examples. As noted previously, *confirmation bias* often causes us to search for and pay attention to evidence that is consistent with our preferred position or outcome, and to ignore or minimize the significance of evidence to the contrary (Bazerman & Moore, 2009; Gilovich, 1991). If we are not careful, it also causes us to see what we want to see in a given situation and to engage in subconscious favorable spinning of potentially relevant facts even if those facts might fairly be treated as pointing in the other direction. Confirmation bias thus can cause us to miss the real lessons from an example that we think we are viewing objectively. (Thus, there is a relationship to another thinking error to which we tend to be subject: missing the point.) To guard against the negative effects of confirmation bias and to learn as much as we can from an example or situation, we need to seek out and pay attention to possible disconfirming evidence: evidence indicating that our preferred position or view may not be correct (Metzger, 2005; Taleb, 2007).

Three other human tendencies that sometimes distort our thinking can adversely affect our ability to learn appropriate lessons about ethical decision making from our own experiences or from examples we observe. They are the *self-esteem motivator, overconfidence bias,* and the *false uniqueness effect.* Each one merits consideration here.

Our need to feel good about ourselves—to bolster our self-esteem—often causes us to lend a favorable characterization to what we have done or failed to do even if that characterization is a strained one. We do not like to admit that we behaved wrongly, so we may take liberties with the facts in order to avoid having to make such an admission, even to ourselves. If we have to concede that we made a mistake, we often try to rationalize it by saying that it was not really our fault, that the circumstances dictated what we did or did not do, or that anyone else in such a situation would have done the same thing (Bazerman & Moore, 2009; Metzger, 2005). The problem, of course, is that it may really have been our fault, or the circumstances did not really dictate the course of action we pursued, or others in the same situation might well have acted differently. Thus, unless we ask ourselves some hard questions and hold our own feet to the fire, the self-esteem motivator may keep us from learning unpleasant but important lessons from our own experiences.

The phenomenon known as overconfidence bias leads us to be more confident than we should be about the extent of our knowledge and our problem-solving skills (Metzger, 2005; Russo & Schoemaker, 1992; Thaler & Sunsteiin, 2009). To the extent that this 'been there, done that—many times' mindset takes hold in a leader, his or her ability to learn helpful lessons from the experiences of others may be compromised. In the realm of ethical decision making, the leader who thinks he or she has mastered everything important and has nothing more to learn may end up teaching those in the organization unfortunate lessons and may unknowingly influence the organization's culture in an undesirable way.

The false uniqueness effect causes us to view ourselves as special. In a room of smart people, each person may tend to view himself or herself as smarter than most or all of the others (Metzger, 2005; Thaler & Sunstein, 2009). If we indulge in the assumption that most people are ethical, we may see ourselves as even more ethical than most. The false uniqueness effect, if left unchecked, can seriously compromise the ability to learn useful lessons about ethical decision making from the examples set by others' actions and decisions. If others' actions and decisions appear to fall short of the mark in an ethical sense, we may see the examples as largely irrelevant to us because we are more ethical than most and never would engage in such behavior anyway. When that happens, potentially valuable lessons go unlearned. To guard against the deleterious outcomes that the false uniqueness effect may help to foster, we need to remind ourselves that those whose actions and decisions were at the heart of high-profile scandals in recent years probably thought of themselves as more ethical than the next person.

5. Keeping Thinking Errors in Check: Implications for Ethical Decision Making

The good news about the thinking tendencies discussed in the previous section is that their negative effects can be minimized if one is aware of them and if one adopts appropriate checks against them. This section explores some appropriate checks, the adoption of which can improve the quality of decisions and can afford a greater likelihood that ethical considerations will receive due treatment in the decision making process.

Maintaining a sense of humility can serve leaders well in more than one way. If they can remind themselves that they may not know everything there is to know, that there is always more to learn, and that they are not necessarily 'special,' the dangers of overconfidence bias and the false uniqueness effect can be minimized (Thaler & Sunstein, 2009). Moreover, the examples set by the humble leader are more likely to be ones that others in the organization want to follow.

Asking the right questions plays a key role in sound critical thinking and affords a further check against the tendencies noted in the previous section. These are among the questions that leaders should routinely ask when reviewing developments, evaluating information, and ultimately making decisions:

- How do we know X is true? Is the sample on which we are relying sufficiently large and representative? If we have a preferred explanation here, are there other possible explanations? Is there evidence that runs to the contrary of our preferred explanation or position? How might we be proven wrong?

- If we do, or not do, A, what happens next? If we do, or not do, B, what happens next? (And so forth.) Who will be affected by our action? How will they be affected? What happens if key consideration Y doesn't materialize? Then what do we do?

- What would constitute success here? What could constitute failure?

- How will others view our action? Can we be comfortable defending it? What is the principle that underlies what we have decided to do? Is that principle

sound? What are we rewarding here? Would we want everyone to do what we are thinking of doing under the relevant circumstances?

If questions of the sort just noted are routinely asked, decisions are more likely to be well-reasoned, soundly based, and sensitive to ethical considerations (Metzger, 2005; Paul & Elder, 2002; Perry, 2011). On the latter front, the questions posed in the final bullet point are especially relevant to practical tests for whether an action or decision adequately takes ethical considerations into account. One such test is sometimes called the '*60 Minutes* test,' the '*New York Times* test', or the '*Wall Street Journal* test' because it contemplates the decision maker's asking himself or herself this question: "Would I be comfortable justifying the decided-upon action in an interview on *60 Minutes* or in an interview for an investigative reporter's story in the *Times* or the *Journal!*" A "no" or "probably not" answer signals that the decided-upon action may require some re-thinking (Badaracco & Webb, 2009; Perry, 2011). The spouse/children/parents/grandparents test operates in a similar fashion. If the decision maker recognizes that he or she would not be comfortable trying to explain and justify the decided-upon action to the persons referred to in the name of the test, the decision maker should take a step back and consider whether another course of action might be both feasible and more ethically defensible.

The beauty of the tests just noted is that they are relatively simple to apply. They do not require deep delving into the intricacies of ethical theories such as utilitarianism (greatest good for the greatest number), rights theory (all have basic fundamental rights that must be respected), justice theory (all have equal entitlement to social benefits, with concerns for the worst-off being paramount in distributional decisions), or virtue ethics, however interesting those intricacies might be (Mallor, Barnes, Bowers, & Langvardt, 2012; Metzger, 2005).

One of the questions posed earlier, however, provides a workable test that does draw heavily on a classic ethics formulation: Kant's Categorical Imperative. The Categorical Imperative is often phrased along these lines: "Act only on that maxim whereby at the same time you can will that it shall become a universal law" (Paton, 1964). The principle is one of universality: Only take an action, or fail to take an action, if you would have everyone take or not take that same action under the same circumstances. Alternatively, as noted in a question raised earlier, would we want everyone to do what we are thinking of doing under the relevant circumstances? If the decision maker applies this test and answers the question with a "no," there may be ethical considerations that merit reexamination in the decision making process.

6. A Final Thought

When organizational leaders learn appropriate ethical decision making lessons from relevant examples, they can effectively teach others in the organization the right lessons through the examples those leaders go on to set. As they help to shape the organization's culture through the examples they provide, leaders also effectively write their own stories and those of their organizations through the actions they take. Effective leaders therefore must remain aware that the failure to pay due heed to ethical considerations in decision making may cause their personal and organizational stories to end with a lament rather than with a triumph. As Joe Paterno reportedly said regarding the matter that led to his firing, "I wish I had done more."

References

Badaracco, J. L, & Webb, A. P. (1995). Business ethics: A view from the trenches. *California Management Review, 37*(2), 8–28.

Bazerman, M. H., & Moore, D. A. (2009). *Judgment in managerial decision making* (7th ed.). Hoboken, NJ: John Wiley & Sons, Inc.

Gilovich, T. (1991). *How we know what isn't so.* New York: Simon & Schuster.

Jackall, R. (1988). *Moral mazes: The world of corporate managers.* New York: Oxford University Press.

Mallor, J. P., Barnes, A. J., Bowers, T., & Langvardt, A. W. (2012). *Business law: The ethical, global, and e-commerce environment.* New York: McGraw-Hill/lrwin.

Metzger, M. B. (2005). Bridging the gaps: Cognitive constraints on corporate control & ethics education. *University of Florida Journal of Law and Public Policy, 16*(3), 436–577.

Paton, H.J. (1964). Translation of Immanuel Kant (1785), *Groundwork of the metaphysics of morals.* New York: Harper & Row.

Paul, R. W., & Elder, L. (2002). *Critical thinking: Tools for taking charge of your professional and personal life.* Upper Saddle River, NJ: Pearson Education, Inc.

Perry, J. E. (2011). Managing moral distress: A strategy for resolving ethical dilemmas. *Business Horizons, 54*(4), 393–397.

Rubin, J. D. (2012). Fairness in business: Does it matter, and what does it mean? *Business Horizons, 55*(1), 11–15.

Russo, J. E., & Schoemaker, P. J. (1992). Managing overconfidence. *Sloan Management Review, 33*(2), 7—17.

Taleb, N. N. (2007). *The black swan: The impact of the highly improbable.* New York: Random House, Inc.

Thaler, R. H., & Sunstein, C. R. (2009). *Nudge: Improving decisions about health, wealth, and happiness.* New York: Penguin Books.

Trevino, L. K., & Nelson, K. A. (2010). *Managing business ethics: Straight talk about how to do it right* (5th ed.). New York: John Wiley & Sons, Inc.

Critical Thinking

1. Having read the summary of the Penn State sexual abuse scandal addressed in the article, what is your opinion of what happened?
2. How could those things that happened have been prevented?

Unfair Business Practices

Are Perks Dividing Your Company?

VADIM LIBERMAN

It Begins with a Cup of Coffee. Suppose your company were to restrict access to the corporate coffee machine to senior executives only. Why? Because busy bigwigs shouldn't have to wait with plebeians for caffeine jolts. Sure, assistants to assistants also battle endless to-do lists, but let's be blunt: Regardless of who prizes whose time more, a senior leader's minutes are certainly more valuable to the organization. Thus, for everyone else, there's a Starbucks around the corner.

An executive coffee policy—absurd, right? But replace coffee with a company jet, and the ridiculous suddenly appears sensible. Maybe.

What might start with coffee and end with air travel bursts with a cornucopia of corporate perquisites: car allowances, country-club memberships, home security, financial-planning assistance, corner offices, telecommuting, reserved parking, reserved restrooms, reserved dining rooms. Reserved—that is, nonmonetary compensation restricted to individuals or groups based on any number of criteria.

Perks are unlike benefits, which employers offer to *all* workers: medical insurance, a communal cafeteria, on-site dry cleaning, a foosball table, several colorful items that pop up when you Google "Google benefits," and, thankfully, coffee. Whereas benefits can distinguish your company from others, perks mainly differentiate workers *within* your organization. And because the list of possible perks stretches wide, so can the gulf between your firm's haves and have-nots.

Who Gets and Who Doesn't

What does it mean to treat people fairly? Ultimately, that's the central question here. While protestors pose it to Wall Street from the outside, it's worth asking it of corporations from the inside. Perks are ideal conduits to get at an answer because they're the most visible manifestations of how your organization sets people apart. (You may not know others' salaries, but you're painfully aware that the company isn't paying for you to tee off at the club this weekend.)

How do—how ought—you draw lines between who will have and who will have not? A common reply: Distribute perks that jibe with your company's culture. Obviously.

Not. Accepting this illogic legitimizes corporate-cultural relativism, whereby your company's approach is best because your organization says it is.

"Companies should ask, 'Which perks would align best with the culture we're trying to create?'" says Gaye Lindfors, a Minnesota-based consultant and former HR director at Northwest Airlines. Put differently, apportioning perks is not a *consequence* of but how you *create* corporate culture. "Actually, perks deserve more attention than other business decisions when defining culture because they are so personal," adds Jennifer Robin, a research fellow at the Great Place to Work Institute, a research, consulting, and training firm.

What do people deserve? When do they deserve it? Why do they deserve it? What does it mean to *deserve* anything? Your answers will shape your culture.

Yes, this is more philosophy than it is HR strategy. There's scarce research on corporate perks that pushes beyond describing to prescribing, which means that an HR director who wants to get perks right must aim to turn philosophy into practice.

> **What do people deserve? When do they deserve it? Why do they deserve it? What does it mean to deserve anything? Your answers will shape your culture.**

Here's how to ponder who flies in first class, who's in economy; who'll play golf, who'll watch it on TV; who gets an office with a window, and who gets an office with a window working from home. Who gets and who doesn't.

Diminished Expectations

If only it were as simple as coffee. As the competition dangles more, and more valuable, shiny things to recruit and retain, you're perpetually forced to play a Darwinian game of Keeping Up With the Googles. Don't want to play? You'll still lose. You won't make best-places-to-work lists; talent will head elsewhere.

You've witnessed this with skyrocketing executive compensation. To an extent, similar criticisms apply regarding perquisites. "Just ten years ago, executive perks were based on competitive practices almost exclusively," explains Don Lindner, executive-compensation practice leader at World at Work, a provider of HR education, conferences, and research. "They would get out of hand." It took only one CEO down the street to get a new car to compel other corporate boards to channel Oprah: And *you* get a car, and *you* get a car, and *you* get a car. And you, Karen Kozlowski, get a Tyco-sponsored $2 million birthday party. And you, Jack Welch, get an $11 million GE apartment. Legalities aside, the dotcom era produced a golden age of perks.

Today, it's more of a copper age. Businesses began seriously slashing perks five years ago, after the SEC mandated disclosure of perks and personal benefits with an aggregate value of more than $10,000, down from $50,000. "Other compensation," the proxy-statement pay category that includes perks, fell from $338,815 to $228,929 between 2005 and 2010 for the top one hundred CEOs, according to compensation-analysis firm Equilar.

A bigger factor than the prospect of having to publicly defend the indefensible: the economy. Now that just having a job feels like a perk, it's unsurprising that the number of companies granting perks to CEOs has slipped, from 90 percent of organizations in 2009 to 78 percent in 2010 to just 62 percent in 2011, according to compensation trackers at Compdata Surveys. "The nature of perks is nowhere near what we've seen in the past," says Brett Good, senior district president at Robert Half International, a consulting and staffing firm. Good predicts that even when the economy gathers steam, no one should expect companies to start picking up birthday-party tabs. Instead, anticipate a continued rise in things you won't see on proxies: hoteling, flex workweeks, job-sharing, and other work/life perks that, for many workers, aren't perks at all.

Everyone Deserves (to Desire) a Trophy

So what does a CEO perk look like these days? In 2010, the most prevalent were supplemental life insurance (offered to 29 percent of CEOs), company cars (24 percent), and club memberships (22 percent), according to Compdata. There is, after all, cachet attached to perks perceived to have high monetary value—which begs another question: Does value reside in the perk or its status?

Decades ago, where you peed signified who you were. An executive-restroom key unlocked far more than a physical door. Where you urinate today typically holds less exclusivity, but some perks, like a company car, still carry trophy value. Except: Don't title and salary (known or perceived) already sufficiently convey status?

In a 2006 paper, "Are Perks Purely Managerial Excess?", University of Chicago B-school professor Raghuram Rajan and Harvard Business School's Julie Wulf write: "There are only so many corner offices or so many places on the corporate jet, and who gets them can signal the recipient's place in the pecking order better than cash compensation can." Does a leader also need a corporate Mercedes to flaunt feathers?

Rajan and Wulf speculate that "the CEO needs to be offered perks (in fact, the most perks) so as to legitimize the status attached to the perk: a prestigious country club membership would not convey as much status for other executives if the CEO did not belong to it." However, this fails to address perks that accrue only to the CEO, and it doesn't justify something like club memberships overall.

Interestingly, the authors reference the military, where medals confer status. They ask, "[W]hy can corporations not invent their own medals or ribbons, which will cost them virtually nothing, instead of paying with perks?"

Good question. Employers invented their own ribbons long ago—plaques and certificates. They don't convey status—you can't park a framed certificate in front of the HQ building, in a space emblazoned with your title—so much as reward performance. Rewards, like plaques, gift certificates, and other recognition tools, don't typically stoke feelings of injustice the way perks do because they seem more meritocratic. You do something well: You get something good. Perks, by contrast, accrue regardless of job performance.

Of course, when asked, corporations invariably insist that they link most perks to performance. Of those that actually mean it, some may even believe it. But what do they believe?

If—*if!*—considering performance at all, companies don't grant top officers perks such as subsidized apartments and business-class plane tickets with the goal of motivating low-level daydreamers. That's not to say a mailroom clerk isn't fantasizing right now about reclining, Prada-clad feet perched atop a big desk twenty floors up, but that's a mere side effect of executive perks. Rather, we think of perks more as components of compensation packages that aim to optimize the work of leaders.

Truthfully, Rajan and Wulf's question about perks versus rewards is a nonstarter. Companies can—and should—use each differently. One may lead to better performance, the other recognizes it, and it probably makes little difference which you offer first to improve performance. "It's management's job to start the chicken-and-egg cycle," recommends Jennifer Robin.

The more relevant issue: If a car, or any perk, were turned into a reward instead—that is, something you got as a consequence of rather than a precursor to doing a good job—would that impact performance? It's a tough question to answer because most companies don't dangle such extravagant rewards in front of anyone outside of the sales department. (Then, too, all this assumes that a link between perks and performance actually exists. For more on making—or not—the business case for perks.)

The Price of Perks

None of us works for a corporation just for the fun of it. We're all paid salaries. Some of us get bonuses. A few of us enjoy stock options. We're all acutely aware of the numbers on our pay stubs—and what those numbers can buy. So why view perks differently than cash?

Because perks have a different perception value than cash. We emotionally connect to perks in ways we don't to dollars because we think of them less as standards and more as extras, and who doesn't like a little—or a lot of—extra? It's as though we're getting something for free—even if it's preposterous to stick a "free" tag on something over which companies and individuals haggle.

We emotionally connect to perks in ways we don't to dollars because we think of them less as standards and more as extras, and who doesn't like a little—or a lot of—extra?

It's often easier for companies, particularly those strapped for cash—as well as candidates and employees—to negotiate perquisites rather than salary. "You can't replace big chunks of pay with perks," points out Don Lindner, "but if you're paying an executive at the median instead of the sixtieth percentile, then offering perks may be a way to keep that person."

Then again, because the greater currency of perks lies in perception, some corporations hesitate to offer them in lieu of cash. A country-club membership costs pennies next to a $20 million pay package, but on a proxy statement, those can be some contentious coins. For example, in 2008, General Motors CEO Rick Wagoner flew to Washington to ask Congress for a bailout aboard the company's $36 million jet. Twenty grand, the trip's approximate cost, pales in comparison to the $12 billion Wagoner asked from Uncle Sam, but it's probably a salary for someone's uncle Sam.

"If you're getting paid $2 million and the proxy reveals that you're also getting a $5,000 financial-planning allowance, it gives the impression that you're piggish," argues Steve Gross, a senior partner at HR consultancy Mercer. To fend off criticism, he recommends, the company should just increase salary by the perk's pecuniary cost.

And yet, the more firms pay execs, the more perks they give them. This indicates not only the obvious—some companies boast deeper pockets than others—but another explanation posited by Rajan and Wulf: "A senior executive may not be willing to pay out of his own pocket for executive jet travel if it were not offered as a perk since his private value for it may be far smaller than the benefit to the company."

Even so, not everyone is convinced that a person joins or leaves an organization based on first-class rides in planes, trains, and automobiles. "Perks make up only 5 to 8 percent of an executive-compensation package," Lindner explains. "They're not going to make the difference in recruiting or retention."

Agrees Gaye Lindfors: "People don't go to organizations and stay because of perks. What keeps them there is a feeling of engagement."

Because You're Worth It?

Till now, an 800-pound gorilla has been lurking in this article—the entitled executive. Though no enterprise will cop to basing actions on entitlement, "it's probably the main basis on which companies continue to make decisions about perks," reveals Laura Sejen, global practice leader for rewards at Towers Watson. The problem isn't that people feel entitled to perks, it's that—

Actually, that *is* part of the problem. Steve Gross recalls working with an executive who demanded matching corporate sedans for him and his wife. The employee explained that should his car need repairs, his wife's would be a backup. "He was obviously a pig," Gross says.

"People begin to assume that perks are like benefits," adds Jennifer Rosenzweig, research director at The Forum, an HR consultancy affiliated with Northwestern University. "Companies have to be careful about getting into patterns of people expecting them."

"Hey," you might be thinking, "I worked hard to get to where I am, so damn it, I deserve a club membership." But you'd be confusing perks for position with perks for performance, which aren't perks but rewards. Also, you'd have to be high to think a high title accompanies high performance. A glance around your company should confirm the two are hardly synonymous. "But hold on again—I earn more money than others, meaning the company values me more, so give me my friggin' club membership too!" That argument would hold if cash and perks traded in equivalent currency, but since they don't, entitlement by any other name is still greed.

So: If employees who feel entitled are just part of the problem, the other part are the companies that inflate their egos. In the end, it's not someone who thinks the "C" in his title warrants entitlement but the organization that deserves an "F" for perpetuating it. The problem, of course, is that the "C" people run the company. It's a lot to ask the entitled to put down the Kool-Aid.

But that doesn't mean we shouldn't ask. "You face a challenge then," Sejen cautions. "If perks are not about hierarchy, you'll have a hard time defending why you've decided to make Person X eligible and Person Y ineligible." It is not, however, impossible. "As long as there are development opportunities and encouragement to get into higher positions, then differential perks based on one's position are less important," explains Jennifer Robin. Here's another way to look at it: If you give a perk to someone who feels entitled, that's OK—as long you don't grant the perk *because* someone feels entitled. Otherwise, adds Robin, "you create an environment of haves and have-nots, which can be damaging because that kind of mentality will work against you in the long run."

Entitlement by any other name is still greed.

Fairness Through Inequality

Let's be real: No workplace ever could be completely egalitarian.

No workplace ever *should* be completely egalitarian.

Many of us assume the fact of the former to justify the latter, but even if total egalitarianism were impossible, shouldn't we at least earnestly push toward it and not let perfect stand in the way of good? And isn't workplace egalitarianism, you know, *good?*

"You don't want to create perceptions and resentment that top people are getting more at the expense of everyone else," says Steve Gross. "It's like asking me to go from an office to a cubicle while my boss keeps his giant office. 'If I'm making a sacrifice, where's yours?' The more perception of unfairness, the less likely you'll have engaged workers."

You don't want to create perceptions and resentment that top people are getting more at the expense of everyone else.

Sure, pay and other factors already buttress office classism, but this article isn't *The Communist Manifesto,* and just because divisions exist in the workplace doesn't imply we shouldn't strive to minimize—or at least not maximize—them via perks.

The Proof is in the Perk

Businesses aren't as eager today to offer perks simply because the competition does. Instead, there must be a "business case," says practically every observer. But doesn't vying for talent serve a business purpose? You probably hear the business-case imperative so often that you nod approvingly without pausing to ponder the term's meaning or relevance. *Because you know it.* A perk must aid performance, engagement, productivity, *business.*

Indeed, "companies are now being more thoughtful about what's appropriate," says World at Work's Don Lindner. "Today, most companies are asking, 'Do we really need to offer a country-club membership?' They can't answer that, so we're seeing a lot of perks go away because they can't be shown to support attraction or retention."

Yet one in four organizations still offer CEOs club memberships. Do they have a business case? Yes, no, and maybe. It's no secret that a company can rationalize anything—everything—with a business purpose. Perhaps club memberships allow CEOs unique opportunities to broker deals. Perhaps not. Maybe the perk really does attract and keep talent. Maybe not. The point is, dig deep enough and you'll always unearth a business case for a perk. The real question is whether you can *prove* it. "If you can't show how perks support business strategy, you shouldn't be using them," Lindner suggests.

The "proof," however, tends to be anecdotal and correlative, at best. That doesn't mean you should dismiss such data or trash your perks. Rather, an absence of harder evidence likely reinforces what Albert Einstein knew: "Not everything that counts can be counted."

—V.L.

While some organizations have eschewed perks in the spirit of fairness (see "The End of the Perk?"), others use them to promote fair treatment. But what does that mean? It does *not* mean that everyone is equal, or even equally valuable. After all, each of us has different strengths and weaknesses. So when your CEO claims he values every employee, he's not lying. He's simply failing to add "just not equally."

Instead, think of fairness as equal consideration of workers' interests, or needs. For example, Google's benefits-and-perks priority is "to offer a customizable program that can be tailored to the specific needs of each individual."

"Too many times, organizations assume that fairness means equal treatment, but we have people performing different roles at different levels, so their needs will be different," explains Jennifer Robin. By matching perks to individual needs, she continues, "companies can send a signal: 'We understand you, and here are things that will make your job and life easier and that will also help the organization.'" You'll end up distributing perks unevenly, not unfairly.

Having Needs

Sometimes needs pertain to the job. For example, only staffers who must be on call get to make calls from company cell phones. Or only a few leaders get private security due to their high-profile positions. "It's declassifying and re-crafting what have traditionally been status symbols into more functional perks," explains Jennifer Rosenzweig. In other words, providing people with the tools they need to do their jobs. But if something is necessary, not just nice, are we really still talking about perks?

Yes, because anything an organization gives to you and not me is technically a perk. Yet a nagging feeling remains: It's weird to regard necessities as perks. And that's OK. When employees cease to view perks as perks, class divisions erode, supporting teamwork and engagement.

Perks catering to personal needs are thornier. Often, these are work/life perks, such as telecommuting or Google's reimbursement of up to $500 for takeout meals to new parents during a newborn's first three months so employees can concentrate more on work. When a perk doesn't directly relate to a job, some may grumble, "Why don't I get that too?"

For instance, "I don't have, nor want, children, but I'm also crunched for time. Give me $500 for food so I can be more productive!" Jennifer Benz, a San Francisco-based HR consultant, parallels this example to tuition reimbursement. Imagine a staffer insisting, "I don't want to go to school, but give me the tuition money anyway." As if. "There's no need to justify every perk just because 100 percent of the workforce can't take advantage of it," Benz explains. "The important thing is to meet as many needs as possible." Indeed, employees eligible for other perks will rarely protest, as complaints usually arise in cultures of perceived disenfranchisement. At Google, you'd be hard-pressed to point to a neglected group.

Nevertheless, timesaving perks are hardest to defend. We're all squeezing ninety into sixty minutes of work, so why should CEOs fly aboard a corporate plane while you languish in

The End of the Perk?

To promote greater egalitarianism, or at least the perception thereof, some companies seek to shun perks. "Intel does not have programs for providing personal benefit perquisites to executive officers, such as permanent lodging or defraying the cost of personal entertainment or family travel," reads the company's 2011 proxy statement. The company also boasts a goal "to maintain an egalitarian culture in its facilities and operations." In fact, former CEO Andy Grove, who said he despised "mahogany-paneled corner offices," famously worked out of an 8 ft. by 9 ft. cubicle, as does current chief Paul Otellini.

"[W]e do not normally provide perquisites or other benefits to our named executive officers that are not generally available to all eligible employees," reads the current proxy for JDS Uniphase, a communications-products manufacturer. The company adds that "executive officers are not entitled to operate under different standards than other employees"—meaning they don't get subsidized financial and legal advice, personal entertainment, recreational club memberships or family travel, reserved parking spaces, and separate dining facilities.

But might abolishing perks in the spirit of equality beget anything but? Does it merely spread unfairness equally?

Other firms that tout egalitarian environments include Nvidia, Dell, and Hewlett-Packard. Not surprising that they are giants in the tech industry, where massages, dry cleaning, photo-processing services, catered meals, monthly wine tastings, and foosball tables continue to define workplaces. A true egalitarian enterprise, it seems, provides benefits to all, not perks to some.

But might abolishing perks in the spirit of equality beget anything but? Does it merely spread unfairness equally? "I've seen companies that have said they won't do anything unless it's equal across the board," reveals Jennifer Robin, co-author of *The Great Workplace: How to Build It, How to Keep It, and Why It Matters,* "so even if it makes sense for you to work from home, you're not allowed because another group of workers can't. Even if it makes sense to have a laptop because you travel, 'You can't have one because we can't give everyone a laptop.' You end up with an over-structured organization." Impressive intentions with oppressive outcomes.

Ultimately, it's impossible and impractical to treat everyone identically—*someone* has to sit in the corner office, or corner cubicle. Someone will always get something that someone else does not. Some people need laptops, some need to telecommute, some need (depending on how you define the word) to fly on the corporate jet. "Intel's company-operated aircraft hold approximately 40 passengers and are used in regularly scheduled routes between Intel's major United States facility locations, and Intel's use of non-commercial aircraft on a time-share or rental basis is limited to appropriate business-only travel," the company's proxy continues. JDS's proxy also points out: "[CEO] Mr. Heard received a total of $95,125 to assist with his relocation to Germantown, Maryland. Additionally, Mr. Heard received a commuter allowance of $20,000 for the period from October 2010 through May 2011."

Intel and JDS—and, no doubt, other businesses—don't have true zero-perks policies. Thus, JDS's statement that it does "not normally provide perquisites or other benefits to our named executive officers" is true only so long as the emphasis is on *normally*.

—V.L.

baggage check? "The CEO has to spend most of his time and energy on the job. This isn't as much the case lower down," explains Don Lindner. "This perk will do the most good at the highest level." In other words, your CEO values every employee, just not equally—*and he (and the board) values himself most.*

Subsequently, the perk becomes not the plane but, rather, time itself. It makes sense for an enterprise to give more to those who have less of it. Overall, though, time-related perks are perhaps the only ones for which you become increasingly ineligible the higher up you go. It's easier to grant flextime to an accountant than to the CFO.

True Value

Because people have different needs, they predictably value perks differently. "What is important to you may be unimportant to me," says Steve Gross, who cites a Mercer executive who worked his way up to a senior level but turned down a larger office. "He couldn't care less," recalls Gross.

Not everyone wants to work in pajamas, park near the entrance, or fly Air Your-Company-Name-Here. Suppose a company were to extend corporate-aircraft access to everyone (about as likely as restricting coffee to the C-suite). If 99 percent of workers have no business need to fly, what good is access without usage? The organization would be boasting nothing but lip service to egalitarianism based on a worthless perk to most employees. Take note: Individuals, not the company, determine the subjective values of perks.

Now, some people—get ready for this—desire status. Should the company satisfy that need too?

Equal consideration of interests is just that—consideration. It is not equal fulfillment. All needs are not of equal value, so the best, if imperfect, approach is to carefully weigh different interests when deciding on perks, including one's need for status versus everyone's perceptions of fairness. "I worked with a company that offered reserved parking to directors and above. It was clearly a status thing," recounts Laura Sejen. "The company consistently talked about valuing teamwork. There was a disconnect for lots of employees, who saw who the company thought was really important." Everyone already *knew* who was important; there was no need for parking spots to reinforce that.

Of course, you can argue that a director's time is more valuable so he should get to park upfront, but you can make the my-time-is-more-important-than-your-time case for almost every perk. That doesn't mean you should, especially when balancing it against perceptions of injustice and possible disengagement. At Google, for example, special parking spots go only to pregnant women, the handicapped, and people needing outlets to plug in electric cars.

Similarly, you could argue that financial-planning services for top leaders save them (their more valuable) time, but "it's probably not your senior executives but your lower-paid individuals who need help with financial planning most," says Jennifer Benz. "Why not offer it to everyone?"

*W*hy not? Silicon Valley has been transforming perks into benefits for years. Whether tech companies such as Google offer endless lists of benefits to recruit and retain, allow employees to do their jobs better, or simply keep workers tethered to the office, the search giant is inching closer to an egalitarian environment and engaging people. "Slanting things that can support the whole workforce toward senior executives is not the best use of resources," Benz says. "A lot of companies are still very shortsighted and have traditional views of their workforce and are hesitant to implement programs that we know help people do their jobs better."

Other times, you may have to remove perks because revenues are down or they don't seem to impact performance positively. Taking them away can feel like a breach of an emotional contract for employees. "It's like ripping off a bandage; it's going to hurt," says Jennifer Rosenzweig. "But being forthright and transparent will go a long way to keeping employees' trust."

Ultimately, you'll need to develop a fair system of perks to compete in the marketplace and function well. Whether you add or subtract perks or turn them into benefits, you may still never purge your organization of entitlement or meet everyone's job and personal needs. But isn't it worth trying?

Critical Thinking

1. What happens when some employees receive perks, those employees most likely being in senior-level positions, and lower-ranking employees do not receive perks?

2. Are there questions of ethics and fairness in such situations?

3. What is meant by the concept of fairness through inequality?

4. Assume you are a consultant advising management about perks and their distribution. What would be your advice to management and why?

5. The article concludes with a statement, "... you may still never purge your organization of entitlement or meet everyone's job and personal needs." Do you agree with this statement? Why or why not?

Liberman, Vadim. From *The Conference Board Review*, Winter 2012, pp. 42–51. Copyright © 2012 by Vadim LIberman. Reprinted by permission of the author.

Under Pressure, Teachers Tamper with Test Scores

TRIP GABRIEL

The staff of Normandy Crossing Elementary School outside Houston eagerly awaited the results of state achievement tests this spring. For the principal and assistant principal, high scores could buoy their careers at a time when success is increasingly measured by such tests. For fifth-grade math and science teachers, the rewards were more tangible: a bonus of $2,850.

But when the results came back, some seemed too good to be true. Indeed, after an investigation by the Galena Park Independent School District, the principal, assistant principal and three teachers resigned May 24 in a scandal over test tampering.

The district said the educators had distributed a detailed study guide after stealing a look at the state science test by "tubing" it—squeezing a test booklet, without breaking its paper seal, to form an open tube so that questions inside could be seen and used in the guide. The district invalidated students' scores.

Of all the forms of academic cheating, none may be as startling as educators tampering with children's standardized tests. But investigations in Georgia, Indiana, Massachusetts, Nevada, Virginia and elsewhere this year have pointed to cheating by educators. Experts say the phenomenon is increasing as the stakes over standardized testing ratchet higher—including, most recently, taking student progress on tests into consideration in teachers' performance reviews.

Colorado passed a sweeping law last month making teachers' tenure dependent on test results, and nearly a dozen other states have introduced plans to evaluate teachers partly on scores. Many school districts already link teachers' bonuses to student improvement on state assessments. Houston decided this year to use the data to identify experienced teachers for dismissal, and New York City will use it to make tenure decisions on novice teachers.

The federal No Child Left Behind law is a further source of pressure. Like a high jump bar set intentionally low in the beginning, the law—which mandates that public schools bring all students up to grade level in reading and math by 2014—was easy to satisfy early on. But the bar is notched higher annually, and the penalties for schools that fail to get over it also rise: teachers and administrators can lose jobs and see their school taken over.

No national data is collected on educator cheating. Experts who consult with school systems estimated that 1 percent to 3 percent of teachers—thousands annually—cross the line between accepted ways of boosting scores, like using old tests to prep students, and actual cheating.

"Educators feel that their schools' reputation, their livelihoods, their psychic meaning in life is at stake," said Robert Schaeffer, public education director for FairTest, a nonprofit group critical of standardized testing. "That ends up pushing more and more of them over the line."

Others say that every profession has some bad apples, and that high-stakes testing is not to blame. Gregory J. Cizek, an education professor at the University of North Carolina who studies cheating, said infractions were often kept quiet. "One of the real problems is states have no incentive to pursue this kind of problem," he said.

Recent scandals illustrate the many ways, some subtle, that educators improperly boost scores:

- At a charter school in Springfield, Mass., the principal told teachers to look over students' shoulders and point out wrong answers as they took the 2009 state tests, according to a state investigation. The state revoked the charter for the school, Robert M. Hughes Academy, in May.
- In Norfolk, Va., an independent panel detailed in March how a principal—whose job evaluations had faulted the poor test results of special education students—pressured teachers to use an overhead projector to show those students answers for state reading assessments, according to The Virginian-Pilot, citing a leaked copy of the report.
- In Georgia, the state school board ordered investigations of 191 schools in February after an analysis of 2009 reading and math tests suggested that educators had erased students' answers and penciled in correct responses. Computer scanners detected the erasures, and classrooms in which wrong-to-right erasures were far outside the statistical norm were flagged as suspicious.

The Georgia scandal is the most far-reaching in the country. It has already led to the referral of 11 teachers and administrators to a state agency with the power to revoke their licenses. More disciplinary referrals, including from a dozen Atlanta schools, are expected.

John Fremer, a specialist in data forensics who was hired by an independent panel to dig deeper into the Atlanta schools, and who investigated earlier scandals in Texas and elsewhere, said educator cheating was rising. "Every time you increase the stakes associated with any testing program, you get more cheating," he said.

That was also the conclusion of the economist Steven D. Levitt, of "Freakonomics" fame and a blogger for The New York Times, who with a colleague studied answer sheets from Chicago public schools after the introduction of high-stakes testing in the 1990s concluded that 4 percent to 5 percent of elementary school teachers cheat.

Not everyone agrees. Beverly L. Hall, who, as the superintendent of the Atlanta Public Schools has won national recognition for elevating test scores, said dishonesty was relatively low in education. "Teachers over all are principled people in terms of wanting to be sure what they teach is what students are learning," she said.

Educators ensnared in cheating scandals rarely admit to wrongdoing. But at one Georgia school last year, a principal and an assistant principal acknowledged their roles in a test-erasure scandal.

For seven years, their school, Atherton Elementary in suburban Atlanta, had met the standards known in federal law as Adequate Yearly Progress—A.Y.P. in educators' jargon—by demonstrating that a rising share of students performed at grade level.

Then, in 2008, the bar went up again and Atherton stumbled. In June, the school's assistant principal for instruction, reviewing student answer sheets from the state tests, told her principal, "We cannot make A.Y.P.," according to an affidavit the principal signed.

"We didn't discuss it any further," the principal, James L. Berry, told school district investigators. "We both understood what we meant."

Pulling a pencil from a cup on the desk of Doretha Alexander, the assistant principal, Dr. Berry said to her, "I want you to call the answers to me," according to an account Ms. Alexander gave to investigators.

The principal erased bubbles on the multiple-choice answer sheets and filled in the right answers.

Any celebrations over the results were short-lived. Suspicions were raised in December 2008 by The Atlanta Journal-Constitution, which noted that improvements on state tests at Atherton and a handful of other Georgia schools were so spectacular that they approached a statistical impossibility. The state conducted an analysis of the answer sheets and found "overwhelming evidence" of test tampering at Atherton.

Crawford Lewis, the district superintendent at the time, summoned Dr. Berry and Ms. Alexander to separate meetings. During four hours of questioning—"back and forth, back and forth, back and forth," Dr. Lewis said—principal and assistant principal admitted to cheating.

"They both broke down" in tears, Dr. Lewis said.

Dr. Lewis said that Dr. Berry, whom he had appointed in 2005, had buckled under the pressure of making yearly progress goals. Dr. Berry was a former music teacher and leader of celebrated marching bands who, Dr. Lewis said, had transferred some of that spirit to passing the state tests in a district where schools hold pep rallies to get ready.

Dr. Berry, who declined interview requests, resigned and was arrested in June 2009 on charges of falsifying a state document. In December, he pleaded guilty and was sentenced to probation. The state suspended him from education for two years and Ms. Alexander for one year.

Dr. Lewis, now retired as superintendent, called for refocusing education away from high-stakes testing because of the distorted incentives it introduces for teachers. "When you add in performance pay and your evaluation could possibly be predicated on how well your kids do testing-wise, it's just an enormous amount of pressure," he said.

"I don't say there's any excuse for doing what was done, but I believe this problem is going to intensify before it gets better."

Critical Thinking

1. What is the potential impact of tying student test scores to teacher tenure, compensation or benefits?

2. How do educational stakeholders (students, teachers, parents, individual schools, school systems) benefit or lose as a result of state, federal, and municipal achievement testing?

Investigation into APS (Atlanta Public Schools) Cheating Finds Unethical Behavior Across Every Level

Heather Vogell

Across Atlanta Public Schools, staff worked feverishly in secret to transform testing failures into successes. Teachers and principals erased and corrected mistakes on students' answer sheets.

Area superintendents silenced whistle-blowers and rewarded subordinates who met academic goals by any means possible.

Superintendent Beverly Hall and her top aides ignored, buried, destroyed or altered complaints about misconduct, claimed ignorance of wrongdoing and accused naysayers of failing to believe in poor children's ability to learn.

For years—as long as a decade—this was how the Atlanta school district produced gains on state curriculum tests. The scores soared so dramatically they brought national acclaim to Hall and the district, according to an investigative report released Tuesday by Gov. Nathan Deal.

In the report, the governor's special investigators describe an enterprise where unethical—and potentially illegal—behavior pierced every level of the bureaucracy, allowing district staff to reap praise and sometimes bonuses by misleading the children, parents and community they served.

The report accuses top district officials of wrongdoing that could lead to criminal charges in some cases.

The decision whether to prosecute lies with three district attorneys—in Fulton, DeKalb and Douglas counties—who will consider potential offenses in their jurisdictions.

For teachers, a culture of fear ensured the deception would continue.

"APS is run like the mob," one teacher told investigators, saying she cheated because she feared retaliation if she didn't.

The voluminous report names 178 educators, including 38 principals, as participants in cheating. More than 80 confessed. The investigators said they confirmed cheating in 44 of 56 schools they examined.

The investigators conducted more than 2,100 interviews and examined more than 800,000 documents in what is likely the most wide-ranging investigation into test-cheating in a public school district ever conducted in United States history.

The findings fly in the face of years of denials from Atlanta administrators. The investigators re-examined the state's erasure analysis—which they said proved to be valid and reliable—and sought to lay to rest district leaders' numerous excuses for the suspicious scores.

Deal warned Tuesday "there will be consequences" for educators who cheated. "The report's findings are troubling," he said, "but I am encouraged this investigation will bring closure to problems that existed."

Interim Atlanta Superintendent Erroll Davis promised that the educators found to have cheated "are not going to be put in front of children again."

Through her lawyer, Hall issued a statement denying that she, her staff or the "vast majority" of Atlanta educators knew or should have known of "allegedly widespread" cheating. "She further denies any other allegations of knowing and deliberate wrongdoing on her part or on the part of her senior staff," the statement said, "whether during the course of the investigation or before."

Don't Blame Teachers?

Phyllis Brown, a southwest Atlanta parent with two children in the district, said the latest revelations are "horrible." It is the children, she said, who face embarrassment if they are promoted to a higher grade only to find they aren't ready for the more challenging work.

Still, she doesn't believe teachers should be punished.

"It's the people over them, that threatened them, that should be punished," she said. "The ones from the building downtown, they should lose their jobs, they should lose their pensions. They are the ones who started this."

AJC Raised Questions

Former Gov. Sonny Perdue ordered the inquiry last year after rejecting the district's own investigation into suspicious erasures on tests in 58 schools. The AJC first raised questions about some schools' test scores more than two years ago.

The special investigators' report describes years of misconduct that took place as far up the chain of command as the superintendent's office. The report accuses Hall and her aides of repeatedly tampering with or hiding records that cast an unflattering light on the district.

In one case, Hall's chief Human Resources officer Millicent Few "illegally ordered" the destruction of early, damning drafts of an outside lawyer's investigation of test-tampering at Atlanta's Deerwood Academy, the report said.

Another time, Few ordered staff to destroy a case log of cheating-related internal investigations after The Atlanta Journal-Constitution requested it, the report said. Few told staff to replace the old log with a new, altered version. When the district finally produced the complaints, the investigators wrote, it illegally withheld cases that made it "look bad"—either because its investigation was poor or because wrongdoing received minimal sanction.

Few also made false statements to the investigators, the report said.

Few, who could not be reached for comment Tuesday, denied to the investigators that she tampered with documents or ordered anyone else to do so.

Lying to investigators and destroying or altering public records are felonies under Georgia law with a maximum penalty of 10 years in prison.

Deputy Superintendent Kathy Augustine, as well as area superintendents Michael Pitts and Tamara Cotman, also gave the investigators false information, the report said, and the district's general counsel Veleter Mazyck "provided less than candid responses."

The report also said Hall and Augustine illegally suppressed a report by a testing expert last year. Andrew Porter, dean of the University of Pennsylvania Graduate School of Education, largely confirmed an AJC analysis that suggested cheating occurred, but the district withheld his findings from the media and public.

Augustine, Pitts and Cotman could not be reached Tuesday. Mazyck referred questions to her attorney. "I'm shocked that they would characterize her statements as less than candid," said Richard Sinkfield, Mazyck's attorney. "She was fully cooperative, fully open, and has not participated in any wrongdoing."

The investigators said district officials misled them and hampered their investigation.

"Dr. Hall pledged 'full cooperation' with this investigation, but did not deliver," the report said. "APS withheld documents and information from us. Many district officials we interviewed were not truthful."

"The Chosen Ones"

The district passes its scores on to the state each year and pledges they are accurate. Giving a "false official writing" is also a felony.

In some schools, the report said, cheating became a routine part of administering the annual state Criterion-Referenced Competency Tests. The investigators describe highly organized, coordinated efforts to falsify tests when children could not score high enough to meet the district's self-imposed goals.

The cheating cut off struggling students from the extra help they would have received if they'd failed.

At Venetian Hills, a group of teachers and administrators who dubbed themselves "the chosen ones" convened to change answers in the afternoons or during makeup testing days, investigators found. Principal Clarietta Davis, a testing coordinator told investigators, wore gloves while erasing to avoid leaving fingerprints on answer sheets.

Davis refused to answer the investigators' questions. She could not be reached Tuesday.

At Gideons Elementary, teachers sneaked tests off campus and held a weekend "changing party" at a teacher's home in Douglas County to fix answers.

Cheating was "an open secret" at the school, the report said. The testing coordinator handed out answer-key transparencies to place over answer sheets so the job would go faster.

When investigators began questioning educators, now-retired principal Armstead Salters obstructed their efforts by telling teachers not to cooperate, the report said.

"If anyone asks you anything about this just tell them you don't know," the report said Salters said. He told teachers to "just stick to the story and it will all go away."

Salters eventually confessed to knowing cheating was occurring, the report said. He could not be reached Tuesday.

At Kennedy Middle, children who couldn't read not only passed the state reading test, but scored at the highest level possible. At Perkerson Elementary, a student sat under a desk, then randomly filled in answers and still passed.

At East Lake Elementary, the principal and testing coordinator instructed teachers to arrange students' seats so that the lower-performing children would receive easier versions of the Fifth Grade Writing Tests.

Principal Gwendolyn Benton, who has since left, obstructed the investigation, too, the report said, when she threatened teachers by saying she would "sue them out the ass" if they "slandered" her to the GBI.

When the investigators interviewed Benton, she denied knowing cheating took place. She could not be reached Tuesday.

District employees suffered intense stress—enough to send at least one to the hospital—in a workplace where threats from supervisors kept them from reporting wrongdoing for fear of losing their jobs.

Area superintendents, who oversee clusters of schools, enforced a code of silence. One made a whistle-blower alter his reports of cheating and placed a reprimand in his file—and not the cheater's. Another told a teacher who saw tampering that if she did not "keep her mouth shut," she would "be gone."

"In sum, a culture of fear, intimidation and retaliation permeated the APS system from the highest ranks down," the investigators wrote. "Cheating was allowed to proliferate until, in the words of one former APS principal, 'it became intertwined in Atlanta Public Schools . . . a part of what the culture is all about.'"

Three Key Reasons

The investigators gave three key reasons that cheating flourished in Atlanta: The district set unrealistic test-score goals, or "targets," a culture of pressure and retaliation spread throughout the district, and Hall emphasized test results and public praise at the expense of ethics.

Because the targets rose each time a school attained them, the pressure ratcheted up in classrooms each year. Cheating one year created a need for more cheating the next.

"Once cheating started, it became a house of cards that collapsed on itself," the investigators wrote.

Educators most frequently cited the targets to explain cheating.

"APS became such a 'data-driven' system, with unreasonable and excessive pressure to meet targets, that Beverly Hall and her senior cabinet lost sight of conducting tests with integrity," the report said.

The investigators said Hall's aloof leadership style contributed directly to an atmosphere that fueled cheating.

She isolated herself from rank-and-file employees, the report said. Mazyck, the district's general counsel, told investigators that her job was to provide Hall with "deniability," insulating Hall from the need to make tough choices.

Sinkfield, Mazyck's attorney, said the investigators took her statements about law practice in general "totally out of context."

A major reason for the ethical failures in Hall's administration, the investigators wrote, was that Hall and her senior staff refused to accept responsibility for problems.

"Dr. Hall and her senior cabinet accepted accolades when those below them performed well, but they wanted none of the burdens of failure," the report said.

The district's priority became maintaining and promoting Hall's image as a miracle worker.

After an earlier investigation into cheating by a group of civic and business leaders, Hall was under pressure to crack down. The investigation was flawed, however, producing allegations but no confessions.

Nonetheless, Hall forwarded the names of about 100 Atlanta educators to the teacher licensing board for possible disciplinary action. She did so based on statistics showing high erasures in certain classrooms, despite the fact that someone other than the teacher could easily have done the erasing.

The investigators said Hall made the referral so it appeared she was taking a tough stance.

They called her actions "unconscionable."

The report also touched on the support the Atlanta business community has provided Hall for years.

Her supporters were so concerned the district's problems would reflect poorly on the Atlanta "brand," the report said, that they attacked those who asked questions about the district's purported success. A senior vice president at the Metro Atlanta Chamber, for instance, suggested a report commissioned by business and civic leaders that found cheating was limited to a dozen schools would need to be "finessed" past Gov. Sonny Perdue, the report said.

That effort failed. Perdue appointed the special investigators in August 2010.

Hall preferred to spend her time networking with philanthropic and business leaders rather than walking the halls of her schools, the investigators found.

But when the scandal erupted, she withheld key information—state data on the suspicious erasures—even from executives and civic leaders who the school board, at Hall's urging, appointed to conduct the inquiry.

"In many ways, the community was duped by Dr. Hall," the report said. "While the district had rampant cheating, community leaders were unaware of the misconduct in the district. She abused the trust they placed in her.

"Hall became a subject of adoration and made herself the focus rather than the children," the investigators wrote. "Her image became more important than reality."

Critical Thinking

1. Have you witnessed cheating among your classmates? How did you feel about it? Were you tempted to do it yourself?

2. To what do you attribute cheating and do you see any hope that it will someday largely go away? Explain your answer.

When You're Most Vulnerable to Fraud

In the best of times, entrepreneurs tend to take their eye off the ball.

ROB JOHNSON

Five years ago, Ed Couvrette was on top of the world. The manufacturing company he founded, E.F. Couvrette Co., was ringing up sales of $10 million a year and was negotiating contracts for triple that amount. On employees' birthdays, he routinely gave out bonus checks—a week's pay for every year they'd been at the company.

"Now I can hardly afford birthday cards," he laments.

His revenue is down more than half, customers have abandoned him in droves, and he has been forced to severely slash jobs. He can't line up credit, and some weeks there's not enough money in the bank to cover payroll at his Salem, Va., operation, which does business as Couvrette Building Systems.

Mr. Couvrette didn't get trapped by the collapsing economy or a shrinking industry. Instead, he says he was the victim of massive fraud by his chief operating officer—who, among other things, pocketed over $300,000 he was supposed to send to the Internal Revenue Service to cover payroll taxes. The former officer is now in prison; his attorney, Tony Anderson of Roanoke, Va., declined to comment on the case.

Mr. Couvrette's case offers a hard lesson for small businesses: When times are great—watch out. Because that's when you're most vulnerable to fraud. Sales are soaring, and the biggest problem seems to be where to fit all the new equipment and employees. But those heady days can be perilous, since success can distract the founder from such mundane financial duties as collecting payroll taxes and verifying the accuracy of bills.

"It's often when things are going well in a small business that betrayal strikes," says Walter Jones, a fraud examiner and retired IRS agent who's now a consultant to Mr. Couvrette. "In an atmosphere where sales and profits are increasing, the diversion of funds is masked by success."

'Small on Administration'

For some entrepreneurs, another factor makes them prime targets for fraud: Overseeing finances doesn't come naturally. That was the case with Mr. Couvrette, who has an engineering background. He was most comfortable on the factory floor at his company, which makes kiosks to house drive-up automated teller machines at banks; he enjoyed supervising everything from the welding of the steel housings to painting them with banks' logos.

"I was big on production, small on administration," says Mr. Couvrette, now 58.

Mr. Couvrette had also long taken his books for granted, thanks in large part to a series of dependable company controllers, including his father, a certified public accountant. Further, Mr. Couvrette says he couldn't imagine his company getting victimized—given that its mission involved *preventing* crime. "We got into the drive-up ATMs at a time when banks were becoming more security conscious about customers being robbed while walking up to the machines," Mr. Couvrette says. "More banks were interested in ATM facilities where the customers could stay in their cars and leave quickly if they felt threatened."

He admits his guard was down in 2001 when he hired Roy Dickinson, an accountant with a sound track record, as the growing company's chief operating officer.

After hiring Mr. Dickinson, Mr. Couvrette says he made a mistake in judgment that is common in small-business embezzlement cases: He put the same employee—Mr. Dickinson—in charge of both receipts and disbursements. While entrusting both ends of the money-moving chores to one employee may seem to streamline paperwork, it's just too risky, says Mr. Jones, the fraud expert. "I believe in what Reagan said about nuclear-missile treaties: Trust but verify."

In February 2005, Mr. Couvrette says he noticed that a high-profile new area of his business being run by Mr. Dickinson—making software and hardware adjustments on dozens of ATMs around the country—wasn't producing a profit. "I kept waiting for our cash flow and margins to get where they should be with expenses, and they didn't," says Mr. Couvrette.

In March 2005, Mr. Couvrette scheduled a meeting with his chief operating officer, calling him back to Salem from a

How to Steer Clear of Fraud? The Experts Weigh In

Small businesses are victimized by embezzlement far more often than bigger companies, according to a survey this year by the Association of Certified Fraud Examiners, a trade group based in Austin, Texas.

In fact, 31% of all business frauds nationally were in companies with fewer than 100 employees, according to the study, and an additional 23% were suffered by those with under 999 workers. Only 21% were committed in companies with more than 10,000 employees.

What's more, small businesses in the U.S. typically suffer larger losses than big companies do. The median loss for companies with fewer than 100 employees was about $150,000–compared with $84,000 in businesses with payrolls exceeding 10,000.

Andi McNeal, director of research at the ACFE, says small businesses are relatively easy targets for internal fraud "because there are usually less formal financial controls. There's usually a lot of trust put in one person, which may be necessary for these businesses to run, but it can come back to haunt."

So, how to protect your company from fraud? Here are some tips from the association.

- If you're delegating responsibility for accounts receivable and the company's disbursements, don't put the same person in charge of both, even if it means you have to hire an additional employee.
- Bring in an outside accountant at least once a year to review your business financial records. Typical fees are $100 to $150 an hour, depending on how organized your records are. Consider retaining different outside accountants occasionally to have a fresh eye involved in the review.
- Be aware of employees who are involved with your company's finances and never take time off. Embezzlers rarely take vacations for fear their theft will be discovered by someone filling in.

- Embezzlers usually spend the money they steal very quickly. Tip-offs include changes in lifestyle such as spending on expensive cars and vacations.
- One common internal fraud is kickbacks involving vendors, so stay alert to unusually close relationships between employees responsible for finances and suppliers and customers.
- Be the first person to open your monthly business bank statements. Even if you don't have time to examine them closely, your attention sends a message to any potential fraudster.
- When perusing your bank statements, don't just look at the numbers; examine the actual images of canceled checks. Otherwise you can't confirm where the money really went.
- Remember that some internal theft doesn't leave an audit trail.

For example, skimming involves stealing a company's cash before the receipts are entered into the accounting ledger. In a sales skim, the fraudster collects a customer's payment at the point of sale and simply pockets the money without recording it. The loss may come to light only via clues such as inventory shortages or lower-than-expected cash flow.

- Look at receipts for deposits of both federal and state taxes.
- Remember that liabilities can double the amount of taxes due, including penalties and interest, within a year, so don't take more than a few months between your informal audits.
- Maintain an open-door policy that encourages employees who have suspicions about misappropriations or questionable spending to tell you in confidence.

—Rob Johnson

New York business trip. "He didn't show, so I fired him," says Mr. Couvrette.

That confrontation led to the hiring of an outside auditor, Mr. Jones. The examination revealed myriad financial problems, including payroll taxes that had been collected but not forwarded to the IRS, according to Mr. Jones. Mr. Couvrette was ultimately responsible for paying the IRS; the agency agreed to a settlement of about $320,000, according to Mr. Jones, who was Mr. Couvrette's intermediary with the government. "Stealing payroll taxes is a form of misappropriation that small-business owners don't catch because the money isn't going for company expenses anyway," says Mr. Jones.

In February of last year, meanwhile, Mr. Dickinson pleaded guilty in the U.S. District Court in Roanoke to

conspiracy to commit mail and wire fraud, and attempting to interfere with IRS laws. He was sentenced to three years in prison—a term he's currently serving—and ordered to pay restitution of more than $300,000.

Beyond pocketing the money intended for the IRS, Mr. Dickinson pleaded guilty to several acts of fraud. He used company money to cover remodeling costs for his home, for instance, and covered his tracks by altering company records, according to his plea. And he used his company American Express card to purchase items such as a $6,850 Rolex watch and altered the bills to show those transactions as business expenses, according to his plea.

In 2005, word that the IRS had issued tax liens against Couvrette Building Systems spread to the company's creditors and customers, according to Mr. Jones. Both categories consisted largely of banks, and "tax problems are the kiss of death when you're dealing with banks," says Mr. Jones. "So, Ed's credit quickly dried up and he lost millions of dollars in contracts."

Now Mr. Couvrette's annual revenue has been slashed by 60% and so has his production line—to about 30 workers, down from 150 five years ago. The hulking gray manufacturing plant on his company's 10-acre site contains pockets of workers, but most of the production line is quiet. Many of his former bank customers have found other suppliers. And Mr. Couvrette's credit is shot.

"I have zero elasticity of funds right now," he says. "I need loans to rebuild my delivery trucks and pay vendors," and of course meet payroll.

A Death in the Family

Sometimes it isn't just success that distracts entrepreneurs. Personal issues can also take owners' focus off the business and leave them vulnerable to fraud. Consider **Interactive Solutions** Inc. in Memphis, Tenn. In 2002, the videoconferencing company achieved its then-highest annual sales, about $6 million, and was recording double-digit profit margins.

"Things were going so well I bought a brand-new BMW 525 for my company car, and paid cash for it," says Jay Myers, the 53-year-old founder and chief executive.

Amid the success, Mr. Myers suffered a personal loss: His brother, John, died at age 50. The two had been close, and Mr. Myers started taking occasional days off while in mourning. His attention wandered from the company's finances, and he began relying more heavily on Linda Merritt, a bookkeeper who had come on board a month before John's death, to keep things straight.

"I wasn't paying the attention I should have to the business," says Mr. Myers, adding that his trust in Ms. Merritt was based on her solid job references, which he says included "a lawyer and someone who sang with her in the church choir."

"It was dumb luck," he says, that finally caused him to become suspicious in May 2003, after he read a magazine article detailing a case of internal fraud at a small machinery supplier in Illinois. "Something clicked as I read the story: That could happen to me."

Although he vowed to have his books checked by an outside auditor, Mr. Myers feared what might be found—a common reaction that fraud investigators say sometimes delays the uncovering of embezzlement. After all, says Mr. Myers, "this was humiliating—a potential disaster if my employees found out. It might sink the company. What about my clients and vendors?"

The thefts—in the form of bogus bonuses and commissions by the dozens, according to evidence later presented in court—weren't difficult to verify. When the outside auditor

showed Mr. Myers some of the checks for such payments, he says, "Some of them were to a receptionist. I thought, 'A receptionist doesn't get commissions, she answers the phone.' I felt like such a fool for not knowing this was going on."

In November 2005, Ms. Merritt pleaded guilty to misappropriating funds in federal district court in Memphis, and is now serving an eight-year term in a Texas federal prison. According to the sentencing document in the case, she was ordered to repay more than $260,000, to Mr. Myers and an insurance company and bank involved in Interactive Solutions' finances.

Ms. Merritt's attorney, Stephen Shankman, a federal public defender in Memphis, declined to comment on the case.

New Vigilance

Mr. Myers was able to recover $80,000 via a "dishonest employee liability" rider on his insurance policy. Such clauses can be written to cover everything from credit-card fraud to embezzlement.

Today, Mr. Myers says, he's insured for about $240,000 in losses due to employee dishonesty. He also made an arrangement for partial restitution from an accounting firm that had failed to uncover the embezzlement in a routine examination of Interactive Solutions' books a few months before it was discovered.

Since the fraud episode, Interactive Solutions is riding high. Sales have more than doubled to about $14 million annually. In part, that's thanks to timing; the videoconferencing business is surging as companies look to cut travel costs during the recession. The company has also branched into new areas that are proving popular, such as telemedicine, in which doctors and patients can huddle over long distances.

Mr. Myers is being careful not to get taken unawares again. In fact, he credits part of his recent success to better hiring and employee-retention practices. He takes more time to get to know prospective workers and to check out their backgrounds. These days, Mr. Myers has separate employees who are responsible for handling accounts receivable and paying the company's bills. What's more, he says, he's much more vigilant personally. "When those monthly bank statements come in, nobody opens them now before me."

Mr. Myers now makes it a point to let employees know that if they betray his trust, they could risk jail time. In a recent meeting he warned his 40 workers: "I said if you steal a dollar or a thousand dollars, and I catch you, I will prosecute."

Meanwhile, at Couvrette Building Systems, the employees soldier on. Matt Musselman, a Couvrette design engineer, works at his computer screen on a recent afternoon with an eye to the future. Hoping innovation can win more orders, Mr. Musselman, a member of Couvrette's research-and-development team, diagrams a solar-powered ATM for one of the company's longtime bank customers that has remained loyal, Wells Fargo & Co.

"We're going into green technology," Mr. Musselman says.

Ross Campbell, a painter, sticks around even though he occasionally isn't paid for weeks at a time. He says, "Ed Couvrette is a good guy. I have a lot of faith in him."

Critical Thinking

1. Why are entrepreneurs vulnerable to fraud?
2. What can they do to protect themselves?

MR. JOHNSON is a writer in Roanoke County, Va. He can be reached at reports@wsj.com.

When Good People Do Bad Things at Work

Rote behavior, distractions, and moral exclusion stymie ethical behavior on the job.

Dennis J. Moberg

The news is full of the exploits of corporate villains. We read about how officials at Lincoln Savings and Loan bilked thousands out of their customers' retirement nest eggs. There are stories of the lies Brown and Williamson Tobacco executives told about the addictive nature of cigarettes and the company's subsequent campaign to destroy whistle-blower Jeffrey Wigant. Also in the news are the top managers at Time Warner who looked the other way rather than forego millions from the sale of rap music with lyrics that advocated violence directed at women and the police. Such acts are hard to forgive. Scoundrels such as these seem either incredibly weak or dangerously flawed.

Yet not all corporate misdeeds are committed by bad people. In fact, a significant number of unethical acts in business are the likely result of foibles and failings rather than selfishness and greed. Put in certain kinds of situations, good people inadvertently do bad things.

For those of us concerned about ethical actions and not just good intentions, the problem is clear. We must identify the situational factors that keep people from doing their best and eliminate them whenever we can.

Problem No. 1: Scripts

One factor is something psychologists call scripts. This term refers to the procedures that experience tells us to use in specific situations. When we brush our teeth or congratulate a friend on the arrival of a new grandchild, we probably use scripts.

Unlike other forms of experience, scripts are stored in memory in a mechanical or rote fashion. When we encounter a very familiar situation, rather than actively think about it, we reserve our mental energy for other purposes and behave as though we are cruising on automatic pilot.

In a classic psychological experiment, people approached someone at an office machine making copies and asked, "May I please make just one copy because . . ." The person at the machine generally complied with this request, but the really interesting finding was that the likelihood of compliance was totally independent of the reasons stated. In fact, superfluous reasons such as "because I need to make a copy" were just as successful as good reasons such as "because my boss told me she needed these right away." Apparently, we have all experienced this situation so often that we don't give the reasons our full attention, not to mention our careful consideration.

One ethical lapse clearly attributable to scripts was Ford Motor Co.'s failure to recall the Pinto in the 1970s. The Pinto was an automobile with an undetected design flaw that made the gas tank burst into flames on impact, resulting in the death and disfigurement of scores of victims. Dennis Gioia, the Ford recall coordinator at the time, reviewed hundreds of accident reports to detect whether a design flaw was implicated. Later, he recalled,

> When I was dealing with the first trickling-in of field reports that might have suggested a significant problem with the Pinto, the reports were essentially similar to many others that I was dealing with (and dismissing) all the time. . . . I was making this kind of decision automatically every day. I had trained myself to respond to prototypical cues, and these didn't fit the relevant prototype for crisis cases.

Situations like this occur frequently in the work world. Repetitive jobs requiring vigilance to prevent ethical lapses can be found in quality control, customer service, and manufacturing. In this respect, consider what happened when a nurse with a script that called for literal obedience to a doctor's written orders misread the directions to place ear drops in a patient's right ear as "place in Rear." Good people can inadvertently do very bad things.

Scripts may also be at work when we come face to face with those who are suffering. In situations where we observe the pain of those in need, scripts permit us to steel ourselves against feelings of empathy. Most of us have been approached by the homeless on the street, exposed to horrific images on the television news, and asked for donations on behalf of the victims of natural disasters.

According to research at the University of Kansas, scripts allow people to avoid responsibility for the suffering of others in situations when providing help appears costly. In work contexts, this might explain why businesspeople do not always respond philanthropically to documented cases of human suffering. What appears to be calculated indifference may actually not be calculated at all.

Whenever there is repetition, there are likely to be scripts. Accordingly, the best way to eliminate the potential of scripts to result in unethical behavior is to keep people out of highly repetitive situations. Technology can and has been used to eliminate highly routine tasks, but job rotation is also an option. For example, *The Daily Oklahoman* newspaper of Oklahoma City cross-trains most of its editors and schedules them to switch roles often. This helps keep the editors mentally sharp.

One editor who often switches roles from night to night commented: "You're fresh when you come to a particular job. Like last night I did inside [design], and it was a long and torturous night because of the large paper. But then again I turn around and do something thoroughly different tonight, so I don't feel like I'm trudging back to the same old rut again."

Oklahoman News Editor Ed Sargent thinks editing quality has improved because those who switch roles are exposed to the different approaches their colleagues take to the job. "Every editor has different opinions, obviously, about what's a big error and what's a little error," he said. Although the original intent of the role switching was to distribute stress more evenly, a side effect is that the paper is probably less prone to ethical lapses.

Problem No. 2: Distractions

Scripts are cognitive shortcuts that take the place of careful thinking. A similar human tendency is our mindless treatment of distractions. Think for a moment about the last time you drove to a very important meeting. Once there, were you able to recall any details of your journey? Most of us cannot, which demonstrates that when concentrating on completing an involving task, we don't deal well with distractions.

This inattention to what is happening on the periphery can get us into trouble with our spouses and significant others, and it can also result in ethical lapses. In one very telling experiment, divinity students were told that they had to deliver a lecture from prepared notes in a classroom across campus. Half the students were told they had to hurry to be on time, and the other half were told they had more than ample time.

On the way, the students came across a person in distress (actually an actor), who sat slumped motionless in a doorway, coughing and groaning. Shockingly, only 16 of the 40 divinity students stopped to help, most of them from the group that had ample time. To those in a hurry, the man was a distraction, a threat to their focus on giving a lecture. Ironically enough, half of them had been asked to discuss the parable of "The Good Samaritan."

Mindlessness about distractions at work is most pronounced when employees, with limited means of gaining perspective, are encouraged to be focused and driven. The best way to combat this tendency is for senior managers to model the virtue of temperance. If the president of a company is a workaholic, it is difficult to convince employees to be open to problems on the outskirts of their commitments. In contrast, an organizational culture that facilitates work-family balance or encourages employee involvement in the community may move experiences that should not be seen as mere distractions onto the center stage of consciousness.

Problem No. 3: Moral Exclusion

A final problem that brings out the worst in good people is the very human tendency to morally exclude certain persons. This occurs when individuals or groups are perceived as outside the boundary in which moral values and considerations of fairness apply. The most striking example occurs during warfare when the citizens of a country readily perceive their enemies in demonic terms. Yet, this tendency to discount the moral standing of others results in us discounting all kinds of people, some of them as close as co-workers and valued customers.

Greater awareness and extensive training have reduced some of the exclusion women and people of color have historically experienced. More work needs to be done in this area, as well as in other equally insidious forms of exclusion.

One way such exclusion shows up is in our use of pronouns. If *we* are in marketing and *they* are in production, the chances are that the distance may be great enough for us to be morally indifferent to what happens to them. Similarly, if we use stereotypic terms like *bean counter* or sneer when we say *management,* then it is clear that people in these categories don't count.

Not surprisingly, one way to expand the scope of justice is to promote direct contact with individuals who have been morally excluded. One company that applied this notion in an intriguing way is Eisai, a Japanese pharmaceutical firm. In the late 1980s, Haruo Naito had recently become CEO, and his closest advisers expressed concern that his managers and employees lacked an understanding of the end users of Eisai's products.

Hearing this, Naito decided to shift the focus of attention from the customers of his company's products—doctors and pharmacists—to *their* customers—patients and their families. Eisai managers, he decided, needed to identify better with end users and then infuse the insights from this sense of inclusion throughout the organization. This was a revolutionary idea for this company of 4,500 employees, but Naito believed his employees needed a more vivid reason to care deeply about their work.

"It's not enough to tell employees that if they do something, the company will grow this much or their salary will increase this much. That's just not enough incentive," says Naito. "You have to show them how what they are doing is connected to society, or exactly how it will help a patient." Accordingly, Naito decided to send 100 managers to a seven-day seminar: three days of nursing-home training and four days of medical care observation.

These managers were then sent to diverse regions throughout Japan, where they had to deal with different people, many of whom were in critical condition. They met patients with both physical and emotional problems; some of the patients they came in contact with died during their internships.

This pilot program grew to include more than 1,000 Eisai employees. Pretty soon, even laboratory support personnel had to leave their benches and desks and meet regularly with pharmacists and hospital people.

"Getting them out of the office was a way to activate human relationships," says Naito. Another way was to institute hotlines, which have generated product ideas. As a consequence, many new Eisai drugs were produced, including some that have promise in dealing with Alzheimer's disease. Clearly, moral inclusion was stimulated at Eisai at least insofar as the end users of its products are concerned.

Failing to Bother

Jesuit scholar James F. Keenan reminds us that "sinners in the New Testament are known not for what they did, but for what they failed to do—for failing to bother." We are all prone to this failure, but not necessarily because we are sinners. Repetition, distractions, and our natural tendency to exclude those unfamiliar to us cloud our best thinking and forestall the expression of our virtues. We owe it to ourselves to resist these pernicious influences, and we owe it to those in our work communities to help them to do the same.

Critical Thinking

1. What are the reasons people do bad things at work?
2. Select one of the reasons people do bad things at work and develop arguments for and against the reason.
3. Based on your experience, what are other reasons people do bad things at work? What is "failure to bother" as discussed in the article? Develop a statement in bullet point format supporting or not supporting the concept of failure to bother.

From *Issues in Ethics*, Vol. 10, No. 2, Fall 1999. Copyright © 1999 by Markkula Center for Applied Ethics. Reprinted by permission.

Behind the Murdoch Scandal? Scandalous Governance

GEOFF COLVIN

Two important themes are already clear in the News Corp. drama, though it still has a long way to run. No matter what happens next—events are galloping ahead faster than in any scandal in memory—large ideas emerging from the story so far will influence companies of all types for years to come.

The One-Man Problem

The companies in the most infamous scandals of the past several years—Enron, WorldCom, Tyco, Adelphia, Parmalat, HealthSouth, and now News Corp.—were in widely different industries but shared one trait: All had risen from nothing to huge size and spectacular success as publicly traded companies under one man. (Obviously it could happen under a woman also, but all the outstanding examples so far are male.) These companies never made the transition, which every entrepreneurial success must make, from the magnified reflection of a single person to an institution with a life of its own. They were still Mr. Big's candy store, a baby company in a giant's body. Despite fine-sounding mission statements, the internal reality was that no value outranked pleasing the all-powerful and invulnerable boss, an environment that generally produces trouble.

Yet in recent decades plenty of other companies have risen to greatness under one man and become living institutions without scandal or disaster. Think of Microsoft under Bill Gates, FedEx under Fred Smith, or Charles Schwab under Charles Schwab. What accounts for the difference? A few telltale signs show reliably whether a company will succumb to the one-man problem, and they all blared loud warnings at News Corp.

The most important factor is governance: Does that one man wield power grossly disproportional to his economic stake in the company? Rupert Murdoch does. He owns only about 12% of News Corp., but he exercises control through a mechanism used by many badly governed companies, dual-class stock. Most News Corp. shareholders own class A shares, but only class B shares can vote on directors or anything else, and Murdoch has almost 40% of those shares. Another 7% is held by Saudi Prince Alwaleed bin Talal; he's unlikely to oppose Murdoch, who owns

14% of Alwaleed's media company, Rotana. The other class B shareholders (about 1,300 of them) could in theory gang up and outvote Murdoch, but in practice that doesn't happen.

Result: Legally News Corp.'s directors can fire Rupert Murdoch, but practically he can fire the directors, and they know it. That's why the Corporate Library, a research firm that grades companies' governance, has for the past six years given News Corp. an F—"only because there is no lower grade," says the firm's Nell Minow.

By contrast, companies that have avoided the one-man problem have much-higher-quality governance. The CEO's power reflects his ownership, which generally falls well below 50% as a company grows large; Fred Smith can't fire FedEx's board, for example. Directors are genuinely subject to shareholders' will, and everyone knows it.

Another tip-off to one-man trouble is pay. The founder's stake, even if far less than half, usually remains enough to make him seriously rich. He probably needn't be paid magnificently as well, but at the scandal companies he generally is. Murdoch is a multibillionaire, but he still pays himself a salary of $8.1 million. You might see little purpose in his directors giving him stock awards of $4 million on top of that, since he already owns $5.2 billion of company stock, and it's hard to see the point of giving him additional "incentive compensation" of $4.4 million, since the effect of a $1 increase in the stock price—increasing his wealth by over $300 million—would seem more than enough incentive. Nor is there much apparent logic in awarding him a mammoth pension or a car allowance and personal use of the company jet at shareholder expense. Yet he got all those things in 2010. For perspective, note that Whole Foods founder and CEO John Mackey, whose company stock is worth $80 million, is paid $1 a year.

A third reliable warning sign of the one-man problem is family favoritism. Adelphia and HealthSouth, for example, bought supplies from the founders' families. News Corp. paid Murdoch's wife, Wendi, $92,000 last year for "strategic advice for the development of the MySpace business in China" (News Corp. recently sold MySpace at a staggering loss). The company paid $350,000 last year to the public relations firm of Murdoch's son-in-law and $11.9 million to the TV production company controlled by his daughter Elisabeth, then bought the company this year for $675 million. And Murdoch has openly positioned his sons, first Lachlan and now James, as his heir apparent, placing both in jobs far beyond their demonstrated abilities.

Despite the shareholder devastation wrought by the one-man problem, it may live on. Mark Zuckerberg's Facebook, with its dual-class stock, and Mark Pincus's Zynga, with triple-class stock, are a long way from being examples, but the early signs aren't encouraging. Prospective investors should at least remain vigilant.

Reputation's Moment

We've long heard that reputation is the new currency of corporate success, and "reputation economy" became a fashionable term a few years ago. The News Corp. affair may be looked back on as the moment that companies broadly became believers.

Previous major scandals were mostly financial; the numbers were lies. Not this time. The damage so far derives entirely from behavior—phone hacking and possible police bribery—that appears to be illegal but has nothing to do with reported financial results. Whether it's illegal doesn't matter anyway; it's slimy, and that's enough. News Corp. is deeply tarnished, and the financial effects could be significantly bad.

The company has lost about $5 billion of value in the few weeks since the scandal hit. Longer-term effects could be much worse. "The greatest reputational threat to News Corp., aside from criminal prosecution of Murdoch family members, lies within regulatory and policy circles," says Rupert Younger, director of the Centre for Corporate Reputation at Oxford University's Saïd Business School. News Corp.'s television

businesses—TV networks, TV stations, and satellite broadcasting services worldwide—are together a major source of profit, and they're all subject to government regulation. Government leaders have treated News Corp. gingerly for years, but now "politicians who have been afraid to tackle such an important company are starting to feel that it may be possible to do so," says Younger. "This could literally destroy News Corp.," in the sense that the company could be broken up.

Long-term damage to the company's reputation among customers, employees, communities, and others could also hurt. "In this new reputation economy, people care about whether a company shares the same values as they do," observes Leslie Gaines-Ross, chief reputation strategist at the Weber Shandwick communications firm. Her reading on the scandal so far: "A clearer demonstration of the direct relationship between corporate reputation and corporate well-being is hard to imagine."

These two ideas, the one-man problem and corporate reputation, are obviously related. At News Corp. they're two sides of the same coin. Yet Rupert Murdoch never seemed to put them together. Long before this scandal, he said, "Our reputation is more important than the last $100 million." He was right.

Critical Thinking

1. What is the "one-man problem" identified in the article?
2. Explain the concept of a "new reputation economy" discussed in the article.
3. What are your recommendations for managing in a new reputation economy?
4. Why, as stated in the article, will the "large ideas" from the News Corp. allegations influence other companies in the future?

From *Fortune*, August 15, 2011. Copyright © 2011 by Fortune Magazine. Reprinted by permission of Time, Inc. via Pars International Corp.

American Apparel and the Ethics of a Sexually Charged Workplace

Gael O'Brien

American Apparel finds itself once again in a familiar place—sued again for sexual harassment and creating a hostile work environment, because of the vulnerability its CEO's philosophy of sexual freedom in the workplace creates for the publicly held company.

In discussing a 2006 sexual harassment suit, founder, chairman and CEO Dov Charney expressed the belief that consensual sexual relationships in the workplace were appropriate: "I think it's a First Amendment right to pursue one's affection for another human being."

Recently, Irene Morales, 20, sued Charney, 42, American Apparel, and its directors for about $250 million, alleging Charney forced her into sex acts when she was 18 and an employee. The company has accused Morales of extortion. A lawyer for the company dismissed the allegations, saying when Morales left the company and accepted severance, she signed a statement saying she had no claims against the company and agreed that any future claims would be addressed by confidential arbitration. A judge has halted Morales' suit until March 25, pending a decision on whether it should go to arbitration or trial.

Notwithstanding the distinction of being dubbed "American Apparel's chief lawsuit officer," Charney is a complex figure. His website, filled with photos of him and provocative shots he took of the company's young models, tells the story of his immigrant family, religion, creating the company as a teenager, philosophy on sexual freedom, and politics. Passionate about immigration reform, proud his clothing is "made in America," he pays his 10,000 workers well above garment industry rate.

Charney owns 51.8 percent of the company and the board has thus far apparently gone along with his philosophy of sexual freedom. However, the company is no longer on solid financial footing. Blame the recession or other factors, but it appears that sexy marketing isn't selling American Apparel the way it did several years ago; stock prices have been dropping.

Among the questions Dov Charney's philosophy raises is whether there really can be consensual sex in a workplace if both parties aren't equal in status, salary and intention?

Is the term a delusion if one of the parties is the CEO? For example, how can both parties freely accept responsibility for the consequences of a relationship when one party has power over the other's salary, promotion, or keeping the job?

If tone at the top encourages workplace sexual expression, what are the constraints to protect employees? American Apparels' ethics policy talks about "promoting ethical conduct, including the handling of actual or apparent conflicts of interest between personal and professional relationships."

So who decides if a conflict of interest has occurred between personal and professional relationships and if harm was done in a fleeting or more sustained expression of sexual interest? What about harm to bystanders who just want to do their job and are made uncomfortable by sexual innuendo and graphic language?

If you were doing a cost/benefit analysis of sexual drama (which is an inevitable byproduct of a sexually charged workplace), would the benefits come out ahead if everyone affected got to weigh in?

In interviews, Charney has tied the importance of sexual energy to creative energy on which he says the fashion industry depends. No argument about the value of released endorphins.

Interesting to note that many leaders have championed endorphin highs to stimulate creativity. Among dozens of examples, they set aside areas for ping pong, volleyball, or fitness equipment, or hold events recognizing employee achievements—few, if any of which, have resulted in litigation and loss of company and CEO reputation.

Every leader gets to figure out if what she or he is doing is working and what to change (before a board answers that question for them). Charney enjoyed the reputation as a wunderkind. Now the company is in a different phase facing financial and strategic challenges, as well as another lawsuit about its culture.

The irony of sexual freedom in the workplace is that it is about power, not romance. It often ends up exploiting those most vulnerable—the way, for example, immigrants have often been treated in some workplaces; it also gives ammunition to those who, seeing where a company has made itself most vulnerable, move in for their own kill.

Update–March 28, 2011: Justice Bernadette Bayne held a hearing March 25, 2011 with counsel from both sides in the sexual harassment suit, Morales v. American Apparel. Judge Bayne initially indicated the case should go to arbitration and later said she'd review the additional documents. She gave no indication when she'd rule if the case can go to trial. On March 23, Apparel chairman and CEO Dov Charney was hit with the second sexual harassment suit this month. Kimbra Lo, 19, a former sales associate, alleges she was sexually assaulted when she went to Charney's LA home seeking to be rehired as a model and photographer. Both Lo and Morales went on the Today Show to talk about their lawsuits. The company contends the relationships were consensual.

Critical Thinking

1. What is meant by the allegations of a sexually charged workplace and a hostile work environment?
2. How are the allegations related to ethics and ethical behavior?
3. What lessons for management might be drawn from the article?
4. Identify one lesson for management and defend its importance.

GAEL O'BRIEN is a Business Ethics Magazine columnist. Gael is a thought leader on building leadership, trust, and reputation and writes The Week in Ethics, a weekly column where this article was first published.

From *Business Ethics*, March 15, 2011. Copyright © 2011 by New Mountain Media, LLC. Reprinted by permission.

What the Wal-Mart Ruling Means for Big Business

The Supreme Court ruling in favor of Wal-Mart in a closely watched sex discrimination class action suit will have a far-reaching impact on businesses—and on female workers.

ROGER PARLOFF

Fortune—Today's ruling in the *Dukes v. Wal-Mart* sex discrimination class action—the largest such suit ever and the most important case on the U.S. Supreme Court's business docket this term—is a powerful, multipronged victory for business, though not necessarily for businesswomen.

One key ruling—that most class actions seeking monetary compensation cannot be brought under lenient procedures that were originally designed for suits seeking only injunctive relief—was unanimous, sending a sharp rebuke to the U.S. Court of Appeals for the Ninth Circuit, which had held otherwise by a 6–5 margin.

At the same time, the more far-reaching rulings in the case, which relate to the more fundamental question of just how much in common a million and a half women must have before than can sue as a class for gender discrimination, were decided along narrow, familiar ideological lines, 5–4.

Justice Antonin Scalia wrote the opinion of the Court, and Justice Ruth Bader Ginsburg wrote the partial dissent.

Here are the headlines:

Unconscious Discrimination

The majority drove a stake—multiple stakes, really—through the heart of a very common, powerful genre of employment discrimination class action that revolves around the claim that a company gives its managers excessive discretion in making pay and promotion decisions, allowing those managers to engage in *unconscious* discrimination. In the past, similar suits have been brought against the likes of Costco (COST), Home Depot (HD), and FedEx (FDX), and a group of other large corporations, including Altria (MO), Bank of America (BAC), and Hewlett-Packard (HPQ), had filed amicus briefs in which they admitted feeling vulnerable to suits brought on the Wal-Mart (WMT) template.

Category of Class Action

The Court unanimously agreed that this case—and possibly any class action seeking monetary compensation—*cannot* be brought (as this one was) using the lenient and minimal procedural safeguards that the Federal Rules of Civil Procedure require of suits seeking only injunctive or declaratory relief. This is a ruling of broad significance, *not* confined to the employment discrimination context.

Commonality

The majority decided that for plaintiffs to win the right to proceed as a class, they must demonstrate a relatively high degree of "commonality" between their claims. "Commonality requires the plaintiff to demonstrate that the class members have suffered the same injury," Justice Scalia wrote. "This does not mean merely that they have all suffered a violation of the same provision of law.... What matters ... is not the raising of common *'questions'* ... but rather the capacity of a classwide proceeding to generate common *answers* apt to drive the resolution of the litigation."

Individual Hearings

The Court unanimously agreed that the lower courts' attempts to streamline the adjudication process in this case to accommodate the litigation of more than a million claims at once deprived litigants—not just Wal-Mart, but also absent class members—of needed statutory safeguards. The lower court had let the case to go forward on the theory that it could be decided based on elaborate computer models, but without hearings ever being held to determine whether individual class members were entitled to relief. The Court unanimously rejected such a "Trial by Formula," as Justice Scalia dubbed it.

The Judge's Fact-Finding Role

The majority said that in performing its gatekeeping function in ensuring that classes are composed of plaintiffs whose legal situations share a sufficient minimum degree of "commonality," judges are permitted to make some findings about disputed questions of fact—a role that many judges had thought had to be reserved for later resolution by a jury. In addition, the majority suggested that judges at the class certification stage can probably also make gatekeeping decisions about whether expert witnesses are engaging in junk science.

Victimization Ratio

The majority noted in passing that while the Court had, in a previous case, permitted plaintiffs to allege a "pattern and practice" of discrimination by an employer where one in eight class members claimed victimization, in the *Dukes* case the plaintiffs had only demonstrated that one in 12,500 class members had complained of wrongdoing. The court implied that such a sparse showing was insufficient. Though the majority insisted that it was not setting up any new statistical threshold for making "pattern and practice" claims, the Court's citation of these ratios clearly invites such inferences in the future by lower court judges, who crave bright-line rules of thumb of this type.

To recap the basics, in 2004 a San Francisco federal judge allowed six female Wal-Mart employees to sue on behalf of every one of the nearly 1.5 million female employees who then worked, or had worked, at any of Wal-Mart's 3,400-plus stores nationwide since December 26, 1998. The suit alleged gender discrimination with respect to promotions and pay. (Had the case been allowed to proceed, it would actually have been much bigger than what the Court described—Wal-Mart now has more than 4,300 stores nationwide, for instance—but the Court cites statistics that were accurate when the lower court record on class certification was created in 2004.) In April 2010, the Ninth Circuit pared the class very slightly, but generally approved the lower court's ruling.

The plaintiffs alleged that Wal-Mart allowed individual store managers to make pay and promotion decisions based on excessively subjective criteria. As a consequence, these store managers (who are more often than not men) *unconsciously* tended to choose people like themselves (i.e., other men) to receive career advancements, it was claimed. Over time, Wal-Mart's failure to curb store-manager discretion in the face of continuing statistical gender disparities in pay and promotion rates was then said to amount to intentional discrimination by the company.

Since individual store managers made most promotion and pay decisions at Wal-Mart, one obvious question was whether the alleged abuse of discretion by certain store managers at a small percentage of stores could be extrapolated to establish abuse of discretion at all Wal-Mart stores. In response, the plaintiffs argued that Wal-Mart's strong corporate culture led store managers to unconsciously abuse the discretion they were granted in uniform ways.

At oral argument in March, Justice Scalia had protested that he felt whipsawed by that argument, commenting: "On the one hand, you say the problem is that [the decisions] were utterly subjective, and on the other hand you say there is a strong corporate culture that guides all of this. Well, which is it?"

In today's ruling he rejected almost every aspect of this theory, including the core notion that excessive subjectivity in personnel decisions could amount to a "general policy of discrimination" susceptible to a class-action remedy. Scalia stressed that while Wal-Mart's expert on organizational sociology, William Bielby, said he believed Wal-Mart's procedures were "vulnerable" to discrimination, Bielby admitted that he could not say whether 0.5% or 95% of store manager employment decisions were actually motivated by improperly stereotyped thinking. "Whether 0.5 percent or 95 percent of the employment decisions at Wal-Mart might be determined by stereotyped thinking is the essential question on which respondents' theory of commonality depends," Scalia wrote. "If Bielby admitted he has no answer to that question, we can safely disregard what he has to say."

Though some will interpret today's majority ruling as reflecting the conservative majority's pro-business tilt, an alternative explanation is more likely. There was always a thermonuclear issue lurking just beneath the surface of this case, though it was not one of the specific technical issues the Court asked the parties to brief.

Conservatives view lawsuits like this one as coming very close to permitting gender (or race) discrimination to be proven on the basis of little more than statistical disparities in the workforce that are extremely widespread in our society and which might simply result from a stew of complex, innocent, cultural causes. Many conservatives fear that if employers have to avoid statistical disparities to avoid getting sued, they will feel pressured to adopt secret quotas, which are illegal.

Critical Thinking

1. What allegations of workplace sex discrimination are identified in the article?

2. How might a code of ethics have prevented the alleged sex discrimination discussed in the article?

3. What lessons for management might be drawn from the article? Identify one lesson for management and defend its importance.

Older Workers: Running to the Courthouse?

Do greater numbers of aging baby boomers result in more age discrimination suits?

ROBERT J. GROSSMAN

In March, when the U.S. Equal Employment Opportunity Commission (EEOC) issued its annual report of private-sector discrimination charges, the data painted a disheartening picture. All told—with charges based on age, race, disability, sex and gender, religion, and retaliation— almost 83,000 claims were filed in 2007, representing the largest year-over-year increase since 1993. Age discrimination claims, with 19,103 charges, had the dubious distinction of increasing the fastest, with a caseload 15 percent greater than the prior year.

Reflecting on the numbers, EEOC Chair Naomi Earp voices sharp criticism of employers. Corporate America needs to do a better job of proactively preventing discrimination and addressing complaints promptly and effectively," she wrote in a press release earlier this year.

But a closer look at EEOC data raises an interesting question about age discrimination: In 2007, according to the U.S. Bureau of Labor Statistics (BLS), 76.9 million people in the workforce were age 40 and older. Last year, 99.98 percent of them did not complain to the EEOC about age discrimination. In contrast, people were more than six times more likely to allege race discrimination.

Tempest in a Teapot?

The relative scarcity of age discrimination cases is perplexing in light of the rationale the EEOC offers for last year's increase in complaints: "The jump in filings may be due to a combination of factors, including greater awareness of the law, changing economic conditions, and increased diversity and demographic shifts in the labor force."

True, age filings did inch up, but in context the overall number remains minuscule. By EEOC officials' own reasoning, if age discrimination exists, cases should be pouring in because:

- Older workers have AARP, one of the most vocal and influential lobbies in the country, in their corner educating and advocating for them.

- Workers age 40 and older—who are protected by the Age Discrimination in Employment Act (ADEA)—now account for more than 50 percent of the workforce, according to the BLS.
- The percentage of older workers will continue to trend up as baby boomers move through their work lives.
- The faltering economy is forcing people who had intended to retire to extend their time at work.

Still, last year only 0.02 percent of workers age 40 and older complained of age bias. So, when it comes to age discrimination, is the EEOC's criticism of employers over-the-top?

Brenda McChriston, SPHR, a principal at Spectrum HR Solutions in Baltimore, formerly an HR executive with an international hospitality company, says so: "Age discrimination is not as rampant as the EEOC suggests. The agency is just trying to beef up its case for what it does. In fact, employers have become increasingly savvy about how to keep their workplaces free from litigation—and the EEOC numbers show it."

On the other hand, is it really possible for there to be so little age bias and negative stereotyping? Or has the EEOC, the federal government's star player in the fight against discrimination, moved from center court to the sidelines? Belying the EEOC statistics, workers, job seekers and even employers say the scourge of age discrimination continues to be endemic. For example, in a survey of 5,000 workers age 50 and older conducted by Bob Skladany, vice president of research for RetirementJobs.com in Waltham, Mass., 77 percent said they have experienced or observed workplace age bias. In a companion survey of 165 employers, 78 percent indicated that age discrimination was "a fact of life".

These findings parallel a study prepared by RoperASW for AARP, finding that two-thirds of workers ages 45 to 74 had experienced or observed age bias on the job and that 80 percent of job seekers said they were facing age discrimination.

Why So Few?

Perceptions, of course, are not necessarily reality. But with so many people acknowledging and experiencing bias, why so few EEOC cases? Among the reasons:

- Older workers are less likely to complain, especially if they're still employed. "People don't want to be at war," says Robert Gordon, a partner at Ropes & Gray in Boston and author of *Dealing with Employee Lawsuits: Strategies for the Prevention & Defense of Workplace-Related Claims* (Aspatore Books, 2005). "They don't want to paint a bull's-eye on the back of their heads. Perhaps with some justification, they feel [if they make noise] it will place a taint on them. Instead, they suffer in silence."

- Employers, in the main, are practical and compassionate. They offer face-saving severance tied to counsel-approved releases that ease nonperforming workers out the door. "I find myself advising clients, 'If you want to get rid of Joe Doakes, isn't it better to pay him three months' severance than paying the money to your lawyer?'" Gordon says.

- "Most people are willing to sign the release if they get financial incentive," says Donna Ballman, an attorney in Fort Lauderdale, Fla., who represents claimants.

- High-powered executives and star performers trade in the right to sue when they're hired. Employers tie them to binding arbitration clauses in employment contracts, ensuring that discrimination claims will be handled quickly and quietly.

- The legal process is costly and creeps along. Though lawyers for plaintiffs still take cases on a contingency fee basis, many charge fees, requiring the complainant to pony up at least some money early on. Of course, employers could include arbitration clauses in employment contracts for everyone, but the speed, lower cost and easier access to a hearing might encourage more people to come forward.

Heart of the Storm

Despite the low number of age discrimination claims being filed, HR professionals know too well that quantity means little when you're in the heart of the storm. Even one case wears HR professionals and other managers down. And almost everyone has at least one. "It's a huge drain on an organization's resources; it eats away in terms of morale and productivity," says Michael Buda, SPHR, a consultant in Atlanta who served for seven years as executive vice president of HR and legal counsel at Jackson Healthcare Solutions in Alpharetta, Ga., a health care staffing and software company.

For HR managers, a charge filing from the EEOC marks the onset of a time-consuming, emotionally draining journey. Some insights into the agency will help you prepare—and endure.

A charge filing marks the onset of a time-consuming, emotionally draining journey.

America's Watchdog

EEOC officials have near-impossible jobs. Citizens ask them to serve as champions for workers who see themselves as victims of discrimination, but the agency has limited leverage and resources. For example, it has the power to investigate and conciliate claims, issue findings of "reasonable cause," and bring cases to court. But it lacks authority to render final judgments on the merits of cases or issue financial awards to aggrieved parties.

Hence, EEOC officials learn to cherry-pick from among the charges, looking for obvious winners, especially those that will have an impact beyond the complainant and, perhaps most important, generate publicity, serving as a deterrent.

As complaints flow in, they're assigned to three baskets: Basket A, which contains potentially high-profile claims and those where discrimination seems apparent; Basket B, which holds claims that could go either way; and Basket C, which contains claims that don't look promising. When employers receive a charge, they are not told what basket it falls in. For cases in baskets B and C, the EEOC generally offers parties a chance to settle through mediation.

The EEOC is not the only game in town. Most states and many municipalities have comparable agencies. Their powers vary depending on state laws. Most have work-sharing arrangements with EEOC officials, so claims can be handled interchangeably.

If the complainant has a lawyer, the lawyer often will try to select the forum that can generate the best payday. For example, under the ADEA, when discrimination is found and the employer has acted willfully, the victim may be awarded "liquidated damages" of double the salary he or she lost. In some state courts, such as California and Ohio, the plaintiff may be awarded more-lucrative "punitive" damages.

Toll Booth to a Big Payday

While the EEOC or a state or municipal agency investigates, mediates and conciliates, plaintiffs' lawyers wait in the wings. They can't move cases to court until the agency issues a right-to-sue letter giving them access to what plaintiffs yearn for: a jury of their peers. On occasion, the EEOC may issue a letter soon after the charge is filed. However, it does not have to provide one until the case has been in-house for at least 180 days while EEOC officials investigate "reasonable cause" to suspect the employer has violated the ADEA. In at least one state, Ohio, a complainant can bypass agency consideration and file directly in court, however.

When the EEOC finds reasonable cause, it may go on to federal court on behalf of the complainant, who may choose to also be represented by private counsel. But with only 200 attorneys for the whole country, the EEOC initiates relatively few cases. For example, in 2007, a year when EEOC investigators found reasonable cause in 625 age discrimination cases, the agency's general counsel filed 32 lawsuits, the majority alleging discriminatory discharge. Overall, in 2006, for all types of discrimination, the EEOC filed 383 suits. Of these, 339 ended in consent decrees or settlements and 11 were resolved by voluntary dismissal; of the 33 cases actually resolved by court orders, the EEOC prevailed nine times.

Questionable Victories

When the EEOC finds "no reasonable cause," as it did 10,002 times in 2007, employers feel vindicated. That number represents 62 percent of the age discrimination cases resolved that year. But plaintiffs' lawyers soldier on, undaunted. "Some employers think they're home free, but they're not," says Janet Hill of Hill & Associates in Atlanta, former president of the National Employment Lawyers Association of San Francisco. EEOC lawyers are "hugely overworked, and they don't have the personnel to do complete investigations. The fact that they don't find cause indicates little about the merits of the cases."

During an EEOC investigation, the employer's response to the charge is not shared with the complainant. Unless attorneys for both sides talk or unless a lawsuit is filed, the complainant's lawyer may not know the strength of the employer's defense. Usually, it's during the discovery phase of a suit that the complainant's lawyer knows for sure whether he has a case worth pursuing.

"If I gave up on every case where the EEOC or a state EEO agency didn't find reasonable cause, I wouldn't have a career in employment law," says Rik Siro, principal at Siro Law in Kansas City, Mo. Siro recently won a $2.7 million court verdict for a client who was denied a reasonable cause finding by the Missouri Commission on Human Rights. "Ninety-nine percent of the time when I take a case, there was no reasonable cause." In 2007, the EEOC found reasonable cause in 3.9 percent of the age discrimination cases investigated.

"Employers always try to make a big deal about reasonable cause findings, but judges usually refuse to admit the result into evidence because juries might think the EEOC [officials] investigate more than they actually do," says Dennis Egan, of The Popham Law Firm PC in Kansas City, Mo. Egan, who has been a lawyer for 30 years, has represented plaintiffs in 92 jury trials, winning 72. He says the EEOC failed to find reasonable cause in all of those cases.

But winning a jury trial is one thing; surviving preliminary steps leading to the trial is another. More than 70 percent of federal cases, including those under the ADEA, never get to a jury; they're dismissed by judges granting motions in favor of the employer. "Most court cases settle," says Condon McGlothlen, a partner at Seyfarth Shaw in Chicago. "Of those that don't, employers usually prevail by winning a motion for a summary judgment. At that point in the process, the judge is presented extensive documentation from both sides and is required to apply it in the most favorable light from the plaintiff's perspective."

Winning a jury trail is one thing; surviving preliminary steps leading to the trial is another. More than 70 percent of federal cases . . . are dismissed by judges granting motions in favor of the employer.

In 2007, through settlements and conciliations, the EEOC collected $66.8 million, an average of $4,140 for every claim filed. In addition, the negative publicity that companies suffer after agreeing to high-priced settlements—rather than litigating—serve as not-so-subtle signals to employers of what happens when the EEOC puts them under its microscope.

Sources of Complaints

Complaints of age discrimination generally involve hiring, treatment at work, or termination and dismissal. Dismissal cases account for more than half the cases filed and represent the ones most likely to move beyond the agency to court.

"These cases account for 99 percent of the litigation because that's where the money is," Gordon says. "People who don't get hired usually don't bring lawsuits because in those cases all the employer has to show is a more qualified hire. And people who are still working tend to keep their problems to themselves."

Lisa Whitmore, SPHR, director of HR for Johnson Controls in Waukesha, Wis., an automotive products company with 140,000 employees, agrees. "Our cases almost always are termination cases," she says.

Predominantly, age discrimination cases are based on disparate treatment—requiring the complainant to demonstrate how the employer or its agents acted or failed to act because of age bias or stereotyping, says Dianna Johnston, an EEOC assistant legal counsel in Washington, D.C. The employer must show that reasons for the actions—right or wrong—were not tainted by discrimination. Typical termination cases might encompass scenarios such as the following:

- The person supported a mainframe computer that's being phased out and replaced with a system that he's unable to operate.
- The pace of work has increased, and the person is unable or unwilling to keep up.
- The person is not excited about her job; she has lost her spark and is not performing as well as in the past.

Disparate Impact

Beginning in 2005, the U.S. Supreme Court in *Smith v. City of Jackson* established that the ADEA included a right to sue under a theory of disparate impact. In such cases—and usually when reductions in force occur—if the complainant can demonstrate that a disproportionate number of older workers were laid off, the employer is required to demonstrate that the decisions were made for legitimate, nondiscriminatory business reasons.

So far, employers have been successful in defending all disparate impact cases that have gone to trial. "If your business reason is not outright discriminatory, you'll be OK," McGlothlen says. "Since the *City of Jackson* case, virtually every federal court has bought the defendant's story."

But court decisions don't tell the whole story. At least some cases—class actions involving hundreds of employees—have settled without employers admitting liability. One age discrimination case involving 1,697 former employees laid off by Sprint Nextel settled in 2005 for $57 million, with attorneys for the plaintiffs walking off with a cool $19.4 million in legal fees. "When companies are having trouble hewing to the nutty imperative of Wall Street, they have to slash and burn," says Egan, one of the plaintiffs' lawyers. "If you leave management undirected to decide who should stay or go, they'll drift into saying, 'I'm going to keep the person who is blessed with plenty of runway ahead of them.'"

The Economy's Effect

With the economy in turmoil, employment lawyers on both sides report that the EEOC's prophecy of an increase in age discrimination cases may still come true. "There's a lag between the start of an economic downturn and the legal consequences," McGlothlen says. "We're seeing a steady stream of EEOC charges and lawsuits alleging age discrimination and expect to see more."

The prospect of more claims—no matter the merit—discourages HR professionals. "The entire organization has to be engaged in pulling together documentation, meeting with counsel, interviewing witnesses, answering interrogatories; it's an enormous burden," McChriston says. "In the end, we win, but when you factor in the lost time and expense, what did we win?"

Critical Thinking

1. Why have age discrimination suits decreased in recent years?
2. What is the economic impact of age discrimination suits on the employer?
3. What is meant by "disparate impact"?

ROBERT J. GROSSMAN, a contributing editor of *HR Magazine*, is a lawyer and a professor of management studies at Marist College in Poughkeepsie, N.Y.

From *HR Magazine*, June 2008, pp. 63–64, 66. Copyright © 2008 by Society for Human Resource Management (SHRM). Reprinted by permission of SHRM and via the Copyright Clearance Center.

Fighting the High Cost of "Getting Even" at Work

Employee retaliation lawsuits are at a record high, and they're hard for companies to win. So what can companies do?

ANNE FISHER

For many years, race discrimination charges were the most common complaint against employers, but that has changed. The new no. 1, reports the U.S. Equal Opportunity Commission, is retaliation, meaning alleged actions by employers aimed at getting even with workers who have made other complaints.

In 2010, these cases—36,258 of them—cost companies $404 million, the highest annual total the EEOC has ever obliged private-sector employers to pay. Not only that, but "each one costs six figures to fight in court, regardless of the outcome," notes Kelly Kolb, an employment lawyer at Fowler White Boggs. "They're expensive even if the company wins."

Not that the company is likely to win, for a couple of reasons. First, the definition of retaliation is a bit slippery. Until a few years ago, an employee who filed a retaliation charge had to show some financial loss, such as a firing or demotion, that a boss meted out as punishment for complaining about, say, sexual harassment in the workplace.

Then, in 2006, the Supreme Court decided that definition was too narrow. The upshot of a landmark case, *Burlington Northern Santa Fe v. White,* is that plaintiffs no longer need to have suffered a monetary setback in order to make a charge of retaliation stick.

"Now, anything that would discourage someone from complaining about unfair practices at work can be considered retaliation," notes Kolb. "It could range from passing you over for a promotion to refusing to let you leave early for your kid's softball game."

A second reason why employers usually lose retaliation lawsuits: Juries don't trust them. Says Kolb, "Jurors are predisposed to believe that employers retaliate."

So what can companies do? One tactic: If you're planning to fire someone, don't telegraph the fact in advance. Kolb says that plaintiffs' attorneys often engineer "a set-up": "If you say to an employee, 'Be in my office tomorrow at 2:00 to discuss whether you're going to be let go or quit,' that person can call a lawyer who will instruct him or her to email you a barrage of complaints before 2:00 so they can claim that the firing was 'retaliatory.'"

As a broader matter of policy, Kolb says many retaliation complaints could be avoided if managers took "a more structured approach than in the past. Everything having to do with a person's performance needs to be documented, so that you have a clear paper trail showing the exact reasons for whatever actions someone's boss may have taken."

Just as important, human resources staffers need to be kept apprised of everything that happens, Kolb adds: "In court, you need to be able to show that there was an objective third party involved, so that any personal animus between a boss and a subordinate was not the motivation behind the company's actions."

Of course, HR departments decimated by outsourcing and layoffs may find such painstaking prevention a tall order and that, Kolb, says, may be a big part of the problem.

"So many HR functions now are so shrunken that managers may be tempted to say, 'Instead of bothering HR with this, we can just handle it ourselves,'" he says. "But letting individual managers make [these] decisions all on their own can be a very costly way to go."

Critical Thinking

1. Why are more allegations of retaliation at work lawsuits being filed now than in previous years?

2. What reasons are given in the article why employers often lose retaliation at work lawsuits?

3. What is the importance of an employer establishing a "paper trail" about an employee's performance?

4. What is the role of a Human Resource department in employee retaliation situations?

5. What statement concerning retaliation at work should be in a code of ethics? Write a statement and defend it. If you do not believe such a statement belongs in a code of ethics, explain your reasoning why such a statement should not be included in a code of ethics.

From *Fortune*, August 16, 2011. Copyright © 2011 by Fortune Magazine. Reprinted by permission of Time, Inc. via Pars International Corp.

Values-Driven HR

Juniper Networks is turning words on the wall into behaviors in action.

BILL ROBERTS

Folks at Juniper Networks Inc. have lofty goals. Last year, one goal embraced by company leaders was to help end worldwide slavery. As Juniper employees see it, this goal aligns with the company's values, talent, technology and another lofty goal to change the world—in part, by designing and developing hardware and software for high-performance networks.

Led by its chief executive officer and HR executive, the 15-year-old Sunnyvale, Calif., enterprise is in the process of re-energizing company values among its more than 9,100 employees in 46 countries. As corporate leaders seek more effective ways to put values into action, they want to align corporate giving with those values.

Hence, the Juniper Foundation supports Not for Sale, a nonprofit in Half Moon Bay, Calif., whose mission is to abolish slavery, indentured servitude and other human trafficking and to use social and other technologies in that effort. Some high-tech companies have begun to target these issues because perpetrators can be found within their sprawling supply chains. Juniper contributes money, technology and expertise. "We want to do more than write checks," explains Steven Rice, executive vice president of HR.

Rice says supporting Not for Sale is just one example of how Juniper's leaders strive to create a culture where the company that customers see on the outside matches the one on the inside. The notion of narrowing the gap between values as words on the wall and values as behaviors is starting to permeate HR processes from recruiting to talent management. In pursuit of this quest, Juniper's HR professionals draw on recent research and emerging practices regarding corporate values, cultural transformation and the neuroscience of leadership.

Finding the Way

Juniper's approach represents the future of corporate leadership, says Chris Ernst, co-author of *Boundary Spanning Leadership* (McGraw-Hill, 2010) and a senior faculty member at the Center for Creative Leadership in Greensboro, N.C. He calls Juniper a bellwether for "creating more connected, collaborative, cross-boundary ways of working. The pieces are in place, but there is hard work ahead for Juniper."

A Page from Juniper's Values Blueprint

Value
We are about trust.

Definition
We inspire confidence in colleagues, customers and partners by always acting with integrity, fairness, respect and reliability.

Behaviors
- Acts with the highest level of honesty and integrity.
- Shares agendas and objectives, encouraging feedback and discussing things in an open, collaborative and respectful manner.
- Takes responsibility and delivers on commitment.
- Acts confidently but never arrogantly.
- Respects decisions and supports them with enthusiasm and follow-through.
- Assumes positive intentions, viewing conflict as an opportunity to find constructive solutions that help all succeed.

Rice similarly believes that the journey has just begun. The values, known as The Juniper Way, are as follows: We are authentic, we are about trust, we deliver excellence, we pursue bold aspirations, we make a meaningful difference.

"One definition of our values is to be confident but not arrogant," says Rice, an effervescent proponent of the cause. Rice spent 25 years in HR at Hewlett-Packard Co. in Palo Alto, Calif., before joining Juniper in 2006, where he leads a global HR team of 108. The team includes an HR leader assigned to each business unit, centers of excellence in various disciplines, and a shared services group that relies heavily on employee and manager self-service for HR transactions.

Tone at the Top

After its launch in 1996, Juniper became one of the most watched Internet startups. Its mission was simple and bold: "Connect everything. Empower everyone." Facing formidable rivals, Juniper emerged as one of the leading providers of switches, routers, software and other networking equipment for global networks such as the New York Stock Exchange. In 2011, annual revenue topped more than $4 billion, up 9 percent from 2010 and a record for the company. The company was less affected by the recession than many other businesses, growing its workforce every year since 2009.

Juniper has always attracted some of the best and brightest talent—veterans and new grads with master's and doctoral degrees in science, math, engineering and computer science—to work on hardware systems, computer chip designs, network architecture and software. More than 4,200 employees conduct research and development. The company has a reputation as an innovative, collaborative, high-performance meritocracy. So why focus on values and culture?

Enter Kevin Johnson, a longtime Microsoft executive who became chief executive officer in September 2008, replacing Scott Kriens, who remains chairman of the board.

"Juniper was founded with a thought leadership agenda: to be a disruptive innovator in new ways to power the networks that power the world today," Johnson says. At the core: "When people around the world are connected, it is transformative for business, society, education, social causes, for the good and advancement of people."

Johnson spent his first year clarifying strategy with his leadership team, including Rice. Thus was born The New Network, a theme that encapsulates Juniper's dedication to fast, flexible hardware and software for networks capable of handling ubiquitous voice, data, video and other traffic, wired or wireless, at ever-increasing volume and speed.

With that strategy in place, Johnson turned to culture. "There was an opportunity to shape the cultural values and environment that will allow great people to do their best work," he says. "We had to embrace the concept of the importance of talent and culture in achieving goals. It is not HR's responsibility, but the business leaders' responsibility. And that is where the CEO has a role to play." Rice agrees: "I am the caretaker of the culture; the executive team owns the culture."

As caretakers, Rice and his HR team face the challenge of making sure the company hires, develops, retains, and properly compensates and recognizes workers that have the requisite science, engineering and business skills, plus the personal traits of collaboration and high energy. While offering competitive salaries and benefits, Juniper needs people who are willing to collaborate across business units, driven to innovate, and passionate about their work and how it will change the world, according to Rice.

Ernst, who studied Juniper in his research, says as many as three-fourths of organizational change efforts fail because the focus is misplaced on management systems, structure and process, rather than on leadership. "Real change requires a change in leadership," he says. "And leadership is about culture, beliefs

---

Juniper Networks Inc.

Products and services: Designs, develops and sells products and services for network infrastructure.
Ownership: Publicly held (NYSE: JNPR).
Key executives: Kevin Johnson, chief executive officer; Steven Rice, executive vice president of HR.
2011 revenue: $4.5 billion.
Employees: More than 9,100.
Locations: Headquarters in Sunnyvale, Calif., with operations in 46 countries. The largest concentrations of employees are in the Silicon Valley, the Boston area and India.
Connections: www.juniper.net, www.juniper.net/us/en/company/careers.

---

and values." Ernst is conducting workshops with Juniper's executive team "so they can role-model collaborative behavior for the entire organization. This is one way Juniper is trying to beat the odds," he says.

Values-Centric Cultures

Rice and Greg Pryor, HR vice president for leadership and organization effectiveness, retained Ann Rhoades, head of People Ink Corp. in Albuquerque, N.M., to help build what she calls a values-centric culture. She uses Juniper as an example in her book *Built on Values* (Jossey-Bass, 2011).

Rhoades says some Juniper executives were initially confused by the new approach. They said, "We have great values, why change them?" But Rhoades says those values "were not defined. They did not have behaviors behind them." To infuse values into the culture, they must be spelled out as behaviors that are sought, developed and prized. In her patent-pending process, a group of employees examines existing values and explores new ones, defines them, and identifies behaviors associated with them. The result is a values blueprint.

Juniper chose more than 200 employees from around the world—including new hires, senior engineers, managers and the CEO—to participate in creating the blueprint. "I had a chance to listen and understand the perspectives of others," Johnson says. To identify behaviors associated with desired values, the group used the Organizational Cultural Inventory from Human Synergistics Inc. and produced a draft blueprint in two days.

The 35-member executive team reviewed the blueprint and then held discussions among 120 top leaders. "The executive staff decided on its own, without any coaching, to share this in small sessions with employee groups of no more than 100," Pryor says.

Thus was born the Trio Tour: Groups of three senior executives, often including Johnson, conducted 75 meetings with groups of employees, mostly in person but some virtual, to promote the strategy, the values and the company's promise to customers: a workforce dedicated to innovation, collaboration, authenticity, trust, high performance and leadership in its field. "We framed this incredibly powerful culture work as a renewal of our culture and values, like a long-married couple would renew their wedding vows," Pryor says.

Rhoades applauds the executives' rare commitment to the values rollout.

Hiring to Build the Brand

Rice's HR team began to look for ways to infuse the values throughout talent management processes. The goal was to hire, retain and develop people who have the right skills and knowledge and who share the company's values, too. "If the customer sees you as team-oriented and such and the customer service guy is different, you have a problem," Rice says. "You have to hire against the brand."

In Rice's view, a strong culture has these three components:

- Employees who agree with the mission.
- The ability to identify, keep and develop those types of employees.
- Willingness on the part of corporate leaders to let values drive decisions—from talent management processes to corporate giving.

Juniper's HR team began to identify key attributes, based on the values, that should be sought in any employee and to create about 300 job descriptions (called "architectures") that include the skills, knowledge, behaviors and values associated with each role in the company. The central values of collaboration, authenticity and trust define employees the company calls its J Players. "Our aspiration is 100 percent J players," Rice says.

In conversations and through other communications, business-unit leaders and others asked employees where The Juniper Way fell short in practice. Trust came up, with the annual performance review seen as a culprit. "We got feedback that our existing performance management process was not consistent with the values," Pryor says, so HR professionals revamped the process.

About this time, Pryor discovered David Rock, founder and CEO of Results Coaching Systems LLC, with headquarters in New York City and Sydney, Australia. Rock coined the term "neuroleadership" and founded the NeuroLeadership Institute to promote leadership training.

He uses a model for influencing behavior called SCARF—which stands for status, certainty, autonomy, relatedness and fairness. The model gave Pryor and Rice hard evidence to show engineers and scientists, who were initially skeptical of some of the changes included in the new performance management process.

Culture Shift

Juniper executives point out that the changes are rooted in the need to achieve authenticity with customers. "We are dealing

---

Performance Management Redux

When asked which Juniper value was least apparent in practice, employees said trust. They cited the annual performance review as an example of lack of trust.

Employees expressed concern about the lack of positive feedback, the forced labeling from a ranking system, and even the use of words like "review" and "appraisal."

"We fundamentally rethought our performance management process," says Greg Pryor, HR vice president for leadership and organization development. "It was inspired by the managers who brought this to our attention."

The old performance review was a typical backward-looking process to identify where the employee needed to improve and involved rating each employee. A distribution curve was imposed on the ratings of the entire population.

The process was replaced with a semiannual "conversation day." On these days, employees and managers discuss areas for improvement and areas for new growth, set stretch goals, and align the goals with employees' career aspirations. There is no rating given or a specific measure of improvement expected.

Internal surveys indicated that 93 percent of employees participated in the first conversation day and 66 percent of participants found it "helpful" to "extremely helpful," Pryor says. Conversation days would not be possible without other practices introduced by HR. For example:

- Goal alignment became a separate activity. Employees and managers set goals aligned with the business unit's and the company's overall strategy. More employees are included in this activity than were included in the past.
- Compensation planning now involves a statement of guidance that gives local managers more leeway in distributing merit pay, rather than rigid guidelines for doing so.
- Instead of imposing a distribution curve on employees' ratings, there is now relative laddering within each occupational and geographical group. There are 300 such ladders.
- Detailed talent scenarios for each group now give managers and employees guidance for steps to take based on the scenario in which each employee best fits.

—Bill Roberts

---

with the most richly informed buyers in history," says Lauren Flaherty, executive vice president and chief marketing officer, who adds that when companies don't act genuinely, they "do so at their own peril."

Flaherty and Rice work together on overseeing the brand and values rollout internally and externally. "You always hope that what you present to the marketplace externally has an authentic origin from within. But you often hope more than it is reality," Flaherty says.

Juniper is different from most companies, she admits. "It has a very open, collaborative culture. It is not burdened by turf. Synergies are seen as a good thing. That's why you can get a marketing team and HR team to work together to change the external face and internal face of the company."

Juniper's efforts are unusual, even for Silicon Valley standards, but other HR executives are taking note. "There is a cultural shift happening more generally, and a lot of HR organizations are waking up to it," says Paul Whitney, vice president of HR and site services for Infinera Corp., an optical networking company based in Sunnyvale, Calif. Whitney is familiar with Juniper's leaders' efforts.

Ernst acknowledges that Juniper might appear to be so different that it does not offer any direct analogy to traditional industries. But he cautions that more corporate leaders are experiencing or soon will experience similar demands for creativity, flexibility and collaboration.

"Even in government, education and family-owned business, all organizations are dealing with challenges they have not seen before and need to learn to work in new ways," Ernst says.

Critical Thinking

1. Read over the behaviors specified in Juniper's Values Blueprint. Do you agree with these behavioral expectations? Why or why not?

2. Can you suggest other behaviors to strengthen Juniper's Values Blueprint? Why do you believe the other behaviors would strengthen the blueprint?

3. What is a values-centric culture?

4. How does a manager determine if such a values-centric is in place in an organization?

5. Can you suggest metrics for a manager to use in measuring the presence of a values-centric culture in an organization?

The author is technology contributing editor for HR Magazine and is based in Silicon Valley.

Cost Reductions, Downsizing-related Layoffs, and HR Practices

FRANCO GANDOLFI

Introduction

Organizational decimation, or downsizing, has been a pervasive managerial practice for the past three decades. If a firm finds itself in financial difficulties, the widely accepted corporate panacea has been to cut personnel. While strong empirical evidence suggests that reduction-inforce (RIF) activities rarely return the anticipated economic and organizational gains (Cascio, Young, and Morris, 1997), there is increased understanding and awareness that downsized companies are forced to deal with the human and societal after-effects, also known as secondary effects, in a post-downsizing phase (Gandolfi, 2007). Research shows that the human consequences of layoffs are costly and devastating for individuals, their families, and entire communities (Macky, 2004). While workforce reductions cannot always be completely avoided, downsizing-related layoffs must be a managerial tool of absolute last rather than first resort (Gandolfi, 2006).

During an economic downturn, a company must carefully consider its options and assess the feasibility and applicability of cost-reduction alternatives prior to adopting RIF-related layoffs. While a large body of research presenting and discussing the alternatives to downsizing has emerged (Littler, 1998; Mirabal and De Young, 2005), there is still a lack of conceptual understanding of downsizing-related layoffs as part of an organization's cost-reduction stages (Gandolfi, 2008). It is vital for a firm to factor in the concept of cost-reduction and recognize the specific cost-reduction stage that characterizes the firms' current business position and environment. Ideally, a company should be in a position to determine the expected duration and severity of the business downturn as accurately as possible. To perform that task successfully, the executives need to know the cost-cutting phase that the firm is currently in (Vernon, 2003). A firm's cost-reduction stage refers to the time-frame the organization requires to be able to reduce operational expenditures

(George, 2004). In reality, however, accurately forecasting a business downturn can be extremely difficult. Thus, firms have a natural tendency to react to rather than anticipate economic declines (Gandolfi, 2006).

The primary objective of this paper is to present a methodology enabling firms to minimize, defer, or avoid the adoption of RIF, layoffs, and downsizing-related activities. The research introduces and showcases a conceptual framework presenting the cost-reduction stages of a firm coupled with a brief introduction of contemporary human resources (HR) practices that some firms have adopted. Fundamentally, the paper builds upon Vernon's (2003), George's (2004), and Gandolfi's (2008) work of three cost-reduction stages: short-range, mid-range, and long-range phases. Technically speaking, the article constitutes a review and extension of previously published work. The underlying conceptual framework of the cost-reduction stages is depicted in Figure 1.

Cost-reduction Stages

The conceptual framework shown in Figure 1 encompasses three timeframe-related phases commanding several internal cost adjustments that have produced a variety of stage-related HR practices. It is important to note that the HR practices are cumulative. In other words, the practices in each stage are not unique to the actual phase, but applicable in subsequent phases in a cumulative fashion.

First Stage: Short-range Cost Adjustments

The first stage of the cost-reduction framework represents short-range cost adjustments in response to a short, temporary decline in business activities (Vernon, 2003). These business slowdowns are expected to last less than six months (Gandolfi, 2008). Most likely, the firm resorts to minor, moderate cost-reduction measures in this stage.

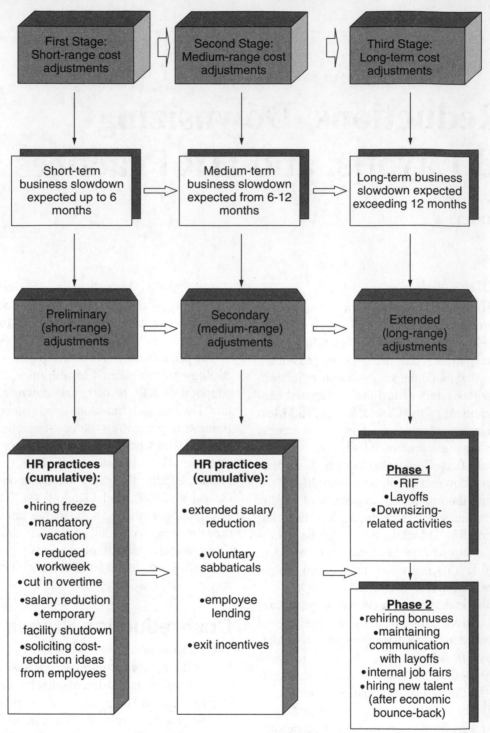

Figure 1   Conceptual framework of cost-reduction stages.

Source: Adapted from Vernon (2003), George (2004), and Gandolfi (2008).

These preliminary adjustments should enable the firm to shun RIF-related layoffs and involuntary cutbacks and return to normal business activity within four to six months (Gandolfi, 2008). Typically, this phase originates with an unexpected drop in sales or a decline in sales forecast. It is characterized by short-term expenditure adjustments to prevent a medium-range downturn or a more lasting, long-range decline. The immediate recognition of a temporary business slip and the resolute engagement in preliminary cost-reduction methods should allow the firm to focus its operations in a cost-sensitive mode for a quick recovery (Vernon, 2003).

The probability of success for the short-range cost adjustments hinges on a number of factors: First, senior management must be able to articulate the business necessity for the cost-adjustment measures effectively and stress the short timeframe of the strategy. A firm's ability to convey the message that preliminary cost-reduction measures at the present time will likely prevent RIF-related layoffs in the future is critical. Second, the HR's role is to communicate decisions made by the board of directors to the entire workforce promptly and to implement the cost-reduction methods swiftly. Third, the employees' flexibility in allowing the firm to modify cost structures increases the chance of success for the planned cost alterations. Therefore, a firm's capacity to overcome a business downturn in the first stage will depend to a large degree on its organization's ability to respond to the new environment by immediately and resolutely modifying expenditures (Vernon, 2003).

Suggested HR Practices for Short-range Cost Adjustments

A review of the literature and the popular press reveals several HR-related practices that firms have implemented for preliminary cost reductions. The following is a non-exhaustive overview and explanation of some of the approaches suggested by scholars and implemented by firms in the global corporate landscape.

• Hiring freeze

A hiring freeze is a mild form of downsizing that reduces labor costs in the short term (Littler, 1998). However, a hiring freeze does not imply that there is no hiring activity at all. Some firms hire new employees while cutting jobs at the same time (Vernon, 2003). While this practice may make sense in terms of supplying the firm with key personnel, it tends to send a confusing message to the workforce. As an example, in its latest attempt to fight rising jet fuel costs and a deteriorating U.S. economy, American Airlines imposed an immediate hiring freeze on all management and support staff (Maxon, 2008).

• Mandatory vacation

Mandatory vacation involves requiring employees to use their accrued vacation days or requiring them to take a number of unpaid vacation days during a certain time period. While employees might not want to be told when and how to use their entitlements, they will nonetheless appreciate the reaffirmed job security (Vernon, 2003). At the time of writing. Chrysler plans a corporate-wide shutdown of its U.S. operations during two weeks in July 2008 to improve the automaker's efficiency and boost productivity (Govreau, 2008).

• Reduced workweek

Firms sometimes resort to a reduced workweek. This may translate into a reduction from 40 to 35 or fewer hours, thereby reducing short-term payroll expenditures. While most employees appreciate being able to spend more time with their families, a reduced paycheck is not always welcomed. Also, employees may find that the same amount of work still needs to be performed while they spend less time on the job (Gandolfi, 2008). Nucor Steel Corporation in South Carolina has avoided layoffs for 35 years by resorting to two and three workdays for its employees during downturns (George, 2004). In a similar vein, in 2008, workers at a St. Thomas automotive parts plant in the U.K. voted a reduction in their workweek rather than see 200 employees leave permanently (De Bono, 2008).

• Cut in overtime pay

Minimizing or abolishing overtime pay for employees can be a powerful technique of reducing operational costs in the short term (Vernon, 2003). Firms may institute an across-the-board (i.e., all employees) abolition or confine the cut to selected categories, such as nonmanagerial, blue-collar, or salaried employees (Gandolfi, 2008). In 2004, GM and Ford and car-supplier Visteon Corporation slashed overtime pay for most employees indefinitely (Dybis and Garsten, 2004).

• Salary reduction

Salary reduction methods have been standard practice for firms experiencing unexpected financial pressure. Whereas salary reductions mitigate financial concerns in the short run, extended salary reductions can negatively affect employee morale and loyalty. Also, while companywide salary reductions prevent layoffs, there is a clear risk that top performers will be encouraged to leave for competitors that dangle superior compensation (Gandolfi, 2008). In 2006, White Electronics Designs introduced salary reductions of 5% for salaried employees and 10% for management, while the hourly workers remained unaffected. In 2006, a collation of Intel managers agreed to take a temporary 100% pay cut to avoid permanent layoffs. Prior to that, Intel announced that it had planned to cut 10,000 employees, including 1,000 managers (Paul, 2006).

• Temporary facility shutdown

Temporary facility shutdowns occur when a work site closes for a designated period of time, while some administrative functions still perform (Vernon, 2003). A shutdown allows employees to have time off without using their vacation days. While overall company production decreases, the firm can achieve considerable costs savings, thereby avoiding layoffs. In early 2008, Aleris International shut down its rolling mill production in Virginia to align production with demand. As a consequence, production for customers was phased out and transferred to other facilities within the U.S. (Aleris, 2008).

- **Soliciting cost-reduction ideas from employees**

Employees appreciate the opportunity to make a positive impact on their workplace and environment. Firms frequently solicit cost-reduction ideas from employees, who are often creative in producing such solutions. This HR practice has proven to be most effective when employees are able to make suggestions in the early stages of cost cutting (Vernon, 2003). At Martin Heyman Associates, all professional construction consultants are encouraged to contribute cost-reduction ideas. Unfortunately, many executives still do not realize that employees are the best source of such ideas because workers on the job are in a prime position to identify and recognize waste (Yorke, 2005).

This overview has shown that there are numerous HR tools at an executive's disposal to reduce short-term expenditures. While some firms have come up with innovative ideas, others have used layoffs as a very first resort. Again, it must be understood that the techniques introduced in this stage are cumulative and applicable in other stages. Moreover, the utilization of each HR practice is unique in that each selected tool will have certain consequences that need to be carefully considered by management prior to adoption.

Second Stage: Medium-range Cost Adjustments

The second stage of the cost-reduction framework comprises medium-term cost adjustments in response to a medium-range business downturn exceeding six months (Vernon, 2003) and up to 12 months (Gandolfi, 2008). These secondary cost-reduction adjustments are frequently signaled through extended company-wide or industry-wide forecasts of diminished sales activity. If properly recognized and executed, the firm may be able to transition to mid-range cost adjustments and thus prevent long-term, RIF-related layoffs and forced downsizing. In this phase constituencies need to recognize that deeper cost-reduction strategies may be required to avert downsizing-related layoffs. Senior management must be able to present the purpose and objectives of the expenditure adjustments convincingly to the entire workforce. This should ensure employee buy-in and commitment. Adopting HR practices in this stage could potentially alter employees' work environment. Therefore, the HR department will play an essential role in the conduct and transition of these practices (Gandolfi, 2008).

Suggested HR Practices for Medium-range Cost Adjustments

A review of the literature and the popular press reveals several HR-related practices that corporations have used trying to obtain secondary cost reductions. The following is a non-exhaustive summary of practices recommended by scholars and introduced in the corporate landscape.

- **Extended salary reductions**

Extending salary reductions can be a method of choice if an economic downturn exceeds six months (Vernon, 2003). While the extension of salary reductions can negatively affect employee commitment and morale, advocates stress that employees would prefer a smaller income temporarily than a permanent loss of their jobs. As with short-term salary reductions, there is a risk that high-performing individuals are encouraged to pursue external employment opportunities (Gandolfi, 2008). Firms have generally been innovative regarding altering variable pay options. Specifically, while some firms balance the reduced salaries by distributing once-a-year payments over 12 months, others substitute stock awards for variable cash payment. For example, U.S. firm 415 Production offered an overall 5% pay cut or a four-day work week reflecting the appropriate decrease in pay to its employees (Morss, 2008).

- **Voluntary sabbaticals**

Voluntary sabbaticals, also called furloughs, allow salaried employees to take voluntary leaves for a designated period of time. Companies may offer sabbaticals with considerably reduced or no pay. Most firms continue to provide benefits during sabbaticals. Sabbaticals enable firms to reduce their medium-term expenditure and can be effective in avoiding downsizing-related layoffs (Gandolfi, 2008). While employees may feel motivated and re-energized upon their return, HR professionals point out that medium-and long-term sabbaticals may cause employees to lose their leading edge and to return with outdated skills. Interestingly, evidence suggests that firms offer generous sabbaticals during times of economic growth but refrain from this HR practice during tough financial periods (Vernon, 2003). Practical examples abound. For example, in 2001, consulting firm Accenture announced that 800 employees qualified for a special voluntary sabbatical program, while 600 employees were going to be laid off permanently (Taub, 2001). In 2001, Information and Communication Mobile, a Siemens division, offered its employees a one- year time-out at reduced pay without losing their jobs permanently (Perera, 2001). Siemens was thus able to reduce costs without losing high- performing employees during difficult economic times.

- **Employee lending**

With this HR practice, the current employer lends an employee to another employer firm for a set period of time while continuing to pay salary and providing benefits

(Vernon, 2003). The borrowing firm, which can be a competitor, in return, reimburses the lending company for part or all of the salary. While employee lending can dramatically decrease medium-range expenditure of the lending firm, some employees may not wish to work for a third party. There is also the risk that the borrowing firm decides to hire the employee permanently once the contracted period is lapsed. As a consequence, the lending firm would loose a critical knowledge base (Gandolfi, 2008). Texas Instruments engaged in lending HR staffers to vendors for up to eight months with the intention of bringing them back to their original jobs at the end of that period. The supplier reimbursed Texas Instruments for their staffers' salaries during the loan period and agreed not to offer them permanent jobs (Morss, 2008).

- **Exit incentives**

Exit incentive options give employees the option of leaving the firm and collecting severance pay or taking early retirement (Vernon, 2003). This strategy enables firms to target jobs while recognizing employees for their service and helps the firm retain the remaining employees (Gandolfi, 2008). Exit incentives can be costly and may create an entitlement mentality for the remaining workforce in the future (George, 2004). In 2007, technology-outsourcing firm EDS (Electronic Data Systems) offered extra retirement benefits to its 12,000 U.S. employees in an offer to accept early retirement (EDS, 2007).

Corporate leaders need to be innovative about reducing medium-term expenditures. As with the previous stage, some firms have demonstrated creativity and resourcefulness regarding the design and implementation of medium-range cost-reduction practices. Anecdotal evidence indicates a natural tendency for firms to resort to layoffs hastily by default without considering legitimate alternatives (Gandolfi, 2008).

Third Stage: Long-range Cost Adjustments

The third stage of the cost-reduction framework represents long-term adjustments that are necessary if a firm experiences a prolonged business downturn exceeding 12 months. This stage may be recognized through an extended decline of current and projected customer demand or extremely volatile economic conditions (Vernon, 2003). The third stage generally requires extended expenditure adjustments by the firm (Gandolfi, 2008). In this timeframe RIF, layoffs, and downsizing-related activities are frequently inevitable. The third stage has two phases (see Figure 1). Phase 1 contains workforce reduction strategies that firms commonly adopt after a prolonged business downturn. While RIF and downsizing activities should always be seen as a last resort, firms should avoid mass layoffs at all costs (Macky 2004; Gandolfi, 2007). Companies who find themselves engaged in deep workforce cuts must adopt HR practices that instill loyalty and commitment in the remaining and exiting workforces (Vernon, 2003). In contrast. Phase 2 encompasses HR activities that aim to re-attract formerly laid off individuals and hire new employees in a post-downsizing period. This presupposes that the RIF have been implemented, that the business downturn has ended and reversed, and that the firm is able and willing to re-hire.

Suggested HR Practices for Long-range Cost Adjustments

Firms forced to embrace permanent RIF and layoffs have reported mixed results. While the execution of downsizing promises immediate financial relief, considerable empirical evidence demonstrates that downsizing-related strategies do not automatically translate into improved organizational performance (Littler, 1998; Macky, 2004). Such strategies have significant secondary consequences for the firm and its stakeholders (Gandolfi, 2006). While downsizing and RIF-related layoffs should always be a strategy of absolute last resort (Gandolfi, 2007), it is clear that layoffs are at times warranted, desirable, or unavoidable. Once the firm has conducted RIF-related activities, the firm will need to re-position itself to be able to re-attract those laid off or hire new employees. Again, this presumes that the economy has bounced back sufficiently and that the firm is in a position to hire again. Some firms re-hire formerly laid off employees, whereas others opt to return to the labor market and seek out new talent. How does the firm attract previous employees? The following constitutes a brief summary of three commonly-used practices.

- **Rehiring bonuses**

While some firms provide a monetary rehiring bonus for veterans to return within a specified period, others hire laid-off employees as external consultants. In some cases, firms realize that they cut too many or the wrong employees, while in other cases management decides to hire back after the economic downturn (Vernon, 2003). Evidence suggests that employees and consultants return to the downsized firm with improved monetary rewards (Gandolfi, 2006). For instance, in 2001 and after two rounds of deep layoffs, Charles Schwab Corp. offered a $7,500 hiring bonus for any previously downsized employee rehired by the firm within 18 months following the layoffs (Morss, 2008).

- **Maintaining communication with laid-off employees**

Firms frequently make a concerted effort to maintain friendly relations with laid-off employees (Vernon, 2003). Modern-day technology, including Internet forums, 24-7 hotlines, and e-mail, provides effective ways to foster and sustain positive employer-employee relationships (Lublin, 2007). This is particularly important if firms intend to rehire the former employees when the economic climate has improved.

- **Internal job fairs**

Firms should make every possible attempt to retain high-performing employees (Gandolfi, 2008). A powerful method is an internal job fair, where firms host events to help place and redeploy downsized employees within the company. For example, the Ford Motor Company is currently putting on internal job fairs in its U.S. plants to entice employees to find new careers beyond the assembly-line (Vlasic, 2008).

Concluding Comments

This paper has presented a methodology of cost-reduction stages enabling firms to minimize, delay, or circumvent reductions-in-force, layoffs, and downsizing-related activities. The depicted conceptual framework is an extension of Vernon's (2003), George's (2004), and Gandolfi's (2008) original work on cost-reduction stages, including an expansion of the third stage incorporating two distinct phases. The research has shown that the key to responsible cost reduction and the selection of appropriate cost reduction methods can be found in the alignment of a firm's cost reduction practices with its current cost-reduction stage. The paper has further established that it is difficult for a firm to accurately forecast the duration and magnitude of a business downturn. Consequently, firms have a natural tendency to respond reactively rather than to anticipate economic declines.

References

Aleris. (2008). Aleris announces temporary shutdown of its Richmond, Virginia, rolling mill facility. Retrieved from www.prnewswire.com/cgi-bin/stories,pl? ACCT =]09&STORY=/www/story/Ü2-22-2008/00047 60651&EDATE=

Cascio. W. F.. Young. C., and Morris, J. (1997). Financial consequences of employment-change decisions in major U.S. corporations. *Academy of Management Journal, 40(5),* 1175-1189.

DeBono. N. (2008, March 18). Presstran workers vote for reduced work week. *Sun Media.* Retrieved from http://Ifpress.ca/cgi-bin/publish.cgi?p=2281OO&s=wheels

Dybis, K., and Garsten, E. (2004, March 18). Michigan firms cut overtime. *The Detroit News.* Retrieved from www.detnews.com/2004/specialreport/0403/18/a0196041.htm

EDS. (2007, September 13). EDS offers exit incentives lo 12,000 workers. *The New York Times.* Retrieved from www.nytimes.com/2007/09/13/technology/13data.html?partner=rssnyt&emc=rss

Gandolfi, F. (2006). *Corporate downsizing demystified: A scholarly analysis of a business phenomenon,* Hyderabad. India: ICFAI University Press.

Gandolfi, F. (2007). How do large Australian and Swiss banks implement downsizing? *Journal of Management & Organization, 13*(2), 145–159.

Gandolfi, F. (2008, July/August). HR strategies that can take the sting out of downsizing-related layoffs. *Ivey Business Journal.*

George, J. (2004). Cutting costs: should personnel be the first to go? *Employment Practices Solution.* Retrieved from www.epexperts.com/modules.php?op=modload&name=News&file=article&sid=1409

Govreau, J. (2008, March 14). Chrysler announces mandatory two-week shutdown of all plans in July 2008. *Market Watch from Dow Jones.* Retrieved from www.marketwatch.com/news/story/chrysler-announces-mandatory-two-week-shutdown/siory.aspx?guid=%7BD7228E3E-9177-4EC7-A0EB-3946EAA50A66%7D

Littler, C.R. (1998). Downsizing organisations: The dilemmas of change. *Human Resources Management Bulletin.* CCH Australia Limited, Sydney.

Lublin, J. (2007, September 24). Employers see value in helping those laid off. *The Watt Street Journal Online.* Retrieved from http://online.wsj.com/public/article/SB119058596757936693.html

Macky, K. (2004). Organizational downsizing and redundancies: The New Zealand workers' experience. *New Zealand Journal of Employment Relations, 29*(1), 63-87,

Maxon, T. (2008, April 4). American Airlines imposes hiring freeze on management and support staff. *The Dallas Morning News.* Retrieved from www.dallasnews.com/shared content/dws/bus/stories/040508dnbusaafreeze. 368d67e.html

Mendels, P. (2001, April 18). Downsizing pay, not people. *BusinessWeek.* Retrieved from www.businessweek.com/careers/content/apr2001/ca20010418_060,htm

Mirabal, N., and De Young, R. (2005). Downsizing as a strategic intervention. *Journal of American Academy of Business, 6(1).* 39—5.

Morss, R. (2008). Creative layoff policy and alternatives to layoffs, *Salary.com.* Retrieved from www.salary.com/personal/layoutscripts/psnl_articles.asp?tab=psn&cat=cat011&ser=ser032&part=par276

Paul. (2006), 100 % pay reduction for all Intel employees. Retrieved from www.starkedsf.com/archives/100-pay-reduction-for-all-intel-employees-a-tnt-special-report/

Perera, R. (2001, August 31). Siemens offers workers 'time outs ' to save cash. *IDG News Service.* Retrieved from www.thestandard.com/article/0,1902,28858.00.html

Taub, P. (2001, June 7). Accenture to cut 600 jobs, *CFO.com.* Retrieved from www.cfo.com/article.cfm/2996624?f=search

Vernon, L. (2003, March). The downsizing dilemma; a manager's toolkit for avoiding layoffs. *Society for Human Resources Management (SHRM),* White Paper.

Vlasic, B. (2008. February 26), Ford is pushing buyouts to workers. *The New York Times*. Retrieved from www.nytimes.com/2008/02/26/business/26ford.html?_r=1&oref=slogin

Yorke, C. (2005). Why employees are the best source of cost-cutting ideas. Ezine Articles. Retrieved from http://ezinearticles.com/?Why-Employees-Are-the-Best-Source-of-Cost-cutting-Ideas&id=66695

Critical Thinking

1. As an employee, what is your opinion of reduced salaries, voluntary sabbaticals or furloughs, or reduced workweek to help avoid layoffs?

2. As an employer, what must you do to maintain satisfactory morale in the face of solutions such as those listed in this article?

3. Is implementing solutions such as these ethically preferable to layoffs even when they affect all employees instead of just a percentage of employees?

DR. GANDOLFI, currently director of the MBA/EMBA programs at Regent University, specializes in human resource management and change management and regularly advises corporations in Australia and Switzerland. His published books include *Corporate Downsizing Demystified: A Scholarly Analysis of a Business Phenomenon.*

People Have to Come Before Profits, Even in a Crisis

The Fukushima Daiichi power plant disaster has become a textbook example of what not to do in an emergency.

ALISTAIR NICHOLAS

After a gigantic earthquake and a devastating tsunami, Japan now has a nuclear crisis which is becoming a case study in bad crisis management. The Fukushima Daiichi nuclear power plant disaster may overshadow the 1984 Union Carbide Bhopal chemical leak, the 1989 Exxon Valdez oil spill or last year's BP oil spill in the Gulf of Mexico as a textbook example of what not to do.

This is not just Japan's problem. A cloud now hangs over the future of nuclear power throughout the "Pacific Ring of Fire" earthquake zone as locals stage traditional and online protests against nuclear energy.

A few organizations will need to adopt new ways of operating after this situation is brought under control. The regulatory authority responsible for nuclear power plants in Japan needs to reassess how to build plants in an earthquake zone. (It appears that the design and location of the Fukushima Daiichi plant was just plain wrong.)

The Tokyo Electric Power Company (TEPCO), which runs the plant, and the Japanese government need to change the way they release critical information in a crisis. (The New York Times has documented the failure of communications.) The flow of information has been slow and vague. In the West we'd describe it as stonewalling. Possibly for the first time in Japanese history, people started seriously questioning those in positions of authority. They felt they had a right to get accurate and truthful updates in a timely manner and that it was not forthcoming.

Japanese authorities also need to assess how they make decisions in a crisis. It appears that much of the decision-making, at least at first, placed a higher value on profit than it did on human life. For example, the Wall Street Journal claims that TEPCO delayed using sea water to cool the reactors because it was concerned about the damage salt water would do to its assets. At least 80 people's lives (those working in the plant at the time of the accident) are at risk because of this decision, plus others involved in the response later on.

This points to a bigger problem in crisis management, worldwide and not just in Japan: lack of training in ethical decision-making in emergencies. Crisis-preparedness training normally focuses on technical details of how to fix problems and how to communicate with the media.

But executives are poorly prepared for making ethical decisions under pressure. When lives are at stake—particularly as they are in a potential nuclear meltdown—you can't stage an escalated response. You must have an ethical response. You should be throwing everything you have at the situation from the beginning.

Japan is not facing a Chernobyl-style full meltdown. All the reactors at Fukushima have been successfully shut down and the focus has been on cooling the plant. The worst case scenario for Fukushima Daiichi is probably the Three Mile Island nuclear accident of 1979. This may mean a contaminated area of 30 kilometres around the plant. This is not great news—but it is not bad for a serious nuclear accident.

Could the outcome have been better? Possibly—if sea water had been used at the outset of the crisis. But we'll have to wait for the final report following the inevitable investigation.

What does this mean for the future of nuclear energy, especially in earthquake-prone regions? China, which is part of the Pacific Rim of Fire and has experienced its own devastating earthquakes (Tangshan in 1976 and Sichuan in 2008), plans to build a staggering 40 new nuclear power plants by 2015. Since the incident in Japan Beijing has halted approvals for these pending an investigation into its own safety standards. But the plants will almost certainly proceed. Asia and the rest of the world need energy to sustain economic growth and development. Nuclear power is the best source because, accidents like this notwithstanding, it is much cleaner than oil and coal which contribute substantially to global warming.

Abandoning nuclear energy would be like refusing to cross roads because you might be run over. If you know the risks you can manage them. The nuclear energy industry now has a better understanding of the risks as a result of this unfortunate accident. (Here's a stock tip: buy uranium mining and nuclear energy shares now. While prices have fallen close to 30 percent since the tsunami, they will surely rise again. The future is in nuclear energy.)

Lessons will be learned about the design and location of power plants. To start with, they won't be placed too close to the coast or major rivers. It wasn't the earthquake itself that created the problems, but the flooding from the tsunami.

Lessons also will be learned about communications during an Asian crisis. The basic principles are: communicate often; communicate clearly; communicate truthfully; and communicate transparently. This may be more difficult in Japan. Japanese, like Chinese, is not a direct language; it is much more nuanced and intuitive than European languages. (At one point a Japanese official dealing with the crisis apologized publicly for causing "bother". In the context of normal Japanese interaction this might have made sense; in a nuclear crisis it seemed out of touch with reality.) Japan's agony may teach other Asian nations how to convey information quickly and accurately.

As I tell my clients in crisis situations: stop talking and start communicating. What the public expects—and has a right to expect—is the truth. But the most important lesson of the last ten days should be to incorporate training on ethical decision making into crisis preparedness training. People must come before profits—always and unconditionally.

Critical Thinking

1. Why does it allegedly appear that the Tokyo Electric Power Company (TEPCO) placed a higher value on profit than on human life in the early period after the Fukushima Daiichi nuclear power plant disaster?

2. How might training in ethical decision making as part of crisis preparedness training ensure that people come before profits?

ALISTAIR NICHOLAS is Executive Vice President, Asia Pacific, with public relations firm Weber Shandwick and its public affairs arm Powell Tate. He is also a member of the Advisory Board of the China Global Risk Council. The views expressed herein are entirely those of the author and do not necessarily reflect those of his employers or their clients, or of any other organizations with which he is associated. Alistair Nicholas has represented nuclear energy companies and companies involved in the nuclear energy supply chain. He blogs about China, reputation management, and everything else at Off The Record.

Deep Throat's Lessons for Whistle-Blowers

Plenty of folks have taken Mark Felt's lonely path since Watergate days. Here's a look at what it takes to successfully reveal wrongdoing.

PATRICIA O'CONNELL

Becoming a whistle-blower is one of the loneliest and most difficult choices one can make in life. Those who come clean on the wrongdoing they witness in the corporate suite or in government risk immediate ostracism. They open themselves up to counterattacks, loss of livelihood, and sometimes long, costly litigation, just for the act of speaking out against a perceived injustice or crime. And even when their disclosures are revealed to be true, they often have a difficult time finding work again, as potential employers fear they can't be trusted. All of which makes the spate of splashy whistle-blowing cases in recent years remarkable indeed. Former Big Tobacco exec Jeffrey Wigand spilled the beans about what the industry knew and when, rousing the ire of cigarette giants. (His story was so dramatic, Hollywood made a movie, *The Insider,* about it.)

Sherron Watkins famously—and futilely—warned former Enron CEO and Chairman Ken Lay about the energy giant's financial house of cards. Watkins, persona non grata at Enron after writing her memo, left several months later. Since then, she has co-authored a book, *Power Failure,* and does consulting and gives lectures.

Now Out of Sight

FBI agent Coleen Rowley wrote about intelligence failures leading to 9/11—now she's mulling a run for Congress. Army Private Joseph M. Darby stepped forward after seeing the now-notorious pictures of Iraqi prisoners being abused in Abu Ghraib. He was recently given the Kennedy Library Foundation's Profile in Courage Award by Caroline Kennedy for "upholding the rule of law that we embrace as a nation." But he and his family have largely dropped out of sight.

It was a still-anonymous tipster who informed New York Attorney General Eliot Spitzer about insurance kickbacks, setting off a chain of events that left the industry reeling—and former AIG (AIG) CEO Maurice R. Greenberg, an icon of the business, in disgrace. What fate awaits the tipster when his or her identity is revealed?

Yet, when it comes to whistle-blowing, none of them comes close to Mark Felt, aka Deep Throat, the recently revealed source who helped *Washington Post* reporters Bob Woodward and Carl Bernstein unravel the Presidential scandal Watergate—and the Presidency of Richard Nixon.

Hero or Traitor?

Whistle-blowing is a funny thing: For every person who thinks it's noble, someone else thinks such a break in ranks is the ultimate disloyalty. Indeed, look at the reaction to the revelation about Felt. Some praise him as a hero. Others—most vociferously and not suprisingly, former members of the Nixon Administration—are now calling him a traitor.

Patrick Buchanan, a former Nixon speechwriter, was quoted in *The New York Times* on June 2 as saying, "I think Deep Throat is a dishonorable man. I think Mark behaved treacherously. I'm unable to see the nobility of the enterprise, sneaking around in garages, moving pots around, handing over material he got in the course of the investigation."

With the "final secret"—in the words of former *Washington Post* editor Ben Bradlee—now broken, it's worth looking back at the granddaddy of all whistle-blowers and see what lessons can be learned:

Follow the Money

That was the advice Deep Throat gave Bernstein and Woodward, and the money trail was one of the things that led them to the White House. In corporate scandals, it's usually all about money, and often the cash leads to the very top as well—with a few stops along the way, at various high-ranking executives' offices. In her memo to Enron's Lay, Watkins raised pointed questions about aggressive accounting. She was following the money.

Cover Your Tracks

According to Woodward, Felt was adamant about not talking on the phone, and he insisted on meeting in underground garages, communicating through an elaborate series of signals that involved moving a flower pot and flag on Woodward's apartment balcony, and a hand-drawn clock in Woodward's copy of *The New York Times*. And according to Woodward and Bernstein, Felt was careful in what he said to them, mindful not to break the law.

Clearly, such subterfuge helped keep Felt's identity secret—and his job at the FBI—safe, which presumably kept him in the loop and enabled him to be a long-term asset to the investigation. And Felt was smart, but he was also very lucky that his identity wasn't revealed sooner. Just witness the fury now aimed at a 91-year-old man in frail health.

Better Yet, Don't Leave Any Tracks

It's interesting to wonder how Felt, a old-fashioned G-man right down to his wool-checkered blazers and fedora, might have inadvertently spilled the beans in this age of e-mail, security cameras, and corporate computer networks. It's hard enough not to leave a paper trail, much less a digital trail. On the bright side, it's also harder for the bad guys to cover their tracks these days. Spitzer, for one, has shown how modern prosecutors can make amazingly strong cases out of e-mail trails.

One Person Can Make a Difference

It's tempting to be cynical and think an individual can't take on a corporation like Enron or an institution like the military or the White House. Watkins' warning was for naught—at least in terms of preventing a problem. But her actions and information were critical in helping to shed light afterward on the mess at Enron, which in part centered on such specious accounting schemes and vehicles as Raptor and Condor.

But One Person Isn't Enough

To be effective, a whistle-blower has to find the right conduit. And chances are good it might not be someone the whistle-blower trusts in the next cubicle or in the office down the hall. For all the criticism leveled at Felt for not following "procedure" and not bringing his concerns to his superiors at the FBI or the Justice Dept., it's hard to imagine that going to FBI Director L. Patrick Gray—Nixon's hand-picked choice for the job—about illegality at the White House really would have been a great idea.

Make Sure Your Confidant Is Trustworthy

No doubt *The Washington Post* was deeply chagrined at having been scooped by *Vanity Fair* on the story it's famous for. Yet Woodward—who still works for the *Post*—and Bernstein

were right to honor the pledge they made to keep Felt's identity a secret until his death or his releasing them from their promise. Kudos also to former editor Bradlee, the only other person privy at the time to Deep Throat's identity. Laws protecting whistle-blowers are imperfect at best. If someone goes to the press, they should feel safe doing so.

"All That Is Necessary for the Triumph of Evil Is That Good Men Do Nothing"

So wrote 18th century Irish philosopher and politician Edmund Burke. O.K., so he excluded "women" from that phrase, but considering when he lived, he can be forgiven. However, include both genders, and his wisdom shines brightly still.

When good men and women do something true and right, evil is sometimes vanquished. That's the highest ideal that a whistle-blower can aspire to, even if others may question his or her motives. Critics think Felt's motives were less than pure. He never hid his disdain for Nixon and his minions, whom he regarded as "Nazis," Woodward revealed in the *Post*'s June 2 editions. Felt was also passed over for the FBI director's job twice. But he did what he thought was right.

Perhaps Woodward and Bernstein would have untangled the gnarly mess of Watergate without Felt's help. Maybe someone else would have come forward to reveal the prisoner abuse at Abu Ghraib if Darby hadn't. Rowley wasn't the only person in the FBI, let alone elsewhere, to point out the intelligence failures surrounding 9/11. Had Wigand lost heart, another exec might have told the truth about the tobacco industry. But as any historian will tell you, such speculation—while fun—ultimately leads to a futile dead end. We'll never know. What's important is what did happen. Felt, and many whistle-blowers after him, made a difference. But first, they made a choice.

Critical Thinking

1. What is whistle-blowing?
2. Is whistle-blowing a noble thing to do or is it an act of disloyalty?
3. What is the highest ideal to which a whistle-blower aspires?
4. What are the lessons for whistle-blowers identified in the article?
5. Which lesson do you believe is the most important lesson? Why?

Whistleblowers: Why You Should Heed Their Warnings

The media loves them, but most businesses treat them as loudmouth malcontents. They do so at their own peril.

JACK AND SUZY WELCH

"Ignore him. He's a wack job."

"She's just bitter she didn't get promoted."

"He's been shooting his mouth off for years—and it's always nothing."

Those lines sound familiar? If you work in business, they probably do—it's how people talk about whistleblowers. Whistleblowers may have a noble reputation in the media, but when they surface within a company, management almost always brushes them off with a discrediting back story or a little piece of history that explains away all their annoying accusations. And here's why that happens: In the vast majority of cases whistleblowers are, to some degree, crazy or vengeful or both. Until one terrible, awful day when, speaking out of vengefulness or ethical earnestness, the whistleblower also happens to be telling the truth. And then, well, you get a crisis like the one Wal-Mart finds itself tangled in today.

Make no mistake. We think Wal-Mart (WMT), which was accused of bribing Mexican officials, is a great company. It has created upward mobility for thousands of people and 1 million—plus jobs around the world, and it remains the American consumer's greatest ally in the war against inflation. Furthermore, the recent accusations against Wal-Mart are just that—accusations. But those allegations, proven true or not, offer an important lesson to everyone in business, and we don't mean the one that's being widely bandied about right now—that big companies like Wal-Mart, because of their size and power, engage in corruption because they can. We don't think that's generally true. Nor do we think the biggest takeaway from the Wal-Mart story is how hard it is for American companies to do business abroad without bribery. It's perfectly possible to operate globally—and win—while playing by good old American rules and regulations.

More: Wal-Mart's 6 biggest blunders

No, to us the Wal-Mart story is most importantly a reminder of the pervasive, even understandable, impulse within companies to ignore whistleblowers because they're so often time wasters. And it's a reminder of why you can't turn your back on them. Ever. In fact, the only way to deal with a whistleblower's accusations—again, every single time and often against your own instincts—is with a hyperbias toward believing that the informant is onto something big. Such a bias must impel you to investigate every claim ferociously. You may think it's a waste of time and money, and will go nowhere; you should be so lucky. And for goodness' sake, don't let the investigation be conducted by the boss who's been accused of wrongdoing! Bring in an outside agency to do the sleuthing, or at the very least executives outside the scope of the alleged problem, with no relationship to the people involved. Yes, you may hate the whole meshugaas and so might everyone it touches. But it's the only way to overcompensate for the propensity to wish whistleblowers away with the perfunctory spot check or the "Everything okay?" kind of look-see that usually occurs.

In the months ahead Wal-Mart (No. 2 on the Fortune 500) will very likely experience the steps that characterize virtually every organizational crisis. First, the company will quickly come to see that its problem is actually much worse than it originally appeared. That's the nature of these kinds of things. Wal-Mart will also find that there are no secrets in this world. Every last detail of the Mexico situation—and of the corporate coverup, if there was one—will seep out. Third, Wal-Mart's handling of the crisis will be depicted in the press in the worst possible light. Being vilified goes with the territory. Finally, there will be "changes." That is, someone will be fired.

It's too bad this crisis had to happen in the first place. And it wouldn't have, if Wal-Mart had done a very hard, very necessary thing: taken every whistleblower at his word.

This story is from the June 11, 2012 issue of Fortune.

Critical Thinking

1. Why do you think it is that whistleblowers are easily ignored?

2. What might management do in terms of policies and procedures to ensure that whistleblowers are heard rather than ignored?

3. What do you think of the advice to take every whistleblower at his word? What are the upsides and/or downsides to this advice?

Welch, Jack and Suzy. From *Fortune*, June 11, 2012. Copyright © 2012 by Fortune Magazine. Reprinted by permission of Time, Inc. via Pars International Corp.

The Unexpected Cost of Staying Silent

Not blowing the whistle may seem like the easy way out, but those who choose silence pay a price.

AMY FREDIN

66 . . . and another massive fraud was just uncovered today thanks to a whistleblower who came forward with critical information . . ." We've all heard these reports on the news and read about them in the newspapers, but this type of activity wouldn't happen in *my* organization, right? And even if it did, certainly *my* employees would quickly take corrective action, right? Let's take a look at the current landscape for organizational wrongdoing, including fraud, as well as the prevalence of whistleblowing in response to these activities. The findings alone may be surprising.

To bring these topics a little closer to home, additional analysis outlines the situations of wrongdoing some of our fellow IMA members encountered. Many individuals in the survey did blow the whistle in these wrongdoing cases, but others chose not to report the situations. This article looks further at their reasons for staying silent and their subsequent feelings of regret associated with that decision.

What Do the Surveys Say?

PricewaterhouseCoopers (PwC) has conducted several global studies of economic crime over the past decade. Most recently, its 2011 study reports data from nearly 4,000 companies worldwide, including 156 from the United States. (See www.pwc .com/gx/en/economiccrime-survey/index.jhtml for PwC's 2011, 2009, and 2007 Global Economic Crime Surveys.)

Data from the 2011 study indicates that 34% of all companies (45% of U.S. companies) reported having uncovered a significant economic crime during the previous 12-month period. The term "significant" means the crime had a definite impact on the business, either from direct, tangible damage or from collateral or psychological damage. These crimes occurred in companies of all sizes and industries. The noted wrongdoings included such instances as cybercrime, bribery and corruption, accounting fraud, and, most frequently, asset misappropriation.

Just two years earlier, more than 3,000 companies worldwide (71 U.S. companies) responded to PwC's 2009 survey where 30% of companies (35% of U.S. companies) reported experiencing a significant economic crime over the previous 12-month period. Considering both of these recent surveys, the prevalence of these crimes is disturbing, to say the least. The loss amounts are staggering as well. In 2011 (and 2009), 54% (44%) of U.S. companies estimated their fraud losses to be between $100,000 and $5 million, with another 10% (8%) reporting that their losses amounted to more than $5 million.

PwC also identified detection sources for these crimes. In 2009, 34% of the incidences worldwide were initially found because of internal or external "tips," but the largest source of detection during that time frame came from companies' own internal controls, which accounted for 46%. In 2011, the global survey reported similar rankings but an even larger disparity between these two detection methods, with only 23% of frauds being detected by "tips," while 50% were detected from a variety of internal control procedures. Kalaithasan Kuppusamy and David Yong Gun Fie reported similar rankings in their October 2004 article, "Developing Whistleblowing Policies: An Aid to Internal Auditors," in *Accountants Today.* They reported global survey results where auditors ranked first and whistleblowers ranked second in terms of detection sources for economic crime.

Though detail for U.S. detection sources in 2011 wasn't reported, the sources of detection in the U.S. in 2009 looked very different from the global results. "The single most common way that fraud was detected among U.S. survey respondents was through tip-offs," the report notes, where whistleblowers alerted officials to 48% of the crimes; internal controls initially detected 28% of the crimes during this time period.

With the prevalence of crime and the importance of whistleblowing well-documented, it might lead you to believe that more and more individuals are coming forward to report organizational wrongdoing. But what percentage of individuals who either know about or suspect wrongdoing come forward?

Going back to 1992, a U.S. federal government survey of its own employees reported that as many as 50% of individuals who were aware of a crime chose to remain silent.

A slightly later study, "Whistle-Blower Disclosures and Management Retaliation" by Joyce Rothschild and Terance Miethe, published in the February 1999 issue of *Work and Occupations,* reported a similar level of nonreporting, but does that level still apply today? As we head into a new era where whistleblowers have the potential to be rewarded financially for their information because of the recently instituted Dodd-Frank Wall Street Reform and Consumer Protection Act, it seems appropriate to take an even more current look at the landscape around those who observe organizational wrongdoing.

The IMA Study

In an effort to understand this issue from an insider's perspective, I surveyed attendees at IMA's Annual Conference & Exposition in 2007. Attendees could complete an anonymous survey, which included questions predominantly related to whistleblowing and internal controls, in exchange for a chance to win one of 10 $50 cash prizes. Of the 75 individuals who completed the survey, 45 reported having observed wrongdoing within their organizations, and 27 of these 45 individuals stated that they reported this information to the appropriate authorized party, suggesting a 60% report rate.

The 60% rate suggests we may be making strides in encouraging whistleblowers to come forward. Yet five of the 27 individuals who blew the whistle on one situation admitted to staying silent on at least one other. The remaining 18 of the 45 individuals who had observed one or more incidences of wrongdoing didn't report any of them. If this last group of 18 nonreporters is analyzed on its own, it suggests that the nonreporter rate is 40%. But if the five individuals who both reported and stayed silent on different issues are allowed to be included in both groups, then the nonreporter rate goes up to 51% (23 out of 45). At this level, we're back to where we started-the 50% range of reporting and nonreporting that previous studies have documented.

In order to better understand the situations behind these reports (and nonreports), the survey asked respondents to describe incidence(s) of wrongdoing that they observed. Table 1

Table 1   Instances of Reported Wrongdoing

Type of Activity Observed	No. of Reports	Examples Noted
Theft of Company Property/Cash	2	Theft of company computer Mishandling of petty cash
Unauthorized/Inappropriate Use of Company Assets	5	Unauthorized use of company vehicle Misappropriation of funds Inappropriate use of grant money Purchase misuse Irrelevant advertising expenditures that weren't approved
Financial Statement Manipulation	5	Misstated product line P&L Aggressive estimates affecting income Income statement misrepresentation Financial statement misstatements Overstatement of inventory value
Claiming Personal Expenses for Reimbursement	4	Airfare for spouse purchased with company credit card Inappropriate personal spending on company credit card Improper expense submission Questionable expense receipts/charges
Sexual Harassment	2	Sexual harassment of a coworker Sexual harassment
Inappropriate Human Resources/Payroll Practices	4	Fraud in the selection process Hiring spouse of executive Back pay being withheld inappropriately Inappropriate untaxed bonuses
Other	5	Kickbacks Overbilling client Employee using counterfeit money in vending machine Inappropriate use of cash-basis accounting Violation of corporate risk management policy
TOTAL	27	

outlines the situations on which individuals blew the whistle. These reported wrongdoing activities varied greatly from mishandling petty cash to misrepresenting the company's income statement to sexual harassment.

Table 2 describes the other situations-the ones on which individuals remained silent. These unreported situations of wrongdoing also varied greatly-from an employee stealing company supplies to manipulating revenues and expenses to claiming personal expenses for reimbursement. When comparing the situations in Tables 1 and 2, the uncanny crossovers are hard to dismiss. The situations described in both tables are very similar, suggesting that it isn't just the event's nature or the significance that drives an individual to report-or not report-wrongdoing.

Table 3 provides a closer look at the survey respondents to see if there are any key demographic differences between those who reported wrongdoing and those who didn't. This information is provided for the entire group of survey respondents along with comparison detail for the two different reporter groups (reporters-the 27 who reported at least one situation of wrongdoing; nonreporters-the 23 who stayed silent on at least one instance of wrongdoing). There doesn't appear to be much difference in the ages and length of time at current companies of those who blew the whistle as opposed to those who stayed silent. The average age across the board was approximately 47, and average time with their current company was also quite steady at approximately eight or nine years.

But there are some gender differences between the groups. Though 55% of the entire sample was male, only 48% of those blowing the whistle were male. Further, of the individuals who remained silent, 70% were male. A meta-analysis by Jessica Mesmer-Magnus and Chockalingam Viswesvaran, "Whistle-blowing in Organizations: An Examination of Correlates of Whistleblowing Intentions, Actions, and Retliation," in the Spring 2005 issue of the *Journal of Business Ethics,* looked

Table 2 Instances of Unreported Wrongdoing . . . and Regret Associated with Staying Silent

Type of Activity Observed	No. of Similar Reports	Examples Notes	Level of Regret Experienced*
Theft of Company Property/Cash	2	Employee stealing supplies from the company	no regret
		Unauthorized purchases; incorrect recording of cash	some regret
Inappropriate Use of Company Assets	1	Accessing pornography on work computer	little regret
Financial Statement Manipulation	5	Inappropriate month-end adjustments	great regret
		Accounting estimate adjustments for bad debt	no regret
		Manipulating revenue and expenses	some regret
		Earnings manipulation	some regret
		Income smoothing using accrual manipulation	little regret
Claiming Personal Expenses for Reimbursement	4	Personal travel of children	great regret
		Misclassifying expense reports	little regret
		Personal assets purchased by company	no regret
		Personal expenses purchased on corporate card	little regret
Sexual Harassment	1	Sexist comments	little regret
Inappropriate HR/Payroll Practices	3	Inappropriate time-sheet reporting	little regret
		Profit-sharing calculations unverifiable	little regret
		Reporting payments to employees as travel vs. wages to avoid payroll taxes	little regret
Other	7	Collusion within upper management; sharing inside information	great regret
		Executive cover-up	some regret
		Violation of federal manufacturing law	great regret
		Fraudulent information reported on tax returns	little regret
		Controller cover-up on missing equipment	great regret
		Noncompetitive supplier selected	no regret
		Sabotage of a new process change	great regret
TOTAL	23		

* Subjects were asked if they were currently experiencing (or had in the past experienced) any regret associated with their decision to stay silent. They were asked to respond in one of the following ways: no regret, little regret, some regret, great regret.

Table 3 Survey Respondents

	All		Reporters		Nonreporters	
Age (in years)						
Mean	47.5		46.7		49.1	
Range	27 to 71		29 to 67		30 to 71	
Tenure with Organization (in years)						
Mean	8.6		9		8.3	
Range	0.25 to 31		2 to 20		0.75 to 30	
	N	Percentage	N	Percentage	N	Percentage
Gender						
Male	41	55 percent	13	48 percent	16	70 percent
Female	33	44 percent	14	52 percent	7	30 percent
Missing Data	1	1 percent	0		0	
Total	**75**		**27**		**23**	
Industry Membership						
Manufacturing	27	36 percent	10	37 percent	7	30 percent
Professional Services	17	23 percent	7	26 percent	6	26 percent
Education	7	9 percent	2	7 percent	5	22 percent
Government	5	7 percent	1	4 percent	1	4 percent
Pharmaceuticals/Healthcare	4	5 percent	1	4 percent	0	0 percent
Other/Missing	15	20 percent	6	22 percent	4	17 percent
Total	**75**		**27**		**23**	
# of Employees in Company						
Less than 100	20	27 percent	11	41 percent	6	26 percent
101 to 500	19	25 percent	5	19 percent	6	26 percent
501 to 2,000	10	13 percent	5	19 percent	5	22 percent
2,001 to 10,000	11	15 percent	1	4 percent	3	13 percent
More than 10,000	13	17 percent	4	15 percent	3	13 percent
Missing	2	3 percent	1	4 percent	0	0 percent
Total	**75**		**27**		**23**	
Certifications Held						
CMA (w/o CPA)	22	29 percent	8	30 percent	7	30 percent
CPA (w/o CMA)	16	21 percent	6	22 percent	3	13 percent
CMA & CPA	20	27 percent	8	30 percent	5	22 percent
Others (no CMA or CPA)	3	4 percent	1	4 percent	1	4 percent
None/Missing	14	19 percent	4	15 percent	7	30 percent
Total	**75**		**27**		**23**	
Highest Degree Completed						
Associate's	1	1 percent	1	4 percent	1	4 percent
Bachelor's	29	39 percent	10	37 percent	7	30 percent
Master's	41	55 percent	16	59 percent	14	61 percent
Doctorate	3	4 percent	0	0 percent	1	4 percent
Missing	1	1 percent	0	0 percent	0	0 percent
Total	**75**		**27**		**23**	

at four specific studies on actual whistleblowers and noted a similar gender difference across those studies: Women blew the whistle more often than men did.

In addition to a gender difference in my study's respondents, the remainder of the data shows that these individuals come from businesses of all types and sizes and that the whistleblowing reports are spread fairly evenly among all such companies. Further, both the reporter and nonreporter groups appear to be composed of similar individuals in regard to their certifications held and degrees completed: The vast majority are either a CMA® (Certified Management Accountant) or CPA (Certified Public Accountant) or both, and the majority in both groups also have a master's degree. In other words, even these highly educated individuals with valued credentials and experience find it difficult to deal with wrongdoing in the workplace.

... the most common reason for not blowing the whistle was fear of retaliation in one form or another . . .

Although this detail portrays the background information of all respondents as well as the wrongdoing situations that they observed, the survey asked more probing questions of the silent observers. Since the rate of whistleblowing has remained constant at around 50% for at least the past 18 years, there must be something more that we can learn from these nonreporters-something that can help us "break through" to future observers that may give them the courage to come forward with their information.

One such survey question asked these individuals to explain why they chose to remain silent. Table 4 reports the reasons they gave. Not surprisingly, the most common reason for not blowing the whistle was fear of retaliation in one form or another, including job loss and difficult working conditions. Others noted reasons such as the wrongdoing wasn't serious enough to worry about; they didn't feel they had enough proof to bring the allegation forward; and/or they felt somebody else would report the situation. Two individuals further noted that they voluntarily left the company because of what was going on.

Regret from Not Blowing the Whistle

But what have these individuals experienced since their decision to remain silent? Did they avoid the retaliation they were hoping to avoid, or were there other negative consequences associated with staying silent, too? One question asked these silent observers whether they were currently experiencing (or had in the past) any regret associated with their decision to remain silent. This data speaks for itself. Presented alongside the unreported situations in the last column of Table 2, the vast majority of silent observers, 19 of the 23 individuals who chose

Table 4   Reasons for Not Reporting the Wrongdoing

Reason Given	Number of Similar Reports
Fear of job loss and/or other retaliation	10
Not that big of a deal	4
Didn't have enough proof	3
Thought somebody else would report it	2
Chose to leave the company instead	2
Other	5
Total*	**26**

* Three individuals each gave two reasons for staying silent, thus the total adds up to 23 + 3 = 26.

not to report the wrongdoings, acknowledge having experienced at least some regret (rated as either little, some, or great) associated with their decision to remain silent.

It further appears that these individuals have experienced regret-to varying degrees-for many different types of wrongdoing situations. Not only did some experience regret for the "bigger" issues, such as "fixing" the numbers or theft of property, but individuals also experienced regret for letting "smaller" issues go unreported, including such things as bypassing proper procedures in order to justify a purchase or letting some personal expenses count for reimbursement.

Tone at the Top

It's clear that there's no easy way to deal with wrongdoing in the workplace. Once an individual becomes aware of illegal and/or unethical activity, there are ramifications for reporting and not reporting it. Unfortunately, organizational wrongdoing occurs in companies of all sizes and in all industries. Further, given that many businesses today find themselves in fragile financial positions with lower-than-desired headcounts, there are fewer resources to allocate toward enhanced internal controls and ethics training.

But there's still something companies can do, at relatively no cost to them, to combat and prevent fraud and wrongdoing. Businesses can espouse an ethical culture, one that truly is motivated from the top tiers of the organizational chart, to show their employees that they mean business. The importance of a company's "tone at the top" certainly it isn't a new phenomenon (see "Tone at the Top: Insights from Section 404" by Dana Hermanson, Daniel Ivancevich, and Susan Ivancevich in the November 2008 *Strategic Finance*). And this is getting even more pronounced attention as a fraud prevention factor in today's fast-paced, risk-laden marketplace. PwC captured this message loud and clear when it concluded its 2011 global economic crime survey with the following statement: "Establishing the right 'tone at the top' is key in the fight against economic crime."

No Easy Way Out

The data in this article suggests that the level of whistleblowing has stayed relatively constant over the past two decades at around 50% and gives reasons as to why the remaining 50% chose to remain silent on these issues. Yet through this analysis it becomes clear that these silent observers don't come out unscathed because they have to live with their decision, knowing that some individuals are benefitting at the expense of others. They have to live with their regret-knowing that their silence may be perpetuating fraud, harassment, law violations, and the like, within that company. The stress associated with this regret may be a cost that they didn't anticipate, but it's a cost nonetheless. Perhaps the potential for financial rewards will now give some of these otherwise silent observers enough incentive to come forward with their information. And perhaps these and other reward opportunities will eventually give all whistleblowers the compensation they desire and deserve to help offset the personal costs that come with whistleblowing.

Once an individual becomes aware of illegal and/or unethical activity, there are ramifications for reporting and not reporting it.

One thing is certain, though. We can all learn something from the survey respondents. Blowing the whistle on organizational wrongdoing isn't an easy thing to do, but staying silent on these issues may not be an easy way out, either.

Critical Thinking

1. Comment on the methodology used in the IMA Study reported in the article. Are the results of the study generalizable given its methodology? Why or why not?

2. Examine Table 4 in the article. Of the reasons given for not reporting wrongdoing (i.e., not blowing the whistle), which of the reasons do you find most compelling? Why? Which the least compelling? Why?

3. Examine Table 2 in the article. What might be the reasons for a finding of great regret versus a finding of no regret? Make a list of possible reasons for feeling or not feeling of regret for use in class discussion.

4. Examine Table 1 – Instance of Reported Wrongdoing. Develop a table or a chart in which you analyze the seriousness of the reported wrongdoing. Then, relate your analysis of Table 1 to the results reported in Table 2. What conclusion might you draw from Table 1 and Table 2?

AMY FREDIN, PhD, is an assistant professor of accounting at St. Cloud State University in St. Cloud, Minn. She also is a member of IMA's Central Minnesota Chapter. You can reach her at (320) 308-3287 or ajfredin@stcloudstate.edu.

SEC Rule Will Let Whistle-Blowers Bypass Internal Programs

JESSE HAMILTON

The U.S. Securities and Exchange Commission will let corporate whistle-blowers collect as much as 30 percent of penalties when they report financial wrongdoing, even when they bypass companies' internal complaint systems.

SEC commissioners voted 3-2 today in Washington to establish a whistle-blower program to "reward individuals who provide the agency with high-quality tips that lead to successful enforcement actions." The program, part of the SEC's rulemaking under the Dodd-Frank Act, expands a bounty system that was previously limited to insider-trading cases.

In setting the rules, the SEC rejected appeals to require that whistle-blowers make reports through companies' internal compliance programs before going to the agency. Instead, the regulator increased incentives for internal complaints by permitting bounties for people whose tips are passed along on to the agency and expanding the time whistle-blowers can maintain their place in line at the SEC while reporting to the company.

"Incentivizing—rather than requiring—internal reporting is more likely to encourage a strong internal compliance culture," SEC Chairman Mary Schapiro said in prepared remarks before the vote.

Commissioner Kathleen Casey, who joined fellow Republican Troy Paredes in opposing the final rule in today's vote, said it "significantly underestimates the negative impact on internal compliance systems" and could lead to a flood of complaints the agency would be unprepared to handle.

Madoff Tips

Dodd-Frank called for the SEC to establish the expanded bounty system after the agency was faulted by lawmakers for fumbling tips about Bernard Madoff's multibillion-dollar fraud. Commissioners voted unanimously on Nov. 3 to seek comment on the program, which will cover whistle-blower complaints dating from the enactment of the regulatory overhaul last July.

The rule approved today allows the SEC to consider awards for whistle-blowers ranging from 10 percent to 30 percent of penalties collected in case where sanctions exceed $1 million. To qualify, tipsters must voluntarily provide information based on their own independent knowledge before it is requested by the SEC or other regulators.

SEC commissioners and staff members received 1,210 comment letters through yesterday and held more than 50 face-to-face meetings trying in vain to assuage concerns that the program would undermine internal systems that were mandated by the Sarbanes-Oxley Act of 2002.

"In the Dark"

"Armed with trial lawyers and new large financial incentives to bypass these programs, whistle-blowers will go straight to the SEC with allegations of wrongdoing and keep companies in the dark," the U.S. Chamber of Commerce said in a statement after the vote. "This leaves expensive, robust compliance programs collecting dust."

In a step aimed at bolstering internal programs, the SEC measure includes a provision for saving a whistle-blower's place in line for 120 days if they chose to report to their company first. It will also consider participation in a company program in determining the percentage of sanctions awarded as a bounty.

The rules were endorsed by the Securities Industry and Financial Markets Association, which released a statement applauding "the SEC's willingness to work with the industry and make important and necessary changes to the internal reporting provisions and the provisions on who can collect monetary awards."

Grimm Legislation

U.S. Representative Michael Grimm, a New York Republican who serves on the House Financial Services Committee, said he may propose legislation that would reverse the SEC's action by barring whistle-blowers from bypassing internal programs.

"The SEC's ruling will do more harm than good as potential victims may go months or years waiting for relief from unscrupulous employees," Grimm said in a statement after the vote. "I look forward to introducing legislation to correct the over-reaching whistleblower provisions in Dodd-Frank and today's

SEC ruling, in a way that catches criminal activity early while protecting whistleblowers from retaliation."

The SEC rules contain provisions designed to protect whistle-blowers against retaliation, which has been the focus of a lawsuit in U.S. District Court for the Southern District of New York. A May 4 opinion from Judge Leonard Sand held that Dodd-Frank says a person has to report wrongdoing to the SEC—or be able to seek protection under other laws—before receiving legal sanctuary.

The final rule won't provide protections to those who don't report to the SEC, reinforcing the court's interpretation.

Separately, commissioners voted 3-2 today to propose limits on the involvement of "bad actors" in Rule 506 securities sales and offerings. The measure, open for comment until July 14, would disqualify people barred from the securities business or convicted of a securities-related felony from exemptions that let issuers raise unlimited capital from accredited investors.

Critical Thinking

1. Should whistle-blowing be incentivized by offering a reward of 30 percent of penalties for financial wrongdoing?

2. What are arguments in favor of incentivizing whistle-blowing? Defend the arguments.

3. Having developed arguments in favor of incentivizing whistle-blowing, what are arguments against incentivizing whistle-blowing? Defend the arguments.

4. Do you agree or disagree with the statement by the U.S. Chamber of Commerce about rewarding whistle-blowers. Why do you agree or disagree?

The Parable of the Sadhu

After encountering a dying pilgrim on a climbing trip in the Himalayas, a businessman ponders the differences between individual and corporate ethics.

BOWEN H. MCCOY

Last year, as the first participant in the new six-month sabbatical program that Morgan Stanley has adopted, I enjoyed a rare opportunity to collect my thoughts as well as do some traveling. I spent the first three months in Nepal, walking 600 miles through 200 villages in the Himalayas and climbing some 120,000 vertical feet. My sole Western companion on the trip was an anthropologist who shed light on the cultural patterns of the villages that we passed through.

During the Nepal hike, something occurred that has had a powerful impact on my thinking about corporate ethics. Although some might argue that the experience has no relevance to business, it was a situation in which a basic ethical dilemma suddenly intruded into the lives of a group of individuals. How the group responded holds a lesson for all organizations, no matter how defined.

The Sadhu

The Nepal experience was more rugged than I had anticipated. Most commercial treks last two or three weeks and cover a quarter of the distance we traveled.

My friend Stephen, the anthropologist, and I were halfway through the 60-day Himalayan part of the trip when we reached the high point, an 18,000-foot pass over a crest that we'd have to traverse to reach the village of Muklinath, an ancient holy place for pilgrims.

Six years earlier, I had suffered pulmonary edema, an acute form of altitude sickness, at 16,500 feet in the vicinity of Everest base camp—so we were understandably concerned about what would happen at 18,000 feet. Moreover, the Himalayas were having their wettest spring in 20 years; hip-deep powder and ice had already driven us off one ridge. If we failed to cross the pass, I feared that the last half of our once-in-a-lifetime trip would be ruined.

The night before we would try the pass, we camped in a hut at 14,500 feet. In the photos taken at that camp, my face appears wan. The last village we'd passed through was a sturdy two-day walk below us, and I was tired.

During the late afternoon, four backpackers from New Zealand joined us, and we spent most of the night awake, anticipating the climb. Below, we could see the fires of two other parties, which turned out to be two Swiss couples and a Japanese hiking club.

To get over the steep part of the climb before the sun melted the steps cut in the ice, we departed at 3:30 A.M. The New Zealanders left first, followed by Stephen and myself, our porters and Sherpas, and then the Swiss. The Japanese lingered in their camp. The sky was clear, and we were confident that no spring storm would erupt that day to close the pass.

At 15,500 feet, it looked to me as if Stephen were shuffling and staggering a bit, which are symptoms of altitude sickness. (The initial stage of altitude sickness brings a headache and nausea. As the condition worsens, a climber may encounter difficult breathing, disorientation, aphasia, and paralysis.) I felt strong—my adrenaline was flowing—but I was very concerned about my ultimate ability to get across. A couple of our porters were also suffering from the height, and Pasang, our Sherpa sirdar (leader), was worried.

Just after daybreak, while we rested at 15,500 feet, one of the New Zealanders, who had gone ahead, came staggering down toward us with a body slung across his shoulders. He dumped the almost naked, barefoot body of an Indian holy man—a sadhu—at my feet. He had found the pilgrim lying on the ice, shivering and suffering from hypothermia. I cradled the sadhu's head and laid him out on the rocks. The New Zealander was angry. He wanted to get across the pass before the bright sun melted the snow. He said, "Look, I've done what I can. You have porters and Sherpa guides. You care for him. We're going on!" He turned and went back up the mountain to join his friends.

I took a carotid pulse and found that the sadhu was still alive. We figured he had probably visited the holy shrines at Muklinath and was on his way home. It was fruitless to question why he had chosen this desperately high route instead of the safe, heavily traveled caravan route through the Kali Gandaki gorge. Or why he was shoeless and almost naked, or how long he had been lying in the pass. The answers weren't going to solve our problem.

Stephen and the four Swiss began stripping off their outer clothing and opening their packs. The sadhu was soon clothed from head to foot. He was not able to walk, but he was very much alive. I looked down the mountain and spotted the Japanese climbers, marching up with a horse.

When I reached them, Stephen glared at me and said, "How do you feel about contributing to the death of a fellow man?"

Without a great deal of thought, I told Stephen and Pasang that I was concerned about withstanding the heights to come and wanted to get over the pass. I took off after several of our porters who had gone ahead.

On the steep part of the ascent where, if the ice steps had given way, I would have slid down about 3,000 feet, I felt vertigo. I stopped for a breather, allowing the Swiss to catch up with me. I inquired about the sadhu and Stephen. They said that the sadhu was fine and that Stephen was just behind them. I set off again for the summit.

Stephen arrived at the summit an hour after I did. Still exhilarated by victory, I ran down the slope to congratulate him. He was suffering from altitude sickness—walking 15 steps, then stopping, walking 15 steps, then stopping. Pasang accompanied him all the way up. When I reached them, Stephen glared at me and said: "How do you feel about contributing to the death of a fellow man?"

I did not completely comprehend what he meant. "Is the sadhu dead?" I inquired.

"No," replied Stephen, "but he surely will be!"

After I had gone, followed not long after by the Swiss, Stephen had remained with the sadhu. When the Japanese had arrived, Stephen had asked to use their horse to transport the sadhu down to the hut. They had refused. He had then asked Pasang to have a group of our porters carry the sadhu. Pasang had resisted the idea, saying that the porters would have to exert all their energy to get them-

selves over the pass. He believed they could not carry a man down 1,000 feet to the hut, reclimb the slope, and get across safely before the snow melted. Pasang had pressed Stephen not to delay any longer.

The Sherpas had carried the sadhu down to a rock in the sun at about 15,000 feet and pointed out the hut another 500 feet below. The Japanese had given him food and drink. When they had last seen him, he was listlessly throwing rocks at the Japanese party's dog, which had frightened him.

We do not know if the sadhu lived or died.

For many of the following days and evenings, Stephen and I discussed and debated our behavior toward the sadhu. Stephen is a committed Quaker with deep moral vision. He said, "I feel that what happened with the sadhu is a good example of the breakdown between the individual ethic and the corporate ethic. No one person was willing to assume ultimate responsibility for the sadhu. Each was willing to do his bit just so long as it was not too inconvenient. When it got to be a bother, everyone just passed the buck to someone else and took off. Jesus was relevant to a more individualistic stage of society, but how do we interpret his teaching today in a world filled with large, impersonal organizations and groups?"

I defended the larger group, saying, "Look, we all cared. We all gave aid and comfort. Everyone did his bit. The New Zealander carried him down below the snow line. I took his pulse and suggested we treat him for hypothermia. You and the Swiss gave him clothing and got him warmed up. The Japanese gave him food and water. The Sherpas carried him down to the sun and pointed out the easy trail toward the hut. He was well enough to throw rocks at a dog. What more could we do?"

"You have just described the typical affluent Westerner's response to a problem. Throwing money—in this case, food and sweaters—at it, but not solving the fundamentals!" Stephen retorted.

I asked, "Where is the limit of our responsibility in a situation like this?"

"What would satisfy you?" I said. "Here we are, a group of New Zealanders, Swiss, Americans, and Japanese who have never met before and who are at the apex of one of the most powerful experiences of our lives. Some years the pass is so bad no one gets over it. What right does an almost naked pilgrim who chooses the wrong trail have to disrupt our lives? Even the Sherpas had no interest in risking the trip to help him beyond a certain point."

Stephen calmly rebutted, "I wonder what the Sherpas would have done if the sadhu had been a well-dressed Nepali, or what the Japanese would have done if the sadhu had been a well-dressed Asian, or what you would have done, Buzz, if the sadhu had been a well-dressed Western woman?"

"Where, in your opinion," I asked, "is the limit of our responsibility in a situation like this? We had our own well-being to worry about. Our Sherpa guides were unwilling to jeopardize us or the porters for the sadhu. No one else on the mountain was willing to commit himself beyond certain self-imposed limits."

Stephen said, "As individual Christians or people with a Western ethical tradition, we can fulfill our obligations in such a situation only if one, the sadhu dies in our care; two, the sadhu demonstrates to us that he can undertake the two-day walk down to the village; or three, we carry the sadhu for two days down to the village and persuade someone there to care for him."

"Leaving the sadhu in the sun with food and clothing—where he demonstrated hand-eye coordination by throwing a rock at a dog—comes close to fulfilling items one and two," I answered. "And it wouldn't have made sense to take him to the village where the people appeared to be far less caring than the Sherpas, so the third condition is impractical. Are you really saying that, no matter what the implications, we should, at the drop of a hat, have changed our entire plan?"

The Individual versus the Group Ethic

Despite my arguments, I felt and continue to feel guilt about the sadhu. I had literally walked through a classic moral dilemma without fully thinking through the consequences. My excuses for my actions include a high adrenaline flow, a superordinate goal, and a once-in-a-lifetime opportunity—common factors in corporate situations, especially stressful ones.

Real moral dilemmas are ambiguous, and many of us hike right through them, unaware that they exist. When, usually after the fact, someone makes an issue of one, we tend to resent his or her bringing it up. Often, when the full import of what we have done (or not done) hits us, we dig into a defensive position from which it is very difficult to emerge. In rare circumstances, we may contemplate what we have done from inside a prison.

Had we mountaineers been free of stress caused by the effort and the high altitude, we might have treated the sadhu differently. Yet isn't stress the real test of personal and corporate values? The instant decisions that executives make under pressure reveal the most about personal and corporate character.

As a group, we had no process for developing a consensus. We had no sense of purpose or plan.

Among the many questions that occur to me when I ponder my experience with the sadhu are: What are the practical limits of moral imagination and vision? Is there a collective or institutional ethic that differs from the ethics of the individual? At what level of effort or commitment can one discharge one's ethical responsibilities?

Not every ethical dilemma has a right solution. Reasonable people often disagree; otherwise there would be no dilemma. In a business context, however, it is essential that managers agree on a process for dealing with dilemmas.

Our experience with the sadhu offers an interesting parallel to business situations. An immediate response was mandatory. Failure to act was a decision in itself. Up on the mountain we could not resign and submit our résumés to a headhunter. In contrast to philosophy, business involves action and implementation—getting things done. Managers must come up with answers based on what they see and what they allow to influence their decision-making processes. On the mountain, none of us but Stephen realized the true dimensions of the situation we were facing.

One of our problems was that as a group we had no process for developing a consensus. We had no sense of purpose or plan. The difficulties of dealing with the sadhu were so complex that no one person could handle them. Because the group did not have a set of preconditions that could guide its action to an acceptable resolution, we reacted instinctively as individuals. The cross-cultural nature of the group added a further layer of complexity. We had no leader with whom we could all identify and in whose purpose we believed. Only Stephen was willing to take charge, but he could not gain adequate support from the group to care for the sadhu.

Some organizations do have values that transcend the personal values of their managers. Such values, which go beyond profitability, are usually revealed when the organization is under stress. People throughout the organization generally accept its values, which, because they are not presented as a rigid list of commandments, may be somewhat ambiguous. The stories people tell, rather than printed materials, transmit the organization's conceptions of what is proper behavior.

For 20 years, I have been exposed at senior levels to a variety of corporations and organizations. It is amazing how quickly an outsider can sense the tone and style of an organization and, with that, the degree of tolerated openness and freedom to challenge management.

When Do We Take a Stand?

I wrote about my experiences purposely to present an ambiguous situation. I never found out if the sadhu lived or died. I can attest, though, that the sadhu lives on in his story. He lives in the ethics classes I teach each year at business schools and churches. He lives in the classrooms of numerous business schools, where professors have taught the case to tens of thousands of students. He lives in several casebooks on ethics and on an educational video. And he lives in organizations such as the American Red Cross and AT&T, which use his story in their ethics training.

As I reflect on the sadhu now, 15 years after the fact, I first have to wonder, What actually happened on that Himalayan slope? When I first wrote about the event, I reported the experience in as much detail as I could remember, but I shaped it to the needs of a good classroom discussion. After years of reading my story, viewing it on video, and hearing others discuss it, I'm not sure I myself know what actually occurred on the mountainside that day!

I've also heard a wide variety of responses to the story. The sadhu, for example, may not have wanted our help at all—he may have been intentionally bringing on his own death as a way to holiness. Why had he taken the dangerous way over the pass instead of the caravan route through the gorge? Hindu businesspeople have told me that in trying to assist the sadhu, we were being typically arrogant Westerners imposing our cultural values on the world.

I've learned that each year along the pass, a few Nepali porters are left to freeze to death outside the tents of the unthinking tourists who hired them. A few years ago, a French group even left one of their own, a young French woman, to die there. The difficult pass seems to demonstrate a perverse version of Gresham's law of currency: The bad practices of previous travelers have driven out the values that new travelers might have followed if they were at home. Perhaps that helps to explain why our porters behaved as they did and why it was so difficult for Stephen or anyone else to establish a different approach on the spot.

Our Sherpa sirdar, Pasang, was focused on his responsibility for bringing us up the mountain safe and sound. (His livelihood and status in the Sherpa ethnic group depended on our safe return.) We were weak, our party was split, the porters were well on their way to the top with all our gear and food, and a storm would have separated us irrevocably from our logistical base.

The fact was, we had no plan for dealing with the contingency of the sadhu. There was nothing we could do to unite our multicultural group in the little time we had. An ethical dilemma had come upon us unexpectedly, an element of drama that may explain why the sadhu's story has continued to attract students.

I am often asked for help in teaching the story. I usually advise keeping the details as ambiguous as possible. A true ethical dilemma requires a decision between two hard choices. In the case of the sadhu, we had to decide how much to sacrifice ourselves to take care of a stranger. And given the constraints of our trek, we had to make a group decision, not an individual one. If a large majority of students in a class ends up thinking I'm a bad person because of my decision on the mountain, the instructor may not have given the case its due. The same is true if the majority sees no problem with the choices we made.

Any class's response depends on its setting, whether it's a business school, a church, or a corporation. I've found that younger students are more likely to see the issue as black-and-white, whereas older ones tend to see shades of gray. Some have seen a conflict between the different ethical approaches that we followed at the time. Stephen felt he had to do everything he could to save the sadhu's life, in accordance with his Christian ethic of compassion. I had a utilitarian response: do the greatest good for the greatest number. Give a burst of aid to minimize the sadhu's exposure, then continue on our way.

The basic question of the case remains, When do we take a stand? When do we allow a "sadhu" to intrude into our daily lives? Few of us can afford the time or effort to take care of every needy person we encounter. How much must we give of ourselves? And how do we prepare our organizations and institutions so they will respond appropriately in a crisis? How do we influence them if we do not agree with their points of view?

We cannot quit our jobs over every ethical dilemma, but if we continually ignore our sense of values, who do we become? As a journalist asked at a recent conference on ethics, "Which ditch are we willing to die in?" For each of us, the answer is a bit different. How we act in response to that question defines better than anything else who we are, just as, in a collective sense, our acts define our institutions. In effect, the sadhu is always there, ready to remind us of the tensions between our own goals and the claims of strangers.

Organizations that do not have a heritage of mutually accepted, shared values tend to become unhinged during stress, with each individual bailing out for himself or herself. In the great takeover battles we have witnessed during past years, companies that had strong cultures drew the wagons around them and fought it out, while other companies saw executives—supported by golden parachutes—bail out of the struggles.

Because corporations and their members are interdependent, for the corporation to be strong the members need to share a preconceived notion of correct behavior, a "business ethic," and think of it as a positive force, not a constraint.

As an investment banker, I am continually warned by well-meaning lawyers, clients, and associates to be wary of conflicts of interest. Yet if I were to run away from every difficult situation, I wouldn't be an effective investment banker. I have to feel my way through conflicts. An effective manager can't run from risk either; he or she has to confront risk. To feel "safe" in doing that, managers need the guidelines of an agreed-upon process and set of values within the organization.

After my three months in Nepal, I spent three months as an executive-in-residence at both the Stanford Business School and the University of California at Berkeley's Center for Ethics and Social Policy of the Graduate Theological Union. Those six months away from my job gave me time to assimilate 20 years of business experience. My thoughts turned often to the meaning of the leadership role in any large organization. Students at the seminary thought of themselves as antibusiness. But when I questioned them, they agreed that they distrusted all large organizations, including the church. They perceived all large organizations as impersonal and opposed to individual values and needs. Yet we all know of organizations in which people's values and beliefs are respected and their expressions encouraged. What makes the difference? Can we identify the difference and, as a result, manage more effectively?

The word *ethics* turns off many and confuses more. Yet the notions of shared values and an agreed-upon process for dealing with adversity and change—what many people mean when they talk about corporate culture—seem to be at the heart of the ethical issue. People who are in touch with their own core beliefs and the beliefs of others and who are sustained by them can be more comfortable living on the cutting edge. At times, taking a tough line or a decisive stand in a muddle of ambiguity is the only ethical thing to do. If a manager is indecisive about a problem and spends time trying to figure out the "good" thing to do, the enterprise may be lost.

Business ethics, then, has to do with the authenticity and integrity of the enterprise. To be ethical is to follow the business as well as the cultural goals of the corporation, its owners, its employees, and its customers. Those who cannot serve the corporate vision are not authentic businesspeople and, therefore, are not ethical in the business sense.

At this stage of my own business experience, I have a strong interest in organizational behavior. Sociologists are keenly studying what they call corporate stories, legends, and heroes as a way organizations have of transmitting value systems. Corporations such as Arco have even hired consultants to perform an audit of their corporate culture. In a company, a leader is a person who understands, interprets, and manages the corporate value system. Effective managers, therefore, are action-oriented people who resolve conflict, are tolerant of ambiguity, stress, and change, and have a strong sense of purpose for themselves and their organizations.

If all this is true, I wonder about the role of the professional manager who moves from company to company. How can he or she quickly absorb the values and culture of different organizations? Or is there, indeed, an art of management that is totally transportable? Assuming that such fungible managers do exist, is it proper for them to manipulate the values of others?

What would have happened had Stephen and I carried the sadhu for two days back to the village and become involved with the villagers in his care? In four trips to Nepal, my most interesting experience occurred in 1975 when I lived in a Sherpa home in the Khumbu for five days while recovering from altitude sickness. The high point of Stephen's trip was an invitation to participate in a family funeral ceremony in Manang. Neither experience had to do with climbing the high passes of the Himalayas. Why were we so reluctant to try the lower path, the ambiguous trail? Perhaps because we did not have a leader who could reveal the greater purpose of the trip to us.

Why didn't Stephen, with his moral vision, opt to take the sadhu under his personal care? The answer is partly because Stephen was hard-stressed physically himself and partly because, without some support system that encompassed our involuntary and episodic community on the mountain, it was beyond his individual capacity to do so.

I see the current interest in corporate culture and corporate value systems as a positive response to pessimism such as Stephen's about the decline of the role of the individual in large organizations. Individuals who operate from a thoughtful set of personal values provide the foundation for a corporate culture. A corporate tradition that encourages freedom of inquiry, supports personal values, and reinforces a focused sense of direction can fulfill the need to combine individuality with the prosperity and success of the group. Without such corporate support, the individual is lost.

That is the lesson of the sadhu. In a complex corporate situation, the individual requires and deserves the support of the group. When people cannot find such support in their organizations, they don't know how to act. If such support is forthcoming, a person has a stake in the success of the group and can add much to the process of establishing and maintaining a corporate culture. Management's challenge is to be sensitive to individual needs, to shape them, and to direct and focus them for the benefit of the group as a whole.

For each of us the sadhu lives. Should we stop what we are doing and comfort him; or should we keep trudging up toward the high pass? Should I pause to help the derelict I pass on the street each night as I walk by the Yale Club en route to Grand Central Station? Am I his brother? What is the nature of our responsibility if we consider ourselves to be ethical persons? Perhaps it is to change the values of the group so that it can, with all its resources, take the other road.

Critical Thinking

1. If you were Bowen McCoy, what would you have done? Refer to ethical theories to support your answer.

2. How do your personal values express themselves in your business life?

BOWEN H. McCOY retired from Morgan Stanley in 1990 after 28 years of service. He is now a real estate and business counselor, a teacher and a philanthropist.

Editor's Note—This article was originally published in the September/October 1983 issue of *HBR*. For its republication as an HBR Classic, Bowen H. McCoy has written the commentary "When Do We Take a Stand?" to update his observations.

Fact Sheet: We Can't Wait: White House Launches Ethics.gov to Promote Government Accountability and Transparency

THE WHITE HOUSE OFFICE OF THE PRESS SECRETARY

President Obama has consistently made clear that he will strive to lead the most open, transparent, and account-able government in history. For over three years, the Administration has done much to make information about how government works more accessible to the public, and to solicit citizens' participation in government decision-making. We have devised ambitious Open Government Plans designed to increase opportunities for public engagement. We have made a tremendous amount of information newly available on government websites. We have even taken steps to provide more disclosure of sensitive government information. So, we are striving to lead an open and transparent government that works for the American people.

President Obama promised he would "create a centralized Internet database of lobbying reports, ethics records, and campaign finance filings in a searchable, sortable, and downloadable format." Today, with the launch of www.Ethics.gov, he's delivering on that promise. In a single, user-friendly format, anyone can access and search the records of seven different databases:

- White House Visitor Records
- Office of Government Ethics Travel Reports
- Lobbying Disclosure Act Data
- Department of Justice Foreign Agents Registration Act Data
- Federal Election Commission Individual Contribution Reports
- Federal Election Commission Candidate Reports
- Federal Election Commission Committee Reports

Never before has this measure of government-verified data been available and so easily searchable in a centralized location. On www.Ethics.gov, the public will be able to find millions of White House Visitor records. You will be able to see agency reports of payments from non-Federal sources for travel to meetings and conferences.

You'll find records for entities registered with the Federal Election Commission. This includes federal political action committees and party committees, campaign committees for presidential, House and Senate candidates, as well as groups or organizations who are spending money in connection with elections for federal office.

You'll also find records for each candidate who has either registered with the Federal Election Commission or appeared on a ballot list prepared by a state elections office. This includes contributor information for each contribution of $200 or more from an individual to a federal committee.

Finally, you'll be able to find lobbying registrations and reports filed under the Lobbying Disclosure Act.

Ethics.gov takes an important step to increase transparency and accountability. This is good for government and good for the American people.

The President's Record

From the day he took office, the President committed his Administration to work towards unprecedented openness in government. On his first full day in office, President Obama signed the Memorandum on Transparency and Open Government—a document that has helped to guide the federal government as it has worked toward a new era of open government and public engagement.

Since then, the President has redoubled his Administration's efforts to live up to that early promise–creating Data.gov to increase public access to government information, aggressively tracking the federal government's use of federal dollars with websites like Recovery.gov and USASpending.gov, introducing the "We the People" initiative to give all Americans an opportunity to petition the government on a range of issues affecting our nation, calling for a large-scale transformation in how agencies maintain their records, and launching an effort to cut waste and streamline government operations.

Continuing his commitment to an open and transparent government, the President challenged nations to make all governments more open and accountable to their people. To meet that challenge, in September 2011, the United States, with other founding nations, launched the Open Government Partnership (OGP)–a global effort to promote more transparent, effective and accountable governance in countries around the world. As part of OGP, the President unveiled the United States National Action Plan on Open Government, which outlines twenty-six

commitments that the United States is implementing to create a more open and participatory government.

Critical Thinking

1. Go to the federal government's websites to see what they have posted. Are you satisfied with what they have presented? What would you add to the site, based on developments over the last 4–8 years?

2. Do you feel that these efforts at transparency and accountability have paid off? Have you, or do you know of anyone who has "visited" any of these sites listed in the article?

White House Office of the Press Secretary, 2012

UNIT 3

Business and Society: Contemporary Ethical, Social, and Environmental Issues

Unit Selections

Learning Outcomes

After reading this Unit, you will be able to:

- How is trust established in the marketplace?
- How is trust impacted by social media and issues of privacy while in online venues?
- What ethical dilemmas is management likely to face when conducting business in foreign environments?
- Do you agree or disagree that ethics must be global in the conduct of business across national borders? Take a position and defend it.
- Is it possible to develop a framework for global business ethics? What attributes should be included in such a framework? How should a framework for global business ethics be implemented?
- What is corporate responsibility? How does it differ from corporate social responsibility, if at all? How does it differ from ethics? How is it similar to ethics?
- What are the ethical issues in sustainability?

Student Website
www.mhhe.com/cls

This unit, Business and Society: Contemporary Ethical, Social, and Environmental Issues, examines the nature and ramifications of prominent ethical, social, and environmental issues facing management today. The unit's articles are grouped into four subsections—Changing Perspectives in Business and Society, Contemporary Ethical Issues, Global Ethics, and a new subsection Ethics, Environment, and Sustainability.

The first article in this unit scrutinizes the importance of companies gaining and maintaining trust in the marketplace. Trust is a concept that transcends the venue in which business is conducted, whether in the domestic market, online, or in global markets.

In the second subsection, the first article considers how Facebook and Google are facing backlashes from users and regulators alike over the way they have handled sensitive data. Other articles examine various privacy concerns and the emergence of digital-privacy rules. The final two articles examine the ethics of social media.

The third subsection features readings that provide helpful insight on ethical issues and dilemmas inherent in multinational operations. It describes adapting ethical decisions to a global marketplace and offers guidelines for helping management deal with product quality and ethical issues in global markets.

© Design Pics / Darren Greenwood

The final subsection examines the emergent area of ethics, environment, and sustainability. Articles in this subsection focus on corporate social responsibility as well as on a manager's ethical responsibilities for sustainability and the environment.

Internet References

Ethics and Sustainability from AACSB
www.aacsb.edu/resources/ethics-sustainability/default.asp

Ethics and Sustainability from Trigonos
www.trigonos.org/ethics_and_sustainability

Global Ethics—Articles and Cases
www.scu.edu/ethics/practicing/focusareas/global_ethics

Trust in the Marketplace
www.bbb.org/us/leveraging-bbb

Trust Required Here
http://insight.kellogg.northwestern.edu/index.php/Kellogg/article/trust_required_here

United Nations Environment Programme (UNEP)
www.unep.ch

United States Trade Representative (USTR)
www.ustr.gov

Workopolis.com
http://sympatico.workopolis.com

World Trade Data
www.sicex.com

Trust in the Marketplace

JOHN E. RICHARDSON AND LINNEA BERNARD MCCORD

Traditionally, ethics is defined as a set of moral values or principles or a code of conduct.

. . . Ethics, as an expression of reality, is predicated upon the assumption that there are right and wrong motives, attitudes, traits of character, and actions that are exhibited in interpersonal relationships. Respectful social interaction is considered a norm by almost everyone.

. . . the overwhelming majority of people perceive others to be ethical when they observe what is considered to be their genuine kindness, consideration, politeness, empathy, and fairness in their interpersonal relationships. When these are absent, and unkindness, inconsideration, rudeness, hardness, and injustice are present, the people exhibiting such conduct are considered unethical. A genuine consideration of others is essential to an ethical life. (Chewning, pp. 175–176).

An essential concomitant of ethics is of trust. Webster's Dictionary defines trust as "assured reliance on the character, ability, strength or truth of someone or something." Businesses are built on a foundation of trust in our free-enterprise system. When there are violations of this trust between competitors, between employer and employees, or between businesses and consumers, our economic system ceases to run smoothly. From a moral viewpoint, ethical behavior should not exist because of economic pragmatism, governmental edict, or contemporary fashionability—it should exist because it is morally appropriate and right. From an economic point of view, ethical behavior should exist because it just makes good business sense to be ethical and operate in a manner that demonstrates trustworthiness.

Robert Bruce Shaw, in *Trust in the Balance*, makes some thoughtful observations about trust within an organization. Paraphrasing his observations and applying his ideas to the marketplace as a whole:

1. Trust requires consumers have confidence in organizational promises or claims made to them. This means that a consumer should be able to believe that a commitment made will be met.
2. Trust requires integrity and consistency in following a known set of values, beliefs, and practices.
3. Trust requires concern for the well-being of others. This does not mean that organizational needs are not given

appropriate emphasis—but it suggests the importance of understanding the impact of decisions and actions on others—i.e. consumers. (Shaw, pp. 39–40)

Companies can lose the trust of their customers by portraying their products in a deceptive or inaccurate manner. In one recent example, a Nike advertisement exhorted golfers to buy the same golf balls used by Tiger Woods. However, since Tiger Woods was using custom-made Nike golf balls not yet available to the general golfing public, the ad was, in fact, deceptive. In one of its ads, Volvo represented that Volvo cars could withstand a physical impact that, in fact, was not possible. Once a company is "caught" giving inaccurate information, even if done innocently, trust in that company is eroded.

Companies can also lose the trust of their customers when they fail to act promptly and notify their customers of problems that the company has discovered, especially where deaths may be involved. This occurred when Chrysler dragged its feet in replacing a safety latch on its Minivan (Geyelin, pp. A1, A10). More recently, Firestone and Ford had been publicly brought to task for failing to expeditiously notify American consumers of tire defects in SUVs even though the problem had occurred years earlier in other countries. In cases like these, trust might not just be eroded, it might be destroyed. It could take years of painstaking effort to rebuild trust under these circumstances, and some companies might not have the economic ability to withstand such a rebuilding process with their consumers.

A *20/20* and *New York Times* investigation on a recent *ABC 20/20* program, entitled "The Car Dealer's Secret" revealed a sad example of the violation of trust in the marketplace. The investigation divulged that many unsuspecting consumers have had hidden charges tacked on by some car dealers when purchasing a new car. According to consumer attorney Gary Klein, "It's a dirty little secret that the auto lending industry has not owned up to." (*ABC News 20/20*)

The scheme worked in the following manner. Car dealers would send a prospective buyer's application to a number of lenders, who would report to the car dealer what interest rate the lender would give to the buyer for his or her car loan. This interest rate is referred to as the "buy rate." Legally a car dealer is not required to tell the buyer what the "buy rate" is or how much the dealer is marking up the loan. If dealers did most of the loans at the buy rate, they only get a small fee. However, if they were able to convince the buyer to pay a higher rate, they made considerably more money. Lenders encouraged car dealers to charge the buyer a higher rate than the "buy rate" by agreeing to split the extra income with the dealer.

David Robertson, head of the Association of Finance and Insurance Professionals—a trade group representing finance managers—defended the practice, reflecting that it was akin to a retail markup on loans. "The dealership provides a valuable service on behalf of the customer in negotiating these loans," he said. "Because of that, the dealership should be compensated for that work." (*ABC News 20/20*)

Careful examination of the entire report, however, makes one seriously question this apologetic. Even if this practice is deemed to be legal, the critical issue is what happens to trust when the buyers discover that they have been charged an additional 1–3% of the loan without their knowledge? In some cases, consumers were led to believe that they were getting the dealer's bank rate, and in other cases, they were told that the dealer had shopped around at several banks to secure the best loan rate they could get for the buyer. While this practice may be questionable from a legal standpoint, it is clearly in ethical breach of trust with the consumer. Once discovered, the companies doing this will have the same credibility and trustworthiness problems as the other examples mentioned above.

The untrustworthiness problems of the car companies was compounded by the fact that the investigation appeared to reveal statistics showing that black customers were twice as likely as whites to have their rate marked up—and at a higher level. That evidence—included in thousands of pages of confidential documents which *20/20* and *The New York Times* obtained from a Tennessee court—revealed that some Nissan and GM dealers in Tennessee routinely marked up rates for blacks, forcing them to pay between $300 and $400 more than whites. (*ABC News 20/20*)

This is a tragic example for everyone who was affected by this markup and was the victim of this secret policy. Not only is trust destroyed, there is a huge economic cost to the general public. It is estimated that in the last four years or so, Texas car dealers have received approximately $9 billion of kickbacks from lenders, affecting 5.2 million consumers. (*ABC News 20/20*)

Let's compare these unfortunate examples of untrustworthy corporate behavior with the landmark example of Johnson & Johnson which ultimately increased its trustworthiness with consumers by the way it handled the Tylenol incident. After seven individuals who had consumed Tylenol capsules contaminated by a third party died, Johnson & Johnson instituted a total product recall within a week costing an estimated $50 million after taxes. The company did this, not because it was responsible for causing the problem, but because it was the right thing to do. In addition, Johnson & Johnson spearheaded the development of more effective tamper-proof containers for their industry. Because of the company's swift response, consumers once again were able to trust in the Johnson & Johnson name. Although Johnson & Johnson suffered a decrease in market share at the time because of the scare, over the long term it has maintained its profitability in a highly competitive market.

Certainly part of this profit success is attributable to consumers believing that Johnson & Johnson is a trustworthy company. (Robin and Reidenbach)

The e-commerce arena presents another example of the importance of marketers building a mutually valuable relationship with customers through a trust-based collaboration process. Recent research with 50 e-businesses reflects that companies which create and nurture trust find customers return to their sites repeatedly. (Dayal . . . . p. 64)

In the e-commerce world, six components of trust were found to be critical in developing trusting, satisfied customers:

- State-of-art reliable security measures on one's site
- Merchant legitimacy (e.g., ally one's product or service with an established brand)
- Order fulfillment (i.e. placing orders and getting merchandise efficiently and with minimal hassles)
- Tone and ambiance—handling consumers' personal information with sensitivity and iron-clad confidentiality
- Customers feeling that they are in control of the buying process
- Consumer collaboration—e.g., having chat groups to let consumers query each other about their purchases and experiences (Dayal . . . , pp. 64–67)

Additionally, one author noted recently that in the e-commerce world we've moved beyond brands and trademarks to "trustmarks." This author defined a trustmark as a

> . . . (D)istinctive name or symbol that emotionally binds a company with the desires and aspirations of its customers. It's an emotional connection—and it's much bigger and more powerful than the uses that we traditionally associate with a trademark. . . . (Webber, p. 214)

Certainly if this is the case, trust—being an emotional link—is of supreme importance for a company that wants to succeed in doing business on the Internet.

It's unfortunate that while a plethora of examples of violation of trust easily come to mind, a paucity of examples "pop up" as noteworthy paradigms of organizational courage and trust in their relationship with consumers.

In conclusion, some key areas for companies to scrutinize and practice with regard to decisions that may affect trustworthiness in the marketplace might include:

- Does a company practice the Golden Rule with its customers? As a company insider, knowing what you know about the product, how willing would you be to purchase it for yourself or for a family member?
- How proud would you be if your marketing practices were made public . . . shared with your friends . . . or family? (Blanchard and Peale, p. 27)
- Are bottom-line concerns the sole component of your organizational decision-making process? What about human rights, the ecological/environmental impact, and other areas of social responsibility?
- Can a firm which engages in unethical business practices with customers be trusted to deal with its

employees any differently? Unfortunately, frequently a willingness to violate standards of ethics is not an isolated phenomenon but permeates the culture. The result is erosion of integrity throughout a company. In such cases, trust is elusive at best. (Shaw, p. 75)

- Is your organization not only market driven, but also value-oriented? (Peters and Levering, Moskowitz, and Katz)
- Is there a strong commitment to a positive corporate culture and a clearly defined mission which is frequently and unambiguously voiced by upper-management?
- Does your organization exemplify trust by practicing a genuine relationship partnership with your customers— *before, during, and after* the initial purchase? (Strout, p. 69)

Companies which exemplify treating customers ethically are founded on a covenant of trust. There is a shared belief, confidence, and faith that the company and its people will be fair, reliable, and ethical in all its dealings. ***Total trust is the belief that a company and its people will never take opportunistic advantage of customer vulnerabilities***. (Hart and Johnson, pp. 11–13)

References

ABC News 20/20, "The Car Dealer's Secret," October 27, 2000.

Blanchard, Kenneth, and Norman Vincent Peale, *The Power of Ethical Management*, New York: William Morrow and Company, Inc., 1988.

Chewning, Richard C., *Business Ethics in a Changing Culture* (Reston, Virginia: Reston Publishing, 1984).

Dayal, Sandeep, Landesberg, Helen, and Michael Zeissner, "How to Build Trust Online," *Marketing Management*, Fall 1999, pp. 64–69.

Geyelin, Milo, "Why One Jury Dealt a Big Blow to Chrysler in Minivan-Latch Case," *Wall Street Journal*, November 19, 1997, pp. A1, A10.

Hart, Christopher W. and Michael D. Johnson, "Growing the Trust Relationship," *Marketing Management*, Spring 1999, pp. 9–19.

Hosmer, La Rue Tone, *The Ethics of Management*, second edition (Homewood, Illinois: Irwin, 1991).

Kaydo, Chad, "A Position of Power," *Sales & Marketing Management*, June 2000, pp. 104–106, 108ff.

Levering, Robert; Moskowitz, Milton; and Michael Katz, *The 100 Best Companies to Work for in America* (Reading, Mass.: Addison-Wesley, 1984).

Magnet, Myron, "Meet the New Revolutionaries," *Fortune*, February 24, 1992, pp. 94–101.

Muoio, Anna, "The Experienced Customer," *Net Company*, Fall 1999, pp. 25–27.

Peters, Thomas J. and Robert H. Waterman Jr., *In Search of Excellence* (New York: Harper & Row, 1982).

Richardson, John (ed.), *Annual Editions: Business Ethics 00/01* (Guilford, CT: McGraw-Hill/Dushkin, 2000).

_____, *Annual Editions: Marketing 00/01* (Guilford, CT: McGraw-Hill/Dushkin, 2000).

Robin, Donald P., and Erich Reidenbach, "Social Responsibility, Ethics, and Marketing Strategy: Closing the Gap Between Concept and Application," *Journal of Marketing*, vol. 51 (January 1987), pp. 44–58.

Shaw, Robert Bruce, *Trust in the Balance*, (San Francisco: Jossey-Bass Publishers, 1997).

Strout, Erin, "Tough Customers," *Sales Marketing Management*, January 2000, pp. 63–69.

Webber, Alan M., "Trust in the Future," *Fast Company*, September 2000, pp. 209–212ff.

Critical Thinking

1. What is the role of trust in the marketplace?
2. Describe an incident of a violation of trust in the marketplace that you yourself have experienced. When you discovered this violation, what was your response?

DR. JOHN E. RICHARDSON is Professor of Marketing in the Graziadio School of Business and Management at Pepperdine University, Malibu, California. **DR. LINNEA BERNARD MCCORD** is Associate Professor of Business Law in the Graziadio School of Business and Management at Pepperdine University, Malibu, California.

Privacy and the Internet
Lives of Others

Facebook and Google face a backlash, from users and regulators alike, over the way they have handled sensitive data.

THE ECONOMIST

Jennifer Stoddart, Canada's privacy commissioner, is furious with Facebook. In August 2009 the social-networking site struck a deal, agreeing to change its policies within a year to comply with the country's privacy law. Now, says Ms Stoddart, the company appears to be reneging on an important part of that deal, which involved giving users a clear and easy-to-implement choice over whether to share private data with third parties. "It doesn't seem to me that Facebook is going in the right direction on this issue," she says, hinting that, without a change of course, the firm could soon become the subject of another formal investigation by her organisation.

Facebook is not the only internet giant to provoke the ire of data watchdogs. Google endured withering criticism this week following news that it had recorded some personal communications sent over unsecured Wi-Fi data networks in homes and offices in some 30 countries. On May 17th Peter Schaar, Germany's federal commissioner for data protection, called for an independent investigation into Google's behaviour, claiming that it had "simply disobeyed normal rules in the development and usage of software."

The cases highlight rising tension between guardians of privacy and internet firms. And they reflect concern among web users about how private data are made public. Several prominent internet types such as Cory Doctorow, a science-fiction author, and Leo Laporte, a podcaster, have abandoned Facebook. Sites such as QuitFacebookDay.com are urging others to do so, nominating May 31st for a mass Facebook "suicide."

This is unlikely to stop the meteoric rise of Facebook, which is poised to claim half a billion members and which draws even more visitors as a whole to its site. But nerves have been rattled at the company's headquarters in Silicon Valley, where bosses are mulling over how to respond. Several senior folk are now hinting that Facebook will soon roll out simpler privacy controls to make it easier to keep more data hidden. MySpace, a rival, is already making its controls simpler in an effort to woo disaffected Facebookers to its service.

A revolt over Facebook's handling of privacy has been brewing for some time. In December the social network changed the default settings on its privacy controls so that individuals' personal information would be shared with "everyone" rather than selected friends. Facebook argued this reflected a shift in society towards greater openness and noted that users could still adjust privacy settings back again. But incensed privacy activists lobbied for it to be reversed.

The switch should not have come as a surprise. Early on, many social networks impose fairly tough privacy policies in order to attract and reassure users. But as more join, controls are gradually loosened to encourage more sharing. As people share more, Facebook can increase the traffic against which it sells advertising. And the more it learns about users' likes and dislikes, the better it can target ads that generate hundreds of millions of dollars.

Protests grew louder still following a developers' conference last month at which Mark Zuckerberg, Facebook's boss, announced yet another series of policy changes. One that caused irritation was an "instant personalisation" feature that lets certain third-party websites access Facebook data when people visit. Critics say that Facebook has made it tricky to disable this feature, which may explain why Ms Stoddart dislikes it so much.

European officials are grumbling about Facebook too. This month a group of data-protection experts who advise the European Commission wrote to the social network, calling its decision to loosen the default settings "unacceptable." And in the United States, the Electronic Privacy Information Centre, a non-profit group, has asked America's Federal Trade Commission to see if Facebook's approach to privacy violates consumer-protection laws.

Privacy watchdogs are also seeing if Google has broken any laws by capturing Wi-Fi data without permission. The search firm says that an experimental software project designed to gather data from unencrypted Wi-Fi networks was accidentally rolled out along with its Street View initiative, which uses cameras mounted on cars to film streets and buildings. As a result snippets of sensitive private data were collected and stored for years, without the Street View leaders' knowledge.

Street Unwise

Google apologised and stressed that the unauthorised sampling collected only enough data to fill a single computer hard disk. It added that the information had not been used in any products nor shared outside Google. And it said it would appoint an independent body to review the fiasco in addition to conducting an internal review of its privacy practices. "We screwed up," admitted Sergey Brin, a Google cofounder, on May 19th.

Yet Google's reputation has been damaged. The episode shows that it needs to get a better grip on what its staff are up to. Initial denials that it had collected sensitive data, reversed when Germany's privacy watchdog demanded a more detailed review, also look like a public-relations blunder. And doubts have been raised about the quality of some managers. A spokesman for the firm blamed "a failure of communication between teams and within teams." That is a worrying admission, given the vast amounts of sensitive data in Google's digital coffers.

It had already suffered this year during the launch of Buzz, its own social-networking service. Users complained that the search giant had dipped into their Gmail accounts to find "followers" for them without clearly explaining what was happening—a practice that the firm quickly scrapped. Last month ten privacy commissioners from countries such as Britain, Canada and France urged the company not to sideline privacy in a rush to launch new technology.

At Google's European Zeitgeist conference this week, Eric Schmidt claimed that the firm has the most consumer-centric privacy policy of any online service. Google's chief executive added that no harm had been done by the Wi-Fi debacle. Others may reach a similar conclusion. But tussles over privacy issues will persist. "Nobody has a clear view of where to draw the line on privacy matters online," says Jonathan Zittrain, a professor at Harvard Law School. Privacy commissioners will be busy for a while yet.

Critical Thinking

1. What electronic data do you expect to remain private when you post it on Facebook or other social media? How private is "private" on the Internet?
2. How is consumer privacy protected?

Automotive "Black Boxes" Raise Privacy Issues

G. CHAMBERS WILLIAMS III

I f you're involved in a traffic accident with no witnesses except you and the other driver, it's just your word against his, right?

Wrong.

Your own car just might tattle on you if you're at fault.

So-called event data recorders that function much like the "black boxes" on airplanes, and which are now installed on virtually all new vehicles, can give investigators incriminating details about your driving behavior in the final seconds before a crash.

Some motorists—fearful of what they see as an invasion of privacy—aren't too happy about that.

"I didn't think my '98 Saturn was new enough to have the data recorder, but apparently it does, and I think it should be up to me to decide how and when I share that information with someone else," said Bob McClellan Jr., 35, of Antioch.

"If I were given the opportunity to agree to have this on the vehicle when I buy it, then that probably would be OK," McClellan said. "But if I own the car, it's my business what's on the recorder, and no one should be able to access it unless I say so."

Details that can be scrutinized include how fast the vehicle was going, as well as whether the brakes or accelerator were being pressed, which way the car was being steered, and—yes—even whether the occupants were wearing their seatbelts. The data is always being recorded, but it's only saved to the device's memory if an air bag deploys, automakers say.

Critics argue that the system is a snoop and unfair to consumers.

"It's in the cars, it can't be turned off, and the information is available to anyone with a court order," said Gary Biller, executive director of the National Motorists Association, a group that advocates on behalf of drivers in instances of unfair traffic enforcement.

"Our members ask whether these devices can be disabled, but they can't, because they are integral to the computer systems that control modern cars," Biller said.

Laws have been implemented in 13 states to limit access to the information in the recorders, but there are no such regulations on the books in Tennessee and many other states to prevent someone from uploading the data without permission.

Getting that data is easier on some vehicles than others, but a Nashville company, VCE Inc., has been at the forefront of using information from the recorders to reconstruct traffic accidents since the introduction of the devices in the mid-1990s.

"We have been involved from the start and were among the first ones to begin downloading the data from these recorders for the accident reconstructions we do for attorneys and insurance companies," VCI Vice President Todd Hutchison said.

"We typically get permission from the owner of the vehicle, but that's not necessarily who owned it at the time of the accident," he pointed out. "If the insurance company has bought the salvaged vehicle, they can give us permission."

Data Easy to Collect (AT)

Collecting the data is simple. VCE investigators merely connect to the vehicle's diagnostic system using a cord that attaches to a laptop computer, and special software then reads the data, Hutchison said.

Both Metro police and the Tennessee Highway Patrol have the equipment to capture the information after an accident, he said.

It doesn't always take a wired connection to access the data. Beginning with the 2011 Chevrolet Cruze, General Motors will be able to upload the information from the recorders wirelessly through the OnStar system included on most of the automaker's vehicles.

And Biller said his organization has heard of possible transponder-style readers that could upload the data just by coming close to a vehicle that is equipped with special technology similar to that used by automated toll-collection systems.

"It's a valuable tool for insurance companies," said Buddy Oakes, a Columbia-based insurance claims adjuster. "If there is no way to tell right away what happened in an accident, sometimes we request permission from the vehicle owner or through the court to extract the data, which gives us the last 15 seconds of activity before the impact.

"It shows how fast the car was going, how hard it was being braked, what evasive moves were made. We've had people say they were sitting still at a stoplight and got hit, when the data recorder shows they were doing 30 mph through the intersection."

Data Used to Calculate Rates

Some insurance companies also are using the data to help rate customers' driving habits to determine how much their premiums should be, but that would be only with the customers' cooperation, Oakes said.

As for the expectation of privacy, "that pretty much went out the door for most things a long time ago," he said. "I don't know that there's privacy on anything anymore. Every phone call you make can be tracked, and just about anything that becomes a legal matter becomes public information." Automakers defend the development and use of the data recorders as a great research tool to help make vehicles safer.

"For us, the whole purpose was safety research," said GM safety spokeswoman Sharon Basel.

The devices were first installed in conjunction with the introduction of air bags in cars nearly two decades ago to show what forces were involved in activating the bags and to help automakers improve them, automakers say.

"We have them in all of our vehicles, and have had since the mid-'90s," Basel said.

Nissan, Ford, Toyota and most other automakers have been using the technology in their new vehicles since at least the mid-2000s.

There are no requirements for them to put the devices in cars, but beginning with the 2011 model year, the National Highway Traffic Safety Administration requires that automakers state in the vehicle owner's manual whether a recorder is installed and where it is located. Locations vary by make, model and year.

"We feel that, overall, it is a benefit for auto safety, but we also go to great lengths to protect our customers' privacy," said

Ford Motor Co. spokesman Wes Sherwood. "If anyone wants access to the data, they will need the owner's consent or the proper legal authority to do so. But the devices are included on all Ford vehicles now, and we have a supplier that provides a tool for reading the information. It's widely available to law enforcement or anyone else with the authority to download the data."

Dealership service departments can download the data from the recorders, which also store reports about vehicle malfunctions to help pinpoint maintenance problems, said Nelson Andrews, general manager of Nelson Cadillac and Land Rover Nashville. He said the devices go "a long way toward helping us fix" whatever is wrong.

"There's really nothing people can do about it," Andrews adds. "But my cellphone collects more data than these devices do."

Nissan is among automakers that provide dealers with software to collect and analyze data from the recorders, said spokesman Steve Yaeger.

"We have event data recorders on all of our vehicles, and we have software called Consult that can be used by qualified people to read that data," Yaeger said. "All of our dealers have it. But it's protected by a code, and is not available to just everybody."

"If it's requested by law enforcement or court order, though, we can provide the information for that."

Critical Thinking

1. Should a person's driving behavior be recorded if he/she has not given explicit permission for such recording? Why or why not?

2. Does the act of purchasing a new car implicitly give permission to record driving behavior? Why or why not?

3. Why is recording of driving behavior a privacy issue?

4. From an ethical view, what are positive and negative aspects of such recordings?

Digital-Privacy Rules Taking Shape

JULIA ANGWIN

Frustrated by a flood of privacy violations, the Federal Trade Commission on Monday issued a strong call for commercial-data collectors to adopt better privacy practices and called for Congress to pass comprehensive privacy legislation.

In a starkly written 73-page report on privacy in the digital age, the agency called on United States commercial data collectors to implement a "Do Not Track" button in Web browsers by the end of the year or to face legislation from Congress forcing the issue.

"Simply put, your computer is your property. No one has the right to put anything on [your computer] that you don't want," said Jon Leibowitz, chairman of the FTC, at a news conference Monday.

The agency also for the first time turned its attention to offline data brokers—which buy and sell names, addresses and other personal information—calling on them to create a centralized website providing consumers with better access to their data. The agency also wants legislation requiring data brokers to give consumers the right to see and make corrections to their information.

Linda Woolley, executive vice president of the Direct Marketing Association, which represents data brokers, said the group opposes giving consumers access to marketing information because it would be expensive, difficult to keep secure and the type of data used by marketers doesn't harm consumers.

The agency wants internet firms to . . .

- Store data securely, limit collection and retention, and promote data accuracy
- Include a "Do Not Track" mechanism in Web browsers by the end of the year
- Provide consumers access to data collected about them by data brokers that buy and sell names, addresses and other personal information

"We are very wary about taking the information out of the information economy," Ms. Woolley said.

The FTC doesn't have the authority to write new rules for privacy. Instead, it hopes its report will spur the industry to agree to abide by its voluntary guidelines.

The FTC can then use its authority to prosecute "deceptive" behavior if companies that agree to the guidelines don't live up to their promises.

Last month, the FTC notched a win for its guideline approach when the online-advertising industry voluntarily agreed to one of the main privacy recommendations: the development of a "Do Not Track" mechanism that would let users limit Web tracking using a single setting in Web browsing software.

Previously, the industry had urged consumers to individually "opt out" of more than a hundred different companies that track Web browsing behavior.

However, the agreement—which was announced at the White House last month—has been mired in debate about what "Do Not Track" means. The online-ad industry has agreed to what amounts to a "Do Not Target" definition, which would still allow data to be collected for purposes such as market research and product development. Privacy advocates are pushing for it to mean that data won't be collected. An international standards body is working to develop a consensus agreement on the definition of Do Not Track by June.

The Digital Advertising Association, which represents more than 400 companies, said it is pushing ahead to implement its definition of Do Not Track. "We're not at the finish line, but we're pretty close," said the trade group's counsel Stuart P. Ingis.

FTC Commissioner J. Thomas Rosch dissented from the vote approving the report, in part because he said "it is not clear that all the interested players in the Do Not Track arena" will be able to agree on a definition.

Critical Thinking

1. Do you believe that the FTC should require commercial data collectors to implement digital-privacy safeguards? Why or why not?

2. Should so called offline data brokers be allowed to buy and sell personal information without the permission of the individual whose personal information is being bought and sold? Why or why not?

3. Should digital privacy be legislated or should the data collection industry be encouraged to adopt voluntary guideline for digital privacy? Take a position and defend your position.

The Ethics of Social Media—Part I: Adjusting to a 24/7 World

JAMES HYATT

S o your company hasn't had an OMG moment over Facebook ethics?

As they say, Good Luck With That.

It has been almost a decade since Congress passed the Sarbanes-Oxley Act in the wake of the Enron, Tyco and World-Com scandals, seeking to put in place a variety of measures to protect investors and address standards of behavior. Over the years, once-controversial practices about disclosure and ethics have become generally accepted standards.

But the social media explosion—from email and Facebook to blogs and Twitter—is making a hash of once-resolved issues and creating all kinds of new dilemmas.

- Businesses have less and less control over how they communicate with the public, while 24-7 bloggers feel free to snipe away.
- Job seekers find their private lives may no longer be private and employees worry that the boss is electronically looking over their shoulders.
- Consumers can't be sure their account information remains safe and have no way to tell whether favorable on-line comments about products and businesses are legitimate.
- Professionals of all sorts—psychiatrists, attorneys, school teachers, reporters, and even NFL players—are learning to live with new, often controversial, social media rules. A customer's irate blog can undo months and years of corporate image work. A careless email can sabotage delicate contract talks or M&A negotiations. Failure to protect customer information can result in years of costly litigation. An old party-hearty photo may block a chance at a new job. Hitting "send" without thinking can torpedo an executive's career.

In just one recent week:

- an email circulating among male employees at the PricewaterhouseCoopers Dublin offices—rating the 'top 10' new female recruits, with headshots—quickly went "viral" and drew widespread criticism. (Some tut-tutting newspapers, however, also saw fit to run the headshots as news.)
- an executive at Pacific Gas & Electric in California was put on paid leave after seeking to join, under an assumed name, an online discussion group critical of the utility's plans to install "smart meters."
- labor lawyers across the country warned clients that a National Labor Relations Board (NLRB) office planned an unfair labor practice complaint against an ambulance company for firing an employee who posted negative Facebook comments about her supervisor.
- Britain's financial regulator, seeking to address insider trading, ordered financial services firm to keep records of employee cellphone calls.

No wonder companies are rushing to build new defenses and adopt new policies to reinforce ethical behaviors and learning how to use social media to react to real-time problems. At the same time, individuals are rethinking their casual attitude about exposing personal information on the Web. And in Washington, government agencies are adopting new guidelines defining acceptable social media behavior.

Defining Social Media Behavior Is Clearly a Work in Progress

A year ago, the Society of Corporate Compliance and Ethics and the Health Care Compliance Association looked at what organizations are doing about social media issues. Twenty-four percent of those surveyed said an employee had been disciplined in their organization for activities on Facebook, Twitter or LinkedIn, more often in the not-for-profit sector. But half of the respondents said their organization had no policy regarding employee online activity outside of work.

Technology search firm Robert Half in April asked chief information officers about social networking policies; 38% said their companies have tightened social networking policies, while 17% say the policies have eased. And 55% reported "no change".

A recent survey by Deloitte of about 1,700 companies found that 26% said they had no social media policy which 34% answered "not applicable/don't know" even though 84% thought every company should have a social media policy in place.

Your Social Media Profile Can Affect Your Job Prospects

A survey commissioned by Microsoft in December 2009 found that 79% of hiring managers and job recruiters reviewed online information about job applicants, and 70% of U.S. hiring managers surveyed said they'd rejected candidates based on what they found online. "Chances are you already have a reputation online, even if you don't want one," Microsoft says. And three-fourths of the U.S. recruiters and HR professionals said their companies have formal policies requiring hiring personnel to research applicants online.

The survey firm declared that "Now, recruiters can easily and anonymously collect information that they would not be permitted to ask in an interview, and the survey found that recruiters are doing just that."

Corporate and union attorneys went on alert early in November 2010 when word spread of the NLRB's unfair labor practices complaint involving the Facebook posting. The NLRB said the company's social media policies were "overly broad." The LegalTimes blog quoted the company as saying "although the NLRB's press release made it sound as if the employee was discharged solely due to negative comments posted on Facebook, the termination decision was actually based on multiple, serious issues."

Although an administrative law judge will have to rule in the case, Philadelphia-based law firm Morgan, Lewis & Bockius LLP declared that "all private sector employers should take note of this issue, regardless of whether their workforce is represented by a union."

You Need a Social Media Policy

Social media behavior "can have real legal and economic consequences for businesses," writes attorney Michelle Sherman in a Social Media Law Update Blog for law firm Sheppard Mullin Richter & Hampton LLP.

"A post may seem as innocent as an employee expressing a personal opinion. However, if the person describes herself as working for a particular company, and then speaks on a highly controversial subject, her post could damage the 'good will' of the company. Or, the poster may be recommending a product to all of her Facebook friends without sharing that she happens to work for the product manufacturer in violation of fair advertising practices."

Sherman says adopting a social media policy can show compliance with Federal Trade Commission guidelines about endorsements, and can better protect brand value "by ensuring that employees do not post unflattering material in association with the business."

One of the most remarkable studies is the 130-plus-page Social Media White Paper, now in its second edition, prepared by Reed Smith LLP. The paper reviews 13 areas where social media is impacting business—from advertising and marketing to trademarks—and declares "the key lesson is that rather trying to control, companies must adopt an altered set of rules of engagement." Well worth a visit.

It has become increasingly common for major companies to issue specific directives on social media behavior. While most encourage employee efforts to put companies in a positive light, they also spell out acceptable conduct. For example:

(Wells Fargo): "By posting content on this Blog, you expressly grant Wells Fargo (and its affiliates) the right to use or distribute the posted content in any form, worldwide, and in perpetuity."

(Kaiser Permanente): "Be mindful of the world's longer memory—Everything you say is likely to be indexed and stored forever, either via search engines or through bloggers that reference your posts."

(FedEx): By posting to the FexEx Citizenship Blog "you agree not to post or transmit anything unlawful, threatening, libelous, defamatory, obscene, inflammatory or pornographic, or anything that infringes upon the copyright, trademark, publicity rights or other rights of a third party."

(Mayo Clinic): "Where your connection to Mayo Clinic is apparent, make it clear that you are speaking for yourself and not on behalf of Mayo Clinic. In those circumstances, you may want to include this disclaimer: 'The views expressed on this [blog; website] are my own and do not reflect the views of my employer."

(Microsoft): "As a general rule, Microsoft does not review, edit, censor, or, obviously, endorse individual posts. You should 'be smart' and, as an employee of the company, you should not only think about how your blog reflects on you as an individual, but also about how your blog affects Microsoft as a whole."

Concerns go well beyond defining proper behavior and move into legal areas. FINRA, the successor to the National Association of Securities Dealers Inc., stresses that social media postings can violate industry rules about promoting investments and soliciting customers. FINRA says securities firms should take steps to be sure that employees using social media sites for business are "appropriately supervised" and "do not present undue risks to investors."

The Social Media Business Council, a group of large companies that explore social media issues, posts a free "Disclosure Best Practices Toolkit" online suggesting checklists to help companies and employees "learn the appropriate and transparent ways to interact with blogs, bloggers, and the people who interact with them."

It makes recommendations on how to deal with bloggers, on how employees should handle personal and unofficial blogging, on how to be transparent in providing rewards or incentives to bloggers, on best practices for third parties acting on behalf of a company, and on best practices for "artistic/entertainment situations where temporarily obscuring the sponsor of a site is necessary and appropriate." For instance, it is okay to use a pretend blog where someone writes that they may have discovered aliens in their house to promote a science fiction movie. But it is not okay to create "a fake customer blog where the 'author' writes: 'I'd love to go see this movie.'"

Critical Thinking

1. What are new dilemmas for ethics brought about by social media?

2. Why is it important for management to develop a social media policy?

3. Should an employee's social media behavior be covered under a corporate code of ethics? Why or why not?

The Ethics of Social Media— Part II: Playing by New Rules

It has been almost a decade since Congress passed the Sarbanes-Oxley Act in the wake of the Enron, Tyco and WorldCom scandals, seeking to put in place a variety of measures to protect investors and address standards of behavior. Over the years, once-controversial practices about disclosure and ethics have become generally accepted standards. But the social media explosion—from email and Facebook to blogs and Twitter—is making a hash of once-resolved issues and creating all kinds of new dilemmas.

In this second-part of a two-part series, James Hyatt surveys some of the approaches toward social media challenges being pursued by government, corporations and a wide variety of business professionals.

JAMES HYATT

While businesses sort out their social media policies, many federal agencies are wading in to referee the online world.

- The Obama Administration, through the Commerce Department's National Telecommunications and Information Administration, is drafting what it calls "Internet Policy 3.0," to address several issues including privacy and cybersecurity. One proposal: Fair Information Practice Principles, which an official says would be "the information privacy framework in the United States to clarify how personal data on the Internet is protected."

- The Federal Trade Commission in April moved up its review of the Children's Online Privacy Protection Rule to see if changes are needed; the rule requires operators of websites and online services that target children under age 13 to obtain verifiable parental consent before they collect, use, or disclose personal information from children.

- The Food and Drug Administration's division of Drug Marketing, Advertising, and Communications expects to begin issuing as early as December 2010 guidance on a series of social media issues faced by the pharmaceutical industry, such as how manufacturers can address misinformation listed on a third-party site.

- Last December, the Federal Trade Commission revised its guidelines on use of endorsements and testimonials in advertising. Among other changes, the revisions declare that celebrities should disclose their relationships with advertisers "when making endorsements outside the context of traditional ads, such as on talk shows or in social media."

- The Defense Department in February took steps to open up social media links to members of the armed forces, and notes thousands of Facebook, Twitter and other pages have been registered. Failing to obtain the "chain of command's approval, well that's not good—plain and simple," the DOD says.

- The Securities and Exchange Commission has encouraged public companies to expand shareholder and public communication through use of the Internet; the policy has led to some controversy over how a company goes about releasing financial information promptly and widely.

Microsoft in October said it would begin using its Investor Relations website as the "authoritative portal" for financial and other information, and no longer use financial newswires. The move prompted Business Wire, owned by Berkshire Hathaway Co., to label the move "a textbook example of 'worst practices' investor relations." Business Wire, of course, derives much of its revenue from disseminating corporate press releases. Business Wire Chairman and CEO Cathy Baron Tamraz pointedly concluded: "There's a large investor in Omaha who doesn't want to be checking hundreds of websites minute-by-minute throughout the day. But then again, who would?"

Can I Buy a Social Media Fix?

As might be expected, the social media commotion has prompted a wave of products and services intended to help businesses cope with the challenges—much like the trend I chronicled five years ago in the wake of Sarbanes-Oxley.

Cisco Systems Inc. in early November unveiled Cisco SocialMiner, software designed to monitor in real time "status updates, forum posts, or blogs from customers . . . alerting enterprises of conversations related to their brand." Cisco said with 34% of online Americans having used Facebook, Twitter "or other social media to rant or rave about a product, company or brand," businesses need to be aware of what customers are saying and "respond to general inquiries or rectify customer service issues so as to enhance and protect brand reputation."

And Cisco introduced a "rich media capture platform that supports the recording, playback, live streaming and storage of media, including audio and video" to capture, preserve and mine conversations for business intelligence.

(Cisco's Facebook page in mid-November had 113,862 "friends".)

Or consider ReputationDefender, a service that "controls how you look when someone Googles you or your business." The MyEdge Pro product is "proven to increase positive content and actively combat false, misleading or irrelevant Google results for businesses and business owners including doctors, lawyers, executives, contractors, real estate agents—anyone whose business depends on their reputation."

For $9.95 a month, another of the company's products, MyPrivacy, will remove personal information from the web, monitor the Internet, and create a "do not track" list for you at over 100 online networks.

TextGuard provides a service to let businesses record telephone conversations and voicemails on company mobile devices; financial regulators increasingly are requiring that companies keep a record of such communications.

And companies with a long history of document storage and research services are expanding into the wired world. Xerox Litigation Services, which hosts more than two billion pages of data for 20,000 clients, last year added its "E-mail Analytics" service to help aid investigations and help companies respond to requests in legal cases. Xerox said more than 70% of the data it hosts is in email.

Hello Sweetheart, Get Me Twitter

Journalism is awash in hand-wringing over social media issues. Reporters debate using Facebook and Twitter in chasing down story ideas; editors worry about how to link online material to other websites; and readers wonder about how reliable "news" they see on the web really is. (A photo of a tornado passing the Statue of Liberty, widely circulated in September when a storm hit the New York City area, turned out to be from 1976.)

Washington Post managing editor Raju Narisetti in October reminded newsroom employees not to use social media accounts to "answer critics and speak on behalf of the Post." The reminder came after a staffer apparently fired back at critics of a piece the paper had published.

Many major media organizations have revised and reissued their ethical codes to address the concerns.

For example, Reuters' guidelines on "Reporting from the Internet" stress that "discovering information publicly available on the web is fair game. Defeating passwords or other security

methods is going too far." And, "do not use anything from the Internet that is not sourced in such a way that you can verify where it came from." Wikipedia "can be a good starting point for research, but it should not be used as an attributable source," Reuters declares.

National Public Radio in October reminded news staff members that "NPR journalists may not participate in marches and rallies involving causes or issues that NPR covers," and pointedly noted the restriction included the Jon Stewart and Stephen Colbert rallies in Washington. And, the memo added, "you must not advocate for political or other polarizing issues online."

Doctors have their own social media issues; some have abandoned use of Facebook and other venues, deciding the risks of give-and-take with and about patients is too great a threat to privacy. A California psychologist writes that "casual viewing of clients' online content outside of the therapy hour can create confusion in regard to whether it's being done as a part of your treatment or to satisfy my personal curiosity."

Dr. Arthur R. Derse of the Medical College of Wisconsin, in a recent AMA Ethics Forum column, writes "an online consultation using social networks can go wrong in myriad ways. The dissemination of patient information in an electronic form to an open forum is fraught with risk."

And medical students can be just as thoughtless as other students in their social media use. The Journal of the American Medical Association last year surveyed medical schools and found and 47 out of 78 schools reported "incidents of students posting unprofessional online content," including violations of patient confidentiality, use of profanity, discriminatory language, depiction of intoxication and sexually suggestive material. And the survey found 30 schools had informally warned students and three had dismissed students. But only 28 out of 73 deans queried said their schools had policies about student-posted online content.

Co-eds Google Their Dates. What about Lawyers and Litigants?

The answer seems obvious: somebody sues you—see what they've been up to online. Not so fast.

Legal ethics committees in New York and Pennsylvania have addressed the question. In Pennsylvania, an attorney wondered whether a third party could "friend" a witness. The committee said no, calling such a step deception by not revealing the purpose to obtain information for use in a lawsuit.

In New York, the question was whether a lawyer could access a public website. The committee said okay, so long as the profile is generally available and the lawyer doesn't "friend" the other party.

Currently, there are challenges to trial decisions because a juror tweeted during the trial, and debates over letting reporters tweet from the courtroom (some states permit it, federal courts generally oppose). A North Carolina judge was reprimanded for "friending" defense counsel and discussing a pending case with the judge (considered improper ex-parte communications). And many states are instructing jurors against using social media while hearing cases. "The information you are accessing is not evidence," declares a model jury charge in New Jersey.

"Let's Go to the Videotape!"—Not So Fast

The sports business presents a particularly curious set of ethical issues over social media.

Networks, which pay huge sums for exclusive rights to broadcast sporting events, are finding it hard to keep control over the broadcasting of live sporting events. They don't want sportswriters using their content via the Internet and cellphones.

The New York Yankees ban fans from bringing video cameras and laptop computers into Yankee Stadium. The Washington Redskins have banned writers from tweeting or blogging while watching practices. The National Football League bans players and coaches from using social media such as tweeting for 90 minutes before, during, or sometime after a game.

Sports broadcaster ESPN last year temporarily suspended popular "Sports Guy" columnist Bill Simmons for criticizing an ESPN radio station partner on Twitter. ESPN earlier had issued a policy prohibiting reporters and writers from discussing sports on social-networking sites.

The NCAA tries to keep coaches and schools from using social media outlets in recruiting. While they can advertise their programs online, they're prohibited from using a site "for direct person-to-person contact with an individual potential student-athlete." However, signing on as a "friend" doesn't count as direct contact, the NCAA says. (Indiscrete Facebook entries by partying athlete recruits this year has led to legal investigations.)

Critical Thinking

1. What ethical issues of social media are identified in the article?

2. What advice would you offer management about handling the ethical issues of social media?

3. What aspects of or things about an employee's use of social media should be covered in a corporate code of ethics?

Challenges of Governing Globally

A strong understanding of the three distinct corporate governance systems around the world will help managers conduct business more effectively in other countries.

MARC J. EPSTEIN

Shortly after New Year's Day in 2009, just six months after Satyam and its politically influential chairman, Ramalinga Raju, were honored by the World Council for Corporate Governance, the company and its senior leadership became the subject of the largest corporate fraud investigation in India's history. Raju admitted to fabricating 70 billion rupees ($1.5 billion) of Satyam's assets and 95% of the previous year's revenue. Despite its record for good governance, this large, respected outsourcing firm saw its market value fall more than 80% in 24 hours. Long before the confession, shareholders had expressed dissatisfaction with Raju's leadership. Many charged that the board of directors and its members failed to meet their basic responsibilities.

Senior executives aren't the only perpetrators of corporate fraud. A scandal at Volkswagen (VW), Germany's largest carmaker, erupted in 2005 when it was discovered that managers and labor representatives had received improper benefits from the company and its suppliers. A quid-pro-quo agreement had developed between managers and labor that centered around the important role that union representatives play on German boards (workers' representatives have 50% of the seats on the supervisory boards of companies with 2,000 or more employees). In return, the local government, which was the controlling shareholder of the corporation with only 18% ownership (the voting rights of any single share-holder are limited to 20%), was satisfied with the ability to guarantee regional job security. Yet it seemed that the other shareholders may not have been receiving equal benefits, and the VW board found itself unable or unwilling to protect its minority owners from actions that didn't maximize the returns to everyone.

Understanding corporate governance practices globally should be a priority for managers who work in multinational corporations or with international clients.

Not all corporate governance failures involve financial fraud. In 2010, BP, one of the world's largest oil and gas companies, saw its market value fall by more than 50% in less than 60 days after the infamous explosion at a deepwater drilling rig off the U.S. Gulf Coast. The incident killed 11 employees and resulted in the largest marine oil spill in history, costing BP billions of dollars in compensation for victims and cleanup costs. The government investigation of the explosion revealed numerous causes and guilty parties. Many people have suggested that BP's board failed to put the right processes in place to ensure that reasonable safety measures were taken to prevent such a disaster.

These stories occur far too often in corporations all over the world. Enron, WorldCom, and Tyco in the U.S. and Parmalat in Italy immediately come to mind. Sometimes these failures are fraud, and sometimes they're the result of poor oversight. Nevertheless, they have caused us to reexamine the structures, systems, and processes of corporate governance.

As you know, corporate governance is the system by which corporations are directed, controlled, and made accountable to shareholders and other stakeholders. Failures such as those outlined above occur in a wide variety of companies and industries and in different countries around the world. Understanding corporate governance practices globally should be a priority for managers who work in multinational corporations or with international clients.

Here I'll describe three corporate governance systems—Anglo-American, Communitarian, and Emerging Markets—and provide a comparison that you can use to recognize and evaluate differences in practice. This is a summary of extensive work that I recently completed in response to many inquiries from senior managers who want to better understand how to evaluate corporate and board performance in other countries.

Table 1 summarizes some of the major differences in the general characteristics of each system.

Table 1 General Characteristics of Global Corporate Governance Systems

Examples of Countries/Regions General Characteristics	Anglo-American United States, United Kingdom, Australia, Canada, South Africa	Communitarian Japan, Germany, Belgium, Scandinavia	Emerging Markets China, Eastern Europe, India, Brazil, Mexico, Russia
	• Shareholder-centric • Market centered • Unitary board structure	• Stakeholder-centric • Bank centered • Two-tier board structure (supervisory & management)	• Stakeholder-centric • Government/Family centered • Board structure varies
	• Boards primarily composed of nonexecutive directors (and independent directors)	• Labor, founding family, and bank are common members—interlocking common	• Few independent board members
	• Common law legal system • High levels of disclosure and more rules on disclosure	• Civil law legal system • Moderate levels of disclosure	• Legal systems relatively weak • Low levels of disclosure
	• Large pay incentives for managers, including pay for performance	• Pay incentives moderate	• Pay incentives smaller

Global Corporate Governance Systems

Corporate governance practices vary globally as a result of significant country differences, such as culture, history, regulatory systems, and economic and financial development. All of you who interact with corporate managers in other countries or have affiliates or subsidiaries throughout the world must understand these differences because it's critical to the evaluation of corporate board performance and to corporate success. It also has important implications for corporate governance, corporate financial and operational transactions, and global relationships.

Let's look at some of the basic differences.

Anglo-American Corporate Governance System

The Anglo-American system of governance evolved in countries to which the U.K. exported its common law legal system during its colonial period, such as the U.S., Australia, New Zealand, Canada, and South Africa. Originally developed to protect private landholders from nobility, the common law legal system sets a broad legal precedent that protects shareholders and tries to prevent a company's leaders from acting against shareholder interests.

In the Anglo-American system, corporations focus primarily on the shareholder and aim to maximize shareholder wealth. Directors usually are elected by shareholders and can be replaced if shareholders aren't satisfied with the company's financial results. The system emphasizes transparency and disclosure about a company's audited financial status, board composition, and corporate strategy.

Since well-developed financial markets heavily influence corporate governance practices, the Anglo-American system is considered market-based with a large share of corporate ownership traded frequently on large, public exchanges. Under this system, corporate boards are structured as unitary boards and are composed primarily of nonexecutive directors (directors who aren't company employees) who represent the interests of large shareholders. These boards also have independent directors with little financial interest in the future performance of the firm. Critics of this system have argued that boards are frequently too large (with as many as 20 members) and that directors have often failed to dedicate enough time to their roles.

Communitarian Corporate Governance System

A Communitarian corporate governance system has evolved in much of continental Europe and in Japan. This system has its origins in the Romano-Germanic civil law codes developed more than a millennium ago. Instead of relying on strong legal protections for investors, performance is regulated through statutes, codes, and relationships with stakeholders.

The Communitarian system is relationship-based, which provides for a stakeholder-centric approach to governance and focuses on a broader set of stakeholders that often includes lenders, members of supply chains, customers, employees, and the community. These relationships allow stakeholders to wield strong control over corporations and hold them accountable. In Germany and Japan, for example, it's common for companies and banks to cross-invest in their suppliers and customers, creating associations of corporations that play an active role in deciding corporate governance standards. Boards often include representatives from various stakeholders who are representing their own interests. A banking representative may be interested in a decision's impact on the corporation but also on the bank he or she works for. Similarly, a union representative on the board is interested in the impact of a decision on the corporation and its shareholders but particularly on the workers that the union represents. This stakeholder orientation provides for a broader set of interests and representation on the board.

Corporate governance under the Communitarian system relies heavily on banks instead of capital markets for financing, and representatives from these banks often sit on the board of directors of a company that they finance. This system generally uses a two-tier board structure, dividing board functions between a supervisory board and a management board.

Critics of the system have argued that it fails to protect minority shareholders and lacks representation for outside investors.

Emerging Markets Corporate Governance System

Emerging Markets countries—such as China, Brazil, India, Mexico, Russia, and much of Eastern Europe—still have relatively young legal systems that haven't fully developed the legal framework necessary to classify their corporate governance systems into the other categories. In China, for example, the first corporations were founded centuries after countries with more defined corporate governance systems began their corporate history. These countries also differ in legal traditions, language, and culture, so it's still uncertain how corporate governance will likely evolve there.

Strategic oversight is an important board role in all three governance systems.

Yet there are some recognizable patterns. The lack of defined legal systems means that shareholders often have few credible legal protections, so boards are expected to vigorously monitor and protect shareholder interests. Also, low levels of disclosure and a lack of transparency often make it difficult for shareholders to exercise informed control over the company.

Corporate governance in Emerging Markets countries tends to be stakeholder-centric and centered around family or government relationships. In addition, large corporate shareholders dominate boards and are well known worldwide. For example, about 30 Korean family groups that are organized as chaebols (business conglomerates) control almost 40% of that country's economy. There's also a large amount of state participation. Even in countries where the government has privatized its corporate holdings, it often retains significant control over corporations by regulating equity markets or influencing board members. For example, often the government retains a regulatory interest in supervising large transactions that have an impact on the state. (All governments do this to some extent, but it's far more common in the Emerging Markets countries.)

Roles of the Board Globally

Though significant differences in corporate governance practices exist, some general principles are present globally that are critical for effective corporate governance. Boards of directors are usually expected to fulfill three separate but related roles: accountability, senior-level staffing and evaluation, and strategic oversight. (For more details on roles and responsibilities of corporate boards, see Marc J. Epstein and Marie-Josée Roy, "Corporate Governance Is Changing: Are You a Leader or a Laggard?" *Strategic Finance,* October 2010, pp. 31–37).

Accountability

In Anglo-American countries, boards of directors traditionally have been responsible for holding managers accountable to shareholders. In the Communitarian system, it's common for the corporation, management, and board to also be accountable to other stakeholders, such as employees, suppliers, and customers. In the Emerging Markets system, boards are typically accountable to the controlling shareholders in the corporation, which can be the state, a family group, or a corporate conglomerate. Thus, it's common to have representatives of these other stakeholders on boards in non-Anglo-American countries.

Senior-Level Staffing and Evaluation

Evaluating senior management, determining their compensation, and having important input to senior staffing decisions are important roles for the board in all three governance systems. But there are important application differences. In the Anglo-American system, many corporations pay managers a huge amount of compensation for their performance in exchange for relentless attention to financial returns. In the Communitarian and the Emerging Markets systems, pay levels, performance-based pay, and the role of the board in determining pay are considerably smaller.

Strategic Oversight

In all three governance systems, strategic oversight is an important board role. In the Anglo-American system, managers focus on strategy formulation, and the board, though providing some oversight, often plays a more passive role in approving important strategic moves. In the Communitarian system, the management board is more assertive in its strategic oversight role and is often more involved in the formulation of strategy than in oversight only. And in the Emerging Markets system, many board members view the formulation and oversight of strategy as the primary role of the board.

Though these specific roles manifest themselves differently in different settings, they greatly impact the mechanisms that ensure managers fulfill shareholder expectations regarding corporate performance.

Internal Determinants of Corporate Boards

How successfully a board performs its duties depends on several internal factors that differ substantially among the three global governance systems (see Table 2). These factors may

Table 2   Internal Determinants of Corporate Governance Systems

Corporate Governance Mechanism	Anglo-American	Communitarian	Emerging Markets
Board Composition, Systems, & Structure			
Board composition	• Balance between internal and independent directors	• Few independent directors	• Independent directors rare
Board structure	• Unitary	• Two-tier	• Varies
Board accountability	• Shareholders	• Stakeholders (including entire value chain and employees)	• Stakeholders and government or founding family
Executive compensation	• Large performance pay	• Moderate performance pay	• Little performance pay

affect managers' roles and interactions with the board, as well as their compensation. They include:

1. Board composition,
2. Board systems and structure, and
3. Performance evaluation and compensation systems.

Board Composition

Board composition choices determine board competencies, skills, and power structures. Many corporate governance experts and international guidelines advocate increased board member independence and increased numbers of nonexecutive directors on boards, yet the role of nonexecutive and independent directors is markedly different in each corporate governance system.

In the Anglo-American system, boards are composed primarily of nonexecutive directors who represent the interests of large shareholders, as well as independent directors with no significant financial interest in the future performance of the firm. Usually there are stringent requirements for board independence since these board members often have a significant amount of power. In Canada, for example, 70% of companies have independent directors serving as their board chair.

In the Communitarian system, independent directors are less common but still hold a considerable amount of power. Since national codes and companies typically don't stress the independence of board directors, most corporation board members in Japan, Italy, and much of continental Europe are internal. This is partly because of codetermination laws that mandate high levels of employee participation on the supervisory board.

The Emerging Markets system features many of the regulatory requirements of the Anglo-American system with regard to independent directors, but truly independent directors are uncommon and wield little power relative to controlling interests on the board. In China, for example, listed companies are required to have two independent directors. Despite these requirements, many believe that Chinese directors show few signs of true independence and are still strongly influenced by the government.

Board Systems and Structure

Board systems and structure are the mechanisms typically used to translate board roles, responsibilities, and composition into decisions. They also vary significantly across governance systems.

Again, in the Anglo-American system, a unitary board typically combines executive directors (company executives who are on the corporate board) and nonexecutive directors. Boards usually are organized into committees—such as audit, nomination, and compensation—that perform much of the board's functions.

In the Communitarian system, the executive directors and nonexecutive directors are divided into two separate entities. The management board, composed mainly of senior-level management, is primarily responsible for managerial decisions, such as strategy, marketing, and product development. The supervisory board, composed of company insiders, such as employees, as well as company outsiders, such as independent accountants, is primarily responsible for overseeing executive management, accounting, senior-level staffing, and evaluation. Employees also can play a significant role in determining the composition of the supervisory board. Shareholders elect the supervisory board, and the supervisory board appoints members of the management board. In Germany, employees elect a third to a half of the members of the supervisory board. In addition, representatives from founding families or national banks may also serve on this board.

In the Emerging Markets system, the board structure varies between countries and even among corporations in the same country. Some corporations have adopted the two-tier board structure of Communitarian countries, and others utilize the unitary board structure of the Anglo-American system. The largest shareholders, usually the state or family groups, often are permitted to control the boards.

Performance Evaluation and Compensation Systems

Performance evaluation and compensation systems also differ among governance systems. In the Anglo-American system, boards are expected to perform rigorous evaluations of senior manager and corporate performance. It's common to structure executive compensation so that a large percentage of that pay is tied to the financial performance of the corporation. Evaluation procedures only recently have become part of corporate governance in the Communitarian system, and most companies in the Emerging Markets system lack explicit evaluation mechanisms. In the two latter systems, large performance-based pay is significantly less common and accounts for a much smaller percentage of overall executive compensation than in Anglo-American countries.

External Determinants of Corporate Board Systems

External factors also affect how boards of directors perform their roles and responsibilities. Three that determine key components of corporate governance are:

1. Markets,
2. Legal systems, and
3. Ownership and control structures.

These mechanisms (see Table 3) ensure that corporations act according to national expectations regarding corporate governance. An understanding of these external factors will provide managers with insight into board regulation, objectives, operations, and decisions.

Markets

The existence of markets for ownership and control of corporations is an important aspect of corporate governance since the threat of takeovers increases when mechanisms for governance fail. Takeovers are most common in the Anglo-American system, particularly in the U.S., while the existence of a controlling shareholder in the Communitarian and Emerging Markets systems lessens the likelihood of a takeover.

Beyond corporate control, stock markets determine the returns available to stockholders in a corporation and diversify ownership. In the Anglo-American system, these markets are quite active. More than 6,000 domestic companies are listed publicly in the U.S., and more than 1,000 are listed in the U.K. But only a relatively small number of firms are listed in Communitarian countries. In Germany, for example, there are fewer than 500 listed companies. In Emerging Markets, stock exchanges are developing rapidly, although there is a great deal of variation across countries. China, for example, has become a "dominant force" in the initial public offering (IPO) market in the last two years with its large exchange in Hong Kong. Yet in Mexico, only a small percentage of transfers occurs through the public markets.

Market listing requirements play another important role in corporate governance. In the Anglo-American system, these regulations have become a dominant mechanism for implementing corporate governance reforms. Several large stock exchanges in Anglo-American countries have adopted mandatory listing requirements that include more stringent corporate governance measures, such as the qualification and roles of board members, having a majority of independent directors, and having a requirement for certain committees such as audit and compensation for publicly traded companies. Many Communitarian and Emerging Markets stock exchanges have followed suit more recently.

Table 3 External Determinants of Corporate Governance Systems

Corporate Governance Mechanism	Anglo-American	Communitarian	Emerging Markets
Markets			
Financial markets	• Strong and active	• Weak and not commonly used	• Volatile
Investment purpose	• Short-term return	• Long-term return	• Policy and political goals
Methods of finance	• Financial markets	• Bank credit and retained earnings	• Private and state-owned banks
LEGAL SYSTEMS			
Legal history	• Common law system	• Civil law system	• Combined systems that are still rapidly evolving
Transactional methods	• Contracts	• Relationship-based transactions	• Relationship-based transactions
OWNERSHIP & CONTROL STRUCTURES			
Ownership structure	• Diverse individual and institutional ownership	• Concentrated family and corporate ownership	• Concentrated family, corporate, and government ownership
Minority shareholder protections	• Strong	• Moderate	• Weak
Dominant control	• Voting and board representation	• Cross-holding, pyramidal groups, lending relationships	• Internal mechanisms and external mechanisms

Legal Systems

Legal systems affect other aspects of corporate governance, including investor protection for minority shareholders, ownership structure, and financial markets. They also are an important aspect of how investors are protected. The Anglo-American corporate governance system, developed from the common law tradition, often exhibits the best legal protection for investors and tends to provide better enforcement of these laws. The Communitarian corporate governance system, derived from the civil law system, has developed other mechanisms to ensure that capital is allocated efficiently. These include concentrated ownership and control, mandatory dividends, and limited equity markets. Countries in the Emerging Markets system have even fewer shareholder protections than in civil law countries and have evolved a severely concentrated ownership structure to compensate for these weak protections. In addition, the state often plays a much more active role as a corporate owner.

Ownership and Control Structures

Concentrated ownership and minority control mechanisms can be viewed as corporate governance mechanisms that evolve in the absence of basic shareholder protections. As a result, the most concentrated ownership structures are usually in Emerging Markets economies. One of the most glaring examples of this concentration is in China, where the state still owns majority holdings in most of the large firms, and Hong Kong, where a small group of business tycoons controls most large companies through concentrated shareholdings.

There's considerable ownership concentration in Communitarian countries as well. In Germany and Japan, for example, large banks, corporate groups, or families can control large portfolios of companies. Although these groups don't always hold majority stakes, they use a variety of tactics to steer the company in the direction that they prefer. These tactics include cross-shareholding, where two or more companies controlled by the same family group or government invest in each other, and pyramidal shareholding, where a company owns a sizable minority stake in a holding company that owns smaller stakes in more companies.

In Anglo-American countries, financial institutions, including pension funds, own more than 60% of all equity capital, yet ownership is quite dispersed. In this system, countries typically lack a controlling shareholder, so officers and directors have more control over decisions. This means that boards are responsible for ensuring that these decisions are in the best interests of the shareholders.

Closely related to ownership and control of corporations are the existence and enforcement of minority shareholder rights. These rights deal with voting privileges, corporate meetings, and dividends. For example, can major shareholders control corporate decisions, and must these decisions be for the benefit of the entire corporation, for all of its shareholders, for all of its stakeholders, or for only the small limited set of controlling shareholders? For an individual small owner of stock, the Anglo-American system provides far more protection both by regulation and through the legal system. In other systems, small shareholders must often just go along with what a major shareholder wants whether it is in their best interests or not.

In Emerging Markets economies, the state is frequently the controlling owner and can use its political power to derive wide control over corporations. In China, for example, rules surrounding the boards of directors of major corporations and financial markets are structured to give the state control over corporations. Even in countries where the state has started to turn control of corporations over to the private sector—such as in India, Brazil, and Russia—governments continue to wield significant power because of their ability to control the legal framework and market environment.

Understanding the Systems is Critical

As corporations become more global, senior financial executives constantly deal with international contractors, licensees, affiliates, suppliers, and subsidiaries. Since these global associations and entities are often subject to different regulatory regimes and corporate governance systems, their decision-making processes can provide surprises. They may choose to ignore that your bid is the lowest and choose a higher-cost bid from a controlling shareholder, but it may be that the decision is to choose a contract from a controlling shareholder that benefits their relationship and benefits the other corporation—who is a common shareholder on multiple entities. Also, it may seem strange to a U.S. manager that a corporation might decide to make decisions that benefit the environment or the labor union over shareholders since the U.S. model is shareholder focused. Remember: The other systems aren't better or worse, but they *are* different—and it's important for managers to understand this as they are doing business in other countries. To better understand decisions and constraints and to conduct business around the world more effectively, executives must understand the context, regulations, and processes of corporate governance in other countries. Without this understanding, evaluating and/or improving performance globally is difficult.

Note

1. This article draws heavily from Marc J. Epstein, "Governing Globally: Convergence, Differentiation, or Bridging," in Eds. Antiono Davila, Marc J. Epstein, and Jean-François Manzoni, *Performance Measurement and Management Control: Global Issues,* Emerald: U.K., 2012.

Critical Thinking

1. What are the salient characteristics of the three different global corporate governance systems presented in the article? List the characteristics and be prepared to discuss them during class.

2. What are the implications for placing a firm's code of ethics in a host country plant given different governance systems in the host country than in the home country?

3. What are the internal determinants of corporate boards?

4. What are the external determinants of corporate boards?

5. How do differing legal systems in various countries affect corporate governance?

6. How do differing legal systems in various countries affect implementation of a firm's ethics programs?

MARC J. EPSTEIN is Distinguished Research Professor of Management at the Jesse H. Jones Graduate School of Business at Rice University in Houston, Texas. He also is a member of IMA®. You can reach Marc at (713) 348-6140 or epstein@rice.edu.

Ethics Must Be Global, Not Local

To build a truly great, global business, business leaders need to adopt a global standard of ethical practices.

BILL GEORGE

In business school, we used to debate whether your business ethics should adapt to the local environment or be the same around the world. Many of my classmates argued, "When in Rome, do as the Romans do." In other words, follow local practices. Those were the days when leading ethicists like Joseph Fletcher and James Adams at Harvard were promoting "situation ethics," based on flexible, pragmatic approaches to complex dilemmas.

I listened to their arguments but never could figure out how leaders of business organizations could operate with one set of principles in their homeland and another overseas.

In the 1970s, the Foreign Corrupt Practices Act (FPCA) sent a chill throughout the business community by criminalizing the act of making payments outside the U.S. in pursuit of contracts. Yet the practice persisted. Many U.S. executives lobbied to relax the FPCA's provisions, arguing that they were at a competitive disadvantage in bidding against non-U.S. companies.

Risking the Company's Reputation

These days the business world has gone global, which has intensified the ethics debate. Making payments to obtain business is common practice in many developing markets in Asia, Africa, the Middle East, and Eastern Europe, and some companies feel obliged to play the game to compete. Witness Germany's Siemens (SI), which has admitted to nearly $2 billion in bribes, leading to the resignations of both its board chairman and its CEO in 2007. Then there's Britain's BAE Systems, which has been accused of making a $2 billion payment to a Saudi prince to secure $80 billion in government contracts. (The company denied the allegation, which is being investigated by the U.S. Justice Dept.)

What's significant about these ethical scandals is the damage they do to great institutions. If you were leading such an organization, would you risk permanently damaging your company in order to win a few overseas contracts? Regrettably, for some executives the answer is yes.

Forty years of experience has strengthened my belief that the only way to build a great global company is with a single global standard of business practices, vigorously communicated and rigorously enforced. Applying "situation ethics" in developing countries is the fastest way to destroy a global organization. To sustain their success, companies must follow the same standards of business conduct in Shanghai, Mumbai, Kiev, and Riyadh as in Chicago.

Engage the CEO in the Process

How else will employees in far-flung locations know what to do when pressured by customers or competitors to deviate from company standards? If overseas managers miss their financial targets because they adhere to strict ethical standards, can they be confident management will back them up?

Operating ethically requires much more than a code of conduct. The CEO and top management must engage with employees around the world to insist on transparency and compliance. Otherwise, they will never know what's going on. The company must have a closed-loop system of monitoring and auditing local marketing practices. The "don't look, don't tell" approach is bound to destroy your company's reputation. High standards must be enforced with a zero tolerance policy.

This well-established approach is employed by the companies on whose boards I serve—ExxonMobil (XOM), Goldman Sachs (GS), and Novartis (NOVN). Their employees throughout the world know precisely what is expected of them. Nothing is more important to these companies than their reputations, and they know that nothing destroys reputations faster than ethical violations.

Ethics Create Shareholder Value

General Electric's (GE) former general counsel, Ben Heineman, writes in "Avoiding Integrity Land Mines" in the *Harvard Business Review* about high performance with high integrity, proposing that performance and ethics go hand in hand. Heineman argues persuasively that CEOs can't just publish their policies and enforce them. Rather, they must get personally involved in ensuring ethical behavior and engaging employees in vigorous discussions of real-world issues. Otherwise, marginal practices like using agents to make payments will abound.

Despite the best efforts, there will be deviations. That's when leaders are watched most closely by their subordinates. Will management make an exception for a top performer?

Early in my time as CEO of Medtronic (MDT) I had to deal with numerous such deviations that led to the termination of such high-performing executives as the president of our European operations and country managers of Japan, Argentina, and Italy. These actions sent a powerful message that we were serious about company standards, and no one was exempt.

The bottom line is that good ethics is good business. There is a direct correlation between behaving ethically and creating long-term shareholder value. Furthermore, high integrity in external business dealings goes hand in hand with creating greater transparency and increased integrity in internal relationships. This necessitates choosing leaders who are not only ethical themselves but also committed to ensuring their organizations operate ethically at all times.

Bill's True North Principle: Great global organizations can be built only from a solid ethical foundation.

Critical Thinking

1. Should a business firm adapt its business code of ethics to local host-country environments or use the firm's home-country code of ethics in every country in which it operates around the world? Take a position and defend your position.

2. What is the role of a CEO in managing a firm's global ethics?

BILL GEORGE is professor of management practice at Harvard Business School and author of *7 Lessons for Leading in Crisis, True North,* and *Authentic Leadership.* The former chair and CEO of Medtronic, he currently serves on the boards of ExxonMobil and Goldman Sachs. Read more at www.BillGeorge.org, or follow him on Twitter@Bill_George.

From *Bloomberg BusinessWeek*, February 12, 2008. Copyright © 2008 by Bill George. Reprinted by permission of the author.

Conceptualizing a Framework for Global Business Ethics

WILLIAM J. KEHOE

The imperative of globalization arguably is one of the more significant changes experienced by business in the past several decades (Levitt, 1983; Kehoe and Whitten, 1999; Hill, 2001; Cateora and Graham, 2002; Czinkota, Ronkainen and Moffett, 2002; Keegan, 2002; Griffin and Pustay, 2003; Hill, 2003; Lascu, 2003; Yip 2003). In pursuing globalization, firms analyze and debate various entry strategies to host-country markets; carefully consider the appropriateness of sourcing equipment, financing, materials, personnel and other factors of production across the global arena; argue the merits of operating in a home-country currency versus host-country currencies; and study the cultures of host countries. However, the challenges of implementing an ethical system globally sometimes are addressed only as an afterthought, particularly when an ethical problem occurs.

This manuscript addresses the importance of developing and implementing an ethical framework to facilitate the application of ethics across the expanse of a global firm's operating arena. Prior to presenting the framework, the field of global business ethics is summarized, and the more interesting, well-conceptualized, and significant literature in the field is reviewed. Then, unethical business practices in global business are identified and discussed, so as to present a platform for the development of a framework for global business ethics. The framework is conceptualized and discussed and implementation suggestions for management are presented.

Global Business Ethics as a Field of Study

Almost a decade ago, DeGeorge (1994) opined, "business ethics is still a young field, and its international dimensions have scarcely been raised, much less adequately addressed." While still relatively a young field,

the literature base of global business ethics is developing rapidly and has a richness of content.

Literature of 1960s and 1970s

Among the more interesting and well-conceptualized literature in the field during the 1960s and 1970s is the work of such scholars as Baumhart (1961) introducing the concept of ethics in business and exploring the ethics of business practitioners. Raths, Harmin and Simon (1966) provided important underpinnings on values and teaching for the new field of business ethics; Smith (1966) advanced a theory of moral sentiments; Boulding (1967) provided important underpinnings to business ethics in his scholarly examination of value judgments in economics; and Perlmutter (1969) reflected on the difficult evolution of a multinational corporation. Other notable literature of the period includes work by Kohlberg (1971) conceptualizing stages of moral development, by Bowie (1978) developing an early taxonomy of ethics for multinational corporations, and by Carroll (1979) presenting a model of corporate social performance.

Literature of the 1980s

Moving to the 1980s, significant scholarship included such literature as Engelbourg (1980) in a significant examination of the early history of business ethics and Drucker (1981) examining the concept of business ethics. Nash (1981), enlivening Bowie's (1978) taxonomy, posited twelve questions for managers to ask when considering the ethical aspects of a business decision and offered a taxonomy of shared conditions for successful ethical inquiries. Berleant (1982) explored problems of ethical consistency in multinational firms, raising questions relevant to this day.

Lacyniak (1983) developed one of the first primers in ethics for managers. McCoy (1983), in a classic article, presented a parable that is used to differentiate corporate and individual ethics. Donaldson (1985) reconciled international norms with ethical business decision-making, Kehoe (1985) examined ethics, price fixing, and the management of price strategy, and Lacaznik and Murphy (1985) published a book of ethical guidelines for marketing managers. Ferrell and Gresham (1985) conceptualized a contingency framework for understanding ethical decision-making, Hoffman, Lange and Fedo (1986) examined ethics in multinational corporations, and Murphy (1988) focused on processes for implementing business ethics. The literature period of the 1960s/1970s/1980s closed with a comprehensive work by Donaldson (1989) examining the ethics of international business.

Overall, the literature of the 1960s/1970s/1980s tended to be descriptive in methodology, nature, and tone. Of course, a descriptive nature is to be expected, as business ethics was an embryonic field at that time then. The literature introduced ethical concepts and theories to academics and practitioners in business. It anchored the field of business ethics, conceptualized its early content, developed taxonomies, and established the importance and the validity of the concept of ethics in business with both academics and practitioners.

Literature of the Early 1990s
The period of the early 1990s saw the field of business ethics begin to flourish conceptually, empirically, and operationally. Bowie's (1990) article on business ethics and cultural relativism signaled a movement from the field's descriptive tone toward higher levels of abstraction and inquiry. DeGeorge (1990) authored a book chapter examining international business systems and morality, while Donaldson (1992) presented a classic article on the language of international corporate ethics. Koehn (1992) examined the ethic of exchange, an important article in that the concept of exchange is a central underpinning of business. Velasquez (1992) explored questions of morality and the common good in international business. DeGeorge (1993) addressed the concept of competing with integrity. Green (1993) placed business ethics in a wider global context, while Kehoe (1993) examined theory and application in business ethics.

The Business Ethics Quarterly heralded a defining moment in the scholarship of business ethics by publishing an entire issue (January 1994) devoted to international business ethics. Nicholson (1994) presented a framework for inquiry in organizational ethics, the first such framework in the literature. Fraedrich, Thorne and Ferrell (1994) assessed the application of cognitive moral development theory to business ethics. Rossouw (1994) addressed the ethics of business in developing countries, an important article given that many ethical abuses occur in developing countries.

Delener (1995) advanced earlier scholarship on ethical issues in international marketing, Smith (1995) described marketing strategies for an ethics era, while Rogers, Ogbuehi, and Kochunny (1995) raised troubling questions of the ethics of transnational corporations in developing countries. Perhaps fittingly, given the emerging questions about ethics of transnational corporations, the Caux Roundtable's Principles for Business (1995) were published at this time, believed to be the first international code of ethics created through collaboration of business leaders in Europe, Japan, and the United States (Skelly, 1995; Davids, 1999).

Literature of the Later 1990s
Donaldson (1996), perhaps building from the troubling questions about ethics in the early 1990s, examined values in tension when home-country ethics are employed in host-country markets away from a home country. Bowie (1997) posited the moral obligations of multinational corporations, while Johnson (1997) foreshadowed ethics during turbulent times as he examined ethics in brutal markets. Kung (1997) reminded scholars that globalization calls for a global ethic. Becker (1998) applied the philosophy of objectivism to integrity in organizations. Costa (1998) argued that moral business leadership is an ethical imperative, and Dunfee (1998), in an article based on a 1996 speech, explored the marketplace of morality from the focus of a theory of moral choice. Hasnas (1998), in an article subtitled "a guide for the perplexed," attempted to clarify the field of business ethics in an interesting article examining three leading normative theories of business ethics—the stockholder theory, the stakeholder theory, and the social contract theory.

A more scholarly tone in business ethics is found particularly in works by Brock (1998), questioning whether corporations are morally defensible and by Collier (1998), theorizing the ethical organization. Other significant literature includes Ferrell (1998) examining business ethics in a global economy, Bowie (1999) reaffirming the place of a Kantian perspective in business ethics, and Buller and McEvoy (1999) examining how to create and to sustain an ethical capability in a multinational corporation. Lantos (1999) considered how to motivate moral corporate behavior, Mackenzie and Lewis (1999) focused on the case of ethical investing, and Weaver, Trevino and Cochran (1999) posited corporate ethics programs as control systems.

In each of these articles of the later 1990s, a more scholarly, more theoretical, and less descriptive approach is manifest than in many earlier articles in the field, particularly in the literature of the 1960s, 1970s, and early 1980s.

A New Century's Literature

Continuing the scholarly tone of the later 1990s, Chonko and Hunt (2000) presented an important retrospective analysis and prospective commentary on ethics and marketing management, while Freeman (2000) examined business ethics at the millennium. Robin (2000) developed a hierarchical framework of ethical missions and a model of corporate moral development. Velasquez (2000) considered globalization and the failure of ethics. Werhane (2000) authored a seminal work on global capitalism in the 21st Century—a work that foreshadows the level of analysis and depth of scholarship to which business ethics aspires and which it must attain.

A question for consideration is whether business ethics is moving toward a postmodern phase (Carroll, 2000; Gustafson, 2000), in which it is not the rules of ethics but rather the "questions that raise issues of responsibility" that will guide business ethics to its tomorrows beyond. Is the field moving toward an interesting future for scholarship in ethics in which content and issues about ethical issues not envisioned in the early 1980s will emerge for serious reflection and scholarship? Contents and issues such as a cross-cultural comparison of ethical sensitivity (Blodgett, Lu, Rose and Vitell, 2001); myth and ethics (Geva, 2001); an examination of questions at the intersection of ethics and economics (Hosmer and Chen, 2001); ethics and perceived risk (Cherry, 2002); ethics and privacy (Connolly, 2000; McMaster, 2001); ethics and stakeholder theory (Cragg, 2002; Jensen 2002; Kaufman, 2002; Orts and Strudler, 2002); religiosity and ethical behavior (Weaver and Agle, 2002), and multinationality and corporate ethics (van Tulder and Kolk, 2001; Singer 2002). All of these emergent areas of reflection and scholarship are areas of inquiry important in a home country, but exponentially more critical for examination as organizations move increasingly to host-country markets throughout the world.

From Literature Emerges Imperatives for Research

As the tomorrows emerge for the field of business ethics, several imperatives flow from an examination of the extant literature. One, the field of business ethics, over the past several decades, has been descriptive in nature and tone. It is imperative that business ethics rises above its descriptive beginning. Second, is the necessity to develop a replication tradition. It is troubling that the field of business ethics is somewhat lacking of a replication tradition, possibly due to being an emergent field of inquiry. There is little replication in the field, even into the 1990s or so it seems. A third imperative, possibly related to the lack of a replication tradition or perhaps causative of a lack of

replication, concerns a low heuristic power of much of extant research. It is imperative that scholars in the field replicate research and build from and upon the research of others.

Diversity in Understanding of Ethics

Just as there is diversity in research in business ethics, so, too, is there diversity in the understanding of systems of ethics in the conduct of global business, a diversity of understanding that is a function of a host of economic, political, religious, and social variables that define the differences between peoples, nations, and cultures. As an example, Donaldson and Dunfee (1994), postulated that "Muslim managers may wish to participate in systems of economic ethics compatible with the teachings of the Prophet Muhammad, European and American managers may wish to participate in systems of economic ethics giving due respect to individual liberty, and Japanese managers may prefer systems showing respect for the value of the collective." In each of these situations and in similar situations within the many countries of the world, a given system of ethics, particularly a system of ethics that is home-country specific, may not be accepted, respected, understood, or practiced by host-country nationals.

While the ethics of individuals differ around the world and while a system of ethics from a home country may not be embraced by host-country nationals, managers of global firms nevertheless must raise ethics in the consciousness of their employees regardless of where employees are assigned in the world or whatever their national origins. In raising ethical consciousness, it is insufficient to do so simply by establishing a code of ethics in an organization. Rather, management must develop an ethical culture across an organization (O'Mally, 1995) and put in place an organizational structure or framework for ethics, perhaps a framework such as is advocated in this manuscript.

By advocating an ethical culture as well as having an ethical framework, Paine (1994) argued that the reputation of a firm is enhanced and its relationships with its constituencies are strengthened. Sonnenberg and Goldberg (1992) found that employees feel better about a firm and perform at higher levels when they sense ethics as part of its culture. As a result, it is posited in this research that a firm will realize higher-level results when a concern for ethics pervades the organization and is a part of its culture.

A concern for ethics and ethical values must be developed for a global firm to be holistic, to be greater than the sum of its many parts, whether a firm and its operating units are located in the home country and/or in host countries. Global holism is a necessity for success in global business and requires that "the organization has shared beliefs, attitudes, and values," including a system of ethics, which, when taken together, "creates a consistency in the way the firm treats customers, vendors, other business partners, and each other, wherever business is being done" (Daniels and Daniels, 1994). A concern for ethics in global business is a major responsibility of management, is an integral aspect (Roddick, 1994) of international trade, contributes to global holism, and is an imperative for success in global business (Trevino, Butterfield and McCabe, 1998).

Unethical Practices in Global Business

There are many ways in which a firm might engage in unethical business practices in the global business arena, hopefully inadvertently rather than deliberately. Unethical corporate behavior may have genesis in a lack of understanding of, or an appreciation for, the culture of a host country in which a firm is operating. Many examples of unethical practices are reported in the literature. Presented below are examples developed by Kehoe (1998) and selected by a panel of executives as being among the most egregious. Since being developed as twelve examples in 1998, the research has been updated to include fifteen examples reported in the following paragraphs in no particular order of significance.

- The first egregious example is an unethical practice of making of payments, often unrecorded, to officials in a host country in the form of bribes, kickbacks, gifts, and/or other forms of inducement (Landauer, 1979; Kimelman, 1994; Rossouw, 2000; Sidorov, Alexeyeva and Shklyarik, 2000; Economist Reporter, 2002c; Hanafin, 2002). These payments often are made in spite of prohibitions of the U.S. Foreign Corrupt Practices Act (1977) against such practices.

- A second egregious example is management representing a firm as financially healthier than its actual condition. This allegedly occurred by managers requiring employees to alter forecasts, plans, and budgets in order to mirror market expectations (Fuller and Jensen, 2002), to report sales or business activity at inflated levels (Leopold, 2002), or to inflate pro forma earnings (Roman, 2002). Additionally, some managers allegedly established complex and off-balance-sheet financial structures (Colvin, 2002;

Economist Editorial, 2002; Elins, 2002; McLean, 2002; Zellner and Arndt, 2002; Zellner, France and Weber, 2002) with assets of dubious quality designed to cause an organization to appear financially healthier than was actually its true condition.

- A third egregious example is for an individual to use a position within a firm to advance one's personal wealth at the expense of others, as is alleged to have occurred in Enron (Colvin, 2002; Elins, 2002; McLean, 2002; Nussbaum, 2002; Schmidt, 2002; Schwartz, 2002; Zellner, Anderson and Cohn, 2002) and Nortel Networks Corporation (Crenshaw, 2002).

- A fourth egregious example, related to the first, second, and third examples and as equally egregious, and is a situation of management punishing those employees who come forward to report or blow a whistle about an unethical practice or practices (Alford, 2001; Economist Reporter, 2002a; Economist Reporter, 2002b; Mayer and Joyce, 2002). Posited as perhaps even more egregious is to ignore or to marginalize a whistleblower, alleged to have occurred in the Enron bankruptcy situation (Arndt and Scherreik, 2002; Krugman, 2002; Mayer and Joyce, 2002; Morgenson, 2002; Sloan and Isikoff, 2002; WSJ Editorial, 2002; Zellner, Anderson and Cohn, 2002).

- A fifth example is the marketing of products abroad that have been removed from a home-country market due to health or environmental concerns. Examples given by Hinds (1982) include chemical, pharmaceutical, and pesticide products, as well as contraceptive devices, which were removed from the U.S. market allegedly for being unsafe to the environment and/or to health, but for which marketing in other countries was continued, and, in some cases, was accelerated.

- Marketing products in host countries that are in questionable need or which are detrimental to the health, welfare, and/or economic well being of consumers is a sixth egregious unethical practice. An often-cited example (Willatt, 1970; Post, 1985; French and Granrose, 1995; Ferrell, Fraedrich and Ferrell, 2002) is the marketing of infant formula in developing countries by Nestle S.A. (www.nestle.com). Parents in developing countries are alleged to have been unable to afford the formula, unable to read directions to use the formula appropriately, unable to find sanitary sources of water for preparing the formula, and not to have needed the formula until Nestle convinced them that its use was necessary. Another example (White, 1997; Ferrell, Fraedrich and Ferrell, 2002) is marketing of cigarettes in developing countries by advertising that implies that most people in the United States smoke and that smoking is "an American thing to do."

- A seventh example is a firm operating in countries that are known to violate human rights and/or failing to be an advocate for human rights in such countries. During the apartheid era in South Africa, U.S. firms were criticized for doing business in the country and for failing to advocate human rights by publicly opposing the discrimination, oppression, and segregation of apartheid (Deresky, 1994; Sethi and Williams, 2001).

- An eight example is a firm moving jobs from a home country to low-wage host countries. When this occurs, workers in the home country are hurt because of loss of jobs (Kehoe, 1995), while workers in a host country are exploited by low wages. For example, Ballinger (1992) argued that Nike's (www.nike.com) profits increased due, in part, to the lower wages paid to workers in Nike-contracted plants outside the United States. Employees in these plants allegedly worked in excess of ten hours per day, six days a week, for a weekly salary of less than U.S. $50 for their efforts. The Associated Press (1997) reported that employees in Nike-contracted plants in Vietnam were paid U.S. 20 ¢ per hour for working a 12-hour day. Encouragingly, reports in *The New York Times* (Staff Report, 1997), *Time* (Saporito, 1998) and *Fortune* (Boyle, 2002) imply that Nike is correcting the alleged abuses of employees in contracted plants in Vietnam.

- Utilizing child labor (Nichols, et.al., 1993) in host countries when the law in a firm's home country prohibits such use is the ninth example of an unethical practice. While the use of child labor in a host country may be a necessity to support a child and her/his family, be preferable to unemployment, and not be of a concern to the host government, is it ethical to use children as laborers? In the past several years, a group of firms, including Nike, Reebok, L.L. Bean, Liz Claiborne, and Toys R Us, committed to a policy of prohibiting the employment of children younger than 15 years of age in factories in host countries (Headden, 1997; Bernstein, 1999; Singer, 2000). Additionally, Toys R Us has requested suppliers to seek SA 8000 certification, an international standard certifying working conditions (Singer, 2000).

- Tenth is a practice of operating in countries whose environmental standards are lax, or, the converse, being lax in respect for a host country's environment. In the Amazon, global corporations are reported (Thomson and Dudley, 1989) to have ignored their own and the host country's environmental guidelines in extracting oil. In Ireland, global firms are suspected (Keohane, 1989) of ignoring environmental regulations and to be illegally dumping hazardous waste throughout the country. In several countries, large agriculture conglomerates are bioengineering and genetically modifying crops, perhaps to the determent of the environment, animals, and people (Comstock, 2000). Finally, an emerging issue under the tenth example is the dumping of waste materials in less-developed host countries, sometimes waste of a hazardous nature that would require special handling in a home country but which is dumped carelessly in host countries (Ferrell, Fraedrich and Ferrell, 2002).

- Eleventh is operating in a host country with a lower regard for workers' health and well being than in the home country. Japanese companies are alleged (Itoh, 1991) to have over worked their employees both in Japan and in host countries and to have been indifferent to their health. Union Carbide is alleged (Daniels and Radebaugh, 1993) to have operated a plant in Bhopal, India with lower safety standards than its plants in more developed countries.

- Conducting business in a developing nation in such a manner as to dominate the nation's economy is a twelfth example of an unethical practice. Several rubber companies have been accused of dominating the economies of the developing nations in which they operated rubber plantations. Such domination has been called *dependencia* (Turner, 1984), and has been shown to be damaging to a host country's economy, demoralizing to its people, and of questionable ethics.

- A thirteenth example is intervening in the affairs of a host country through such activities as influence peddling or other efforts to affect local political activity. In Italy, for example (Anonymous, 1993a), an investigation was undertaken into the alleged illegal financing of political parties by Italian business firms, as well as by foreign business entities operating in the country.

- Taking actions abroad that would be unpopular, controversial, unethical, or illegal in the home country is a fourteenth example. For instance,

MacKenzie (1992) raised the controversial issue of whether, given advances in DNA research, a business firm has a right to patent a life form? Officials at the European Parliament in Brussels debated the legal and moral issues of this question. While a conclusion has not been reached, assuming an affirmative conclusion, may a non-European firm, operating in a European market, patent life forms in Europe if such patenting activity is unethical or illegal in the firm's home country?

• A fifteenth and final example is an egregious practice of a firm reinvesting little of the profit realized in a host country back in that country due to a restrictive covenant in corporate policy requiring that a majority of profit earned in a host country be repatriated back to the home country. This means that a global firm may reinvest very little back in a host country, and the citizens of the country may be exploited as a result.

Conceptualizing a Framework for Global Business Ethics

It is posited in this research that a framework for ethics is needed for firms engaged in global business across the many cultures that are encountered. A framework that points a firm safely along the global road—a code for the road, as in the lyrics of Crosby, Stills and Nash (1970), "you, who are on the road, must have a code that you can live by. . . ." Is it possible to design such a framework and to develop a code by which global businesses might live? Where do managers begin the process?

The framework for global business ethics presented here has eight stages. A firm ideally should progress through all eight stages in designing and implementing a global ethical system. The framework begins with the stage of understanding the orientation of a firm, and concludes with recommendations for promulgating and using a framework of global business ethics.

Step One—Orientation of a Firm

The first step in a framework for global business ethics is to define a firm's orientation in the global business arena. A firm may participate in global business as an exporter, a multinational firm, a multilocal multinational firm, a global firm, or some combination of these methods. Each of these methods of participation moves a firm further from being a domestic firm and gives it an increasing array of experiences in world markets. The orientation of a firm may be ethnocentric—home-country oriented; polycentric—adaptive to host countries; or geocentric—open to using the best resources wherever they are

available in the world. Each of these orientation positions has implications for ethics.

As an exporter, the orientation of a firm may be generalized as primarily ethnocentric. The logic-in-use of an exporter may be generalized as being that home-country approaches should be applied wherever in the world the firm may operate. This ethnocentric logic means that home-country approaches to ethics are considered to be superior to those elsewhere in the world and may be applied whenever possible.

When a firm moves toward multinational operations, management's orientation will evolve, as the result of the experiences in host countries, from an ethnocentric viewpoint of an exporter toward a polycentric orientation as its managerial logic-in-use. This orientation recognizes that a firm must adapt to the unique aspects of each national market in which it operates. The logic-in-use is broadened by a willingness to adapt the home-country's ethical system in the various host countries in which the firm operates. This willingness to adapt its home-country ethical system is strengthened as a firm focus astutely on each host country, develops a multilocal approach to its multinational operations, brings host-country national into management positions, and grants greater autonomy from the home-country parent. All of these things heighten a firm's willingness to adapt and/or to customize its ethical system to fit the culture of a host country.

When a firm evolves to being a global firm, management's orientation becomes geocentric, with an acceptance of and openness to concepts, ideas, processes, and people from throughout the world, including approaches to ethics. The implication of a geocentric orientation is that a firm will be more amenable to addressing values that are inherent in the culture of a host country as a system of ethics is developed.

In developing a framework for global business ethics, a global firm, with a geocentric orientation of its management, is posited to be more open to using a system of global ethics than is an exporter, whose orientation tends to be ethnocentric. In terms of orientation, a global firm generally exhibits a greater readiness to develop ethical systems that appreciate and include the diversity of culture differences found in the world. An exporter, by contrast, is a domestic firm and is posited generally to prefer home-country ethical systems.

Step Two—Differences and Similarities between Countries

The second step toward a framework for global business ethics is to appreciate and understand the differences and similarities between countries. In global business, there obviously are significant differences between peoples, countries, and cultures. This diversity adds richness to the experience of living on the earth, but may be problematic in establishing an ethical culture in a firm.

Comparing any two countries in regard to ethics in business would find striking differences as well as similarities. For example, consider a comparison of Japan and the United States.

Japan's business culture is characterized (Shimada 1991) as having excessive corporate competition and a focus on rationality in decision making, based on economic factors at the expense of human factors. Itoh (1991) reported that Japanese managers are criticized for being indifferent to the health of their employees. Hammer, Bradley and Lewis (1989) found cases of influence-peddling scandals involving leading business executives and Japanese politicians. In fact, breaches in business ethics was suggested by Whenmouth (1992) to be part of the system of doing business in Japan, with unethical behavior having origins deep in the country's cultural tradition.

In comparison, business in the United States has experienced some of the same ethical lapses as in Japan. For example, Labich (1992) presented evidence showing that for some U.S. managers, ethics had an economic basis. These managers became lax in regard for ethics during difficult economic times, but returned to a stronger appreciation of ethics when business conditions improved. The increasing number of whistle-blowing cases in the United States argues that something may be remiss in corporate ethics programs (Driscoll, 1992; Dworkin and Near, 1997; Mayer and Joyce, 2002). Research by Sandroff (1990) and others found such ethical abuses as lying to employees and clients, expense account padding, favoritism, nepotism, sexual harassment, discrimination, and taking credit for the work of others are part of U.S. business culture. All of which has led to an increasing number of business firms offering in-house training in ethics (Hager, 1991), developing games and simulations in ethics (Ireland, 1991), establishing permanent ethics committees (Labrecque, 1990), publishing codes of ethics (Court, 1988), and contracting with ethics' consulting firms for advice and programs, in what Cordtz (1994) has called an *ethicsplosion*. One consulting firm, Transparency International, is reported (Anonymous, 1993b) to have programs to improve ethics and standards of conduct, and to have worked with companies to prevent bribe paying in the conduct of global business.

Step Three—Identify Things of Broad Agreement

While there are differences and similarities in the appreciation for ethics among countries of the world, and while there are differences and similarities in lapses of ethics among businesses from various countries, there are things about ethics to which peoples across the world may agree. This is the third step in the framework. To identify those things, or values, in which there may be common agreement around the world.

Valasquez (1992, p. 30) identified the *global common good* as an area of worldwide agreement. He argued that individuals in international business have a responsibility to contribute to the global common good, including "maintaining a congenial global climate, . . . maintaining safe transportation routes for the international flow of goods, . . . maintaining clean oceans, . . . and the avoidance of global nuclear war. The global common good is that set of conditions that are necessary for the citizens of all or of most nations to achieve their individual fulfillment. . . . "

Beyond the aspects of a global common good to which people in international business might agree, there are certain attributes of life in any society to which a majority might agree (Kehoe, 1994). These include such values and principles (Goodpaster, Note 383-007) as, obeying the law; not harming others; respecting the rights and property of others; never lying, cheating, or stealing; keeping promises and contracts; being fair to others; helping those in need; and encouraging and reinforcing these values in others, all of which Goodpaster called *moral common sense*. These moral values are reaffirmed and enlarged by Scott (2002) in identifying honest communications, respect for property, respect for life, respect for religion, and justice as important organizational moral values.

Another example of attributes to which people throughout the world agree is found in a code of ethics of Rotary International. The attributes to which some 1.2 million Rotarians in 162 countries (Rotary, 2002) agree are: truth telling, fairness to others, goodwill toward others, and acting in ways beneficial to others. These concepts are embodied in a code called the 4-Way Test of Rotary International. The code, consisting of twenty-four words, is as follows: 1. Is it the truth? 2. Is it fair to all concerned? 3. Will it build goodwill and better friendships? 4. Will it be beneficial to all concerned?

Step Four—Find Voice to Express Agreement

Having identified the things of broad agreement, the fourth step of the framework is to identify a voice or way of expressing those things. Understanding voice is important because it is arguably likely that there are different voices used by people in different countries to express the same value or ethical concept. In fact, within the same country, an ethical concept may be voiced differently (Gilligan, 1982) by men than by women. The challenge is to find a voice or moral language appropriate for each culture wherein a global firm may operate. The challenge further is to recognize when a change in voice is required in order to express an ethical concept in a different culture.

In order to find a voice appropriate for situations in global business ethics, an underpinning of ethical theory is an initial step. In brief, ethical theory might be presented from a teleological or a deontological frame.

Teleological theory is concerned with the *consequences* of an action or business decision. The teleological principle of utilitarianism requires that an individual act in a way to produce the greatest good for the greatest number. In acting in this manner, an individual considers not only self in a decision or action, but the impact of the act on others. An individual applying utilitarianism in decision-making "would determine the effects of each alternative and would select the alternative that optimizes the satisfactions of the greatest number of people." (Kehoe, 1993, p.16)

Deontological theory is concerned with the *rules* used to arrive at an action or a decision rather than the consequences of the action; that is, deontological theory is rule based, whereas teleological theory is consequences based. The deontological principle of the categorical imperative (Kant, 1785) is: "Act only according to that maxim by which you can at the same time will that it should be a universal law." In other words, the categorical imperative proscribes that individuals only do those things that they can recommend to others. That is, there are certain things that must be done in order to maintain basic humanity in a society, just as there certain things that must be practiced by individuals to maintain order in an organization. These things make up the shared moral values of an organization and are a part of its ethical culture. For example, a manager who does not participate in bribery because he or she could not admit or recommend it to others may be said to be adhering to the categorical imperative. Likewise, as other individuals in a firm adhere to the categorical imperative, it becomes a shared moral value and a part of the ethical culture of a firm.

Kidder (1994) conceptualized an example of shared moral values. He surveyed "ethical thinkers" from around the world and identified eight shared moral values that have broad application across cultures. These included love, truthfulness, fairness, freedom, unity, tolerance, responsibility, and respect for life.

A second example of shared moral values is by DeGeorge (1994). He suggested that there are moral norms that cross cultures that may be used to develop ethical standards for global business. Examples of such shared moral norms are truthfulness, respect for property, fairness, and trust.

Research by Scott (2002) elevated a third example of shared moral values. Arguing that the most important organizational value for analysis is an organization's moral values, she identified five moral values for organizations—justice, honest communication, respect for property, respect for life, and respect for religion.

Perhaps the most useful example of shared moral values is by Donaldson (1992). He analyzed six moral languages for their appropriateness in global business ethics. The languages were: virtue and vice; self-perfection through self control; maximization of human welfare; avoidance of human harm; rights and duties; and social contract. He argues (Donaldson, 1992, p. 280) that "the former three (virtue and vice; self perfection through self control; maximization of human welfare) are inappropriate for establishing a system of ethics in global business," while the "latter three (avoidance of human harm; rights and duties; social contract) are deontological ethical languages with the capacity to establish minimum rather than perfectionist standards of behavior" and are, therefore, better suited for addressing ethical issues in global business. These moral languages give voice to ethics in global business.

Step Five—Use Voice to Develop Ethical Statements

Generalizing from the conclusions concerning the appropriateness of moral languages for global business ethics, the fifth step of the framework emerges. That step is to use voice to develop ethical statements or codes of ethics.

It is posited that the voice used in a framework for global business ethics should be deontological rather than teleological, and minimum rather than perfectionist. This means that the statements developed in a framework for global business ethics should be rule based and be minimum in standard. Said another way, simpler and shorter statements are more appropriate in developing a framework for global business ethics. Parsimony must be the guiding principle in using voice to develop ethical statements.

Step Six—Separate Core and Peripheral Values

Being guided by voice to use rule based, minimum in standard, simple, and short statements, a global business organization, as a sixth step, should determine the core values to be included in its ethical framework and in its global code of ethics. Then identify the peripheral values that may be altered or even deleted from its global code of ethics according to the culture of a host country. This means, for example, if a global firm's home country is the United States, and if it operates also in China, India,

Mexico, and Russia, its global code of ethics should contain core-value statements of the home country as well as statements common across all the countries, but may contain different peripheral-value statements in each of the host countries.

It is an imperative that individuals in a global firm understand its core values and its peripheral values. Collins (1995) defined a core value as something a firm would hold even if it became a competitive disadvantage. Donaldson (1996) identified three core values that have basis in Western and non-Western culture and religious traditions—respect for human dignity, respect for basic rights, and good citizenship through support of community institutions. He postulated (Donaldson, 1996, p. 53) that core values "establish a moral compass for business practice. They can help identify practices that are acceptable and those that are intolerable—even if the practices are compatible with a host country's norms and laws. Dumping pollutants near people's homes and accepting inadequate standards for handling hazardous materials are two examples of actions that violate core values. Similarly, if employing children prevents them from receiving a basic education, the practice is intolerable" and violates core values.

To separate core and peripheral values, consider this situation. If the core values of a firm include acknowledging human equality, promoting human welfare, providing high quality products, having fair prices, contributing to the community, and compliance with national laws, these values should be reflected in a firm's global code of ethics and promulgated to all host-country subsidiaries. If, however, a firm believes that relationships among employees, with customers, and with suppliers are best addressed at the country level, these are peripheral values to be addressed in ethical statements developed by employees in each operating location. In brief, a firm, as noted by Laczniak and Murphy (1993), should strive to have a single worldwide policy on ethics to address its core values, those values never to be compromised, but may allow addenda to its worldwide core-value policy on ethics to address peripheral values that are inherent in the culture of a host country.

Step Seven—Writing a Global Code of Ethics

The seventh step of the framework concerns writing a global code of business ethics that will be a central part of a firm's framework for global business ethics. A global code cannot and should not be written at the home-country headquarters. Rather, contributions to the code must be sought from around the world. Individuals from throughout a firm's global expanse must be involved in developing the code. This means that a committee or task force that is charged with developing the code should have representation from each geographic region in which a firm operates, or even, if possible, from each host country. Likewise, individuals from across functions and levels of hierarchy should be included, so that the result is a multifunctional, multilevel, multinational task force. The goal must be to be as inclusive as possible in developing a global code of ethics.

Global inclusiveness is important so that a code does not contain only the concepts, ideas, prejudices theories, values and words of a firm's home country. This is part of using voice to develop a global code. A firm's values that are reflected in a code must be stated in a globally inclusive manner. This is not easily accomplished. It can only be accomplished by being as globally inclusive in voice as possible in writing the code. This implies that those charged with developing a global code of ethics must be empowered to be in close and regular contact wherever located in the world. This may mean that a firm regularly uses teleconferencing while developing the code. It also may mean that meetings of the task force are held regularly in various host countries while the code is being developed. Put simply, a global code of ethics cannot and should not be developed solely in a home-country venue.

Step Eight—Promulgating and Using a Global Code of Ethics

The final step of a framework for global business ethics is to promulgate and use the code of ethics. This means that the code must be translated effectively to the language of each host country. In each host country, some process for ethics representation should be arranged. It may be that a manager is assigned responsibility for ethics in addition to other duties, or preferably an ethics officer is designated formally in each country. That individual should be charged with promulgating the code of ethics, encouraging its use, and managing and refining the firm's framework for global business ethics. The posited result of having a framework of global business ethics is that there should be higher levels of ethical behavior across a global firm when a framework is in place, as was reported by Ferrell and Skinner (1988) with codes of ethics in domestic firms. Simply put, ethics must be made "salient and be part of an ongoing conversation" within an organization (Freeman, 2001). The goal of developing a framework for global business ethics is to have ethics often considered, rather than seldom or never considered in the conduct of global business (Kehoe, 1998).

Conclusion

A mosaic of diversity continues to shine brilliantly across the landscape of global business. It is a landscape of business firms, large and small, operating in various ways in an increasing number of the countries of the world. It is a landscape of diverse cultures, with differing appreciations for and understandings of ethics. It is a landscape of individual managers encountering choices that reflect all the ambiguities, differences and subtleties of a global mosaic of diversity. It is a landscape of people unified by shared moral values and of global firms in which ethics must be an imperative.

More than forty years ago, Berle (1954) made a statement that is relevant for today's global corporations. The statement addressed ethics and the responsibilities of management. "The really great corporation management must consider the kind of community in which they have faith and which they will serve and which they intend to help construct and maintain. In a word, they must consider the ancient problems of the good life and how their operations in the community can be adapted to affording or fostering it."

The framework conceptualized in this research is anchored in a concept of shared moral values and developed by using moral languages to give meaning to ethics across cultures. The framework allows for a firm to remain loyal to its core values in situations involving questions of ethics, but allows different peripheral-value statements in host countries. When developing a framework for global business ethics, contributions must be sought from throughout the world. This means that individuals from throughout a firm's global expanse must be involved in developing the framework. Such a global corporate community developed framework will contribute to a concept of ethics being embraced throughout a firm, and to ethics being a word often spoken by employees throughout a firm, rather than a word seldom spoken or never spoken.

A report of the Center for Business Ethics (Hoffman, 2000) noted "business ethics is no longer a set of national initiatives, if it ever was. It is now a global affair." Anywhere a firm operates in the world, its activities must be ethical and adapted to affording or fostering the good life. This is an ethical imperative. Simply yet profoundly stated (Freeman, 2002), "ethics is about the most important parts of our lives and must be center stage" in any activity whether of a business or a personal nature. The practice of ethics in global business is posited to enhance a global corporation, uplift it and its stakeholders, and ensure that its actions foster the good life.

References

Alford, C. Fred (2001). *Whistleblowers: Broken Lives and Organizational Power.* Ithaca, NY: Cornell University Press.

Anonymous (1993a). "The Purging of Italy, Inc.," *Economist,* March 20, pp. 69–70.

Anonymous (1993b). "Clean, Not Laundered," *Economist,* May 8, p. 78.

Arndt, Michael and Susan Scherreik (2002). "Five Ways to Avoid More Enrons," *Business Week,* February 18, pp. 36–37.

Associate Press Report (1997). "Conditions Deplorable at Nike's Vietnamese Plants," *The Daily Progress,* March 28, p. A2.

Ballinger, Jeffrey (1992). "The New Free-Trade Hall," *Harper's,* August, pp. 45–47.

Baumhart, Raymond C. (1961). "How Ethical Are Businessmen?" *Harvard Business Review,* July/August, pp. 6–12.

Becker, Thomas E. (1998). "Integrity in Organizations," *Academy of Management Review,* Volume 23 (1), pp. 154–161.

Berle, A. A. (1954). *The 20th Century Capitalist Revolution.* New York: Harcourt, Brace and World, pp. 166–176.

Berleant, Arnold (1982). "Multinationals and the Problem of Ethical Consistency," *Journal of Business Ethics,* 3, August, pp. 185–195.

Bernstein, Aaron (1999). "Sweatshops: No More Excuses," *Business Week,* November 8, pp. 104–106.

Blodgett, Jeffrey G., Long-Chaun Lu, G. M. Rose and S. J. Vitell (2001). "Ethical Sensitivity to Stakeholder Interests: A Cross-Cultural Comparison," *Journal of the Academy of Marketing Science,* Volume 29 (2), pp. 190–202.

Boulding, Kenneth (1967). "The Basis of Value Judgments in Economics," in Sidney Hook, ed., *Human Values and Economic Policy.* New York, NY: New York University Press.

Bowie, Norman E. (1978). "A Taxonomy for Discussing the Conflicting Responsibilities of a Multinational Corporation," in Norman E. Bowie, *Responsibilities of Multinational Corporations to Society.* Arlington, VA: Council of Better Business Bureaus, pp. 21–43.

Bowie, Norman E. (1990). "Business Ethics and Cultural Relativism," in Peter Madsen and Jay M. Shafritz, eds., *Essentials of Business Ethics.* New York: Penguin Books, pp. 366–382.

Bowie, Norman E. (1997). "The Moral Obligations of Multinational Corporations," in Norman E. Bowie, ed., *Ethical Theory and Business.* Upper Saddle River, NJ: Prentice-Hall, pp. 522–534.

Bowie, Norman E. (1999). *Business Ethics: A Kantian Perspective.* New York, NY: Blackwell Publishers.

Boyle, Matthew (2002). "How Nike Got Its Swoosh Back," *Fortune,* Volume 145, June 11, p. 31.

Brock, Gillian (1998). "Are Corporations Morally Defensible?" *Business Ethics Quarterly,* Volume 8, October, pp. 703–721.

Buller, Paul F. and Glen M. McEvoy (1999). "Creating and Sustaining Ethical Capability in the Multinational Corporation," *Journal of World Business,* 34 (4), pp. 326–343.

Business Ethics Quarterly (1994, Volume 4, January). Issue devoted entirely to international business ethics, pp. 1–110.

Carroll, Archie B. (1979). "A Three-Dimensional Conceptual Model of Corporate Social Performance," *Academy of Management Review,* Volume 4, pp. 497–505.

Carroll, Archie B. (2000). "Ethical Challenges for Business in the New Millennium," *Business Ethics Quarterly,* Volume 10, Number 1, pp. 33–42.

Cateora, Philip R. and John L. Graham (2002). *International Marketing.* New York, NY: McGraw-Hill Companies, Inc.

Caux Roundtable, Principles for Business. (1995). *Society for Business Ethics Newsletter,* May, pp. 14–15.

Cherry, John (2002). "Perceived Risk and Moral Philosophy." *Marketing Management Journal,* Volume 12, Issue 1, pp. 49–58.

Chonko, Lawrence B. and Shelby D. Hunt (2000). "Ethics and Marketing Management: A retrospective and Prospective Commentary," *Journal of Business Research,* 50, pp. 235–244.

Collier, Jane (1998). "Theorising the Ethical Organization," *Business Ethics Quarterly,* Volume 8, October, pp. 621–654.

Collins, James M. (1995). "Change Is Good—But First, Know What Should Never Change," *Fortune,* May 29, p. 141.

Colvin, Geoffrey (2002). "Wonder Women of Whistleblowing," *Fortune,* August 12, p. 56.

Comstock, Gary L. (2000). *Vexing Nature? On the Ethical Case Against Agricultural Biotechnology.* Boston, MA: Kluwer Academic Publishers.

Connolly, P. J. (2000). "Privacy as Global Policy," *InfoWorld,* September 11, pp. 49–50.

Cordtz, Dan (1994). "Ethicsplosion," *Financial World,* August 16, pp. 58–60.

Costa, John Dalla (1998). The Ethical Imperative: *Why Moral Leadership Is Good Business.* Reading, MA: Addison-Wesley.

Court, James (1988). "A Question of Corporate Ethics," *Personnel Journal,* September, pp. 37–39.

Cragg, Wesley (2002). "Business Ethics and Stakeholder Theory," *Business Ethics Quarterly,* Volume 12, Number 2, April, pp. 113–142.

Crenshaw, Albert B. (2002). "Nortel Executive Quits Amid Accusations," *The Washington Post,* February 12, pp. E1 and E4.

Crosby, Stills and Nash. (1970).

Czinkota, Michael R., Ilkka A. Ronkainen and Michael H. Moffett (2002). *International Business.* Fort Worth, TX: Harcourt College Publishers.

Daniels John D. and L. H. Radebaugh (1993). *International Dimensions of Contemporary Business.* Boston, MA: PWS-Kent Publishing Company, pp. 79–80.

Daniels John L. and N. Caroline Daniels (1994). *Global Vision: Building New Models for the Corporation of the Future.* New York: McGraw-Hill, Inc., p. 12.

Davids, Meryl (1999). "Global Standards, Local Problems," *Journal of Business Strategy,* January/February, pp. 38–43.

DeGeorge, Richard T. (1990). "The International Business System, Multinationals, and Morality," in Richard T. DeGeorge, *Business Ethics.* New York: Macmillan Publishing Company.

DeGeorge, Richard T. (1993). *Competing With Integrity in International Business.* New York: Oxford University Press.

DeGeorge, Richard T. (1994). "International Business Ethics," *Business Ethics Quarterly,* Volume 4, January, pp. 1–9.

Delener, Nejdet, ed. (1995). *Ethical Issues in International Marketing.* New York: International Business Press.

Deresky, Helen (1994). *International Management.* New York: Harper Collins College Publishers, pp. 516–519.

Donaldson, Thomas (1985). "Multinational Decision Making: Reconciling International Norms," *Journal of Business Ethics,* December, pp. 357–366.

Donaldson, Thomas (1989). *The Ethics of International Business.* New York: Oxford University Press.

Donaldson, Thomas (1992). "The Language of International Corporate Ethics," *Business Ethics Quarterly,* Volume 2, July, pp. 271–281.

Donaldson, Thomas (1996). "Values in Tension: Ethics Away From Home," *Harvard Business Review,* September–October, p. 53.

Donaldson, Thomas and T. W. Dunfee (1994). "Toward a Unified Conception of Business Ethics: Integrative Social Contracts Theory," *Academy of Management Review,* April, p. 261.

Driscoll, Lisa (1992). "A Better Way to Handle Whistle Blowers: Let Them Speak," *Business Week,* July 27, p. 36.

Drucker, Peter (1981). "What is Business Ethics?" *The Public Interest,* Spring, pp. 18–37.

Dunfee, Thomas W. (1998). "The Marketplace of Morality: Small Steps Toward a Theory of Moral Choice," *Business Ethics Quarterly,* Volume 8, January, pp. 127–145.

Dworkin, Terry M. and J.P. Near (1997). "A Better Statutory Approach To Whistle Blowing," *Business Ethics Quarterly,* Volume 7, January, pp. 1–16.

Economist Reporter (2002a). "In Praise of Whistleblowers," *The Economist,* January 12, pp. 13–14.

Economist Reporter (2002b). "As Companies Cut Costs They Cut Corners Too. Time to Blow the Whistle?" *The Economist,* January 12, pp. 55–56.

Economist Reporter (2002c). Special Report: Bribery and Business," *The Economist,* March 2, pp. 63–65.

Elins, Michael (2002). "Year of the Whistleblower," *Business Week,* December 16, pp. 106–110.

Engelbourg, Saul (1980). *Power and Morality: American Business Ethics, 1840–1914.* Westport, CT: Greenwood Press.

Ferrell, O. C. (1998). "Business Ethics in a Global Economy," *Journal of Marketing Management,* Volume 9 (1), pp. 65–71.

Ferrell, O. C. and L. G. Gresham (1985). "A Contingency Framework for Understanding Ethical Decision Making," *Journal of Marketing,* 49 (Summer), pp. 87–96.

Ferrell, O. C. and S. J. Skinner (1988). "Ethical Behavior and Bureaucratic Structure in Marketing Research Organizations," *Journal of Marketing Research,* 25 (February), pp. 103–109.

Ferrell, O. C., John Fraedrich and Linda Ferrell (2002). *Business Ethics.* Boston, MA: Houghton Mifflin.

Fraedrich, John, Debbie M. Thorne and O. C. Ferrell (1994). "Assessing the Application of Cognitive Moral Development Theory to Business Ethics," *Journal of Business Ethics,* 13, pp. 829–838.

Freeman, R. Edward (2000). "Business Ethics at the Millennium," *Business Ethics Quarterly,* Volume 10, January, pp. 169–180.

Freeman, R. Edward (2001). Presentation to the FBI/UVA Annual Meeting, University of Virginia, December 12, 2001.

Freeman, R. Edward (2002). Presentation to Beta Gamma Sigma Ethics Symposium, University of Virginia, February 1, 2002.

French, Warren A. and John Granrose (1995). *Practical Business Ethics.* Englewood Cliffs, NJ: Prentice-Hall, Inc.

Fuller, Joseph and Michael C. Jensen (2002). "Just Say No to Wall Street," *Working Paper 02-01,* Tuck School of Business, Dartmouth College and Harvard Business School.

Geva, Aviva (2001). "Myth and Ethics in Business," *Business Ethics Quarterly,* Volume 11, October, pp. 575–597.

Gilligan, Carol (1982). *In a Different Voice: Psychological Theory and Women's Development.* Cambridge, MA: Harvard University Press.

Goodpaster, Kenneth E. (Note 383-007). "Some Avenues for Ethical Analysis in General Management," *Harvard Business School Note 383-007,* p. 6.

Green, Ronald M. (1993). "Business Ethics in a Global Context," in Ronald M. Green, *The Ethical Manager.* New York: Macmillan Publishing Company.

Griffin, Ricky W. and Michael W. Pustay (2003). *International Business.* Upper Saddle River, NJ: Prentice Hall.

Gustafson, Andrew (2000). "Making Sense of Postmodern Business Ethics," *Business Ethics Quarterly,* Volume 10, July, pp. 645–658.

Hager, Bruce (1991). "What's Behind Business' Sudden Fervor for Ethics?," *Business Week,* September 23, p. 65.

Hammer, Joshua, Bradley Martin and David Lewis (1989). "The Dark Side of Japan, Inc.," *Newsweek,* January 9, p. 41.

Hanafin, John J. (2002). "Morality and Markets in China," *Business Ethics Quarterly,* Volume 12 (January), 1–18.

Hasnas, John (1998). "The Normative Theories of Business Ethics: A Guide for the Perplexed," *Business Ethics Quarterly,* Volume 8, January, pp. 19–42.

Headden, Susan (1997). "A Modest Attack on Sweatshops," *U. S. News and World Report,* April 28, p. 39.

Hinds, M. (1982). "Products Unsafe at Home Are Still Unloaded Abroad," *The New York Times,* August 22, p. 56.

Hill, Charles W. L. (2001). *International Business.* New York, NY: McGraw-Hill.

Hill, Charles W. L. (2003). *Global Business Today.* New York, NY: McGraw-Hill.

Hoffman, W. Michael (2000). *Business Ethics: Reflections for the Center.* Waltham, MA: Center for Business Ethics, p. 6.

Hoffman, W. Michael, A.E. Lange, and D. A. Fedo, eds. (1986). *Ethics and the Multinational Enterprise.* Lanham: University Press of America.

Hosmer, LaRue T. and Feng Chen (2001). "Ethics and Economics: Growing Opportunities for Research," *Business Ethics Quarterly,* Volume 11, October, pp. 599–622.

Ireland, Karin (1991). "The Ethics Game," *Personnel Journal,* March, pp. 72–75.

Itoh, Yoshiaki (1991). "Worked to Death in Japan," *World Press Review,* March, p. 50.

Jensen, Michael C. (2002). "Value Maximization, Stakeholder Theory and the Corporate Objective Function," *Business Ethics Quarterly,* Volume 12, Number 2, April, pp. 235–256.

Johnson, Elmer W. (1997). "Corporate Soulcraft in the Age of Brutal Markets," *Business Ethics Quarterly,* Volume 7, October, pp. 109–124.

Kant, Immanuel (1785). *Foundations of the Metaphysic of Morals,* L. W. Beck, translator. New York: Bobbs-Merrill, 1959, p. 39.

Kaufman, Allen (2002). "Managers' Double Fiduciary Duty: To Stakeholders and To Freedom," *Business Ethics Quarterly,* Volume 12, Number 2, April, pp. 189–214.

Keegan, Warren J. (2002). *Global Marketing Management.* Upper Saddle River, NJ: Prentice Hall.

Kehoe, William J. (1985). "Ethics, Price Fixing, and the Management of Price Strategy," in Gene R. Laczniak and Patrick E. Murphy, eds., *Marketing Ethics: Guidelines for Managers.* Lexington, MA: D. C. Heath and Company, pp. 71–83.

Kehoe, William J. (1993). "Ethics in Business: Theory and Application," *Journal of Professional Services Marketing,* Volume 9, Number 1, pp. 13–25.

Kehoe, William J. (1994). "Ethics and Employee Theft," in John E. Richardson, ed., *Annual Editions: Business Ethics.* Guilford, CT: The Dushkin Publishing Group.

Kehoe, William J. (1995). "NAFTA: Concept, Problems, Promise," in B. T. Engelland and D. T. Smart, eds., *Marketing: Foundations For A Changing World.* Evansville, IN: Society for Marketing Advances, pp. 363–367.

Kehoe, William J. (1998). "The Environment of Ethics in Global Business," *Journal of Business and Behavioral Sciences,* Volume 4, Fall, pp. 47–56.

Kehoe, William J. and Linda K. Whitten (1999). "Structuring Host-Country Operations: Framing a Research Study," *Proceedings of the American Society of Business and Behavioral Sciences,* Volume 5, pp. 1–9.

Keohane, K. (1989). "Toxic Trade Off: The Price Ireland Pays for Industrial Development," *The Ecologist,* 19, pp. 144–146.

Kidder, R.M. (1994). *Shared Values for a Troubled World: Conversations with Men and Women of Conscience.* San Francisco: Jossey-Bass, pp. 18–19.

Kimelman, John (1994). "The Lonely Boy Scout," *Financial World,* August 16, pp. 50–51.

Koehn, Daryl (1992). "Toward an Ethic of Exchange," *Business Ethics Quarterly,* Volume 2, July, pp. 341–355.

Kohlberg, Lawrence (1971). "Stages of Moral Development as a Basis for Moral Education," in C. M. Beck, B. S. Crittenden and E. V. Sullivan, eds., *Moral Education.* Toronto, Canada: University of Toronto Press.

Krugman, Paul (2002). "A System Corrupted," *The Wall Street Journal,* January 18, p. C1.

Kung, Hans (1997). A Global Ethic in An Age of Globalization," *Business Ethics Quarterly,* Volume 7, July, pp. 17–32.

Labich, Kenneth (1992). "The New Crisis in Business Ethics," *Fortune,* April 20, pp. 167–176.

Labrecque, Thomas G. (1990). "Good Ethics Is Good Business," *USA Today: The Magazine of The American Scene,* May, pp. 20–21.

Laczniak, Gene R. (1983). "Business Ethics: A Manager's Primer," *Business,* January–March, pp. 23–29.

Laczniak, Gene R. and Patrick E. Murphy (1985). *Marketing Ethics: Guidelines for Managers.* Lexington, MA: D. C. Heath and Company.

Laczniak, Gene R. and Patrick E. Murphy (1993). *Ethical Marketing Decisions: The Higher Road.* Boston, MA: Allyn and Bacon.

Landauer, J. (1979). "Agency Will Define Corrupt Acts Abroad by U. S. Businesses," *The Wall Street Journal,* September 21, p. 23.

Lantos, Geoffrey P. (1999). "Motivating Moral Corporate Behavior," *Journal of Consumer Marketing,* Volume 16 (3), pp. 222–233.

Lascu, Dana-Nicoleta (2003). *International Marketing.* Cincinnati, OH: Atomic Dog Publishing.

Leopold, Jason (2002). "En-Ruse? Workers at Enron Sat They Posed as Busy Traders to Impress Visiting Analysts," *The Wall Street Journal,* February 7, pp. C1 and C13.

Levitt, Theodore. (1983). "The Globalization of Markets," *Harvard Business Review,* May–June, pp. 92–93.

Mackenzie, Craig and Alan Lewis (1999). "Morals and Markets: The Case for Ethical Investing," *Business Ethics Quarterly,* Volume 9, July, pp. 439–452.

MacKenzie, Debora (1992). "Europe Debates the Ownership of Life," *New Scientist,* January 4, pp. 9–10.

Mayer, Caroline E. and Amy Joyce (2002). "Blowing the Whistle," *The Washington Post,* February 10, pp. H1 and H4–H5.

McCoy, Bowen H. (1983). "The Parable of the Sadhu," *Harvard Business Review,* September/October, pp. 103–108.

McLean, Bethany (2002). "Monster Mess: The Enron Fallout has Just Begun," *Fortune,* February 4, pp. 93–96.

McMaster, Mark (2001). "Too Close for Comfort," *Sales & Marketing Management,* July, pp. 42–48.

Morgenson, Gretchen (2002). "Enron Letter Suggests $1.3 Billion More Down the Drain," *The New York Times,* January 17, pp. C1 & C10.

Murphy, Patrick E. (1988). "Implementing Business Ethics," *Journal of Business Ethics,* Volume 7, pp. 907–915.

Nash, Laura L. (1981). "Ethics Without the Sermon," *Harvard Business Review,* November/December, pp. 79–90.

Nichols, Martha, P. A. Jacobi, J. T. Dunlop and D. L. Lindauer (1993). "Third World Families at Work: Child Labor or Child Care?," *Harvard Business Review,* January–February, pp. 12–23.

Nicholson, Nigel (1994). "Ethics in Organizations: A Framework for Theory and Research," *Journal of Business Ethics,* 13, pp. 581–596.

Nussbaum, Bruce (2002). "Can You Trust Anybody Anymore?" *Business Week,* January 28, pp. 31–32.

O'Mally, Shaun F. (1995). "Ethical Cultures—Corporate and Personal," *Ethics Journal,* Winter, p. 9.

Orts, Eric W. and Alan Strudler (2002). "The Ethical and Environmental Limits of Stakeholder Theory," *Business Ethics Quarterly,* Volume 12, Number 2, April, pp. 215–233.

Paine, Lynn S. (1994). "Managing for Organizational Integrity," *Harvard Business Review,* March–April, pp. 106–117.

Perlmutter, Howard W. (1969). "The Tortuous Evolution of the Multinational Corporation," *Columbia Journal of World Business,* January–February, pp. 11–14.

Post, James M. (1985). "Assessing the Nestle Boycott," *California Management Review,* Winter, pp. 113–131.

Raths, Louis E., Merrill Harmin and Sidney Simon (1966). *Values and Teaching.* Columbus, OH: Merrill Publishing.

Robin, Donald P. (2000). *Questions and Answers About Business Ethics: Running an Ethical and Successful Business.* Cincinnati, OH: Dame, Thompson Learning.

Roddick, Anita (1994). "Corporate Responsibility," *Vital Speeches of the Day,* January 15, pp. 196–199.

Rogers, Hudson P., Alponso O. Ogbuehi, and C. M. Kochunny (1995). "Ethics and Transnational Corporations in Developing Countries: A Social Contract Perspective'" in Nejdet Delener, ed., *Ethical Issues in International Marketing.* New York. International Business Press, pp. 11–38.

Roman, Monica (2002). "Deflating those Pro Forma Figures," *Business Week,* January 28, p. 50.

Rossouw, G. J. (1994). "Business Ethics in Developing Countries," *Business Ethics Quarterly,* Volume 4, January, pp. 43–51.

Rotary (2002). "Rotary at a Glance," *The Rotarian,* January, p. 44. See also the Rotary International website at www.rotary.org /aboutrotary/4way.html.

Sandroff, Ronni (1990). "How Ethical Is American Business? The Working Woman Report," *Working Woman,* September, pp. 113–129.

Saporito, Bill (1998). "Taking a Look Inside Nike's Factories," *Time,* Volume 151, Issue 12, pp. 52–53.

Schmidt, Susan (2002). "Lawmaker Challenges Skilling's Denials," *The Washington Post,* February 12, pp. E1 and E5.

Schwartz, John (2002). "An Enron Unit Chief Warned and Was Rebuffed," *The New York Times,* February 20, pp. C1 and C4.

Scott, Elizabeth D. (2002). "Organizational Moral Values," *Business Ethics Quarterly,* Volume 12, Number 1, January, pp. 33–55.

Sethi, S. Prskash and Oliver F. Williams (2001). *Economic Imperatives and Ethical Values in Global Business: The South African Experience and International Codes Today.* South Bend, IN: University of Notre Dame Press.

Shimada, Hauro (1991). "The Desperate Need for New Values in Japanese Corporate Behavior," *Journal of Japanese Studies,* Winter, pp. 107–125.

Sidorov, Alexey, Irina Alexeyeva and Elena Shklyarik (2000). "The Ethical Environment of Russian Business," *Business Ethics Quarterly,* Volume 10, October, pp. 911–924.

Singer, Andrew W. (2000). "When it Comes to Child Labor, Toys R Us Isn't Playing Around," *Ethikos,* May/June, pp. 4–14.

Singer, Peter (2002). "Navigating the Ethics of Globalization," *The Chronicle of Higher Education,* October 11, pp. B7–B10.

Skelly, Joe (1995). "The Rise of International Ethics," *Business Ethics,* March/April, pp. 2–5.

Sloan, Allen and Michael Isikoff (2002). "The Enron Effect," *Newsweek,* January 28, pp. 34–35.

Smith, Adam (1966). *The Theory of Moral Sentiments.* New York, NY: Kelley Publishers.

Smith, N. Craig (1995). "Marketing Strategies for the Ethics Era," *Sloan Management Review,* Summer, pp. 85–97.

Sonnenberg, Frank K. and Beverly Goldberg (1992). "Business Integrity: An Oxymoron?," *Industry Week,* April 6, pp. 53–56.

Staff Report (1997). "Nike Suspends a Vietnam Boss," *The New York Times,* p. C3.

Thomson, Roy and Nigel Dudley (1989). "Transnationals and Oil in Amazonia," *The Ecologist,* November, pp. 219–224.

Trevino, Linda K., K. D. Butterfield and D. L. McCabe (1998). "The Ethical Context of Organizations: Influences on Employee Attitudes and Behaviors," *Business Ethics Quarterly,* Volume 8, July, pp. 447–476.

Turner, Louis (1984). "There's No love Lost Between Multinational Companies and the Third World," in W. M. Hoffman and J. M. Moore, eds., *Business Ethics.* New York: McGraw-Hill Book Company, pp. 394–400.

U. S. Foreign Corrupt Practices Act (1977). www.usdoj.gov/criminal/ fraud/fcpa/dojdocb.htm

van Tulder, Rob and Ans Kolk (2001). "Multinationality and Corporate Ethics," *Journal of International Business Studies,* Volume 32 (2), pp. 267–283.

Velasquez, Manual (1992). "International Business, Morality, and the Common Good," *Business Ethics Quarterly,* Volume 2, January, p. 30.

Velasquez, Manual (2000). "Globalization and the Failure of Ethics," *Business Ethics Quarterly,* Volume 10, January, pp. 343–352.

WSJ Editorial (2002). "Enron's Sins," *The Wall Street Journal,* January 18, p. A10.

Weaver, Gary R., Linda K. Trevino and Philip L. Cochran (1999). "Corporate Ethics Programs as Control Systems," *Academy of Management Journal,* Volume 42 (1), pp. 41–57.

Weaver Gary R. and Bradley R. Agle (2002). "Religiosity and Ethical Behavior In Organizations," *Academy of Management Review,* Volume 27, Number 1, pp. 77–97.

Werhane, Patricia H. (2000). Exporting Mental Models: Global Capitalism in the 21st Century," *Business Ethics Quarterly,* Volume 10, January, pp. 353–362.

Whenmouth, Edwin (1992). "A Matter of Ethics," *Industry Week,* March 16, pp. 57–62.

White, Anna (1997). "Joe Camel's World Tour," *The New York Times,* April 23, p. A31.

Willatt, Norris (1970). "How Nestle Adapts Products to Its Markets," *Business Abroad,* June, pp. 31–33.

Yip, George S. (2003). *Total Global Strategy II.* Upper Saddle River, NJ: Prentice Hall/Pearson Education, Inc.

Zellner, Wendy and Michael Arndt (2002). "The Perfect Sales Pitch: No Debt, No Worries," *Business Week,* January 28, p. 35.

Zellner, Wendy, Stephanie F. Anderson and Laura Cohn (2002). "The Whistle Blower: A Hero and a Smoking-Gun Letter," *Business Week,* January 28, pp. 34–35.

Zellner, Wendy, Michael France and Joseph Weber (2002). "The Man Behind the Deal Machine," *Business Week,* February 4, pp. 40–41.

File: Framework for Global Business Ethics, RR&R, 2003.

Critical Thinking

1. What are important considerations in developing a global code of ethics?

2. Should a firm change its home-country code of ethics when operating in another country? Why or why not?

3. Of the eight stage framework for developing a global code of ethics presented in the article, what stage do you believe is most critical for a firm operating in the global business arena? Why is it a critical stage?

4. How should a firm promulgate its code of ethics in countries in which it operates?

Revisiting the Global Business Ethics Question

Christopher Michaelson

The Question in Question

When the Beijing skyline was reshaped by the appearance of several colossal structures designed by Western architects in the run-up to the 2008 Olympics, the reviews of Western critics suggested that the additions were signs of aesthetic progress. The general expressions of praise that rang out were tinged with an unstated irony, that it took importing a Western aesthetic to demonstrate that Eastern cultural sophistication had arrived or surpassed that of the West.[1] From the comfortable distance of international television, the iconic buildings alight at night looked like they had taken the country over, but up close, they punctuated the juxtaposition of ancient and modern in China. To suggest that one of the world's oldest continuous civilizations needed the imprimatur of New World artists to demonstrate its cultural maturity was a patronizing sentiment, to say the least. If the strong odor of condescension from abroad offended anyone in Beijing, however, they were not saying so. They were the ones who had hired the architects and invited the attention, who came late to an ancient game that had been revived in the United States a century earlier, the rules of which went something like, the higher you could build a skyscraper, the more powerful you would appear. Today, the "mature" markets of the United States and Europe have left behind that game, whose new capitalist enthusiasts are headquartered in Dubai, Taipei, Kuala Lumpur, and Shanghai.

An analogous tone of moral paternalism lurks in the scholarship and practice of Western business ethics, a paradigmatic question of which is, "When moral business conduct standards conflict across borders, whose standards should prevail?" In a recent special issue of *Business Ethics Quarterly,* entitled "The Changing Role of Business in Global Society: New Challenges and Responsibilities," the special issue editors characterize, in a culturally neutral way, a critical ethical challenge of doing business across borders: "TNCs operate in a complex environment with heterogeneous, often contradictory legal and social demands" (Scherer, Palazzo, and Matten 2009: 328). By itself, this statement implies that whatever the TNC's home country (the United States or China, for example), there will be cultural adaptation challenges to doing business wherever the host country may be (China or the United States, for example). Fair enough. However, the editors and contributors to the Special Issue (including one article accepted for the Special Issue but published in a prior issue), along with the scholarly and practice tradition upon which they build, are generally not as concerned with the ethical challenges faced by the Chinese TNC doing business in the United States. Rather, as in the architecture analogy, the cases of interest generally involve Western multinationals doing business in less economically prosperous countries outside of North America and Western Europe (for example, Texaco in Ecuador [Hsieh 2009], Talisman in Sudan [Kobrin 2009], and private security companies protecting American interests in Iraq and Afghanistan [Elms and Phillips 2009]). In these cases, the developing market actors are perhaps even more likely to be victim than villain. Nevertheless, in the tale as it is commonly told, there is a pervasive underlying vulnerability to misconduct in developing markets.

The shared concern is generally of the form that agents of the firm operating in a developing host market far from their developed home market are more prone to engage in unethical behavior. The parties implicated for unethical behavior may be home country managers who place less value on the well-being of host country employees, society, and the environment; they may be host country managers and employees who fail to abide by corporate ethics policies; and they may be third parties, government officials, or others who intentionally exploit gaps in ethical and legal standards or who unintentionally fall victim to confusion about such gaps. Generally, there is no suggestion that developing host market *people* are less ethical than their developed market counterparts. However, there is often explicit or implied criticism that the ethical and legal framework of the host market, including but not limited to principles and rules, along with the institutions that support those principles and rules, is not sufficient to support fair and responsible free market capitalism. As Hsieh (2009: 267) argues, "MNEs have a responsibility to promote well-ordered institutions in societies where they operate that are not well-ordered."

To claim that in jurisdictions where free market capitalism is newer, where societies have not yet had the time and experience to construct the well-ordered institutions needed to support it—for example, the rule of law, a corporate governance system, and transparency—can be a culturally neutral claim, as innocent as teaching the complex rules of Olympic sports to the newer entrants who are determined to participate in the games. In fact, many business ethicists working in developed and developing markets endorse just such a view, that good business behavior is at risk in developing markets because, well, the markets (and their supporting institutions) are developing (for example, in addition to this sentiment appearing in several of the Special Issue articles, it also is expressed in Donaldson 1996, Donaldson and Dunfee 1999, Enderle 1999, Hanafin 2002, Harvey 1999, and Lu 1997 and 2009). However, the ideal, well-ordered society of the Western imagination does not fit as well in reality in a society ruled by authoritarian regime, military government, or desert kingdom as it does in a Western liberal democracy. The claim can too easily be taken to imply that ancient systems of market exchange do not count as capitalism when they are not supported by the rules of contemporary Western capitalism that, for example, seek to limit conflicts of interest and promote impartial governance. It is akin to suggesting that the only way to run an Olympic race is to measure progress in 100-meter increments, as though the Western obsession with brute speeds usurps the spinning, control, and finesse elements that various cultures insert into their traditional running exercises. The prevailing practice in business ethics has been to depict the home country standards, those of the developed market actor, to be "higher" or more "restrictive" or "well-ordered," while host country standards are the "lower," often unwritten norms of the emerging market actor (for example, in addition to this stated or implied construct in several of the Special Issue articles, it also is expressed in Donaldson 1996, Donaldson and Dunfee 1999, Johnson and Abromov 2004, Santoro 2000, Citigroup 2007, ExxonMobil 2009, and many other practice codes). This use of language may imply that home country standards are better, that home country officials demonstrate a stronger commitment with better governance

to better standards, or both. From the standpoint of the Western business ethics literature, either developing markets' ethics are behind (the blunt charge implying developed market moral superiority), or their economics are behind, resulting in ethics and market institutions that have not caught up to global market standards (a more common, veiled charge of developing market moral ignorance).

The question in question—"When moral business conduct standards conflict across borders, whose standards should prevail?"—brings fundamental theoretical issues about moral absolutism and relativism to bear on basic, pragmatic questions about moral absolutism and relativism to bear on basic, pragmatic questions about what is ethical business conduct amid conflicting norms. Business ethicists have been loath to appear to side with cultural relativists, and in fact I do not mean here to endorse moral relativism. I am suggesting, however, that we should be more open to the possibility that the justification for many of the moral absolutes that have come to align with Western capitalist doctrine may be conferred less by moral authority than by economic power. What might count as well-ordered, free market capitalism may be what those in economically powerful markets determine to be well-ordered, free market capitalism. As much as the global ethics question appears to be culturally neutral, many of those who ask it do so with a culturally specific lens shaped by prevailing conditions of Western economic strength. That is, the relative prosperity of developed economies seems implicitly to be taken as evidence of a sustainable form of free market capitalism that is supposed to be a universal economic destination. However, we need to be prepared for the possibility that as the balance of economic power evolves, the economic conception of global capitalism may also change, and with it so might ethical norms.

The BRIC countries (Brazil, Russia, India, and China) already represent a far greater share of economic growth than the G7 (World Economic Forum 2009), and within a few decades, it is likely that neither the U.S. nor the E.U. will represent the world's largest economy in GDP terms (PricewaterhouseCoopers 2006, Keidel 2008). The G20 has become a more influential political consortium than the G7 or G8 (Andrews 2009; Luce 2009). As a result of burgeoning economies from all corners of the globe, we could already be on the cusp of "when China rules the world" (Jacques 2009) and what Zakaria (2008) calls the "post-American world." With a shift in the global balance of economic power underway, it is time to revisit the question.

Questionable Assumptions

Global market capitalism in Scherer, Palazzo, and Matten 2009 includes a role for the corporation as a political actor that goes beyond traditional notions of corporate social responsibility. In this system, which they assert is an emerging reality, business firms are often as economically and politically powerful, or more powerful, than traditional nation states, and they engage in activities that previously were the sole province of government (Matten and Crane 2005; Scherer, Palazzo, and Baumann 2006). This conceptualization of the corporation as, at the same time, a self-interested market actor and a collaborative participant in global governance, has features in common with the vision of the corporation as a "global corporate citizen" set forth by Klaus Schwab (2008: 114) of the World Economic Forum. Schwab asserts that global corporations have "a civic duty to contribute to sustaining the world's well-being in cooperation with governments and civil society"—a duty that is inseparable from their "license to operate." The ambition of these authors to articulate, descriptively and normatively, an emerging role for the corporation in civil society, transcends the question in question of the present paper. As the nation state's influence recedes, and standard-setting is increasingly a product of democratic discourse that includes TNCs as key participants (Scherer and Palazzo 2007), the likelihood of cross-border conflicts of moral standards should also recede, rendering my question obsolete. Along with it, the impression that capitalism is a Western invention, to which non-Westerners are relative newcomers, should dissipate. However, unless and until that situation is fully realized, the question in question will remain fundamentally important to the exploration of global business ethics.[2]

Scherer, Palazzo, and Matten (2009:335) reference numerous examples of multilateral agreements (including the United Nations Global Compact) and cross-sector engagement (addressing such concerns as environmental protection, human rights, and transparent corporate reporting) that "represent a new form of global governance" that, while involving political actors and relationships, would in its ideal form go beyond what they refer to as "power politics." Indeed, Scherer and Palazzo (2007: 1110) envision a "Habermasian" process of public deliberation to address pressing problems that corporations and governments are either unwilling or unable to solve alone, while providing democratic mechanisms that may not achieve an ideal of "power free discourses of political will formation" but might come realistically close. The vision of global governance expressed in Scherer, Palazzo, and Matten 2009 and several predecessor papers goes a considerable distance toward challenging the Western capitalist stereotype of shareholder primacy and addressing associated concerns about ethical imperialism that have often tarnished well-intended efforts by developed market actors to bring well-ordered market institutions to

developing markets. However, even the notion that true global governance can be brought about through a process of "deliberative *democracy*" (emphasis added) risks being perceived as a peculiarly Western ideal, suggesting that even in the ideas that underlie power free discourse there can be found the influence of the powerful. Similarly, Donaldson's (1996) invocation of a Rawlsian ideal of "overlapping consensus" to underlie his articulation of (cross-cultural) "core human values" appeals similarly to democratic consensus-building, which may seem foreign to alternative political traditions. While the process leading to the formation of the U.N. Global Compact might resemble a deliberative ideal, in reality such negotiations are not power free. For example, there is little doubt that the impact of the Global Compact has had much to do with the endorsement of economically powerful market actors (over the protestations of some advocates of the less powerful), while the legitimacy of the Kyoto Protocol on climate change was harmed by the United States' longstanding resistance to it.

This is to say that, whether Westerners or non-Westerners are perceived to be the cause of social and environmental problems, more often than not, Western economic and ethical constructs are proposed as potential solutions. For example, in his analysis of human rights obligations for TNCs, Kobrin (2009: 351) asserts, "the host country is typically the perpetrator, the primary violator of human rights." This assertion seems clearly to hold in the Sudan case that is his primary object of analysis, but there have been important cases in which the primary violators were outsiders (e.g., the perpetration of the opium trade by Britain in India and China) and in which moral accountability was distributed among multiple internal and external parties (e.g., Shell's historical involvement in Nigeria). It would be simplistic and unfair here to assert that the "emerging transnational order" to which Kobrin appeals as a solution is a conspiracy of the powerful; however, it would also be simplistic and naïve to suppose that this order does not reflect a conception of international law with which Western market actors tend to feel more at home and which seems alien to certain non-Western market actors which depend less on formal institutions to enforce moral norms. Pies, Hielscher, and Beckmann's (2009) use of game theory to support an "ordonomic" approach to corporate citizenship reflects another familiar Western worldview that, even when private and public interest coincide, private interest is the *primary* motivator of individual human behavior. Their use (392–93) of the Google et al. in China example as an example of how private parties can act collectively to benefit their own and others' interests presupposes the priority of the right to free speech, as Western analysis of this case has been prone to do. But it is worth questioning whether free speech, a private interest, necessarily is prior to social order, the public interest which the Chinese government evidently put ahead of private rights in this case. My point here is not to doubt the efficacy of these Western constructs as solutions; rather, it is to ask whether the background assumptions about order, rightness, and deliberative democracy reflect the universal consensus of reasonable human beings or rather the more tenuous consensus of more economically powerful human beings that have had disproportionate influence in the current instantiation of our global economy.

The Special Issue editors' vision of global governance might advance us beyond these power politics, but on the real road to a more ideal global governance system, it is worth revisiting a concern. The concern, as outlined earlier in this paper, is that the justification for global business standards that currently prevail, some of which arise from multilateral discourse, may be conferred less by moral authority than by economic power. In a reality that falls short of the ideal of power free discourse, it is worth recognizing, where possible, the influence that economic power can have over ethical norms in the midst of a historic period of economic rebalancing.

A Question of Fit

Western perspectives on doing business in a global context have been criticized for betraying a Western *ethical* bias; however, the Western *economic* bias that pervades the cultural foundations of market capitalism is less often challenged.[3] We may be sensitive, though not immune, to the specter of moral "imperialism" (Donaldson 1996) if we contend that one culture's ethical systems and practices are more advanced than another's. Yet, we routinely use such terms as "developed" and "developing" when we refer to the level of economic advancement of countries. Therefore, when we grapple with ethical problems of doing business across borders, we often explore what ethical practices and legal and political institutions are needed to regulate free market capitalism as we know it, especially in jurisdictions in which this form of capitalism is relatively new. That is, we examine cross-cultural ethics, or how ethics and law need to adapt to accommodate the smooth functioning of market capitalism as we know it. We less often explore cross-cultural *economics;* that is, how the global market system itself may need to adapt to accommodate cultures that may not share certain ethical tenets about human nature fundamental to Western free market capitalism.

Inevitably, such broad claims and categorizations as these oversimplify the state of play, unfortunately dividing the world into "us" and "them," potentially undermining the goal of harmonious interplay.[4] While exploring progress toward a global market system less susceptible to power politics and more likely to produce coincidence between ethical and economic outcomes, polarities—such as "Western and non-Western," "developed and developing," and "ethics and economics," among others—can be useful for emphasizing contrasts, even though such contrasts are not in reality as stark as depicted. For example, state ownership of corporate enterprises, a model that we may previously have associated with non-capitalist markets, has recently returned in the United States and elsewhere as a result of the global recession (Bremmer and Pujadas 2009). Business ethicists and corporate social responsibility theorists have suggested that there is a polar contrast between United States compliance-oriented and European Union sustainability-oriented approaches to corporate social responsibility (Handy 2002). Meanwhile, the model of family ownership that has sometimes been perceived as contributing to "crony capitalism" in Asia is now seen to be an important driver of entrepreneurial growth (James 2008). That is to say that there is no "capitalism as we know it" in reality, but absent a single reference point, the business ethics debate about whose moral standards should prevail has tended to gravitate toward a dominant ideology emphasizing instrumentalism and rationality. The neo-colonialist literature goes so far as to suggest that globalization is not as much the product of a multiplicity of systems coming together as it is the "assimilation within the dominant ideology" of the economically and politically powerful (Banerjee and Linstead 2001), which can at times have the "dark side" of unintended consequences (Khan, Munir, and Willmott 2007).

In general, Western business ethics are inextricably tied to the ideal of a free market, which is itself a moral ideal worth questioning. Western theories of human nature on which the founding doctrines of free market capitalism are based suppose that people are naturally prone to act in their own narrow self-interest. Accordingly, Western corporate governance prescriptions require oversight that is independent of conflicts of interest. These conceptions presuppose a highly instrumental form of reasoning, in which little is done for its own sake but everything is done for the sake of gaining some other sort of extrinsic advantage. As a moral philosopher before he was an economist. Adam Smith was not alien to the idea of moral sentiments associated with non-market goods (Calkins and Werhane 1998; Heilbroner 1999). However, the emphasis of particular ideas in the practice of Western free market capitalism—especially, individualist instrumentalism and the primacy of scientific rationality—can encourage and exploit these ideas in practice that are supposed to be fundamentally human and yet are alien to many, including some people who were not raised under Western capitalist doctrine. That doctrine takes a self-interested, instrumentalist sentiment that is common to a piece within all of us and then accuses all of us of being all self-interested. Then, because it is a piece of all of us, it uses rationalistic, economic predictive modeling techniques to show that the self-interested assumption is all we need in order to understand human market behavior. Economists and political scientists are aware that what these predictive models say of the instrumental rationality of the collective does not apply equally to each individual within the collective (Fehr and Tyran 2005, Friedman 2005, Inglehart 1990, Sen 1988), while even predictive neuroscientific models of the brain and behavior need to account for the interaction of multiple mechanisms that include the passions (Camerer, Loewenstein, and Prelec 2004, 2005), and those non-economic values and emotions routinely lead people to act in ways that appear to be contrary to their self-interest (Fehr and Gächter 2000). Postmodern and feminist theories have long emphasized the role of the emotions in ethical and economic reasoning (Nussbaum 2001, Solomon 2003, 2004). Notwithstanding these challenges to it, the worldview implied in Western business ethics scholarship suggests that individualist, instrumental rationality holds true of the collective—even in Asian societies which we (often too simplistically) characterize as collectivist and less instrumentalist.

In our current, globalized economy in which the free market may be a means and not an end in itself, in which public markets commingle with a norm of private, family-run enterprise, and private equity competes with sovereign wealth funds, it is time to give up some of our blind fidelity to Western norms of economic behavior to recognize that under an alternative economic scenario, those norms may not be as normal. This is not naïvely to suggest that there are no self-interested abuses of power and influence in developing markets or to suppose idealistically that most people who were raised under Confucian or Communist or Catholic doctrine unwaveringly and always put the common good ahead of individual self-interest. Much has been made, perhaps too much (Koehn 1999), of the stereotypical difference between collectivist and individualist societies (Friedman 2005; Nisbett 2003), but this contrast does do the important service of suggesting that a global population that is a more diverse mix of moral sentiments than Western capitalist doctrine allows us to suppose may defy well-worn assumptions about collective behavior if we are able to see it through non-instrumentalist, less purely rationalistic lenses. It is further to recognize the diverse capitalisms in play across the globe as proof that capitalism is not a constant doctrine, but rather a set of ideas to be put into practice, and how it plays out depends upon who is playing it. It plays out in a seemingly never-ending series of

scandals if the players are taught to pursue profitability within the boundaries of an external regulatory regime which will take care of the boundary-setting. Alternatively, in a global market that is sensitive to the privileges often enjoyed by business managers in juxtaposition with impoverished populations, a form of capitalism begins to emerge in which scholars and practitioners alike get to ask humanitarian—and, I would emphasize, other-regarding—questions such as that asked by the Special Issue editors: "What are the challenges and responsibilities of the changing role of business in global society?"

The global business ethics question, "When moral business conduct standards conflict across borders, whose standards should prevail?" needs to be accompanied by a global business economics question: "What kind (or kinds) of capitalism(s) is (are) the right fit for a rebalancing global marketplace?" This pair of questions suggests that business ethics is not purely a matter of imposing a spurious moral absolutism, nor is it to succumb to moral relativism, but rather it is a matter of "fit"—between ethics, economics, and the people in cultures who practice them.

The *Euthyphro* Question

Are prevailing answers to questions of cross-cultural business ethics conflict accepted because they are right, or are they right because they are accepted? To any reader trained in the Western intellectual tradition, this question will sound familiar as a reformulation of Socrates' question to Euthyphro (10a): "Is the holy loved by the gods because it is holy [o]r is it holy because it is loved by the gods?" Of course, the answer to that question is that the gods love what is holy because it is holy, and likewise, we would like to think that our global business ethics standards are global in virtue of their universality rather than in virtue of their promulgation by the economically powerful. However, if economic strength has been the basis for ethical leverage, then we should be prepared for a tumultuous storm of ethical rebalancing as the global economy rebalances.

When we suggest that developing economies are not as far along in their progression toward free market capitalism, just what are we purporting to suggest is the goal? Is it to be more like that form of Western capitalism that has sanctioned instrumental, individualistic behavior to the point at which it has become a pathology, as demonstrated in the business ethics scandals of 2001–2002 and the global recession of 2008–2009, threatening to undermine the very system that has set it forth as a fundamental human expectation? Is it to embrace a scientific model of reasoning in which self-interested behavior is the acceptable norm but the slippery slope toward self-dealing leads to an unacceptable violation of a moral ideal of impartiality? We should not forget that systems of market exchange predating recent events have been part of the economic and political history of every market—including Brazil, Russia, India, and China, in spite of their recent flirtation with Communist and Socialist ideologies.

In the literature on which the Special Issue builds concerning business ethics across borders, prominent concerns have been raised on numerous critical business ethics issues, including but not limited to climate change, and the challenge of limiting greenhouse gas emissions while preserving legitimate economic development (for example, Benton 2002,2008; Romar 2009; Windsor 2004); the pervasiveness of intellectual property piracy (not incidentally, a value-laden term) (Donaldson 1996; Sybert 2008) and cultural differences in attitudes toward intellectual property (Werhane and Gorman 2005); the trade-off between human rights and controlling costs to attract foreign direct investment (for example, Arnold and Bowie 2007, Campbell 2006, Sethi 2003, Velasquez 2000), and limiting corruption (another value-laden term) (O'Higgins 2006, Windsor 2004), while untangling it from legitimate social relations traditions, such as *guanxi,* which confounds the principle of impartiality (Donaldson 1996; Luo 2007; Warren, Dunfee, and Li 2004). With regard to each of these issues, the Western approach to influencing ethical behavior has been to follow the instrumentalist, rationalist path of setting a minimum standard and then to measure and monitor compliance therewith. However, the level of formalization of market and law enforcement institutions is not necessarily a reliable indicator of the level of moral commitment to enforcing moral standards. Given concerns over the excessive litigiousness of Western, and particularly American, legal institutions, the emerging transnational order may well benefit from applying less formal methods for achieving social compliance familiar in less litigious societies, such as cultural conformity, pressure from community elders, and the threat of being ostracized from the market community. Important and irreducibly complex social traditions give rise to practical differences:

- Climate change places values of natural beauty, poverty alleviation, cultural preservation, future generations, and fairness, among others, in tension with economic competitiveness. A true global capitalism cannot solve such a complex problem by setting standards that focus on preserving economic competitiveness alone, and the present increase in triple bottom line reporting can be taken to reflect openness to a system in which a multiplicity of values vie for importance.
- The notion of human rights derives from an intellectual tradition of liberal individualism that regards each human being as the basic unit for

moral analysis. This rights-based perspective is foreign to societies, often more populous and therefore deriving strength in numbers, in which families and communities are the basic unit for moral analysis. The kinds of tradeoffs foreseen by climate change economists (Stern 2007) between resource conservation and human well-being—which may also entail health, safety, and other material sacrifices that are seen by Westerners as human rights issues—are already familiar in resource-constrained societies.

- Intellectual property is a product of institutional pragmatism aimed at, among other things, promoting competition to innovate on the supposition that instrumental incentives are required to promote intellectual invention. The so-called piracy of intellectual property, which is often cast as a disregard for the rule of law accompanied by inadequate enforcement, can also be seen as a reflection of a cultural sentiment that knowledge is public property (or not property at all), for sharing rather than commoditization. As Appiah (2006: 129) notes, IP protection for the sake of cultural preservation may well "damage, irreparably, the nature of what it seeks to protect . . . making countless mine-and-thine distinctions."
- Bribery is bribery within an instrumentalist framework in which every cause has a transactional effect. *Guanxi* is not necessarily bribery in a relationship oriented framework that is more complex than Western legal institutions allow for, in which moral partiality is not perceived to be an automatic vice.[5]

I am not here condoning a worldview that regards environmental degradation, human rights abuses, piracy, and bribery as mere social constructs. Nor do I mean to imply that a shift in economic and political power relations necessarily entails a shift toward the ethical priorities of the new economic champions. However, I am suggesting that in a rebalancing global economy, when we encounter tension in moral standards across borders, we need to be more open than ever to the possibility of revision. That shift in economic power relations gives us reasons to explore whether what we might have taken to be morally authoritative norms might on further examination turn out to have been the product of pre-existing power relations. Lest the notion of economic-ethical-cultural "fit" appear to be merely cultural relativism under a threadbare and flimsy cloak, it is important to distinguish between moral rationalization (accepting cultural differences as universal moral justification for differing cultural practices) and explanation (using cultural differences to illuminate and resolve legitimate cross-cultural value tensions). Under a different balance of economic power, Western business ethicists may still have reasons to challenge human rights practices in emerged (what else should we call them then?) markets, but we may well see a shift in the tone and tenacity of the argument that reflects compromise among legitimate values. Intellectual property, meanwhile, may someday recede in importance as a legal concept, as we are already seeing it undermined by social networking and mass collaboration vehicles that change the way in which content is produced, distributed, shared, and sold. In this evolving global economy, cross-cultural ethical tensions are unlikely to disappear altogether, even as the role of the corporation in a global society increasingly involves greater cross-sector collaboration and multilateral standard-setting.

Recently, at a business forum that I helped coordinate, business executives from major U.S.-based multinationals were asked whether a change in the economic balance of power might portend a change in ethical influence. The executives, themselves of Western cultural descent, plainly did not even understand the question. The question they heard—not the one they were asked—was whether they should compromise their home country ethical standards when operating in host countries. They reverted to familiar truisms about how their corporate values must be unwavering wherever their businesses were operating. The audience did not press them on their failure to address the question at hand, perhaps because these parties also were conditioned by the power relations that have prevailed since the rise of capitalism in the West. This failure of Western eyes to see the cultural complexity beneath the question is reminiscent of our aesthetic conditioning that leads us to see only the telegenic punctuation points on the Beijing skyline, the ones whose Western architects had the cultural audacity to illuminate more brightly than the rest.[6]

Notes

The author would like to thank the editors and anonymous reviewers for valuable feedback on earlier drafts of this paper. Research that contributed to the ideas in this paper was supported by a grant from the University of St. Thomas, Opus College of Business.

1. The signature structures included Beijing National Stadium, the centerpiece of the Olympic Games that became known as the "Bird's Nest," a collaboration between the Swiss firm of Herzog & de Meuron and the Chinese artist Ai Weiwei; Sir Norman Foster's T3 (Terminal Three) at the Beijing Capital International Airport; and China Central Television's headquarters, designed by the Dutch architect Rem Koolhaas. Ourousoff (2008) notes that the Bird's Nest was "said to embody everything from China's muscle-flexing nationalism to a newfound cultural sophistication"; Slessor (2008) hails T3 as both the arrival of modernity and the Pacific Century; while Rose (2009) wondered whether the firecracker-induced blaze at CCTV's sister building would spook superstitious Chinese from hiring Western architects again.

2. Any such sweeping commentary on the state of global business ethics as this will necessarily betray some oversimplification. This paper, along with many that it references, makes use of such dichotomies as "East and West," "developing and developed" market, "democracy and autocracy," "absolutism and relativism," "ethics and economics," "capitalism and non-capitalism," which are in reality blurry and sometimes counterproductive to collaboration and understanding. These are terms of convenience that can have real impacts on the ways in which we see and act.

3. Both forms of concern are evident in the following examples: Takahashi (1999) asserts that global business standards have tended to reflect a Western ethical bias while also characterizing non-Western economic systems as backward. Thomas Friedman (2008: 343) echoes oft-made charges that developed nations have unfairly benefitted from decades of carbon-intensive production that is now restricted for all nations. Benjamin Friedman (2005: 304) explains globalization critics' concern that "industrialization disrupts previously existing social arrangements." Said's well-known concerns about colonialism are not exclusively focused on business and economic behavior but incorporate examples of the interplay between economic power, ethical imposition, and imperialist tendencies (1993).

4. Both Appiah (2006), who prominently advocates an ideal of cosmopolitanism that deemphasizes cultural differences, and Said (1993), who prominently defends colonized peoples against imperialist empires, express discomfort with the divisions implied by "us" and "them" dichotomies.

5. Luo (2007: 215–18) distinguishes *guanxi* from corruption in that it is a social norm, not a deviation; it is legal, not illegal; it is an exchange of favors rather than money; the reciprocity obligations are implicit rather than transactional; there are no lawful risks if it fails; it is long-term rather than short-term oriented; it is not timebound; it is trust- rather than commodity-based; and it is transferable.

6. In a curious endnote to the Beijing Olympics story, the games ended happily for most people. China won the gold medal count, demonstrating athletic superiority that could well be a proxy for future political and economic superiority. The United States won the overall medal count (again), showing that it still retained the ability to mine the lanes, courts, and fields for the most prodigious material haul. The marathoners ran, even though there had been an ironic concern that the relative economic prosperity that had led many Beijing residents to trade their bicycles for cars was going to plague the games with the primitive industrial specter of pollution. The Uyghur ethnic minority of western China, which had threatened possible terrorist activity to bring attention to its human rights claims, was kept at bay in the eastern capital city. Even though a random act of fatal violence by a deranged Chinese man against an American tourist showed that random acts of violence could emerge under an authoritarian regime, the games, as a whole, were peaceful. The success was celebrated by nearly all but the vice mayor of Beijing, Liu Zhihua, who had supervised the construction projects in preparation for the Olympic Games. Liu was stripped of his post and status in 2006 for corruption, a particularly painful revelation for a country and city seeking to demonstrate the orderliness of its institutions to a global marketplace in which many players are

convinced that corruption is endemic. The indictment of Liu for corruption might have been taken by Western observers as a sign of promise that the rule of law was working; his death sentence (suspended as of this writing) might have been taken by those same observers as a sign of concern that China had yet to wake up to modernity on the ethical issue of human rights (Yardley 2008). Or, might it signal a greater commitment to anti-corruption enforcement?

References

Andrews, E. L. 2009. "Leaders of G-20 Vow to Reshape Global Economy" *New York Times* (September 26).

Appiah, K. A. 2006. *Cosmopolitanism: Ethics in a World of Strangers.* New York: W. W. Norton & Company.

Arnold, D. G., and N. E. Bowie. 2007. "Respect for Workers in Global Supply Chains: Advancing the Debate over Sweatshops," *Business Ethics Quarterly* 17: 135–45.

Banerjee, S. B., and S. Linstead. 2001. "Globalization, Multiculturalism and Other Fictions: Colonialism for the New Millennium?" *Organization* 8: 683–722.

Benton, R. 2002. "Environmental Racism, Consumption, and Sustainability," *Business Ethics Quarterly* 12: 83–98.

_____. 2008. "Review of J. R. Desjardins, *Business, Ethics, and the Environment: Imagining a Sustainable Future,*" *Business Ethics Quarterly* 18: 567–81.

Bremmer, I., and Pujadas, J. 2009. "State Capitalism Makes a Comeback," *Harvard Business Review* 87(2): 32–33.

Calkins, M. J., and P. H. Werhane. 1998. "Adam Smith, Aristotle, and the Virtues of Commerce," *Journal of Value Inquiry* 32: 43–60.

Camerer, C. F., G. Loewenstein, and D. Prelec. 2004. "Neuroeconomics: Why Economics Needs Brains," *Scandinavian Journal of Economics* 106(3): 555–79.

_____. 2005. "Neuroeconomics: How Neuroscience Can Inform Economics," *Journal of Economic Literature* 43: 9–64.

Campbell, T. 2006. "A Human Rights Approach to Developing Voluntary Codes of Conduct for Multinational Corporations," *Business Ethics Quarterly* 16: 255–69.

Citigroup. 2007. Code of Conduct: Our Shared Responsibilities, available at www.citigroup.com/citi/corporategovernance/data/codeconduct_en.pdf, first accessed August 25, 2009.

Donaldson, T. 1996. "Values in Tension: Ethics Away from Home," *Harvard Business Review* 74(5): 48–62.

Donaldson, T., and T. W. Dunfee. 1999. *Ties That Bind: A Social Contracts Approach to Business Ethics.* Cambridge, Mass.: Harvard Business School Press.

Elms, H., and R. A. Phillips. 2009. "Private Security Companies and Institutional Legitimacy: Corporate and Stakeholder Responsibility," *Business Ethics Quarterly* 19: 403–32.

Enderle, G., ed. 1999. *International Business Ethics: Challenges and Approaches.* Notre Dame, Ind.: University of Notre Dame Press.

ExxonMobil. 2009. Code of Ethics and Business Conduct, available at www.exxonmobil.com/corporate/files/corporate/investor_governance_ethics.pdf, first accessed August 25, 2009.

Fehr, E., and S. Gächter. 2000. "Fairness and Retaliation: The Economics of Reciprocity," *Journal of Economic Perspectives* 14(3): 159–81.

Fehr, E., and J. R. Tyran. 2005. "Individual Irrationality and Aggregate Outcomes," *Journal of Economic Perspectives* 19(4): 43–66.

Friedman, B. M. 2005. *The Moral Consequences of Economic Growth.* New York: Alfred A. Knopf.

Friedman, T. L. 2008. *Hot, Flat, and Crowded: Why We Need a Green Revolution—and How it Can Renew America.* New York: Farrar, Straus, and Giroux.

Hanafin, J. J. 2002. "Morality and the Market in China: Some Contemporary Views," *Business Ethics Quarterly* 12(1): 1–18.

Handy, C. 2002. "What's a Business For?" *Harvard Business Review* 80(12): 49–56.

Harvey, B. 1999. "'Graceful Merchants': A Contemporary View of Chinese Business Ethics," *Journal of Business Ethics* 20: 85–92.

Heilbroner, R. L. 1999. *The Worldly Philosophers: The Lives, Times, and Ideas of the Great Economic Thinkers,* rev. 7th ed. New York Simon & Schuster.

Hsieh, N. 2009. "Does Global Business Have a Responsibility to Promote Just Institutions?" *Business Ethics Quarterly* 19: 251–73.

Inglehart, R. 1990. *Culture Shift in Advanced Industrial Society.* Princeton, N.J.: Princeton University Press.

Jacques, M. 2009. *When China Rules the World: The End of the Western World and the Birth of a New Global Order.* New York: Penguin.

James, H. 2008. "Family Values or Crony Capitalism?" *Capitalism and Society* 3(1): 1–28.

Johnson, K. W., and I. Y. Abromov. 2004. *Business Ethics: A Manual for Managing a Responsible Business Enterprise in Emerging Market Economies.* Washington, D.C.: United States Department of Commerce, International Trade Administration.

Keidel, A. 2008. China's Economic Rise: Fact and Fiction. Carnegie Endowment for International Peace Policy Brief 61.

Khan, F. R., K. A. Munir, and H. Willmott. 2007. "A Dark Side of Institutional Entrepreneurship: Soccer Balls, Child Labour and Postcolonial Impoverishment," *Organization Studies* 28: 1055–77.

Kobrin, S. J. 2009. "Private Political Authority and Public Responsibility: Transnational Politics, Transnational Firms, and Human Rights," *Business Ethics Quarterly* 19: 349–74.

Koehn, D. 1999. "What Can Eastern Philosophy Teach Us About Business Ethics?" *Journal of Business Ethics* 19: 71–79.

Lu, Xiaohe. 1997. "Business Ethics in China," *Journal of Business Ethics* 16: 1509–18.

_____. 2009. "A Chinese Perspective: Business Ethics in China Now and in the Future," *Journal of Business Ethics* 86: 451–61.

Luce, E. 2009. "G20 Summit: New Body to Lead Global Recovery," *Financial Times* (September 26).

Luo, Yadong. 2007. *Guanxi and Business.* Singapore: World Scientific Publishing.

Matten, D., and A. Crane. 2005. "Corporate Citizenship: Toward an Extended Theoretical Conceptualization," *Academy of Management Review* 30: 166–79.

Nisbett, R. E. 2003. *The Geography of Thought: How Asians and Westerners Think Differently . . . and Why.* New York: Simon & Schuster.

Nussbaum, M. C. 2001. *Upheavals of Thought: The Intelligence of Emotions.* New York: Cambridge University Press.

O'Higgins, E. R. E. 2006. "Corruption, Underdevelopment, and Extractive Resource Industries: Addressing the Vicious Cycle," *Business Ethics Quarterly* 16: 235–54.

Ouroussoff, N. 2008. "Olympic Stadium with a Design to Remember," *The New York Times* (August 5).

Pies, I., S. Hielscher, and M. Beckmann. 2009. "Moral Commitments and the Societal Role of Business: An Ordonomic Approach to Corporate Citizenship," *Business Ethics Quarterly* 19: 375–401.

Plato. 1984. *"Euthyphro,"* in *The Dialogues of Plato,* vol. 1, trans. R. E. Allen. New Haven, Conn.: Yale University Press.

PricewaterhouseCoopers. 2006. The world in 2050: How Big will the Major Emerging Market Economies Get and How Can the OECD Compete? Available at www.pwc.com/en_GX /gx/world-2050/pdf/world2050emergingeconomies.pdf, first accessed July 31, 2009.

Romar, E. 2009. "Snapshots of the Future: Darfur, Katrina, and Maple Sugar," *Journal of Business Ethics* 85: 121–32.

Rose, S. 2009. "Will the Beijing Blaze Come Back to Haunt European Architects?" *The Guardian* (February 10).

Said, E. W. 1993. *Culture and Imperialism.* New York: Vintage Books.

Santoro, M. A. 2000. *Profits and Principles: Global Capitalism and Human Rights in China.* Ithaca, N.Y.: Cornell University Press.

Scherer, A. G., and G. Palazzo. 2007. "Toward a Political Conception of Corporate Responsibility: Business and Society Seen From a Habermasian Perspective," *Academy of Management Review* 32: 1096–1120.

Scherer, A. G., G. Palazzo, and D. Baumann. 2006. "Global Rules and Private Actors: Toward a New Role of the Transnational Corporation in Global Governance," *Business Ethics Quarterly* 16: 505–32.

Scherer, A. G., G. Palazzo, and D. Matten. 2009. "Introduction to the Special Issue: Globalization as a Challenge for Business Responsibilities," *Business Ethics Quarterly* 19: 327–47.

Schwab, K. 2008. "Global Corporate Citizenship: Working with Governments and Civil Society," *Foreign Affairs* 87(1): 107–18.

Sen, A. 1988. *On Ethics and Economics.* Malden, Mass.: Blackwell Publishing.

Sethi, S. P. 2003. *Setting Global Standards: Guidelines for Creating Codes of Conduct in Multinational Corporations.* Hoboken, N.J.: John Wiley & Sons.

Slessor, C. 2008. "Three is the Magic Number," *The Architectural Review* (August 1).

Solomon, R. C., ed. 2003. *What is an Emotion? Classic and Contemporary Readings.* New York: Oxford University Press.

_____, ed. 2004. *Thinking about Feeling: Contemporary Philosophers on Emotions.* New York: Oxford University Press.

Stern, N. 2007. *The Economics of Climate Change: The Stern Review.* Cambridge: Cambridge University Press.

Sybert, R. P. 2008. "IP Protection and Counterfeiting in China," *Intellectual Property & Technology Law Journal* 20(7): 12–15.

Takahashi, A. 1999. "Ethics in Developing Economies of Asia," in *International Business Ethics: Challenges and Approaches,* ed. G. Enderle. Notre Dame, Ind.: University of Notre Dame Press.

Velasquez, M. 2000. "Globalization and the Failure of Ethics," *Business Ethics Quarterly* 10: 343–52.

Warren, D. E., T. W. Dunfee, and N. Li. 2004. "Social Exchange in China: The Double-Edged Sword of *Guanxi,*" *Journal of Business Ethics* 55(4): 355–72.

Werhane, P. H., and M. Gorman. 2005. "Intellectual Property Rights, Moral Imagination, and Access to Life-Enhancing Drugs," *Business Ethics Quarterly* 15: 595–613.

Windsor, D. 2004. "The Development of International Business Norms," *Business Ethics Quarterly* 14: 729–54.

World Economic Forum. 2009. "The Future of the Global Financial System: A Near-Term Outlook and Long-Term Scenarios," available at www.weforum.org/pdf/scenarios /TheFutureoftheGlobalFinancialSystem.pdf, first accessed July 31, 2009.

Yardley, J. 2008. "Beijing Olympics Chief May Be Executed for Corruption," *New York Times* (October 20).

Zakaria, F. 2008. *The Post-American World.* New York: W.W. Norton & Company.

Critical Thinking

1. What is the "question in question" discussed in the article?

2. What is the Euthyphro question? How is this question informative when considering a firm's global business ethics standards?

3. Should corporate values be unwavering wherever in the world a business firm operates? Answer by developing arguments on both sides of the question.

Taking Your Code to China

KIRK O. HANSON AND STEPHAN ROTHLIN

Introduction

The proliferation of codes of conduct and ethical standards among American and European companies has been dramatic over the past twenty years. It is rare today to find a large publicly held company in the West that does not have some type of ethics code and is not involved in the growing dialogue over global standards of conduct. But one of the most difficult challenges facing these companies is how to apply these codes and these ethical standards to the companies' operations in developing countries, particularly in Africa, the Middle East and Asia. Among these cases, perhaps the most urgent challenge is for each company to decide how to adapt and apply its code to operations in China. Companies such as Rio Tinto, Google, and Foxconn are recent case studies in ethical conflicts arising from doing business in China.

With pressures for human rights, environmental sensitivity, and fighting corruption rising in their domestic homelands and in global commerce, nothing is more critical to these companies' reputation and success than learning how to "take their code to China."

This article presents the learning of the two authors and companies they have consulted and worked with over the last ten years in China. Our experience is that Western companies have generally progressed very slowly in applying their codes to their operations in China. This article summarizes why it is so difficult to do so, and what the most successful companies are doing to make it work.

Pressures for a Global Standard of Company Behavior

The fundamental problem any company faces in creating a global commitment to ethical behavior in its own organization is that cultural, competitive, economic and political conditions vary significantly from country to country. It is often said that ethical values themselves differ significantly between countries. From our experience, however, we believe values do not differ as much as common practice—or how companies typically behave. Actual behavior, of course, depends on historical patterns, government regulation and enforcement, social pressures and acceptance, and the moral resolve of the actors. While corruption is common in many countries of the world, one cannot really say that corruption is welcomed or valued

anywhere. There are anti-corruption coalitions among domestic companies in almost every national setting. Even in those countries with the most corruption, there is an awareness of the corrosive effects it brings to the country, and the drag corruption creates for economic development.

Nonetheless, there are some value and cultural differences of significance, and different countries that are at different stages of development often have different priorities for social and economic progress. Further, the national and local governments in host countries present different challenges depending on their history and leadership.

Western companies really have little choice whether to "take their code to China" and to the other countries they operate in. They are facing four key developments which make "taking their codes" to wherever they operate more important and often more difficult. The first is that global companies are under increasingly insistent demands, both legal and from key constituencies in their home countries to adopt and implement standards of behavior abroad that match those at home. The United States' Foreign Corrupt Practices Act (FCPA), which was passed in 1977, makes some forms of corruption abroad crimes in the USA; in 1999 almost all OECD countries signed similar laws.

Because home country constituencies will not tolerate different (i.e. lower) ethical standards abroad, most large Western companies adopt and implement "global codes of conduct" which are expected to guide company behavior to be the same across all countries in which the firm operates. Many companies have commented that, from a purely practical point of view, adherence to a single global standard of behavior reduces the incidence of rogue local behavior, and rationalizations that the firm's conduct must be "adapted" to local conditions.

The second development is a growing global movement, reflected in an increasing number of developing countries, to deal seriously with bribery and corruption. Thirty-eight countries have now signed up to the OECD's 1997 anti-corruption convention, leading to a spatter of cross-border prosecutions. Local constituencies in host countries then pressure companies from developed Western countries to join the reform coalitions to counter corruption. Local affiliates of Transparency International are most significant in this development.

The third development is a growing global dialogue on "global standards" for business behavior. The United Nations Global Compact is an initiative launched in 1999 at the World

Economic Forum in Davos by former Secretary General Kofi Anan but enthusiastically continued under his successor Ban Kee Moon. Companies and NGOs in over 80 countries have pledged to follow the ten principles of the Global Compact in the crucial area of human rights, labor conditions, environmental protection and anti-corruption. Similar efforts are being pursued in specific industries and in specific dimensions of corporate behavior such as employment policies and environmental behavior. Efforts such as these to promote a global standard of behavior are making it more difficult to operate under different practices in different countries. Such pressure requires companies to commit publicly to various global standards, which are then reinforced in their own company codes.

Finally, the explosive growth of the global media in all its forms has led to an increasing scrutiny of corporate behavior, even in the most distant and remote areas of the developing world. It has become difficult for a company to behave differently abroad without it coming to the attention of its home and host country constituencies. Corporate sweatshops, or environmental practices, can be documented by amateur reporters with cellphone cameras, even in the most restricted societies. Such disclosure dramatically increases pressures on Western companies to behave by a single global standard.

The Realities of Operating in Developing Countries

In each country where a company operates, it must confront a set of unique realities in applying its code of corporate behavior. Among the most important are the following:

Cultural expectations and standards—Each country has a set of cultural standards, or more informal expectations, that may conflict with the ethical standards the company operates by elsewhere. While some cultural expectations are benign—modes of greeting and signs of respect—others can be more problematic. In some societies, vendors are often selected primarily because they are a "related company" or are operated by a local employee's family or by a relative of a government official. In other societies, it is expected that potential business partners will develop a deep and reciprocal relationship before a contract is signed. In discussing China, the cultural tradition of gift giving to support such relationships can be a particularly problematic issue to manage.

Social and business community pressure to conform—Foreign companies operating in any society can be very disruptive, whether it is their pay scales or their insistence on arms-length contracting practices. When the foreign company operates by standards that challenge or constitute implied criticisms of local practices, there will be significant pressure on the foreign firm to conform to local practices, lest their presence create greater costs for indigenous firms, or create dissatisfaction in the local firm's workforce. The Western firm may find itself frozen out of business opportunities or subjected to selective regulatory enforcement if it is considered to be "disruptive."

Local management's comfort and loyalty to local standards—Foreign companies seek to hire local managers as quickly as possible and for as many positions as possible. Often local managers, particularly more senior managers already experienced in local companies, have adopted the local values and ways of doing things. Changing these managers' ways of operating can be particularly difficult.

Priorities of economic and political development—The national and local governments of host countries have many priorities and needs, and often choose to focus on issues unimportant to foreign firms while ignoring issues central to these newcomers. Chinese government decisions about how to deal with copyright violations, liberty issues such as access to the internet, and expressions of dissent may create significant difficulties for Western firms.

Western companies as targets of opportunity—Finally, any firm entering a developing country is a target for opportunistic individuals who seek to take advantage of the firm, particularly the substantial investment capital it plans to commit. They may negotiate deals overly favorable to the local partner, and may enmesh the firm in ethically questionable activities before it knows the local situation well enough to avoid such entanglements. Any firm must exercise particular caution until it develops an understanding of the local culture and acquires trusted business partners.

Special Reasons Why Operating in China Is Harder

China, as the "Middle Kingdom," is acutely proud of its long and complex history and culture. There is a widespread conviction that everything which comes from outside China needs a profound process of adaptation and inculturation in order to become accepted and relevant in the Chinese context. Companies seeking to implement "global standards" are sometimes met with distrust and disdain.

A second consideration is that there is a respect for local hierarchies that appears to be all-pervasive in Chinese society. There is a perceived need to give face to influential officials and individuals, which reflects the history of Chinese dynasties and has become distinctly different than the democratic traditions of other countries. A number of behavior patterns reflect this Imperial style. There are rituals and cultural patterns designed primarily to maintain social stability through these hierarchical relationships. On the level of companies and institutions this means that company leaders tend to be given the status of benevolent dictators who are accountable to no one. The way up to the top positions in many organizations may be paved more by one's ability to flatter a senior person at the right moment than by one's competency.

A third consideration, drawn from the long and revered Confucian tradition is the focus of the morally refined person, a "qunzi", who is expected to inspire much more moral behavior than the mere observance of the law. It is felt that the law cannot quite be trusted to ensure that the rights of every individual to be safeguarded. In its place, family bonds remain the strongest social reference, as also reflected strongly in the Confucian tradition. Thus, doing business with family members is often preferred to conducting arms-length transactions.

Finally, it is also true that the recent history of foreign aggression toward China, such as during the Opium wars or the Japanese invasion and massacres in the 1930s and 1940s, are featured frequently in the media and emerge frequently in the memory of the Chinese. These concerns erupt periodically, and affect attitudes toward all Western companies, not just those from the United Kingdom or Japan. There is a particular sensitivity to the perceived aggression of US support for Taiwan, for example. Eruptions of such feelings can delay or derail deal making and normal operations at unexpected moments.

The Chinese Context in 2010

After the end of the so-called "Cultural Revolution" from 1966 until 1976 and the turmoil of the "Gang of Four", China has witnessed the strongest economic growth in history due to the policies the paramount leader Deng Xiaoping introduced in 1978. Special economic zones have been opened in Shenzhen and other cities in China and foreign companies from the United States and Europe now have substantial investments, as well as substantial manufacturing and outsourcing operations to China.

Not surprisingly, the prospect of getting their teeth into a new huge market created the illusion for many foreign firms that enormous and immediate profits would be theirs for the taking. This has been almost always proven to be an illusion from the very beginning. It has been an extremely difficult challenge to be able to compete in China where the web of relationships—"guanxi" in Chinese—especially with government officials—seems to be crucial for one's success. It took the Swiss Multinational firm Nestle, which settled into Mainland China in 1983, twenty years in order to reach profitability. Many joint ventures—such as Pepsi Cola with its partner in Sichuan, Danone with Wahaha—were arranged in haste and have experienced a long and dreadful divorce and seemingly endless litigation. The Chinese companies involved, mostly state owned enterprises, seemed able to appeal to some government body or appeal publicly to nationalistic pride and xenophobic resentment in order to justify an opportunistic escape from their foreign partnership obligations. Despite a still wide spread "Gold Rush Mentality" to make the big deal quickly, a large majority of foreign business ventures have ended in failure or only limited success.

A major element of discomfort of Western companies in 2010 stems from the ambiguous role of the Chinese government dealing with the phenomenon of wide spread corruption which seems to be deeply engrained in the society. On one side, there have been serious attempts from the Central Government since the 1990s to curb corruption with various anti-corruption campaigns. This has been more than lip service. Several actions have shown how steps have been taken. After the appointment of Zhu Rongji as Prime Minister in 1998 a whole empire of corruption, smuggling and prostitution collapsed in the Eastern province of Fujian as bold actions were taken. The year 2006 sticks out as a year when a number of prominent multinationals such as Whirlpool, McKinsey, and ABB were punished by the Chinese government due to their kickback payments to the local government in Shanghai. In the same year the mayor, Mr. Cheng Liangyu, was sacked. During the last National Parliament Congress, blunt statements denouncing wide spread corruption stunned the public.

However, the same government—especially on lower levels—seems to represent a culture of deeply engrained patterns of soliciting favors and the rampant abuse of power. According to a survey among prominent business schools in China, including Hong Kong and Macau, a record number of 49% of the respondents thought that interacting with lower level government officials would most likely bring them into conflict with their personal value system.

There is a noticeable rise of public concern in China regarding business and government misbehavior. A number of recent incidents have had a significant impact on the Chinese public. When news broke out in 2007 that more than a thousand people, including children and disabled people, were being abused in kiln mines in the Shanxi province, it became surprising news coverage and a national tragedy. The link between the most brutal abuse of human beings and corrupt officials (and also local media) who have been paid to keep their mouth shut became obvious to everyone. An indigenous consumer movement, already strong in Hong Kong and Macau, has grown stronger in the wake of the lead paint scandals in the toy industry, the tainted milk scandals in Anhui Province (2001) and Hebei Province (2008), and the gas explosion in Northern China on the Songhua River in November 2005. This explosion stands out as the most devastating ecological disaster in recent history. The clean up will take at least ten more years under the best circumstances.

It is said the Chinese citizen is also awakening to personal responsibility. The earthquake, which occurred in Wenchuan in the Sichuan province on May 12, 2009, provoked such a surprising outpouring of help and mutual assistance that even critical newspapers were hailing the birth of a civil society in China. Public philanthropy and public scrutiny of powerful companies and government officials are both evidence of a growing civil society.

While stories in the West emphasize limitations on the media in China, and there is the tight control from government censorship, it also seems that the so called "New Media"—a term for aggressive investigative journalism—with newspapers like Southern Weekly, Caijing, China Newsweek—has had a significant impact in featuring stories of the abuse of power by some local officials. This new media has presented stories about both exemplary and shoddy behavior by Western companies operating in China.

There is even an emerging study of ethics and responsibility for the next generation of Chinese leaders. The Central Party School has not only been engaged in integrating Business Ethics and Corporate Social Responsibilities program within their curriculum, but also invited law professors and other experts from other countries to their school in order to engage in a serious debate about the rule of law and how civil society may be implemented in China. And according to a survey conducted by Jiaotong University, Shanghai, 39% of the business schools in China do actually include CSR and business ethics in their program.

Background Issues in Implementing a Code in China

There is much debate in China on several major issues which influence how a code is implemented. The first is the question whether the values of a company's Chinese employees are similar to those of their Western counterparts. Some Party ideologues are strongly arguing that Chinese values are divergent from the rest of the world. If there were no common ground, it would indeed be hard to implement in China the same code used in the West. By contrast, when China joined the World Trade Organization (WTO), in July 2001 it was presumed that the internationally accepted standards of the WTO could be implemented in China, that there were enough common values.

Another debate has been developed regarding the term of "Dignity," a term commonly used in recent Chinese government statements. What in Western terminology might be termed as "human rights" appears quite similar to the Chinese term of "Dignity" ("zuiyan"). Some suggest this represents a commitment to common values and may provide a language to address concerns important to Western companies.

Many Western executives operating in China have come to believe the goal to achieve in implementing a code must be far more than the formal agreement and legal compliance sought in the West. We believe implementing global standards in China will only work if they are formally agreed to AND take into account several aspects of the exceeding complex Chinese organizational culture.

For example, it is a good rule in China to assume that at the beginning of a project or implementation that "Nothing Is Clear." A common source of irritation is that partnerships and projects are formally agreed to, but too hastily arranged. Western companies assume all important details have been taken care of, when they have not. Often, a kind of very brief honeymoon is celebrated, followed by a long and painful divorce due to neglect of informal relationships and agreements, which must also be developed. Countless case studies document this pattern. In the most notorious cases, such as the breakdown of the joint venture between the French company, Danone, with its Chinese partner Wahaha, the relationship deteriorated so badly that the respective governments felt compelled to step in and impose a truce. It is, therefore, wise to understand that any successful cooperation with Chinese partners, or even one's own employees, takes much more time. It is frequently a necessary strategy to adopt stronger methods of control if common agreements are to be properly understood and honored. It is unfortunately common that a Western company's first partnership ends up in failure.

When a misunderstanding arises, one should adopt the Confucian self-critical attitude in figuring out the reasons for such a failure rather than putting the blame on the Chinese side. Most often, it will be the neglect of informal agreements and relationships. Only in a deeper relationship and through much more informal and formal communication can the true meaning of agreements in China be clarified.

Another area of general concern in implementing codes is that Western companies often do not appreciate the strong divide between the city and the countryside in China. Implementing agreements and employee and partner standards can be harder in some rural conditions. Roughly two-thirds of the Chinese still live in the countryside where carefully orchestrated rituals are even more important to the successful implementation of agreements. For example, in some circumstances a host may insist on offering hospitality with excessive drinking. While in the cities the foreign guest may be able to politely refuse at some point to continue with the drinking games, in the countryside it may be considered rude to stop the dynamics of getting drunk together.[1] Clearly, a company must find ways of limiting participation in the most objectionable practices. Besides excessive drinking games, there are some banquets and karaoke sessions where women are hired to act as prostitutes. Such objectionable practices can create significant legal exposure for a company as well.

Codes must be written and implemented with an understanding of extensive new legislation in China addressing labor conditions, corruption, whistle-blowing, sexual harassment, consumer and environmental issues. Despite the difficulties of introducing a global ethics code in China, there are opportunities for Western companies to contribute significantly to the implementation and success of these new laws, all of which will make the companies' task easier in the future. There is an interest in growing segments of the government and the Chinese business community to see these laws made effective.

Finally, Western companies must keep abreast of developments in a growing commitment to the rule of law. In many ways, Hong Kong represents a model of the implementation of the Rule of Law in the Chinese context. Hong Kong, which reverted to China in 1997, continues its role as a beacon of clean government. Forty years ago rampant cases of corruption were common in Hong Kong. However, due to the establishment of the Independent Commission against Corruption (ICAC), significant headway has been made in diminishing corruption so that now Hong Kong ranks besides Singapore as the cleanest country in Asia. This has encouraged greater transparency concerning corruption in other parts of China.

The conclusion of the recent publication of the Anti-Corruption report of Mr. Xiao Yang (2009) who served as Supreme Judge in the PRC has been very clear. He argued that corruption on Mainland China has strongly increased in the last fifteen years and has involved more and more Ministries. He argued for the implementation of an institution modeled on ICAC designed to investigate and prosecute cases of abuse cases of public.

Shaping Your Code to Fit China

The first choice every company faces is whether to operate by global standards or to adjust and adapt to local norms. Our experience suggests there is always some adherence to local norms, though not always by changing the actual words in the code, and hopefully, this adherence is within the framework of global standards a company claims to follow wherever it operates. However, in some settings, more adjustments and more recognition of the ethical traditions of the host country may be necessary. We think this is true of China.

We have observed the most successful Western firms in China following these steps to "take their codes to China":

Inculturate Your Code

The term "inculturation" represents a compromise between unchanging global standards and complete local accommodation. "Inculturation" in China has a long history. The Roman Catholic Church has sought, since the time of Matteo Ricci, a Jesuit priest who came to China in 1583, of "inculturating" the Christian message to Chinese conditions. For Ricci and even for Catholics today, religious "inculturation" indicates the dynamic process when key values enshrined in the Gospel such as truth, honesty, and charity are not just imposed from outside, but get truly integrated within a given culture. This process makes possible global consistency with local sensitivity. This is most important in countries like China that have a history of foreign domination and a sensitivity to imperialistic behavior.

For the company choosing to operate in China, inculturation means adhering to global principles that have specific local meanings and therefore, local rules. The most obvious example is gift giving. In a gift giving culture like China, a company would find it hard to adhere to an absolute "no gift" policy as some companies adopt elsewhere in the world. An inculturated gift policy would permit gift giving, albeit tightly limited, but also scaled so that larger gifts, again within a firmly established upper limit, would be permitted to higher executives or officials. An inculturated Chinese policy would also even permit small but scaled gifts to government officials, as this is in China a show of respect. A top value of $75 or $100 for the highest corporate or government official visited is viable and allows the Western company to respect and adhere to local cultural gift-giving practice, but not to engage in bribery. The company also must make it absolutely clear that gifts of any greater value are forbidden.

Inculturation would also recognize the cultural tradition of relationship building and the necessary entertainment to that purpose. However, a Western company should very explicitly and clearly communicate the limits on the value and frequency of such entertainment. Inculturation in China should also recognize the particular context of ethics hotlines and of whistle blowing. With particular adjustments, even this Western concept can be made to work in China, as noted below.

Make the Company Code Consistent with Chinese Laws

China is proud of the progress made in recent years in promulgating and adopting regulatory standards and laws that protect the interests of employees, consumers, and shareholders. It is a necessary step in taking ones's code to China to assess the alignment of these local laws (many very recently adopted) and the company's code of conduct. This process must, of course, be an ongoing one, making future adjustments to the company's code as new laws are adopted in China.

Align Your Code with Chinese Concepts and Slogans of Key Government Officials

In addition to the laws adopted by the National Congress and Communist Party rules adopted by the every five year Central Party Congress, Chinese party and government leaders introduce key phrases or slogans which are meant to organize and direct the path of Chinese economic and social development.

Under Jiang Zemin the former President of the PRC, there was considerable attention to the "Three Represents," a doctrine by which the all-powerful Communist Party of China represented the masses of people, the productive forces of society, and the culture. The key message was the preeminence of the Party, but the detailed message gave room to cast corporate codes and decisions as advocating the masses, the development of productive capacity, and even the proper cultural development of China. Under the first 5-year term of Hu Jintao, the current President of China, the concept of "Harmonious Society" was adopted as a preeminent national goal. Later, Hu promoted the concept of "a Scientific Society" wherein, among other things, empirical data and facts should drive decisions more than bias or entrenched interests.

Tying corporate norms and standards of conduct to that objective can strengthen corporate efforts, both because employees understand the alignment of corporate objectives, but also because the company could occasionally secure government help in enforcing its code that it would not otherwise receive.

Incorporate References to Global Standards Embraced by the Chinese

Over the past ten years, the Chinese government has participated in the formulation of, and conferences on, many international codes and standards. The United Nations Global Compact has 195 signatories in China. The WTO code was widely publicized to Chinese industries in 2001 when China officially joined the WTO. References to these documents and standards strengthen acceptance of a company's global code.

Publish the Code in Bilingual Format

A company code should be published in both English and in Chinese language versions, perhaps side by side. Any Chinese company and every Western company operating in China will have English speakers, and they or other employees will be eager to *compare* the actual English words with the Chinese characters chosen as direct translations. And of course, any company will have Chinese speakers who do not read English. Translation into Chinese demonstrates a seriousness of purpose and a commitment to enforce the code, which must be addressed in the published document.

Introduce the Code in the Chinese Way

Too often, ethics codes are introduced in the United States and in Western Europe by email or by distribution of a printed booklet, perhaps with a card to return acknowledging receipt of the code. This approach will simply not work in China.

Chinese employees will expect that any code or standard they are actually expected to follow will be introduced with considerable time available for discussion, objection and clarification, and in a workshop conducted in their own dialect. At minimum, they will expect to be able to argue about adaptations to the Chinese context, and the particular Chinese characters used to translate the English or European language concepts. Rather than interpret this as dissent and obfuscation, those introducing the code should consider it a productive opportunity to explain the code and get good feedback on the application of the code to the Chinese context.

Other aspects of the introduction should proceed much as they do in the West. The code must be introduced by line officers of the company with a seriousness that convinces employees that these are actually to be the desired standards. Training must address the most common dilemmas employees will face to give clear and understandable signals about the type of behavior expected. Specific examples are more important in the Chinese context because employees will have generally experienced the rollout of multiple initiatives that have had little impact and less staying power.

Education regarding the code must be given to all new hires. Education in the code must be tailored to the several hierarchical levels within the firm, including senior executives, middle managers, and hourly employees.

Do Whistle-blowing the Chinese Way

Without giving up the principle of reporting violations, a Chinese hotline can be positioned and promoted as a "Help line" designed to advise employees on how a particular action should be taken. This approach has been used by many companies in the West. Further, because of the sensitivity to reporting on a senior, there must be greater opportunity for an employee to have his or her complaint treated as genuinely confidential and anonymous. There is a greater sensitivity to cases where the complaint, by its very nature, might be traced back to an individual employee. A Chinese help line will require more promotion and explanation, and may be more effective if it is structured to have complaints dealt with by the highest authority in a company—for example, by the board of directors. Because of deference to hierarchy, only the board can effectively address wrongdoing by senior level officials.

Extending the Code to Business Partners

There is a growing understanding among Chinese businesses that American and European companies must extend their standards and codes to their business partners, and have a right to expect their partners to adhere to the same standards. In the past, too many Western companies have thrown up their hands and despaired of actually influencing the behavior of business partners, accepting signed assurances of compliance but not really expecting adherence. Today, more Western companies are vetting their partners for their capacity and willingness to conform to codes, and then are monitoring and assessing compliance over time.

The first step in the process must be the selection of partners who have the basic capacity to be in alignment with the values and code of the Western firm. This requires due diligence, either by the company's own managers, or by a firm hired explicitly to evaluate potential partners. Such due diligence is usually hard to accomplish, and virtually every firm reports one or more disasters trying to integrate business partners into the business's activities. Nonetheless, Chinese firms, particularly those with experience operating in an international business environment, and firms with experience in previous partnerships with Western companies, can be effective and ethical local partners. In China, there has developed a language often used to describe projects and companies capable of operating by such standards. This is known as operating by "international standards" as opposed to Chinese or local standards. Projects are said to be built to or operating by international standards. Chinese businesses are said to be "international standards companies." Such firms are more likely to be effective partners.

Preparing Local Leadership to Enforce Your Code in China

As in virtually all settings where a company seeks to infuse a code and its standards into actual behavior, local leadership will exercise the strongest influence in China. Chinese executives and managers will be anxious to adopt the latest developments in leadership. It is important to position the code as a key part of cutting edge and modern management.

An extended dialogue with the chief local official regarding the code before it is introduced is essential. Only a local executive can identify the unavoidable points of stress in the implementation of a code. A local executive will expect to be consulted on the "inculturation" process, and may be the best source of ideas for doing this successfully without abandoning the firm's global standards. And only a local executive can highlight where enforcement must be emphasized.

Much has been made regarding the wisdom of having a Chinese national or a foreign passport holder as a Western company's top officer in China. Both have risks for the implementation of a corporate code of conduct. The foreign executive enforcing the code may make the code seem more foreign and less practical in the local context. On the other hand, some Chinese executives may not believe in the code as fully, or may go through the motions without truly requiring adherence within the organization. A Chinese executive who genuinely believes in the code may be more effective in getting compliance from the organization, or recognizing lip service when it is being given.

Company leaders, both at the Western headquarters and in China, need to create a system of accountability—of monitoring and auditing compliance with the code. This is even more important in China than it is in the West. There are so many initiatives and slogans thrown at Chinese managers, that they are looking for signals that this one is not merely lip service. Too often they conclude that ethics codes are not serious because they are introduced in ineffective ways and without the accountability and follow-up.

It is absolutely essential to the success of any code that the offending employee or manager must be subject to firing, and that occasionally an employee does get fired for violating the code. Even more so than in the West, it is critical all understand that the behavior of senior managers and executives be subject to the code, and risk dismissal if they violate the code. There is a predisposition to believe the code is both lip service and/or applied selectively on lower level employees, and not to those higher in the hierarchy.

In summary, we believe Western companies following the preceding principles can and are making genuine progress "taking their codes to China" and establishing a truly global standard of behavior in their firms.

Note

1. Obviously, such games may seriously harm the health of those who are unable to put a timely end to this ritual. Recently there have again been reports of death of government officials due to excessive drinking.

References

Organization for economic co-operation and development. (2009). *Ratification Status as of March 2009.*

Retrieved from www.oecd.org/dataoecd/59/13/40272933.pdf The Foreign Corrupt Practices Act of 1977 § 15 U.S.C. § 78dd-1(1977).

United Nations Global Compact Office. (2005). *The ten principles.* Retrieved from www.unglobalcompact.org/AboutTheGC/TheTenPrinciples/index.html

United Nations Global Compact Office. (2010). *Participant search* [Data File]. Retrieved from www.unglobalcompact.org/participants/search?business_type=all&commit=Search&cop_status=all&country[]=38&joined_after=&joined_before=&keyword=&organization_type_id=& page=1&per_page=100&sector_id=all

Yang, X. (2009). Fantan baogao (Anti-Corruption Report). Beijing: Law Press.

Critical Thinking

1. What are the realities facing a firm when applying its code of ethics in other countries?
2. What are the reasons why operating in China with a code of ethics is harder than elsewhere in the world?
3. How should a code of ethics be shaped to fit China's marketplace?
4. How should a firm prepare its local managers to enforce a code of ethics in China?

Moral Hazard

Can American Companies Compete Abroad without Bribing?

Rob Cox

National Notebook: How to succeed in emerging markets without really bribing is not the title of a new Broadway musical but the vexing question du jour in the boardrooms of multinational corporations. Companies are wrangling like mad with how to effectively push their wares abroad without running afoul of the Foreign Corrupt Practices Act. This 35-year-old legislation was designed to prohibit firms operating in the United States from bribing government officials around the world to win business. From a strictly moral perspective, it's hard to argue with holding companies to a code of proper conduct wherever they operate. But as the act has been given new oomph by the Justice Department and the Securities and Exchange Commission under the Obama administration, the bright line between what is acceptable behavior and what is not has become muddled. Ironically the law itself, and the way the government enforces the rules, has made matters worse. It may be time to give the FCPA a revamp.

Consider last week's Walmart shocker. According to *The New York Times*, the mega-retailer's Mexican unit sprinkled some $24 million of baksheesh into the pockets of local worthies to enable its store expansion. The alleged cover-up of its own 2005 investigation into the matter suggests a deceptive corporate culture at Bentonville HQ. What Walmart actually did in Mexico, though, may not have been illegal. The Justice Department says the law aims to make "it unlawful for certain classes of persons and entities to make payments to foreign government officials to assist in obtaining or retaining business." But Walmart was not technically obtaining new business—it was already active in Mexico. Second, the retailer handed the money to fixers tasked with helping speed along things like zoning approval processes. These sorts of "ministerial and clerical type payments were meant to be beyond the reach" of the FCPA, according to Mike Koehler, a law professor at Butler University. So had Walmart voluntarily brought the findings of its own internal probe to United States authorities, it might have been cleared of any FCPA wrongdoing.

Why Walmart executives instead sought to sweep the matter under the carpet when they learned of the payments isn't clear. But it's hard not to see the absence of any meaningful judicial challenges involving the law as a factor. Public companies like Walmart almost never fight back in court against the government because the risks of losing are far too great. A successful criminal conviction would essentially mean game over. As a result, virtually every case ends in a settlement. "If we had more judicial interpretations of the law, companies would have a clearer idea of the barriers and the bright lines," says attorney Richard L. Cassin, founder and principal writer for the FCPA Blog. Without this, of course, American companies may take a more conservative approach to doing business abroad. Maybe that's good. But if it impedes the ability of companies to export, expand, and exploit new markets, it's not entirely consistent with broader public and economic policy. That's something lawmakers might want to consider.

Critical Thinking

1. Is it possible for an American company to compete in global commerce without bribery? Using the Internet, find examples of companies competing globally without allegations of bribery. Bring your examples to class discussion?

2. What do you believe will be Wal-Mart's likely response to the bribery allegations?

3. Do you agree with the author's contention that "public companies like Wal-Mart almost never fight back in court against the government because the risks of losing are far too great"? Why or why not?

Rob Cox is United States editor for Reuters Breakingviews.

Wal-Mart Hushed Up a Vast Mexican Bribery Case

DAVID BARSTOW, ALEJANDRA XANIC, AND JAMES C. MCKINLEY JR.

In September 2005, a senior Wal-Mart lawyer received an alarming e-mail from a former executive at the company's largest foreign subsidiary, Wal-Mart de Mexico. In the e-mail and follow-up conversations, the former executive described how Wal-Mart de Mexico had orchestrated a campaign of bribery to win market dominance. In its rush to build stores, he said, the company had paid bribes to obtain permits in virtually every corner of the country.

The former executive gave names, dates and bribe amounts. He knew so much, he explained, because for years he had been the lawyer in charge of obtaining construction permits for Wal-Mart de Mexico.

Wal-Mart dispatched investigators to Mexico City, and within days they unearthed evidence of widespread bribery. They found a paper trail of hundreds of suspect payments totaling more than $24 million. They also found documents showing that Wal-Mart de Mexico's top executives not only knew about the payments, but had taken steps to conceal them from Wal-Mart's headquarters in Bentonville, Ark. In a confidential report to his superiors, Wal-Mart's lead investigator, a former F.B.I. special agent, summed up their initial findings this way: "There is reasonable suspicion to believe that Mexican and USA laws have been violated."

The lead investigator recommended that Wal-Mart expand the investigation.

Instead, an examination by The *New York Times* found, Wal-Mart's leaders shut it down.

Neither American nor Mexican law enforcement officials were notified. None of Wal-Mart de Mexico's leaders were disciplined. Indeed, its chief executive, Eduardo Castro-Wright, identified by the former executive as the driving force behind years of bribery, was promoted to vice chairman of Wal-Mart in 2008. Until this article, the allegations and Wal-Mart's investigation had never been publicly disclosed.

But *The Times*'s examination uncovered a prolonged struggle at the highest levels of Wal-Mart, a struggle that pitted the company's much publicized commitment to the highest moral and ethical standards against its relentless pursuit of growth.

Under fire from labor critics, worried about press leaks and facing a sagging stock price, Wal-Mart's leaders recognized that the allegations could have devastating consequences, documents and interviews show. Wal-Mart de Mexico was the company's brightest success story, pitched to investors as a model for future growth. (Today, one in five Wal-Mart stores is in Mexico.) Confronted with evidence of corruption in Mexico, top Wal-Mart executives focused more on damage control than on rooting out wrongdoing.

In one meeting where the bribery case was discussed, H. Lee Scott Jr., then Wal-Mart's chief executive, rebuked internal investigators for being overly aggressive. Days later, records show, Wal-Mart's top lawyer arranged to ship the internal investigators' files on the case to Mexico City. Primary responsibility for the investigation was then given to the general counsel of Wal-Mart de Mexico—a remarkable choice since the same general counsel was alleged to have authorized bribes.

The general counsel promptly exonerated his fellow Wal-Mart de Mexico executives.

When Wal-Mart's director of corporate investigations—a former top F.B.I. official—read the general counsel's report, his appraisal was scathing. "Truly lacking," he wrote in an e-mail to his boss.

The report was nonetheless accepted by Wal-Mart's leaders as the last word on the matter.

In December, after learning of *The Times*'s reporting in Mexico, Wal-Mart informed the Justice Department that it had begun an internal investigation into possible violations of the Foreign Corrupt Practices Act, a federal law that makes it a crime for American corporations and their subsidiaries to bribe foreign officials. Wal-Mart said the company had learned of possible problems with how it obtained permits, but stressed that the issues were limited to "discrete" cases.

"We do not believe that these matters will have a material adverse effect on our business," the company said in a filing with the Securities and Exchange Commission.

But *The Times*'s examination found credible evidence that bribery played a persistent and significant role in Wal-Mart's rapid growth in Mexico, where Wal-Mart now employs 209,000 people, making it the country's largest private employer.

A Wal-Mart spokesman confirmed that the company's Mexico operations—and its handling of the 2005 case—were now a major focus of its inquiry.

"If these allegations are true, it is not a reflection of who we are or what we stand for," the spokesman, David W. Tovar, said. "We are deeply concerned by these allegations and are working aggressively to determine what happened."

In the meantime, Mr. Tovar said, Wal-Mart is taking steps in Mexico to strengthen compliance with the Foreign Corrupt Practices Act. "We do not and will not tolerate noncompliance with F.C.P.A. anywhere or at any level of the company," he said.

The Times laid out this article's findings to Wal-Mart weeks ago. The company said it shared the findings with many of the executives named here, including Mr. Scott, now on Wal-Mart's board, and Mr. Castro-Wright, who is retiring in July. Both men declined to comment, Mr. Tovar said.

The Times obtained hundreds of internal company documents tracing the evolution of Wal-Mart's 2005 Mexico investigation. The documents show Wal-Mart's leadership immediately recognized the seriousness of the allegations. Working in secrecy, a small group of executives, including several current members of Wal-Mart's senior management, kept close tabs on the inquiry.

Michael T. Duke, Wal-Mart's current chief executive, was also kept informed. At the time, Mr. Duke had just been put in charge of Wal-Mart International, making him responsible for all foreign subsidiaries. "You'll want to read this," a top Wal-Mart lawyer wrote in an Oct. 15, 2005, e-mail to Mr. Duke that gave a detailed description of the former executive's allegations.

The Times examination included more than 15 hours of interviews with the former executive, Sergio Cicero Zapata, who resigned from Wal-Mart de Mexico in 2004 after nearly a decade in the company's real estate department.

In the interviews, Mr. Cicero recounted how he had helped organize years of payoffs. He described personally dispatching two trusted outside lawyers to deliver envelopes of cash to government officials. They targeted mayors and city council members, obscure urban planners, low-level bureaucrats who issued permits—anyone with the power to thwart Wal-Mart's growth. The bribes, he said, bought zoning approvals, reductions in environmental impact fees and the allegiance of neighborhood leaders.

He called it working "the dark side of the moon."

The Times also reviewed thousands of government documents related to permit requests for stores across Mexico. The examination found many instances where permits were given within weeks or even days of Wal-Mart de Mexico's payments to the two lawyers. Again and again, *The Times* found, legal and bureaucratic obstacles melted away after payments were made.

The Times conducted extensive interviews with participants in Wal-Mart's investigation. They spoke on the condition that they not be identified discussing matters Wal-Mart has long shielded. These people said the investigation left little doubt Mr. Cicero's allegations were credible. ("Not even a close call," one person said.)

But, they said, the more investigators corroborated his assertions, the more resistance they encountered inside Wal-Mart. Some of it came from powerful executives implicated in the corruption, records and interviews show. Other top executives voiced concern about the possible legal and reputational harm.

In the end, people involved in the investigation said, Wal-Mart's leaders found a bloodlessly bureaucratic way to bury the matter. But in handing the investigation off to one of its main targets, they disregarded the advice of one of Wal-Mart's top lawyers, the same lawyer first contacted by Mr. Cicero.

"The wisdom of assigning any investigative role to management of the business unit being investigated escapes me," Maritza I. Munich, then general counsel of Wal-Mart International, wrote in an e-mail to top Wal-Mart executives.

The investigation, she urged, should be completed using "professional, independent investigative resources."

The Allegations Emerge

On Sept. 21, 2005, Mr. Cicero sent an e-mail to Ms. Munich telling her he had information about "irregularities" authorized "by the highest levels" at Wal-Mart de Mexico. "I hope to meet you soon," he wrote.

Ms. Munich was familiar with the challenges of avoiding corruption in Latin America. Before joining Wal-Mart in 2003, she had spent 12 years in Mexico and elsewhere in Latin America as a lawyer for Procter & Gamble.

At Wal-Mart in 2004, she pushed the board to adopt a strict anticorruption policy that prohibited all employees from "offering anything of value to a government official on behalf of Wal-Mart." It required every employee to report the first sign of corruption, and it bound Wal-Mart's agents to the same exacting standards.

Ms. Munich reacted quickly to Mr. Cicero's e-mail. Within days, she hired Juan Francisco Torres-Landa, a prominent Harvard-trained lawyer in Mexico City, to debrief Mr. Cicero. The two men met three times in October 2005, with Ms. Munich flying in from Bentonville for the third debriefing.

During hours of questioning, Mr. Torres-Landa's notes show, Mr. Cicero described how Wal-Mart de Mexico had perfected the art of bribery, then hidden it all with fraudulent accounting. Mr. Cicero implicated many of Wal-Mart de Mexico's leaders, including its board chairman, its general counsel, its chief auditor and its top real estate executive.

But the person most responsible, he told Mr. Torres-Landa, was the company's ambitious chief executive, Eduardo Castro-Wright, a native of Ecuador who was recruited from Honeywell in 2001 to become Wal-Mart's chief operating officer in Mexico.

Mr. Cicero said that while bribes were occasionally paid before Mr. Castro-Wright's arrival, their use soared after Mr. Castro-Wright ascended to the top job in 2002. Mr. Cicero described how Wal-Mart de Mexico's leaders had set "very aggressive growth goals," which required opening new stores "in record times." Wal-Mart de Mexico executives, he said, were under pressure to do "whatever was necessary" to obtain permits.

In an interview with *The Times*, Mr. Cicero said Mr. Castro-Wright had encouraged the payments for a specific strategic purpose. The idea, he said, was to build hundreds of new stores so fast that competitors would not have time to react. Bribes, he explained, accelerated growth. They got zoning maps changed.

They made environmental objections vanish. Permits that typically took months to process magically materialized in days. "What we were buying was time," he said.

Wal-Mart de Mexico's stunning growth made Mr. Castro-Wright a rising star in Bentonville. In early 2005, when he was promoted to a senior position in the United States, Mr. Duke would cite his "outstanding results" in Mexico.

Mr. Cicero's allegations were all the more startling because he implicated himself. He spent hours explaining to Mr. Torres-Landa the mechanics of how he had helped funnel bribes through trusted fixers, known as "gestores."

Gestores (pronounced hes-TORE-ehs) are a fixture in Mexico's byzantine bureaucracies, and some are entirely legitimate. Ordinary citizens routinely pay gestores to stand in line for them at the driver's license office. Companies hire them as quasi-lobbyists to get things done as painlessly as possible.

But often gestores play starring roles in Mexico's endless loop of public corruption scandals. They operate in the shadows, dangling payoffs to officials of every rank. It was this type of gestor that Wal-Mart de Mexico deployed, Mr. Cicero said.

Mr. Cicero told Mr. Torres-Landa it was his job to recruit the gestores. He worked closely with them, sharing strategies on whom to bribe. He also approved Wal-Mart de Mexico's payments to the gestores. Each payment covered the bribe and the gestor's fee, typically 6 percent of the bribe.

It was all carefully monitored through a system of secret codes known only to a handful of Wal-Mart de Mexico executives.

The gestores submitted invoices with brief, vaguely worded descriptions of their services. But the real story, Mr. Cicero said, was told in codes written on the invoices. The codes identified the specific "irregular act" performed, Mr. Cicero explained to Mr. Torres-Landa. One code, for example, indicated a bribe to speed up a permit. Others described bribes to obtain confidential information or eliminate fines.

Each month, Mr. Castro-Wright and other top Wal-Mart de Mexico executives "received a detailed schedule of all of the payments performed," he said, according to the lawyer's notes. Wal-Mart de Mexico then "purified" the bribes in accounting records as simple legal fees.

They also took care to keep Bentonville in the dark. "Dirty clothes are washed at home," Mr. Cicero said.

Mr. Torres-Landa explored Mr. Cicero's motives for coming forward.

Mr. Cicero said he resigned in September 2004 because he felt underappreciated. He described the "pressure and stress" of participating in years of corruption, of contending with "greedy" officials who jacked up bribe demands.

As he told *The Times*, "I thought I deserved a medal at least."

The breaking point came in early 2004, when he was passed over for the job of general counsel of Wal-Mart de Mexico. This snub, Mr. Torres-Landa wrote, "generated significant anger with respect to the lack of recognition for his work." Mr. Cicero said he began to assemble a record of bribes he had helped orchestrate to "protect him in case of any complaint or investigation," Mr. Torres-Landa wrote.

"We did not detect on his part any express statement about wishing to sell the information," the lawyer added.

According to people involved in Wal-Mart's investigation, Mr. Cicero's account of criminality at the top of Wal-Mart's most important foreign subsidiary was impossible to dismiss. He had clearly been in a position to witness the events he described. Nor was this the first indication of corruption at Wal-Mart de Mexico under Mr. Castro-Wright. A confidential investigation, conducted for Wal-Mart in 2003 by Kroll Inc., a leading investigation firm, discovered that Wal-Mart de Mexico had systematically increased its sales by helping favored high-volume customers evade sales taxes.

A draft of Kroll's report, obtained by *The Times*, concluded that top Wal-Mart de Mexico executives had failed to enforce their own anticorruption policies, ignored internal audits that raised red flags and even disregarded local press accounts asserting that Wal-Mart de Mexico was "carrying out a tax fraud." (The company ultimately paid $34.3 million in back taxes.)

Wal-Mart then asked Kroll to evaluate Wal-Mart de Mexico's internal audit and antifraud units. Kroll wrote another report that branded the units "ineffective." Many employees accused of wrongdoing were not even questioned; some "received a promotion shortly after the suspicions of fraudulent activities had surfaced."

None of these findings, though, had slowed Mr. Castro-Wright's rise.

Just days before Mr. Cicero's first debriefing, Mr. Castro-Wright was promoted again. He was put in charge of all Wal-Mart stores in the United States, one of the most prominent jobs in the company. He also joined Wal-Mart's executive committee, the company's inner sanctum of leadership.

The Initial Response

Ms. Munich sent detailed memos describing Mr. Cicero's debriefings to Wal-Mart's senior management. These executives, records show, included Thomas A. Mars, Wal-Mart's general counsel and a former director of the Arkansas State Police; Thomas D. Hyde, Wal-Mart's executive vice president and corporate secretary; Michael Fung, Wal-Mart's top internal auditor; Craig Herkert, the chief executive for Wal-Mart's operations in Latin America; and Lee Stucky, a confidant of Lee Scott's and chief administrative officer of Wal-Mart International.

Wal-Mart typically hired outside law firms to lead internal investigations into allegations of significant wrongdoing. It did so earlier in 2005, for example, when Thomas M. Coughlin, then vice chairman of Wal-Mart, was accused of padding his expense accounts and misappropriating Wal-Mart gift cards.

At first, Wal-Mart took the same approach with Mr. Cicero's allegations. It turned to Willkie Farr & Gallagher, a law firm with extensive experience in Foreign Corrupt Practices Act cases.

The firm's "investigation work plan" called for tracing all payments to anyone who had helped Wal-Mart de Mexico obtain permits for the previous five years. The firm said it would scrutinize "any and all payments" to government officials and interview every person who might know about payoffs, including "implicated members" of Wal-Mart de Mexico's board.

In short, Willkie Farr recommended the kind of independent, spare-no-expense investigation major corporations routinely undertake when confronted with allegations of serious wrongdoing by top executives.

Wal-Mart's leaders rejected this approach. Instead, records show, they decided Wal-Mart's lawyers would supervise a far more limited "preliminary inquiry" by in-house investigators.

The inquiry, a confidential memo explained, would take two weeks, not the four months Willkie Farr proposed. Rather than examining years of permits, the team would look at a few specific stores. Interviews would be done "only when absolutely essential to establishing the bona fides" of Mr. Cicero. However, if the inquiry found a "likelihood" that laws had been violated, the company would then consider conducting a "full investigation."

The decision gave Wal-Mart's senior management direct control over the investigation. It also meant new responsibility for the company's tiny and troubled Corporate Investigations unit.

The unit was ill-equipped to take on a major corruption investigation, let alone one in Mexico. It had fewer than 70 employees, and most were assigned to chasing shoplifting rings and corrupt vendors. Just four people were specifically dedicated to investigating corporate fraud, a number Joseph R. Lewis, Wal-Mart's director of corporate investigations, described in a confidential memo as "wholly inadequate for an organization the size of Wal-Mart."

But Mr. Lewis and his boss, Kenneth H. Senser, vice president for global security, aviation and travel, were working to strengthen the unit. Months before Mr. Cicero surfaced, they won approval to hire four "special investigators" who, according to their job descriptions, would be assigned the "most significant and complex fraud matters." Mr. Scott, the chief executive, also agreed that Corporate Investigations would handle all allegations of misconduct by senior executives.

And yet in the fall of 2005, as Wal-Mart began to grapple with Mr. Cicero's allegations, two cases called into question Corporate Investigations' independence and role.

In October, Wal-Mart's vice chairman, John B. Menzer, intervened in an internal investigation into a senior vice president who reported to him. According to internal records, Mr. Menzer told Mr. Senser he did not want Corporate Investigations to handle the case "due to concerns about the impact such an investigation would have." One of the senior vice president's subordinates, he said, "would be better suited to conduct this inquiry." Soon after, records show, the subordinate cleared his boss.

The other case involved the president of Wal-Mart Puerto Rico. A whistle-blower had accused the president and other executives of mistreating employees. Although Corporate Investigations was supposed to investigate all allegations against senior executives, the president had instead assigned an underling to look into the complaints—but to steer clear of those against him.

Ms. Munich objected. In an e-mail to Wal-Mart executives, she complained that the investigation was "at the direction of the same company officer who is the target of several of the allegations."

"We are in need of clear guidelines about how to handle these issues going forward," she warned.

The Inquiry Begins

Ronald Halter, one of Wal-Mart's new "special investigators," was assigned to lead the preliminary inquiry into Mr. Cicero's allegations. Mr. Halter had been with Wal-Mart only a few months, but he was a seasoned criminal investigator. He had spent 21 years in the F.B.I., and he spoke Spanish.

He also had help. Bob Ainley, a senior auditor, was sent to Mexico along with several Spanish-speaking auditors.

On Nov. 12, 2005, Mr. Halter's team got to work at Wal-Mart de Mexico's corporate headquarters in Mexico City. The team gained access to a database of Wal-Mart de Mexico payments and began searching the payment description field for the word "gestoria."

By day's end, they had found 441 gestor payments. Each was a potential bribe, and yet they had searched back only to 2003.

Mr. Cicero had said his main gestores were Pablo Alegria Con Alonso and Jose Manuel Aguirre Juarez, obscure Mexico City lawyers with small practices who were friends of his from law school.

Sure enough, Mr. Halter's team found that nearly half the payments were to Mr. Alegria and Mr. Aguirre. These two lawyers alone, records showed, had received $8.5 million in payments. Records showed Wal-Mart de Mexico routinely paid its gestores tens of thousands of dollars per permit. (In interviews, both lawyers declined to discuss the corruption allegations, citing confidentiality agreements with Wal-Mart.)

"One very interesting postscript," Mr. Halter wrote in an e-mail to his boss, Mr. Lewis. "All payments to these individuals and all large sums of $ paid out of this account stopped abruptly in 2005." Mr. Halter said the "only thing we can find" that changed was that Mr. Castro-Wright left Wal-Mart de Mexico for the United States.

Mr. Halter's team confirmed detail after detail from Mr. Cicero's debriefings. Mr. Cicero had given specifics—names, dates, bribe amounts—for several new stores. In almost every case, investigators found documents confirming major elements of his account. And just as Mr. Cicero had described, investigators found mysterious codes at the bottom of invoices from the gestores.

"The documentation didn't look anything like what you would find in legitimate billing records from a legitimate law firm," a person involved in the investigation said in an interview.

Mr. Lewis sent a terse progress report to his boss, Mr. Senser: "FYI. It is not looking good."

Hours later, Mr. Halter's team found clear confirmation that Mr. Castro-Wright and other top executives at Wal-Mart de Mexico were well aware of the gestor payments.

In March 2004, the team discovered, the executives had been sent an internal Wal-Mart de Mexico audit that raised red flags about the gestor payments. The audit documented how Wal-Mart de Mexico's two primary gestores had been paid millions to make "facilitating payments" for new store permits all over Mexico.

The audit did not delve into how the money had been used to "facilitate" permits. But it showed the payments rising rapidly, roughly in line with Wal-Mart de Mexico's accelerating growth. The audit recommended notifying Bentonville of the payments.

The recommendation, records showed, was removed by Wal-Mart de Mexico's chief auditor, whom Mr. Cicero had identified as one of the executives who knew about the bribes. The author of the gestor audit, meanwhile, "was fired not long after the audit was completed," Mr. Halter wrote.

Mr. Ainley arranged to meet the fired auditor at his hotel. The auditor described other examples of Wal-Mart de Mexico's leaders withholding from Bentonville information about suspect payments to government officials.

The auditor singled out Jose Luis Rodriguezmacedo Rivera, the general counsel of Wal-Mart de Mexico.

Mr. Rodriguezmacedo, he said, took "significant information out" of an audit of Wal-Mart de Mexico's compliance with the Foreign Corrupt Practices Act. The original audit had described how Wal-Mart de Mexico gave gift cards to government officials in towns where it was building stores. "These were only given out until the construction was complete," Mr. Ainley wrote. "At which time the payments ceased."

These details were scrubbed from the final version sent to Bentonville.

Investigators were struck by Mr. Castro-Wright's response to the gestor audit. It had been shown to him immediately, Wal-Mart de Mexico's chief auditor had told them. Yet rather than expressing alarm, he had appeared worried about becoming too dependent on too few gestores. In an e-mail, Mr. Rodriguezmacedo told Mr. Cicero to write up a plan to "diversify" the gestores used to "facilitate" permits.

"Eduardo Castro wants us to implement this plan as soon as possible," he wrote.

Mr. Cicero did as directed. The plan, which authorized paying gestores up to $280,000 to "facilitate" a single permit, was approved with a minor change. Mr. Rodriguezmacedo did not want the plan to mention "gestores." He wanted them called "external service providers."

Mr. Halter's team made one last discovery—a finding that suggested the corruption might be far more extensive than even Mr. Cicero had described.

In going through Wal-Mart de Mexico's database of payments, investigators noticed the company was making hefty "contributions" and "donations" directly to governments all over Mexico—nearly $16 million in all since 2003.

"Some of the payments descriptions indicate that the donation is being made for the issuance of a license," Mr. Ainley wrote in one report back to Bentonville.

They also found a document in which a Wal-Mart de Mexico real estate executive had openly acknowledged that "these payments were performed to facilitate obtaining the licenses or permits" for new stores. Sometimes, Mr. Cicero told The Times, donations were used hand-in-hand with gestor payments to get permits.

Deflecting Blame

When Mr. Halter's team was ready to interview executives at Wal-Mart de Mexico, the first target was Mr. Rodriguezmacedo.

Before joining Wal-Mart de Mexico in January 2004, Mr. Rodriguezmacedo had been a lawyer for Citigroup in Mexico. Urbane and smooth, with impeccable English, he quickly won fans in Bentonville. When Wal-Mart invited executives from its foreign subsidiaries for several days of discussion about the fine points of the Foreign Corrupt Practices Act, Mr. Rodriguezmacedo was asked to lead one of the sessions.

It was called "Overcoming Challenges in Government Dealings."

Yet Mr. Cicero had identified him as a participant in the bribery scheme. In his debriefings, Mr. Cicero described how Mr. Rodriguezmacedo had passed along specific payoff instructions from Mr. Castro-Wright. In an interview with The Times, Mr. Cicero said he and Mr. Rodriguezmacedo had discussed the use of gestores shortly after Mr. Rodriguezmacedo was hired. "He said, 'Don't worry. Keep it on its way.'"

Mr. Rodriguezmacedo declined to comment; on Friday Wal-Mart disclosed that he had been reassigned and is no longer Wal-Mart de Mexico's general counsel.

Mr. Halter's team hoped Mr. Rodriguezmacedo would shed light on how two outside lawyers came to be paid $8.5 million to "facilitate" permits. Mr. Rodriguezmacedo responded with evasive hostility, records and interviews show. When investigators asked him for the gestores' billing records, he said he did not have time to track them down. They got similar receptions from other executives.

Only after investigators complained to higher authorities were the executives more forthcoming. Led by Mr. Rodriguezmacedo, they responded with an attack on Mr. Cicero's credibility.

The gestor audit, they told investigators, had raised doubts about Mr. Cicero, since he had approved most of the payments. They began to suspect he was somehow benefiting, so they asked Kroll to investigate. It was then, they asserted, that Kroll discovered Mr. Cicero's wife was a law partner of one of the gestores.

Mr. Cicero was fired, they said, because he had failed to disclose that fact. They produced a copy of a "preliminary" report from Kroll and e-mails showing the undisclosed conflict had been reported to Bentonville.

Based on this behavior, Mr. Rodriguezmacedo argued, the gestor payments were in all likelihood a "ruse" by Mr. Cicero to defraud Wal-Mart de Mexico. Mr. Cicero and the gestores, he contended, probably kept every last peso of the "facilitating payments."

Simply put, bribes could not have been paid if the money was stolen first.

It was an argument that gave Wal-Mart ample justification to end the inquiry. But investigators were skeptical, records and interviews show.

Even if Mr. Rodriguezmacedo's account were true, it did not explain why Wal-Mart de Mexico's executives had authorized gestor payments in the first place, or why they made "donations" to get permits, or why they rewrote audits to keep Bentonville in the dark.

Investigators also wondered why a trained lawyer who had gotten away with stealing a small fortune from Wal-Mart would now deliberately draw the company's full attention by implicating himself in a series of fictional bribes. And if Wal-Mart de Mexico's executives truly believed they had been victimized, why hadn't they taken legal action against Mr. Cicero, much less reported the "theft" to Bentonville?

There was another problem: Documents contradicted most of the executives' assertions about Mr. Cicero.

Records showed Mr. Cicero had not been fired, but had resigned with severance benefits and a $25,000 bonus. In fact, in a 2004 e-mail to Ms. Munich, Mr. Rodriguezmacedo himself described how he had "negotiated" Mr. Cicero's "departure." The same e-mail said Mr. Cicero had not even been confronted about the supposed undisclosed conflict involving his wife. (Mr. Cicero flatly denied that his wife had ever worked with either gestor.) The e-mail also assured Ms. Munich there was no hint of financial wrongdoing. "We see it merely as an undisclosed conflict of interest," Mr. Rodriguezmacedo wrote.

There were other discrepancies.

Mr. Rodriguezmacedo said the company had stopped using gestores after Mr. Cicero's departure. Yet even as Mr. Cicero was being debriefed in October 2005, Wal-Mart de Mexico real estate executives made a request to pay a gestor $14,000 to get a construction permit, records showed.

The persistent questions and document requests from Mr. Halter's team provoked a backlash from Wal-Mart de Mexico's executives. After a week of work, records and interviews show, Mr. Halter and other members of the team were summoned by Eduardo F. Solorzano Morales, then chief executive of Wal-Mart de Mexico.

Mr. Solorzano angrily chastised the investigators for being too secretive and accusatory. He took offense that his executives were being told at the start of interviews that they had the right not to answer questions—as if they were being read their rights.

"It was like, 'You shut up. I'm going to talk,' " a person said of Mr. Solorzano. "It was, 'This is my home, my backyard. You are out of here.' "

Mr. Lewis viewed the complaints as an effort to sidetrack his investigators. "I find this ludicrous and a copout for the larger concerns about what has been going on," he wrote.

Nevertheless, Mr. Herkert, the chief executive for Latin America, was notified about the complaints. Three days later, he and his boss, Mr. Duke, flew to Mexico City. The trip had been long-planned—Mr. Duke toured several stores—but they also reassured Wal-Mart de Mexico's unhappy executives.

They arrived just as the investigators wrapped up their work and left.

A Push to Dig Deeper

Wal-Mart's leaders had agreed to consider a full investigation if the preliminary inquiry found Mr. Cicero's allegations credible.

Back in Bentonville, Mr. Halter and Mr. Ainley wrote confidential reports to Wal-Mart's top executives in December 2005 laying out all the evidence that corroborated Mr. Cicero—the hundreds of gestor payments, the mystery codes, the rewritten audits, the evasive responses from Wal-Mart de Mexico

executives, the donations for permits, the evidence gestores were still being used.

"There is reasonable suspicion," Mr. Halter concluded, "to believe that Mexican and USA laws have been violated." There was simply "no defendable explanation" for the millions of dollars in gestor payments, he wrote.

Mr. Halter submitted an "action plan" for a deeper investigation that would plumb the depths of corruption and culpability at Wal-Mart de Mexico.

Among other things, he urged "that all efforts be concentrated on the reconstruction of Cicero's computer history."

Mr. Cicero, meanwhile, was still offering help. In November, when Mr. Halter's team was in Mexico, Mr. Cicero offered his services as a paid consultant. In December, he wrote to Ms. Munich. He volunteered to share specifics on still more stores, and he promised to show her documents. "I hope you visit again," he wrote.

Mr. Halter proposed a thorough investigation of the two main gestores. He had not tried to interview them in Mexico for fear of his safety. ("I do not want to expose myself on what I consider to be an unrealistic attempt to get Mexican lawyers to admit to criminal activity," he had explained to his bosses.) Now Mr. Halter wanted Wal-Mart to hire private investigators to interview and monitor both gestores.

He also envisioned a round of adversarial interviews with Wal-Mart de Mexico's senior executives. He and his investigators argued that it was time to take the politically sensitive step of questioning Mr. Castro-Wright about his role in the gestor payments.

By January 2006, the case had reached a critical juncture. Wal-Mart's leaders were again weighing whether to approve a full investigation that would inevitably focus on a star executive already being publicly discussed as a potential successor to Mr. Scott.

Wal-Mart's ethics policy offered clear direction. "Never cover up or ignore an ethics problem," the policy states. And some who were involved in the investigation argued that it was time to take a stand against signs of rising corruption in Wal-Mart's global operations. Each year the company received hundreds of internal reports of bribery and fraud, records showed. In Asia alone, there had been 90 reports of bribery just in the previous 18 months.

The situation was bad enough that Wal-Mart's top procurement executives were summoned to Bentonville that winter for a dressing down. Mr. Menzer, Wal-Mart's vice chairman, warned them that corruption was creating an unacceptable risk, particularly given the government's stepped-up enforcement of the Foreign Corrupt Practices Act. "Times have changed," he said.

As if to underscore the problem, Wal-Mart's leaders were confronted with new corruption allegations at Wal-Mart de Mexico even as they pondered Mr. Halter's action plan. In January, Mr. Scott, Mr. Duke and Wal-Mart's chairman, S. Robson Walton, received an anonymous e-mail saying Wal-Mart de Mexico's top real estate executives were receiving kickbacks from construction companies. "Please you must do something," the e-mail implored.

Yet at the same time, records and interviews show, there were misgivings about the budding reach and power of Corporate Investigations.

In less than a year, Mr. Lewis's beefed-up team had doubled its caseload, to roughly 400 cases a year. Some executives grumbled that Mr. Lewis acted as if he still worked for the F.B.I., where he had once supervised major investigations. They accused him and his investigators of being overbearing, disruptive and naive about the moral ambiguities of doing business abroad. They argued that Corporate Investigations should focus more on quietly "neutralizing" problems than on turning corrupt employees over to law enforcement.

Wal-Mart's leaders had just witnessed the downside of that approach: in early 2005, the company went to the F.B.I. with evidence that the disgraced former vice chairman, Mr. Coughlin, had embezzled hundreds of thousands of dollars. The decision produced months of embarrassing publicity, especially when Mr. Coughlin claimed he had used the money to pay off union spies for Wal-Mart.

Meanwhile, Wal-Mart de Mexico executives were continuing to complain to Bentonville about the investigation. The protests "just never let up," a person involved in the case said.

Another person familiar with the thinking of those overseeing the investigation said Wal-Mart would have reacted "like a chicken on a June bug" had the allegations concerned the United States. But some executives saw Mexico as a country where bribery was embedded in the business culture. It simply did not merit the same response.

"It's a Mexican issue; it's better to let it be a Mexican response," the person said, describing the thinking of Wal-Mart executives.

In the midst of this debate, Ms. Munich submitted her resignation, effective Feb. 1, 2006. In one of her final acts, she drafted a memo that argued for expanding the Mexico investigation and giving equal respect to Mexican and United States laws.

"The bribery of government officials," she noted dryly, "is a criminal offense in Mexico."

She also warned against allowing implicated executives to interfere with the investigation. Wal-Mart de Mexico's executives had already tried to insert themselves in the case. Just before Christmas, records show, Mr. Solorzano, the Wal-Mart de Mexico chief executive, held a video conference with Mr. Mars, Mr. Senser and Mr. Stucky to discuss his team's "hypothesis" that Mr. Cicero had stolen gestor payments.

"Given the serious nature of the allegations, and the need to preserve the integrity of the investigation," Ms. Munich wrote, "it would seem more prudent to develop a follow-up plan of action, independent of Walmex management participation."

The Chief Weighs In

Mr. Scott called a meeting for Feb. 3, 2006, to discuss revamping Wal-Mart's internal investigations and to resolve the question of what to do about Mr. Cicero's allegations.

In the days before the meeting, records show, Mr. Senser ordered his staff to compile data showing the effectiveness of Corporate Investigations. He assembled statistics showing that the unit had referred relatively few cases to law enforcement agencies. He circulated copies of an e-mail in which Mr. Rodriguezmacedo said he had been treated "very respectfully and cordially" by Mr. Senser's investigators.

Along with Mr. Scott, the meeting included Mr. Hyde, Mr. Mars and Mr. Stucky, records show. The meeting brought the grievances against Corporate Investigations into the open. Mr. Senser described the complaints in Mr. Lewis's performance evaluation, completed shortly after the meeting. Wal-Mart's leaders viewed Mr. Lewis's investigators as "overly aggressive," he wrote. They did not care for Mr. Lewis's "law enforcement approach," and the fact that Mr. Scott convened a meeting to express these concerns only underscored "the importance placed on these topics by senior executives."

By meeting's end, Mr. Senser had been ordered to work with Mr. Mars and others to develop a "modified protocol" for internal investigations.

Mr. Scott said he wanted it done fast, and within 24 hours Mr. Senser produced a new protocol, a highly bureaucratic process that gave senior Wal-Mart executives—including executives at the business units being investigated—more control over internal investigations. The policy included multiple "case reviews." It also required senior executives to conduct a "cost-benefit analysis" before signing off on a full-blown investigation.

Under the new protocol, Mr. Lewis and his team would only investigate "significant" allegations, like those involving potential crimes or top executives. Lesser allegations would be left to the affected business unit to investigate.

"This captures it, I think," Mr. Hyde wrote when Mr. Senser sent him the new protocol.

Four days after Mr. Scott's meeting, with the new protocol drafted, Wal-Mart's leaders began to transfer control of the bribery investigation to one of its earliest targets, Mr. Rodriguezmacedo.

Mr. Mars first sent Mr. Halter's report to Mr. Rodriguezmacedo. Then he arranged to ship Mr. Halter's investigative files to him as well. In an e-mail, he sought Mr. Senser's advice on how to send the files in "a secure manner."

Mr. Senser recommended FedEx. "There is very good control on those shipments, and while governments do compromise them if they are looking for something in particular, there is no reason for them to think that this shipment is out of the ordinary," he wrote.

"The key," he added, "is being careful about how you communicate the details of the shipment to Jose Luis." He advised Mr. Mars to use encrypted e-mail.

Wal-Mart's spokesman, Mr. Tovar, said the company could not discuss Mr. Scott's meeting or the decision to transfer the case to Mr. Rodriguezmacedo. "At this point," he said, "we don't have a full explanation of what happened. Unfortunately, we realize that until the investigation is concluded, there will be some unanswered questions."

Wal-Mart's leaders, however, had clear guidance about the propriety of letting a target of an investigation run it.

On the same day Mr. Senser was putting the finishing touches on the new investigations protocol, Wal-Mart's ethics office sent him a booklet of "best practices" for internal investigations. It had been put together by lawyers and executives who supervised investigations at Fortune 500 companies.

"Investigations should be conducted by individuals who do not have any vested interest in the potential outcomes of the investigation," it said.

The transfer appeared to violate even the "modified protocol" for investigations. Under the new protocol, Corporate Investigations was still supposed to handle "significant" allegations—including those involving potential crimes and senior executives. When Mr. Senser asked his deputies to list all investigations that met this threshold, they came up with 31 cases.

At the top of the list: Mexico.

After the meeting with Mr. Scott, Mr. Senser had told Mr. Lewis in his performance evaluation that his "highest priority" should be to eliminate "the perceptions that investigators are being too aggressive." He wanted Mr. Lewis to "earn the trust of" his "clients"—Wal-Mart's leaders. He wanted him to head off "adversarial interactions."

Mr. Senser now applied the same advice to himself.

Even as Mr. Halter's files were being shipped to Mr. Rodriguezmacedo, Mr. Stucky made plans to fly to Mexico with other executives involved in the bribery investigation. The trip, he wrote, was "for the purpose of re-establishing activities related to the certain compliance matters we've been discussing." Mr. Stucky invited Mr. Senser along.

"It is better if we do not make this trip to Mexico City," Mr. Senser replied. His investigators, he wrote, would simply be "a resource" if needed.

Ten days after Mr. Stucky flew to Mexico, an article about Wal-Mart appeared in The Times. It focused on "the increasingly important role of one man: Eduardo Castro-Wright." The article said Mr. Castro-Wright was a "popular figure" inside Wal-Mart because he made Wal-Mart de Mexico one of the company's "most profitable units."

Wall Street analysts, it said, viewed him as a "very strong candidate" to succeed Mr. Scott.

Case Closed

For those who had investigated Mr. Cicero's allegations, the preliminary inquiry had been just that—preliminary. In memos and meetings, they had argued that their findings clearly justified a full-blown investigation. Mr. Castro-Wright's precise role had yet to be determined. Mr. Halter had never been permitted to question him, nor had Mr. Castro-Wright's computer files been examined, records and interviews show.

At the very least, a complete investigation would take months.

Mr. Rodriguezmacedo, the man now in charge, saw it differently. He wrapped up the case in a few weeks, with little additional investigation.

"There is no evidence or clear indication," his report concluded, "of bribes paid to Mexican government authorities with the purpose of wrongfully securing any licenses or permits."

That conclusion, his report explained, was largely based on the denials of his fellow executives. Not one "mentioned having ordered or given bribes to government authorities," he wrote.

His report, six pages long, neglected to note that he had been implicated in the same criminal conduct.

That was not the only omission. While his report conceded that Wal-Mart de Mexico executives had authorized years of payments to gestores, it never explained what these executives expected the gestores to do with the millions of dollars they received to "facilitate" permits.

He was also silent on the evidence that Wal-Mart de Mexico had doled out donations to get permits. Nor did he address evidence that he and other executives had suppressed or rewritten audits that would have alerted Bentonville to improper payments.

Instead, the bulk of Mr. Rodriguezmacedo's report attacked the integrity of his accuser.

Mr. Cicero, he wrote, made Wal-Mart de Mexico's executives think they would "run the risk of having permits denied if the gestores were not used." But this was merely a ruse: In all likelihood, he argued, Wal-Mart de Mexico paid millions for "services never rendered." The gestores simply pocketed the money, he suggested, and Mr. Cicero "may have benefited," too.

But he offered no direct proof. Indeed, as his report made clear, it was less an allegation than a hypothesis built on two highly circumstantial pillars.

First, he said he had consulted with Jesus Zamora-Pierce, a "prestigious independent counsel" who had written books on fraud. Mr. Zamora, he wrote, "feels the conduct displayed by Sergio Cicero is typical of someone engaging in fraud. It is not uncommon in Mexico for lawyers to recommend the use of gestores to facilitate permit obtainment, when in reality it is nothing more than a means of engaging in fraud."

Second, he said he had done a statistical analysis that found Wal-Mart de Mexico won permits even faster after Mr. Cicero left. The validity of his analysis was impossible to assess; he did not include his statistics in the report.

In building a case against Mr. Cicero, Mr. Rodriguezmacedo's report included several false statements. He described Mr. Cicero's "dismissal" when records showed he had resigned. He also wrote that Kroll's investigation of Mr. Cicero concluded that he "had a considerable increase in his standard of living during the time in which payments were made to the gestores." Kroll's report made no such assertion, people involved in the investigation said.

His report promised a series of corrective steps aimed at putting the entire matter to rest. Wal-Mart de Mexico would no longer use gestores. There would be a renewed commitment to Wal-Mart's anticorruption policy. He did not recommend any disciplinary action against his colleagues.

There was, however, one person he hoped to punish. Wal-Mart de Mexico, he wrote, would scour Mr. Cicero's records and determine "if any legal action may be taken against him."

Mr. Rodriguezmacedo submitted a draft of his report to Bentonville. In an e-mail, Mr. Lewis told his superiors that he found the report "lacking." It was not clear what evidence supported the report's conclusions, he wrote. "More importantly," he wrote, "if one agrees that Sergio defrauded the company and I am one of them, the question becomes, how was he able to get away with almost $10 million and why was nothing done after it was discovered?"

Mr. Rodriguezmacedo responded by adding a paragraph to the end of his report: They had decided not to pursue "criminal actions" against Mr. Cicero because "we did not have strong case."

"At the risk of being cynical," Mr. Lewis wrote in response, "that report is exactly the same as the previous which I indicated was truly lacking."

But it was enough for Wal-Mart. Mr. Rodriguezmacedo was told by executives in Bentonville on May 10, 2006, to put his report "into final form, thus concluding this investigation."

No one told Mr. Cicero. All he knew was that after months of e-mails, phone calls and meetings, Wal-Mart's interest seemed to suddenly fade. His phone calls and e-mails went unanswered.

"I thought nobody cares about this," he said. "So I left it behind."

Critical Thinking

1. What is your overall impression about the allegations of bribery being faced by Wal-Mart?

2. Having read the article carefully, preparing talking points for class discussion about the efficacy of Wal-Mart's response to the allegation. Contrast the initial response to a time later when "the Chief (i.e., Mr. Scott) weighs in."

3. If you were an outside consultant advising Mr. Scott on ethical issues involved in the situation of the alleged bribery, what would be your advice?

4. What might Wal-Mart's management have done differently in the aftermath of the bribery allegations?

5. Prepare comments for class discussion on the "case closed" section of the article.

6. What are the lessons to be learned from the allegations of bribery and Wal-Mart's handling of the allegations?

What Really Drives Value in Corporate Responsibility?

Few companies are clear about how investing in social initiatives will change stakeholder behavior or the harm a bad strategy can cause.

CB BHATTACHARYA, DANIEL KORSCHUN, AND SANKAR SEN

Now that stakeholders—including consumers, investors, and employees—pay increasing attention to the social and environmental footprints of business, corporate-responsibility efforts have moved into uncharted management territory. We see companies reengineering supply chains to make them "greener," supporting social causes through volunteer programs for employees, or lobbying for human rights in far-flung corners of the globe.

As this tide swells, many executives are left with the nagging sense that such investments rest on a shaky understanding of how corporate responsibility creates value, both for their companies and for society. Some investments, of course, produce immediate and quantifiable gains, such as those from recycling or from manufacturing processes that save energy. But often, social investments are expected to yield longer-term benefits as engaged consumers step up their purchases, a broader investor base develops, or new talent flocks to a company's recruiters.

In these more ambiguous cases, how is a manager to know whether stakeholders will indeed respond positively? Our research, described in greater detail in our recent book, *Leveraging Corporate Responsibility: The Stakeholder Route to Maximizing Business and Social Value,*[1] suggests that while stakeholders' interpretations of corporate responsibility are multifaceted and far from uniform, it is vital that managers avoid creating an impression that such activities are crowding out core business priorities. In fact, some well-meaning corporate-responsibility activities can actually harm a company's competitiveness.

Consider an experiment. We had consumers rate their own purchase intentions for computer accessories after learning about a company's product quality and corporate-responsibility activities. Descriptions of the company as having high product quality had a modest positive effect, but for a company with low product quality, the consumer's willingness to make a purchase actually *decreased* when it engaged in otherwise positive corporate-responsibility activities. In this second case, consumers were wary of these activities, thinking that the company ought to give precedence to product quality. Related research shows a similar dynamic at work with investors: highly innovative Fortune 1000 companies derive greater financial returns from their corporate-responsibility activities than their less innovative counterparts do.

By following a few basic principles, leaders can increase the likelihood that stakeholders will interpret corporate-responsibility initiatives more accurately and thus more positively.

Don't hide market motives. Stakeholders are remarkably open to the business case for corporate responsibility, as long as initiatives are appropriate given what stakeholders know about the business, and as long as companies genuinely pursue and achieve the accompanying social value. Companies should understand that they can pursue profitable core business and corporate-responsibility objectives in tandem, without trade-offs.

Serve stakeholders' true needs. Consumers are drawn to products that satisfy their needs. Likewise, stakeholders are drawn to companies whose corporate-responsibility activities produce solid benefits, which can be tangible (such as improved health in local communities) or psychological (for instance, volunteer programs that help employees better integrate their work and home lives). Before investing in corporate responsibility, however, managers need to set clear objectives that companies can meet and then, ideally, create programs together with key stakeholder groups.

Test your progress. Corporate responsibility acts as a conduit through which companies can demonstrate that they care about their stakeholders. A company should assess its initiatives regularly to ensure that they foster the desired unity between its own goals and those of stakeholders. Calibrating strategy frequently improves the odds that corporate responsibility will create value for all parties.

Companies with low product quality could reap negative returns from their corporate-responsibility activities.

Example of computer accessories purchase decision: on a scale of 1 to 7, where 1 = not at all likely to buy and 7 = very likely to buy

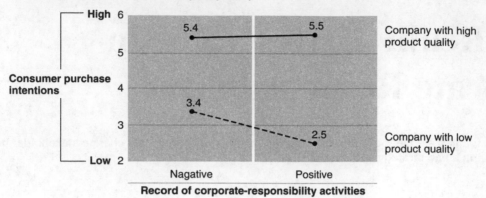

Source: CB Bhattacharya and Sankar Sen

Notes

1. CB Bhattacharya, Daniel Korshun, and Sankar Sen, *Leveraging Corporate Responsibility: The Stakeholder Route to Maximizing Business and Social Value,* New York: Cambridge University Press, November 2011. Our research examines the two most important stakeholder groups—consumers and employees—to understand how and why they react to corporate-responsibility initiatives. The insights we gained helped us show how companies can develop, implement, and evaluate social-responsibility programs that foster stronger relationships with stakeholders and thus create value for them and companies alike.

Critical Thinking

1. The authors suggest three basic principles for having stakeholders interpret corporate-responsibility initiatives more accurately and positively. Pick one of the principles and develop pro and con arguments about its efficacy.

2. Analyze the data presented in the article. Do you agree with the results? Why or why not?

CB BHATTACHARYA is the E.ON Chair in Corporate Responsibility and dean of international relations at the European School of Management and Technology (ESMT), in Berlin; **DANIEL KORSCHUN** is an assistant professor at Drexel University's LeBow College of Business; and **SANKAR SEN** is a professor of marketing at Baruch College's Zicklin School of Business.

Doing More Good

Here are several ways your company can become a better corporate citizen.

JODI CHAVEZ

Today's challenging economic climate has forced many organizations to reduce spending, release workers, and raise fees to consumers. The result is that businesses of all shapes and sizes are being painted in an unfavorable light, inviting criticism from the public and politicians alike.

But the picture being painted—that of a business culture that abandons the public in pursuit of profits—isn't an accurate one. The most effective counter to this depiction is the rise of corporate responsibility initiatives.

The Committee Encouraging Corporate Philanthropy (CECP), an international forum of business leaders focused on measuring and encouraging corporate philanthropy, recently released its *Giving in Numbers* report for 2011. In the report, the CECP noted that one out of every two businesses had actually increased the amount of funds contributed to charity or community organizations since the onset of the recession in 2007. As a matter of fact, a quarter of companies reported increasing their giving by more than 25%. Furthermore, the CECP tracked aggregate total contributions for 110 high-performing companies in 2007–2010 and found that aggregate total giving rose by 23%.

Clearly, many successful businesses are actually augmenting their contributions to society and taking the challenge of good corporate citizenship seriously. But why? Of course, the ability to "do more good" for more people carries intrinsic value and tremendous appeal. Yet there are other significant business benefits that arise out of doing more good.

Here we'll explore some of these benefits, and I'll offer practical ways you can begin to make a difference in your company and, ultimately, society.

The Business Case for Being Charitable

The rise of corporate responsibility and citizenship has been two decades in the making. As detailed in "Responsibility: The New Business Imperative," published in the May 2002 issue of *The Academy of Management Executive,* during the 1990s: "Numerous exposés of labor practices in global supply chains pressured multinational brands and retailers to adopt corporate codes of conduct. Later in the decade, pressure—and expectations—increased further, driving firms not only to introduce codes but also to ensure compliance with these codes by their suppliers." Finally, the fall of businesses like Enron and the recent financial collapse and mortgage crisis forced businesses to reexamine their "anything goes" approach to profitability.

All these are crucial steps in the evolution of corporate responsibility. But today the most important driver of corporate responsibility is the belief that good citizenship makes good business sense.

There are several ways it can give you a competitive advantage.

Building a reputation: Companies large and small impact the neighborhoods, cities, and countries they do business in. By aligning your goals with the goals of the community in which you operate, you're more likely to build a mutually beneficial relationship with potential stakeholders, including employees, customers, investors, suppliers, and business partners.

Setting your company apart: Like an innovative product or a new service offering, a strong record of corporate responsibility is a competitive advantage that you can leverage against others in your industry.

Attracting investment: Businesses with strong records of corporate responsibility generate more interest from investors when compared with apathetic competitors. In a study titled "Institutional and Social Investors Find Common Ground," originally published in the *Journal of Investing* and later cited in the comprehensive article "The Business Case for Corporate Social Responsibility" in the *International Journal of Management Review,* author Timothy Smith lays out why this is the case. "Many institutional investors 'avoid' companies or industries that violate their organizational mission, values, or principles ... [They also] seek companies with good records on employee relations, environmental stewardship, community involvement, and corporate governance."

Reducing costs and risks: Companies that make a concerted effort to contribute to and advance society are more likely to avoid potential penalties or exposure to legal fines and government intervention. This is especially important in a climate of increased regulation and scrutiny. A strong record of corporate citizenship can also help you avoid harm to your reputation and sales that may arise without notice.

Attracting better talent: Great people want to work for great companies. By demonstrating your strong commitment to teamwork, responsibility, community, etc., you can attract employees who share those same values. Furthermore, now may be the opportune time to start reevaluating your corporate responsibility profile so you can connect with future leaders. Research indicates that the Millennial generation, currently entering the workforce in record numbers, is particularly civic minded. Members of this generation want more from their job than just a paycheck—they want an opportunity to make a difference. Why not give it to them and give yourself an edge in the process?

Increasing motivation and retention: In addition to attracting new talent, a demonstrated commitment to corporate responsibility can enhance engagement across your current workforce. It can also help you identify leaders who want to spearhead these important initiatives. This can help you reduce the expenses inherent in high turnover, including recruiting, training, and onboarding, and eliminate productivity gaps that occur when an employee leaves your company.

The Millennial generation wants more from their job than just a paycheck—they want an opportunity to make a difference.

Fostering innovation: By looking beyond the walls of your buildings and understanding the wider impact of your business, you can open your eyes to new opportunities and new avenues for growth. A primary example of this is Xerox, which has shown a continued commitment to sustainability and citizenship in designing "waste free" products and investing in "waste free" facilities. This commitment has led to the development of new products that appeal to corporations, fuel profitability, and set Xerox apart in the marketplace. Toyota is another example of a company that recognized the impact of its business—vehicle emissions—and built a profitable solution to the problem in the form of the popular Prius hybrid. Though other auto manufacturers have followed suit, the development of the Prius and its status as the first commercially viable hybrid gave Toyota a competitive advantage and a leg up on the competition. No matter what product or service you offer, a new perspective gleaned from a commitment to corporate responsibility can help you do the same.

Putting Responsibility into Action

Today, corporate responsibility encompasses many forms, including education about social issues and advancement of different cultures (social responsibility), ensuring the health of the environment (sustainability), and donating funds or time to charitable causes (philanthropy). Corporate responsibility is also concerned with the health and safety of the workforce and providing good working conditions for employees.

With corporate responsibility taking on so many facets, it may be difficult to determine how your company can begin making an impact. The International Institute for Sustainable Development (IISD) recently published *Corporate Social Responsibility: An Implementation Guide for Business* to help companies adapt and facilitate corporate social responsibility. Here is their recommended frame-work for implementation.

Conduct a corporate social responsibility (CSR) assessment: Gather and examine relevant information about your products, services, decision-making processes, and activities to determine your current CSR activity. An effective assessment should give you an accurate understanding of your values and ethics, the CSR issues that are affecting your business now or in the future, key stakeholders, and your leadership's ability to deliver a more effective CSR approach.

Develop a CSR strategy: Using your assessment as a starting point, begin to determine your objectives. Develop a realistic strategy that can help you reach your goals. The IISD recommends these five steps to developing an effective strategy:

- Build support with the CEO, senior management, and employees.
- Research what others (including competitors) are doing.
- Prepare a matrix of proposed CSR actions.
- Develop options for proceeding and the business case for them.
- Decide on direction, approach, boundaries, and focus areas.

Develop commitments: Create a task force to review your objectives and finalize your strategy. The task force should solicit input from key stakeholders—the CEO, department heads, top management, etc.—to gauge their interest and ensure future participation. Using this feedback, prepare a preliminary draft of your CSR commitment, and review this again with those employees who will be affected or who can help effect change. At this point, you can revise and publish your commitments for your internal audience, customers, investors, and potential employees.

Implement CSR commitments: This is the phase where your planning begins to give way to reality. Though each company should approach this critical step in accordance with its unique values and culture, the IISD offers these universal best practices:

- Prepare a CSR business plan.
- Set measurable targets, and identify performance measures.
- Engage employees and others to whom CSR commitments apply.
- Design and conduct CSR training.
- Establish mechanisms for addressing resistance.
- Create internal and external communications plans.
- Make commitments public.

Document progress: It's imperative that you're able to communicate the impact of your efforts to internal and external stakeholders. Reporting tools provide insight into the costs of your initiatives as well as the hard and soft benefits derived from your corporate responsibility program.

Reporting on responsibility initiatives has actually given rise to an entirely new financial model called social accounting. Social accounting is the process of measuring, monitoring, and reporting to stakeholders the social and environmental effects of an organization's actions. Social accounting is conducted by accountants who employ the same tools and knowledge used in traditional financial reporting. Though many larger organizations utilize social accounting, all businesses can benefit from being able to demonstrate the true value of their actions.

In fact, robust social accounting and responsibility reporting is fast becoming the standard for businesses, not the exception. KPMG conducted an *International Survey of Corporate Responsibility Reporting 2011* to review trends of 3,400 companies worldwide, including the top 250 global companies (the G250). The survey indicated that corporate responsibility reporting is undertaken by 95 percent of the G250 and 64 percent of the 100 largest companies across the 34 countries surveyed.

"[Corporate responsibility] has moved from being a moral imperative to a critical business imperative. The time has now come to enhance [corporate responsibility] reporting information systems to bring them up to the level that is equal to financial reporting, including a comparable quality of governance controls and management," said Wim Bartels, global head of KPMG's Sustainability Assurance.

Evaluate and improve: Using the reports and metrics generated, continue to refine your corporate responsibility initiatives. This is critical. Evaluate your performance objectively, identify opportunities for improvement, and engage key stakeholders to plot a course for the future.

The reality of today's economic, political, and social climate necessitates that business leaders rise above their bottom lines and look to make an impact outside their organization. Doing so presents an opportunity to elevate others while elevating your organization.

Critical Thinking

1. What is corporate citizenship?

2. What are the differences between good and bad corporate citizenship?

3. The article suggests a five step process for developing a Corporate Social responsibility strategy. What is your opinion of each of the suggested steps? What other, if any, steps might be added to the five step process?

JODI CHAVEZ is senior vice president of Accounting Principals. You can reach her at Jodi.Chavez@accountingprincipals.com.

Necessary but Not Sufficient

An Exploration of Where CR Begins—and Ends

PETER A. SOYKA

Recent years have witnessed a proliferation of corporate social responsibility (CSR) and corporate responsibility (CR) programs in many industries, along with media, graduate programs and institutes, and other resources to support and promote them. The underlying concept of CSR/CR is deeply rooted in the conviction that corporations have a variety of obligations to their host societies that go well beyond meeting shareholders' expectations of financial returns. A problem, however, complicates reliance on such an approach to guide the behavior of the organization. Setting aside the CR programs that lack substance and appear to be mainly about public relations (we count more than a few), it is not clear within the CR construct how far the responsibility to address environmental, social, and governance (ESG) concerns extends. Nor is it clear how such concerns should be balanced against the need for the corporation to satisfy the demands of its customers and earn the rate of return required by its owners and other capital providers.

The general rule of thumb appears to be to meet certain required minima (e.g., legal compliance, no use of unreasonable labor practices) and as many other "good" things as resources allow, with the proviso that virtually any demand made by a major customer will receive careful consideration. That is, CSR/CR as commonly understood does not provide a clear means for striking the appropriate balance between obligation and opportunity, nor does it place sufficient emphasis on incenting the desired behaviors from companies and their employees. The concept of sustainability, as defined in this article (and more fully in my recent book), provides these missing elements. My concept of sustainability combines CSR/CR and related concepts with aggressive, financially driven assessment of opportunities. Such a balanced approach is the only viable way to get United States business at large on a more sustainable path.

Sustainability Defined

In my view, sustainability is a value set, philosophy, and approach that is rooted in the belief that organizations (corporate and otherwise) can and must materially contribute to the betterment of society. Sustainable organizations must balance their needs, aspirations, and limitations against the larger interests of the societies in which they operate. Only organizations that provide goods and/or services that are of value to people and/or society more generally, and are dedicated to excellence, interested in the full development of human potential, and committed to fairness, are likely to be durable (sustainable) over the long term. Fundamentally, sustainable organizations are purpose-driven, with the purpose being an overarching objective larger and less tangible than self-gratification or profit maximization. Indeed, they accept that their conduct and all their activities in totality must yield an overall benefit-to-cost ratio greater than unity. Accordingly, in my formulation of the concept, sustainable organizations are:

- Mission-driven;
- Aware of and responsive to societal and stakeholder interests;
- Responsible and ethical;
- Dedicated to excellence;
- Driven to meet or exceed customer/client expectations; and
- Disciplined, focused, and skillful.

This view places the conventional emphasis on the "three legs of the stool" (economic prosperity, environmental protection, and social equity) within a larger, more integrative context. It also recognizes that each is a key dimension of any coherent concept of sustainable organizations, past or present. The importance of each of the three major elements of sustainability depends on the organization's nature and purpose. Public sector and nonprofit organizations have been formed and structured specifically to provide some combination of products and services that benefit society, whether that involves forecasting the weather, teaching children, or defending the country from military threats. With the exception of agencies and nongovernmental organizations (NGOs) specifically focused on some aspect of sustainability—such as the United States Environmental Protection Agency (EPA) or the Sierra Club—most such organizations have a primary mission to fulfill that is not directly related to either environmental protection or social equity. Nonetheless, by adopting sustainability as a guiding principle, such organizations commit themselves at the very least to ensuring that they limit any adverse impacts of their operations on the environment and treat all stakeholders fairly. Many public sector organizations, including the federal government and its many parts, have been moving decisively in recent years to institute more sustainable behavior.

Only organizations that provide goods and/or services that are of value to people and/or society more generally, and are dedicated to excellence, interested in the full development of human potential, and committed to fairness, are likely to be durable (sustainable) over the long term.

Corporations are in quite a different place. They are not explicitly supported by and accountable to the American taxpayer and have not (generally) been formed to pursue a mission eligible for tax-exempt status as a nonprofit. Some observers believe that in contrast to the work done by the government and nonprofit sectors, the legitimate role of business is to make money for its owners (shareholders), and the more the better. In this view of the world, time and money invested in improving environmental performance, providing safer working conditions, supporting local communities through philanthropic activity, and other such CR behaviors are an unwarranted and unproductive use of the firm's assets. This view, which has been held and promoted with great conviction by many in the business community and academia, is increasingly being challenged.

Recognizing important sustainability issues and acting on them in an enlightened and sophisticated way has been shown to increase revenue growth and earnings and to strengthen firm positions in terms of the factors that drive long-term financial success.

Corporate leaders should accept and, ideally, embrace the concept of sustainability, for two fundamental reasons. One is that United States corporations, as distinct entities holding enumerated legal rights and receiving numerous public benefits, have an obligation not only to comply with all applicable laws and regulations but also to ensure that their conduct does not harm the broader societies of which they are a part and on which they depend for survival. (Unfortunately, many people in the business community and press seem not to recognize how many benefits the United States federal and state governments provide, and how different this largesse is from the situation in many other countries.) The other is that, increasingly,

recognizing important sustainability issues and acting on them in an enlightened and sophisticated way has been shown to increase revenue growth and earnings and to strengthen firm positions in terms of the factors that drive long-term financial success. In other words, the argument for embracing corporate sustainability (above and beyond CR) has two elements: It is the right thing to do, and it is the smart thing to do.

Beyond Environment and Philanthropy

Each of these other, more limited concepts has considerable merit. However, none is new or sufficient to both address the needs and interests of the broad set of stakeholders to which most organizations are accountable and to position the firm to avail itself of all related opportunities.

Sustainability is often framed in the media as a campaign to "green" the world or "save the planet." When viewed from an appropriately broad perspective, however, sustainability extends beyond the currently fashionable focus on "greening." Greening is, after all, simply the latest manifestation of public interest in the environment, which has come back into vogue during the past three or four years following a multiyear hiatus. As an interested party who has watched several incarnations of a growing public/business interest in improving the environmental performance of organizations (and individuals), I find it both heartening and, in some ways, disturbing to observe the eagerness with which many are now embracing everything "green." Greening sounds and feels admirable, but public interest in this topic tends to wax and wane over time. My fear is that it will again fall out of fashion, unless the renewed focus on environmental performance improvement is coupled with considerations of social equity and both are underlain by rigorous economic analysis. Sustainability, defined in this way, provides the only theoretical and practical environmental improvement framework that can be fully justified and maintained during both good and challenging economic times. Therefore, it is robust and "sustainable" enough for the long haul.

My concerns with the terms CSR and CR are somewhat different. Although in most formulations they include the three "legs of the stool," they really are about delineating and acting on the obligations of the modern corporation to society at large. In contrast, and as highlighted above, sustainability should be considered an imperative that applies to all organizations and political entities (countries, states, municipalities). Each of these is challenged to understand and address the broad conditions under which it operates and its relationships with other entities and the natural world. Each also must chart a course on which it can thrive without undermining its asset base or unfairly precluding or limiting the sustainable success of others. In that context, CR can be thought of as one element of a corporate strategy to address the sustainability imperative. Such an element can, for example, identify the concerns of external stakeholders and define and execute processes to ensure that these external interests are respected as the firm pursues its broader business goals. In other words, CR and its analogues can be an important part of (but in any case are a subset of) an organization's approach to sustainability. In particular, CR can, and often does, comprise an organization's efforts to respond to the imperative to promote sustainable development. Similarly, CR can be used to appropriately target a company's philanthropic activities. Or the firm might separately deploy a strategic philanthropy campaign. But by its nature any such activity is far narrower in scope and effect than organizational sustainability. The two should not be confused or, in my view, ever be used interchangeably.

These distinctions are not trivial. Indeed, understanding and resolving them has proven difficult for many organizations and practitioners. Regardless of what words you choose to employ, the key point is that pursuing sustainability at the organizational level is more complex, more important, and more difficult than simply greening the organization to some arbitrary but comfortable level, or becoming more attentive to particular stakeholders and their views. However, substantial rewards can accompany taking on this greater level of difficulty.

Sustainability has emerged directly from the environmental movement and is often focused on key environmental issues and challenges. However, important opportunities exist for corporate leaders to examine social equity and economic issues in parallel with the environmental aspects of their organizations. The concept of sustainability provides an integrative framework to facilitate this thought process. Moreover, in practice, synergies and scale economies often make it possible to address issues having both environmental and social aspects more effectively and economically than would be possible by pursuing separate, unrelated approaches.

Of Governance and Values

Many stakeholders want assurance that the people at the top of the organization have thought through its important environmental and social issues and that they have developed and deployed effective programs, systems, and practices to address them. Sustainability provides an integrating structure that can both guide and explain how corporate leaders meet these expectations and do so in a way that is far more streamlined, sophisticated, and ultimately less time-consuming than would be possible otherwise.

Environmental and social improvement initiatives are continually underused when they are not seen as contributing to core business drivers or creating financial value in any tangible way.

Illegal and, increasingly, unethical behavior is not well tolerated by regulators, customers, suppliers, and other business partners. Such behavior can have severe financial consequences, both immediately and in the longer term. Understanding what

is legal requires competence and vigilance on the part of one's general or outside counsel, but understanding what is ethical requires a set of organizational values and business norms. It is now widely understood that well-run companies have a core "DNA" or identity that embodies shared values and aspirations and is independent of any individual. This attribute enables the organization to remain strong and vibrant over an extended period even as people enter and depart from it. Moreover, this type of organizational identity provides many advantages under normal circumstances but is especially critical during crisis situations, when people need to know how to act as well as what to do. Sustainability can serve as a common, unifying principle to guide the thinking and behaviors of all members of the organization. This is important when different members are called on to execute their unique functions, some of which may be in conflict. Moreover, sustainability provides the needed flexibility to address the following realities:

- Environmental, social, and economic considerations must be balanced.
- The way in which they are balanced will differ according to the organization, issue, and circumstance in question.
- This balance will likely change over time.

The complexities of, and interrelationships among, ESG issues require a management approach that combines and considers all these disciplines. Such an approach should address all significant needs and requirements (particularly compliance), surface and resolve conflicts among them, provide consistency and predictability, and be both effective and efficient. In other words, some sort of overarching concept and management structure is required, and sustainability provides the "umbrella" under which many organizations are now organizing their previously disparate internal functions. I am unaware of any competing or alternative concept that has been shown to be workable while providing similar benefits.

The best way to pursue sustainability is to consider the three primary determinants of value for any business enterprise:

- The revenue stream and the customer base that generates it;
- Earnings or, in the case of public sector organizations, effective control of costs and management of capital; and
- Adequate understanding and management of risk.

A sensible sustainability strategy embodies careful consideration of how new initiatives or changes to existing programs might affect all three of these determinants of value. History has shown that absent this orientation, environmental and social improvement initiatives are continually underused because they are not seen as contributing to core business drivers or creating financial value in any tangible way. By the same token, a properly specified sustainability approach imposes a new measure of financial discipline on both internal and external proponents of new "greening" ideas and prospective investments in projects or activities having primarily a social orientation.

My fear is that "greening" will again fall out of fashion, unless the renewed focus on environmental performance improvement is coupled with considerations of social equity, with both underlain by rigorous economic analysis.

Entering the Mainstream

EHS issues have in many cases been managed tactically in United States corporations and public sector agencies. Historically, EHS functions were often housed within, and directed by, the organization's legal department because the focus then was on understanding legal requirements and ensuring compliance. More recently, EHS people have reported through various administrative functions (such as human resources), facility maintenance, or manufacturing management. In short, with few exceptions, EHS has been managed primarily as a facility-based tactical function, rather than as a strategic issue or source of potential broad-spectrum financial value creation. Adopting a sustainability framework can help disrupt, and might even compel, dissolution of organizational silos that exist in many companies. This can create the conditions needed for people across the organization to reach out to one another. They can identify and manage environmental and social issues in ways

that limit risk, build brand and market value, and generate new cash flows. In an organization actively pursuing sustainability, achieving better environmental performance or more equitable dealings with stakeholders is not a task to be delegated to someone else. It is an integral part of everyone's job (if only in a small way), from the boardroom to the shop floor.

Critical Thinking

1. What is the relationship of sustainability and corporate responsibility?

2. Using the Internet, identify firms with strong sustainability programs and good corporate responsibility results.

3. For the firms you identified in answering question 2, analysis at least two of those firms on the basis of the six attributes of a sustainable organization presented in the article. Explain how the two firms you chose either exhibit or do not exhibit attributes of a sustainable organization.

4. What is the relationship of ethics and sustainability? To be an ethical firm, does the firm need a sustainability program? Why or why not?

PETER SOKA is founder and president of Soyka & Company. This is the first in a series of excerpts from his new book, *Creating a Sustainable Organization: Approaches for Enhancing Corporate Value Through Sustainability,* reprinted with permission from FT Press, a division of Pearson.

Cause for Concern

Water conservation has been billed as the most important environmental issue of the 21st century, yet few American consumers are altering their behaviors—and fewer companies are trying to motivate them to do so

CHRISTINE BIRKNER

According to the U.S. Environmental Protection Agency, at least two-thirds of the United States is either experiencing or bracing for local, regional or statewide water shortages. Parts of the United States use up to 80 percent of their available freshwater resources, making future water shortages more probable, according to the United Nations Educational, Scientific and Cultural Organization. Globally, 1.2 billion people live in areas with inadequate water supplies and by 2025, two-thirds of the world will contend with water scarcity, according to the International Water Management Institute.

> ## 1.2 billion people live in areas with inadequate water supplies.
> International Water Management Institute

Did you know that the world's water shortages are that dire? You're not alone if you didn't—and you're in good company if you have yet to do anything about it. A 2011 study by the London-based Chartered Institution of Water and Environmental Management says that consumers around the world are generally unaware of their own water consumption, tend not to change their behavior and have a general lack of knowledge about water management issues.

"Water is still a really inexpensive resource across the country and until water rates go up, the vast majority of people aren't going to think twice about conserving water," says Park Howell, president of Park&Co, a Phoenix-based marketing agency that specializes in sustainability and has worked on nationwide water conservation campaigns. "It's a big environmental issue that's creeping up on consumers that they don't even realize is at their doorstep."

While consumer behaviors have yet to change, such change is inevitable, experts say, which makes water conservation a powerful and prescient cause for companies to get behind—incorporating water-saving strategies into both their day-to-day operations and their marketing plans, and taking the lead on water-based public awareness efforts. "It's going to be the No. 1 environmental issue for North America, if not the entire world, in the next few years [because] the population continues to expand and our infrastructure is not keeping up. Consumer product manufacturers are [realizing] this is going to become much more visible over the next decade and if they're there as a pioneer saying, 'Let us show you how to use our product to save water,' then [they're] the hero," Howell says.

Distilling the Message

Howell is no stranger to effective water-based marketing strategies. In 1999, his firm developed a campaign for the city of Mesa, Ariz., aimed at encouraging residents to conserve water. The campaign, called "Water: Use it Wisely," offers simple water conservation tips on a website and in TV, print and radio ads. Initially used by local utilities, the "Water: Use It Wisely" messaging later was adopted by more than 400 public and private entities across the United States, with corporate sponsors including Lowe's and Home Depot, and is still active nationwide. The campaign model is important, Howell says, because it allows utilities that have limited financial and personnel resources to co-brand a national campaign and benefit from its universal theme: "There are a number of ways to save water, and they all start with you."

"We learned early that people across the country said, 'Don't tell me to save water; show me how,' " Howell says. "The campaign demonstrated to corporations that environmental engagement can be fun, thought-provoking and easy for an individual to do."

Corporate Conservation

Many municipalities have no choice but to promote more positive consumer behaviors regarding water usage and on the corporate side, many companies know that it makes good business sense to change their organizational behaviors when it comes to water usage—whether or not they decide to promote it.

"[Water conservation] is a rapidly growing area in the corporate world," says Brian Richter, director of global freshwater strategies at the Nature Conservancy, an Arlington, Va.-based global conservation organization that works with government agencies at local, state and federal levels around the world to evaluate water efficiency. "More and more companies are seeing the need to get involved in looking at their water use: how much they use, where they use it and the certainty or risk associated with that use." Northfield, Ill.-based Kraft Foods Inc., which has worked with the Nature Conservancy in the past, reduced water consumption at its manufacturing plants by 21% from 2005 to 2010 and plans to further reduce water consumption by an additional 15% by 2015, according to a company spokesman.

In 2010, Chicago-based MillerCoors initiated a study of water-related supply risks in its supply chain and worked with the Beverage Industry Environmental Roundtable, a partnership of global beverage companies devoted to environmental issues, to create an industry approach to "water footprinting." "Sustainability benefits the business and benefits the environment, and for us, we really want to be a recognized leader in the space," says Kim Marotta, vice president of corporate social responsibility at MillerCoors. "We need to understand the watersheds of where our breweries are located so we protect the quality and quantity of water long term." MillerCoors also sponsors the beverage page on the Mother Nature Network website, which includes news, educational videos and tips on sustainability issues such as water conservation best practices for businesses.

Other than industry-focused initiatives and some brand sponsorships of clean water efforts, MillerCoors doesn't engage in much water-related cause marketing yet because other environmental issues, such as recycling, attract more consumer attention, Marotta says.

That organizational rather than cause-marketing-related approach to water conservation isn't atypical among American businesses. At Atlanta-based Coca-Cola Co., most water conservation efforts are conducted behind the scenes as well, at least in the United States. As part of its partnership with the Nature Conservancy, Coca-Cola worked with academics at the Global Environment & Technology Foundation on a report detailing methods by which companies can measure and account for the benefits of water conservation work in communities and watersheds. Coca-Cola and the Nature Conservancy also worked with private land owners and cooperatives in north Texas to expand grasslands and reintroduce native species to restore prairies, which helps with water quality.

By 2025, two-thirds of the world will contend with water scarcity.

International Water Management Institute

"We have evolved in our understanding and response to water issues over the last decade," says Greg Koch, Coca-Colas

managing director of global water stewardship. "We've recognized the stresses water is under, from quality, to quantity, to droughts and scarcity. Plant performance is important and we've maintained that, but . . . it's not enough for us to take care of the water we need for our business because water is so fundamental to life. It's in our vested business interest to play a role in watersheds and communities, and in awareness and education."

Richter says that companies must first get a handle on their own water usage before they can engage in any meaningful water-related cause marketing initiatives. "It's difficult for a company to take a position of encouraging its consumers to be responsible for their water use until the company assumes the responsibility for its own water."

From a Drip to a Deluge

Coca-Cola therefore is navigating the "water as a corporate cause" strategy carefully, introducing only a few water conservation programs domestically until consumers are more receptive to water-related messaging. Instead, Cokes environmental messaging in the United States focuses on recycling and species conservation efforts, such as the company's recent holiday campaign in which Coke cans and bottles were white rather than red to support the World Wildlife Fund's polar bear conservation programs. These efforts more closely match the American consumer's mindset, says Lisa Manley, Coca-Cola's director of sustainability communications. "Consumer interests vary country by country. We need to understand areas of interest within our sustainability area that are most relevant to a particular community and work to tailor our communications against those. Here in the United States, we've seen a lot more interest around packaging and recycling. In [global] markets, we see more of a defined interest around water," Manley says.

Overseas, Coca-Cola is doing more overt water conservation initiatives, including running ads such as the one in its Latin American marketing campaign, "Every Bottle Tells a Story," that features a man doing water stewardship work in communities in Mexico. And during the FIFA World Cup in South Africa in 2010, Coca-Cola ran ads promoting the Replenish Africa Initiative, which helps bring water to drought-ridden communities throughout the continent.

Coca-Cola's site-specific and consumer-sensitive strategy is wise, experts say. "[Water conservation] is certainly not on the forefront of American consumers' minds, but it is on the forefront of global consumers' minds," says Karen Barnes, vice president of insight at Shelton Group Inc., a Knoxville, Tenn.-based advertising agency focused on bringing sustainability to the mass market.

When corporations are ready to engage American consumers on water conservation awareness, though, they could take a page from the play-book of Piscataway, N.J.-based faucet and toilet maker American Standard Brands. American Standard's water conservation efforts are organic in that the company's products handle consumers' water use, so water conservation as a corporate cause is an obvious fit. Jeannette Long, vice president of digital marketing, doesn't deny that fact but says that by promoting water efficiency, both the company and the environment can benefit.

Water conservation is part of American Standard's DNA, she says. "Every product that we make is a water receptacle or has water that passes through it, so we feel like it's our responsibility to design products that will function exceptionally well and use as little water as possible. The bathroom accounts for 75% of water used in the home, so if we're designing the products, it's our responsibility to create the best product and still protect our natural resources."

American Standard recently teamed up with the Environmental Protection Agency on a water conservation program called WaterSense and developed water-efficient faucets, showerheads and toilets. As part of that program, American Standard worked to change consumer perception that water-efficient appliances don't perform as well as regular appliances, Long says. "Our biggest goal is to convince consumers that more water does not equal better performance. We've reduced water in the faucet category by 20% and in the showerhead category by 40%, and we do testing to ensure that the performance the customer's going to experience is exactly the same as when they used more water."

To tout its products' water- and money-saving capabilities, American Standard conducted the Responsible Bathroom campaign from late 2009 to early 2011. The campaign included print, TV and mobile marketing, with trailers featuring American Standard product exhibits stopping at home shows around the country. "It was critical for us to demonstrate that you don't need as much water. [We] came up with demonstrations that showed, 'This toilet flushes 24 golf balls with 20% less water,'" Long says. "Everybody walked away saying, 'Wow, that's impressive.'"

Responsible Bathroom ads promoted water-saving behaviors, emphasizing that a family of four, for instance, can save 16,000 gallons of water a year by using water-saving appliances and water-efficient practices. The campaign included a Responsible Bathroom Sweepstakes, which gave away vacations to families who submitted creative ways to save water. A water calculator on the Responsible Bathroom section of American Standard's website also estimated the cost savings of using water-efficient appliances.

Getting consumers to adopt water-saving habits is a challenge, Long admits. "Some of them won't be interested in water conservation, but there is this message that says: 'You're going to use less water; your performance is going to be just as good, actually better than when you were using more water, and you're going to save money on your water bill. You're going to save energy because you're not heating as much water for your shower and your faucets.' We talk to them on that side, for people who aren't environmentally conscious."

To introduce future generations to the issue of water conservation, American Standard partners with the Green Education Foundation on a curriculum for New Jersey schools that shows children how much water is being used in the bathroom. Students conduct audits of plumbing products, figuring out how much water they could save if they replaced fixtures in their school. "We were effective [in] bringing younger generations

into it because they are more socially minded as they start to hear about natural resources being used up," Long says.

The company also donated $1 million to the Nature Conservancy's water conservation awareness programs in 2010, and works with organizations such as the International Association of Plumbing and Mechanical Officials and the EPA on plumbing infrastructure testing. American Standard also meets with congressmen about issues that relate to the plumbing industry and water conservation, all of which are important to the end consumer.

Howell applauds American Standard's conservation efforts. "They've got products that use water and facilitate the flow of water, so they're a good corporate citizen, going out of their way to build water savings into the product and teach the behavior change. Technology alone is not going to save this planet, no matter how energy-efficient the showerhead," he says.

For Cleveland-based Great Lakes Brewing Co., which sells a water-based product with a water-related brand name, water conservation also is a natural fit. "Our product is made of 95% water, so it's the main ingredient of our product," says Saul Kliorys, environmental programs manager at Great Lakes. "We've called our company Great Lakes Brewing Co., Lake Erie is one mile away: Those are the reasons we're interested in [water conservation]. It's a resource that's getting scarcer and scarcer."

The brewer's cause marketing efforts include a music festival in Cleveland called Burning River Fest that's dedicated to promoting water conservation. Money raised at the festival goes to water conservation organizations such as the Doan Brook Watershed Partnership in Northeast Ohio, Lake Erie Waterkeeper and a rain harvesting program for urban gardens at Baldwin Wallace College in Berea, Ohio. Great Lakes also works with organizations that conduct educational projects at local schools, including Drink Local, Drink Tap in Cleveland and Tinkers Creek Watershed Partners in Twinsburg, Ohio.

The brewer's water conservation efforts are an obvious tie-in, Kliorys says, and they help to boost the company's brand image. "In Cleveland, folks like our brand a lot, so we asked them why they do, and the primary reason is for the quality of the beer ... but most people are also supportive of the sustainability initiatives. It's definitely an added benefit."

Be Conservative

As with any cause marketing initiative, authenticity is key to companies' water conservation messages, whether consumer-driven or covert. Water has always been a top priority for MillerCoors as a business, which helps in its bid for authenticity, Marotta says. "Any time you're connecting with a consumer and talking about the importance of any aspect of sustainability, it absolutely needs to be authentic. If you're not walking the walk, then don't talk the talk. If it's about water, you better be operating from the most water-efficient breweries, understanding your footprint and making water conservation efforts in your supply chain. Otherwise, it's going to be noticeable that its greenwashing and not part of the DNA of the brand," she says. "It's not as though we woke up in 2008 and said: 'Boy, there's some successful sustainability campaigns out there. We should really look at this.' It's [been] a decades-long commitment."

Echoes Coca-Cola's Manley: "Today's consumer is incredibly savvy and incredibly aware of a company matching their behaviors with their messaging, so it would be folly for us to communicate with something that we didn't feel we were engaging in a responsible way around. We've got all of the proof points that one might need to feel comfortable beginning to think about how do you convey the message to consumers—and not just convey it in terms of how do you educate them, but... how do you invite them along in the journey? I see it as an area where we'll have increasing engagement with consumers in the future."

"Water is going to be the most important natural resource and environmental issue of the 21st century."

Brian Richter, The Nature Conservancy

Water will never be just the cause du jour. Rather, it's a matter of survival, the Nature Conservancy's Richter says, so it's a worthwhile investment to get behind water conservation now. "Water is going to be the most important natural resource and environmental issue of the 21st century. Population growth is going to put more and more pressure on limited water supplies,

so it's going to be critically important for everyone, especially corporations, to be actively involved in promoting activities that will protect those water supplies and use them more efficiently," he says. "Unlike many other natural resources, water has no substitute."

"Unlike many other natural resources, water has no substitute."

Brian Richter, The Nature Conservancy

Critical Thinking

1. Do you agree that water conservation is the most important environmental issue of the 21st century? Why or why not?

2. Why do you think so few American consumers are ignoring the need for water conservation?

3. If you live in an area of adequate water, should you be concerned about the reported 1.2 billion people in the world without adequate water supplies? Prepare answers on both sides of this question.

4. How might the need for water conservation be instilled in society?

5. If you were to write a paragraph for inclusion in a firm's code of ethics about the importance of water conservation, what would you write? Be prepared to present and explain your paragraph to your classmates.

Birkner, Christine. From *Marketing News*, March 31, 2012. Copyright © 2012 by American Marketing Association. Reprinted by permission.

UNIT 4

Ethics and Social Responsibility in the Marketplace

Unit Selections

Learning Outcomes

After reading this Unit, you will be able to:

- What responsibility does an organization have to reveal product defects to consumers?

- Should executives face criminal charges for unsafe products? Are there situations where an executive should not face criminal charges?

- Which area of marketing strategy (product, price, place, or promotion) is most subject to public scrutiny in regard to ethics? Why? Using Internet or library research, provide examples of unethical techniques or strategies involving each of these four areas. Indicate which of the examples are most egregious and explain why you feel they are most egregious.

- Given the competitiveness of the business arena, is it possible for business personnel to behave ethically and both survive and prosper? Explain. Give suggestions that could be incorporated into business strategy for firms that want to be both ethical and successful.

- Name some organizations that make you feel genuinely valued as a customer. What are the characteristics of these organizations that distinguish them from their competitors? Name organizations that do not make you feel valued as a customer. How are these organizations different from organizations that make you feel valued?

- How does philanthropy fit into a corporation's business model?

Student Website

www.mhhe.com/cls

From a consumer viewpoint, the marketplace is the "proof of the pudding" or where the "rubber meets the road" for business ethics. What the company promulgates about the virtues of its product or service has little meaning if the company's actual marketing practices and its treatment of the consumer contradict and thereby invalidate its claims.

At its core, marketing has a moral and noble purpose: to satisfy human needs and wants and to help people through the exchange process. Marketing involves the coordination of the variables of product, price, place, and promotion to effectively and efficiently address the needs of consumers. Unfortunately, at times, the unethical marketing practices of some firms have cast a shadow of suspicion over marketing in general. Since marketing is the aspect of business that is most visible to the public, it has perhaps taken a disproportionate share of the criticism directed toward the free-enterprise system.

This unit, Ethics and Social Responsibility in the Marketplace, presents articles examining the strategic process and practice of incorporating ethics into the marketplace. The first subsection, Marketing Strategy and Ethics, contains articles describing how marketing strategy and ethics can be integrated in the marketplace. The first article wrestles with how ethical issues in new product development could be affecting innovation growth. The

© Design Pics/Darren Greenwood

second article examines how rude and blatantly unjust customers should be treated.

In the second subsection, Ethical Practices in the Marketplace, one article examines how companies can make money and also do good in the marketplace. A second article enlarges on the concept of doing good to do well.

Internet References

Business and Philanthropy
www.associatedcontent.com/article/7908845/business_and_
philanthropy.html?cat=3

Business for Social Responsibility (BSR)
www.bsr.org

Customer Value—Creating Customer Value
www.1000ventures.com/business_guide/crosscuttings/customer_
value_creation.html

Customer Value—How to Value Customers
www.intangiblebusiness.com/Brand-services/Marketing-services/
News/How-to-value-customers~ 972.html

Customer Value—Valuing Customer Value
www.customerthink.com/blog/valuing_customer_value

Do Well by Doing Good—Benjamin Franklin
www.evancarmichael.com/Famous-Entrepreneurs/624/Lesson-5-
Do-Well-by-Doing-Good.html

Doing Well versus Doing Good
www.recruiter.com/i/doing-well-doing-good

How to Do Well and Do Good
http://sloanreview.mit.edu/the-magazine/2010-fall/52118/
how-to-do-well-and-do-good

Total Quality Management Sites
www.nku.edu/~ lindsay/qualhttp.html

Unsafe Products
http://gmeyerslaw.com/unsafe-products

Honest Innovation

Ethics issues in new product development could be stalling innovation growth.

CALVIN L. HODOCK

Product innovation is the fuel for America's growth. Two Harvard economists described its importance as follows: "Innovation is no mere vanity plate on the nation's economic engine. It trumps capital accumulation and allocation of resources as the most important contributor to growth."

Innovative initiatives are a high risk game; failures widely outnumber successes. While enthusiasm, conviction and creativity should flourish in the hearts and minds of the innovation team, judgments must remain totally, even brutally, objective. But unconscious and conscious marketing dishonesty may make this easier said than done.

Unconscious Marketing Dishonesty

People fall in love with what they create, including movies, television pilots, novels, art and new products. And all too often that love is blind: As objectivity eludes the creator, normally rational people become evangelical rather than practical, rational marketing executives.

The Coca-Cola executive suite was convinced that New Coke was the right thing to do. Procter & Gamble's research and development (R&D) believed that Citrus Hill was a better-tasting orange juice than Tropicana and Minute Maid. The spirited Pepsi Blue team overlooked the obvious knowledge that colas should be brown. Ford's MBA crowd believed in a "cheap Jag" strategy. And Motorola's engineers were misguided in their devotion to the Iridium satellite telephone system.

Crest Rejuvenating Effects was fake innovation: It basically was just regular Crest with a great cinnamon vanilla flavor and feminine packaging, positioned for the "nip and tuck" generation of women aged 30 to 45. Similar to Rice Krispies' famous "snap, crackle, and pop" campaign, it encountered a tepid reception, but the brand's custodians believed that America was ready for "his and hers" tubes of toothpaste in their medicine cabinets.

These were well-meaning people who wandered off course because they became enamored with what they created. But let's face it, optimism has limits. The marketplace disagreed, and that's the only vote that counts in any innovation effort.

Conscious Marketing Dishonesty

Conscious marketing dishonesty is more insidious. Blinded passion may still be part of the equation, but in this case the innovation team consciously pushes the envelope across the line of propriety. Before long, there are disquieting signs or signals that all is not well with the new product.

Unfavorable data or information might be ignored, perhaps even suppressed. There might be the blithe assumption that some miracle will surface, and make it all right. Successful innovation initiatives are not products of miracles, but simply take a good idea and execute all the basic steps that are part of the discovery process. The reward goes to those who excel in executing the thousands of details associated with the dirt of doing.

Either way, conscious or unconscious, marketing dishonesty means resources are wasted, valuable time and energy are lost forever and shareholder value may be diminished (depending on the magnitude of the mistake). Often, nobody takes the blame—and many get promoted, because activity gets rewarded over achievement.

There's often no accountability, even though the new product blueprint is peppered with the fingerprints of many. New product assignments are similar to a NASCAR pit stop. The players are constantly moved around the chess board. The brand manager working on a new product for six to nine months moves to mouthwash. The mouthwash brand manager moves to shampoos. And what we have is a game of musical chairs, with no accountability. It is understandable why innovation teams are willing to "run bad ideas up the flag pole" in lassiez-faire-type innovation environments.

While there are supposed to be security checkpoints in the development process, the marketing "id" finds ways to maneuver around them. When important marketing research findings are ignored or rationalized away, because the innovation team is racing toward a launch date promised to management, the spigot of objectivity is turned off because reality might get in the way. Innovation initiatives build momentum to the point where nothing will stop the new product from being launched—not even dire news.

Marketing Dishonesty

There are eight recurring errors associated with flawed innovation. The most disingenuous is marketing dishonesty, where the innovation team consciously engages in deception—even though there is a red flag flapping in the breeze, indicating that a new product is ill. Six marketing dishonesty scenarios are outlined here.

Campbell's Souper Combo

Souper Combo was a combination frozen soup and sandwich for microwave heating; it tested extremely well as a concept. The product was test marketed, and national introduction was recommended.

Two forecasts surfaced. The new product team estimated that Souper Combo would be a $68 million business. The marketing research department viewed it differently: It would be a $40 million to $45 million business, due to weak repeat purchase rates. Nobody challenged the optimistic forecast. Senior management trusted what they heard, while being fed a bouillabaisse of marketing dishonesty. The national introduction was a disaster, and Souper Combo died on the altar of blemished innovation in nine months.

Crystal Pepsi

Pepsi's innovation team ignored focus group participants who hated the taste of this clear cola. It was forced through the Pepsi distribution system on its journey to failure. When was the last time you saw Crystal Pepsi on the store shelves?

Apple Newton

The Newton was the first (but flawed) PDA rushed to market, because then-CEO John Scully viewed it as his signature product—knowing that Apple loyalists were dismayed that a "Pepsi guy" was running the company. Scully wanted to establish a technical legacy that endured long after he left the Apple campus.

The first Newtons were shipped to market with more than a thousand documented bugs. Nobody had the courage to tell Scully and the Apple board about this.

Arthritis Foundation Pain Relievers

This was a line of parity analgesics, involving a licensing agreement where the company paid the Atlanta-based Arthritis Foundation $1 million annually for trademark use. This analgesic line was a positioning gimmick destined for a law and order encounter, and that doesn't mean the NBC television program. Nineteen states attorney generals said the proposition was deceptive. The drugs contained analgesics common to other pain relievers, and were developed without assistance from the Arthritis Foundation. The Foundation was paid handsomely for the use of its name.

Although McNeil Consumer Healthcare admitted no wrong doing, the case was settled for close to $2 million.

Pontiac Aztek

This was considered the ugliest car ever, and the research verified this. While the research predicted that the Aztek was a hopeless cause, the project team sanitized the research sent to senior management to make the situation look better than it was. Decisions about the Aztek's fate were based on intelligence that was heavily modified and edited. Get it out became more important than "get it right."

Aztek-type decisions became regrettably common in the General Motors culture. John Scully never heard the bad news about the Newton, and the General Motors executive suite didn't want to hear any bad news about their cars. It is a heck of way to run one of America's largest corporations and a bad deal for General Motors shareholders, when a culture of intimidation fuels marketing dishonesty. No wonder things are grim at GM these days.

Polaroid Captiva

This camera was similar to Polaroid's original goldmine product the SX 70, but with a smaller film format. It was priced at $120, although marketing research indicated it would not sell if priced over $60. In this scenario, marketing sold a bad idea supported with a specious assumption; marketing research couldn't sell the truth.

Executive Briefing

Jeffery Garten, former dean of the Yale School of Management and *BusinessWeek* columnist, graded business schools with a C+ in teaching ethics. Sweeping bad news about new product initiatives under the rug can be more costly than embezzlement, and it is just as unethical. A *USA Today* survey says that 52% of students working on their master's of business administration degrees would buy stock illegally on inside information. Business schools need to emphasize ethics training far more than they do now, particularly since unethical behavior can be an underlying dynamic in new product failures.

Captiva's potential sales were inflated with an assumption about high levels of repeat purchases after introduction. Selling cameras is different than selling cookies or shampoo, products that need replacement. Captiva perished in the marketplace, as the company violated its cardinal principle: Make the cash register ring selling film, while offering the cameras at cost.

Ethics Issues

While these new products had varied product deficiencies, they all share a common denominator: an optimistic sales forecast. An innovation team can manipulate the numbers to get any sales level it wants. It's easy to do, use optimistic assumptions. New product teams can, and do, cook the books with creative number crunching.

Most new product failures are heavily researched. It is used to justify moving a bad new product forward. In a recent *Advertising Age* article, Bob Barocci, the CEO of the Advertising Research Foundation, remarked, "There is a general belief that over 50% of the research done at companies is wasted." He attributed this to the desire to "support decisions already made." All too often, innovation teams push questionable new products through the pipeline with the support of "justification research."

Another ethical issue is targeting. It is difficult to imagine that ad agencies and their clients did not know Vioxx and Celebrex were overprescribed drugs, sold to consumers with minor aches and pains who could have used less expensive alternatives like Advil and Aleve. Both clients and agencies mutually formulated target strategies with Celebrex and Vioxx as examples. These drugs were developed for senior citizens with chronic pain. But the target segment was too small, so the focus shifted to aging baby boomers with clients and agencies in agreement on the reconfiguration.

Prescriptives

Here are seven recommendations:

1. **Innovation committee.** Boards have finance, audit, nominating and compensation committees. Why not an innovation committee composed of outsiders who are not board members? Their role is to assist the board in assessing innovation initiatives. The board can then decide what action should be taken, including pressing the "kill button."

Companies sometimes do postmortems after failure. The innovation committee should perform pre-mortems early in the development process, before bad ideas soak up lots of money. There is a rich reservoir of people resources to serve on innovation committees (e.g., academics, retired senior executives, industrial designers, and product and industry specialists). But one thing that they should not be is cronies of professional management.

2. **Find a value-added marketing research department.** The prior case histories illustrate that bad research news often is ignored or rationalized away. Hire a research director who knows how to develop and steward a value-added research department, and that has senior management's respect. The respect factor will protect the function from retribution, should the news be bad. Such a person will not be easy to find. One company's solution was to hire a consultant from McKinsey & Company to steward their research department.

In the early days, pioneer researchers such as Alfred Politz and Ernest Dichter presented their findings to boards of directors. Marketing research lost it status on its journey from infancy to maturity. Today's market research is frequently unseen by the board. The right person in the function—think one with management respect—gives marketing research an influential voice in the innovation process that it currently does not have.

3. **Reinforce the unvarnished truth.** Senior management needs to embrace skeptics, rather than surround themselves with "yes people." Before management reviews a new product plan, key players—manufacturing, finance, marketing, and marketing research—should sign off that the plan's assumptions, the underlying source for rosy sales forecasts, are truthful.

4. **Ethics boot camp.** Corporations spend millions on employee training, but how much is focused on ethics to help marketers navigate through gray areas? The innovation team should attend an ethics boot camp early in the development process. This should include everybody, including the ad agencies. Manipulating the forecast for a new product is unethical. It cheats the shareholders even more than it cheats the public.

5. **Teaching new product development.** In academia, new product courses are taught with a focus on best practices; a different perspective is required. The abysmal failure rate is due to worst practices. Classroom discussions of best practices aren't doing much to reduce failure. Class lectures should focus on ethics issues, like manipulating forecasts and justification research used to keep bad ideas afloat.

6. **Ethics test.** Business schools screen candidates based on their graduate management admission test (GMAT) scores. But there is another much-needed test that business schools should implement: an ethics test. Ethics scores should carry equal weight with GMATs. This demonstrates to candidates that ethics are important, and represent a significant prerequisite for admission. As evidenced in new product cases, ethics is more than simply the despicable acts of WorldCom's Bernie Ebbers and Enron Corporation's Andrew Fastow. And, most important, this should help business schools turn out students with a stronger moral compass—ones who don't feed management a duplicitous forecast for a flawed new product.

7. **Corporate endowments.** Corporations interact with business schools on many different levels. They make sizable donations, fund basic research and send their executives to workshops and seminars. They also need to endow ethics chairs with dedicated academics who are interested in ethics scholarship. Corporations should not hesitate to open up their vaults of information to these academics. What are the ethical patterns that underscore an endless stream of new product failures?

Final Thoughts

Failure is inevitable in product innovation. Perfect success is impossible, even undesirable, because it impedes reaching for the stars like Apple did with iPhone or Toyota with the Prius. Perfect success would be a dull agenda of safe bets like a new fragrance or a new flavor. This means the company has elected to play small ball.

This was the trap that Procter & Gamble fell into for close to three decades, despite having 1,250 PhD scientists churning out a treasure chest of patents—leading to 250 proprietary technologies. Despite all this patent activity, very few market-place hits that made the company famous—think Tide or Pampers as examples—had surfaced from this scientific capability. The innovation focus had drifted to minor product improvements, until the newly anointed CEO A. G. Lafley came along to change all that.

Lafley mandated that P&G be more aggressive, expect failures, and shoot for an innovation success rate in the range of 50% to 60%. And that means having only 4 out of 10 new products fail at Procter & Gamble, well below the industry norm.

The statistic—nine out of 10 new products fail—has hovered over the marketing landscape for six decades. It is estimated that the food industry loses $20 billion to $30 billion annually on failed new products. Would it not be refreshing to attempt to scale this back with a healthy dose of marketing honesty?

Critical Thinking

1. What is the difference between optimism and lying?
2. In what ways does product innovation lend itself to deceptive practices?

CALVIN L. HODOCK is former chairperson of the American Marketing Association board, author of *Why Smart Companies Do Dumb Things* (Prometheus Books, 2007), and professor of marketing at Berkeley College, based in West Paterson, N.J. He may be reached at calhodock@hotmail.com.

Reprinted with permission from *Marketing Management*, March/April 2009, pp. 18–21, published by the American Marketing Association. Copyright © 2009 by American Marketing Association.

Serving Unfair Customers

Leonard L. Berry and Kathleen Seiders

1. Changing Focus: From Unfair Companies to Unfair Customers

Ten years ago, we published an article titled "Service Fairness: What It Is and Why It Matters" (Seiders & Berry, 1998). Therein, we argued that poor service is not always linked to unfair company practices, but that unfair company practices are always linked to customer perceptions of poor service. We also argued that companies can pay a heavy price when customers believe they have been treated unfairly because customers' responses to perceived injustice often are pronounced, emotional, and retaliatory. We concluded by providing guidelines for managers on preventing unfairness perceptions and effectively managing those that do arise.

Fairness remains a critically important topic today, for it is essential to a mutually satisfactory exchange between two parties. Perceived unfairness undermines trust and diminished trust undermines the strength of relationships. Perceived unfairness is always a negative development. The focus of our original article was company unfairness to customers. Fairness, however, is a two-way street; thus, our present focus is customer unfairness to companies. This time, we examine how customers can be unfair, why it is important, and what companies can do about it.

We are ardent champions of the customer, but we do *not* believe in the maxim that "the customer is always right." Sometimes, the customer is wrong and unfairness often results. That the customer is sometimes wrong is a dirty little secret of marketing, known to many but rarely discussed in public—or in print. What better occasion to broach this unmentionable topic than *Business Horizons'* 50th anniversary?

2. What Is Customer Unfairness and Why Does it Matter?

Customer unfairness occurs when a customer behaves in a manner that is devoid of common decency, reasonableness, and respect for the rights of others, creating inequity and causing harm for a company and, in some cases, its employees and other customers. Customer unfairness should be viewed independent of illegality because unfair customer behavior frequently is

legal; repugnant, perhaps, but not necessarily illegal. Our focus in this article is legal customer behavior that is unfair, falling in the so-called "gray area" of company response.

When does a customer's bad judgment (or, when do bad manners) cross the line to "unfairness"? Three concepts are particularly useful in considering this question. The first is the severity of the harm the customer causes. The second is the frequency of the customer's problematic behavior. Figure 1 shows increasing levels of these two factors: "minor," "moderate," and "extreme" for severity of harm and "uncommon," "intermittent," and "recurrent" for frequency of occurrence. Customer behavior that reaches either the "moderate" or "intermittent" level would usually earn the unfairness label. At these levels, the customer crosses a threshold.

The third concept is intentionality. The customer who seeks to take advantage and inflict harm, who willfully disrespects the rights of other parties, will almost always deserve the unfairness label. In some cases, customers may seek to harm a company that they believe has harmed them. The customers' behavior in this case is an act of retaliation. When customers blame a company for unfair treatment, there are fair and unfair ways of responding. Intentionally unfair behavior is usually indefensible.

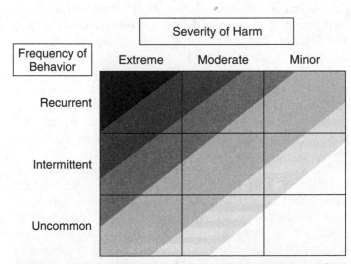

Figure 1 The threshold of customer unfairness. Adapted from Seiders and Berry (1998).

How do companies deal with unfair customers? We contacted executives from a variety of service organizations to solicit their opinions on the topic and to document examples drawn from their experiences. (We restricted our inquiries to consumer services executives based on the assumption that business-to-business services merit a separate exploration.) Our preliminary research reveals that some executives struggle with how to respond to customer unfairness. They don't want to respond in a way that confounds the company's commitment to quality service, which they and others worked hard to instill. Nor do they want to risk offending a still-profitable, albeit problematic, customer. The following comments from four executives illustrate:

- "I think there is a subservient or servant mentality to all service, and to stray from that causes confusion in taking clear and concise action that should be positive for the customer."

- "The lifetime cost of losing a guest exceeds $500, so we go to great lengths to avoid losing them, even when they're wrong. Rather than risk offending guests, we tend to let 'little things' go."

- "My philosophy is that the customer is always right to some degree. It is that matter of degree that determines the action of the company. I believe that if we ever think that the customer is 100% wrong, then we have a high risk of becoming arrogant and not being customer-focused. I know that this may sound crazy, but if we crack open the door to this idea, then I think we can very quickly go down the slippery slope."

- "We are just not used to thinking of guests 'crossing the line.' I don't know that I have ever set up boundaries. I always feel that guests have the right to say what they want and to do what they want, short of inconveniencing another guest or physically harming another guest or employee."

Our position is that companies cannot afford to ignore customer unfairness and should devise a plan to deal with it. Unfair customer behavior can exact a significant toll on employees' job satisfaction and weaken a company's overall service quality. We are not just speculating about this. Recent research by Rupp and Spencer (2006) found that customer injustice increased the degree of effort required for employees to manage their emotions in inter-personal transactions. This increased effort in what is termed *emotional labor* produces added stress, and contributes to employee turnover and overall unwillingness to perform (Grandey, Dickter, & Sin, 2004). Moreover, the injustice of one customer can negatively affect employee behavior toward other customers.

The effects of customer unfairness are often magnified because employees find it difficult to deal with customers who have treated their coworkers disrespectfully, even if the same customers treated them fairly (Rupp, Holub, & Grandey, 2007). Unfair acts are more memorable than typical encounters (Lind & Tyler, 1988), and employees may respond to customer unfairness by discussing incidents with other sympathetic employees, fostering negative word of mouth about customers.

When some customers systematically abuse company policies, such as retail return policies, companies are inclined to either clamp down with tougher rules or increase prices to cover losses. In effect, fair customers are penalized by the actions of unfair customers. Employees are put on the defensive and can become more sensitive to customer manipulation, and more inclined to question the sincerity of customers' communications and the motives that lie behind their actions (Tyler & Bies, 1990). The dynamic can turn adversarial. In short, both employees and customers pay for other customers' misdeeds.

3. Types of Unfair Customers

Over the last 30 years, justice research has focused on three types of justice. *Distributive justice* relates to the outcomes of decisions or allocations; *procedural justice* relates to the procedures used to arrive at those outcomes; and *interactional justice* relates to interpersonal treatment and communication. Interactional justice is demonstrated by interpersonal fairness (i.e., when individuals are treated with dignity and respect) and informational fairness (i.e., when communications are truthful and important decisions are explained) (Rupp & Spencer, 2006). Many studies have found that interactional injustice produces particularly strong responses.

Our exploration of customer unfairness led us to identify distinct types of problem customers. The categories we discuss are neither mutually exclusive nor comprehensive, but describe the most common and problematic types of unfair customers. Each category highlights a different facet of customer unfairness, although some behaviors may logically fit into more than one category. We exclude customers who use stolen credit cards, manipulate price tags, steal merchandise, and stage 'accidents' in service facilities (see, for example, Fullerton & Punj, 2004). The scenarios we consider involve more ambiguity than clear-cut illegality.

3.1. Verbal Abusers

Verbal abusers lash out at employees in a blatantly offensive and disrespectful manner whether in face-to-face transactions, over the telephone, or via the Internet. The verbal abuser capitalizes on the power imbalance commonly present in service encounters: the customer who is 'always right' has the upper hand by default and an opportunity to push the boundaries of fair behavior. One healthcare executive profiled this customer type as "patients and family members who belittle, demean, intimidate, and abuse staff members, and threaten litigation at the slightest lapse in service." Verbal abusers bully front-line employees who typically lack the freedom to defend themselves and, in fact, are expected not to react visibly to unfair treatment by customers. Given the importance of interactional injustice, it is no surprise that the verbal abuser's behavior can have such negative effects on employees.

Customers' verbal abuse of employees is probably more pervasive than most service industry executives would want to admit. There is no accepted protocol for managing a verbal abuse episode, and we suspect that most often this type of incident is not managed. Our favorite story involves the owner of a bicycle store well known for its dedication to customer service. A father was picking up a repaired bicycle for his daughter, who, without telling him, had approved the recommended replacement of both tires (a $40 service). Although the employee patiently and repeatedly explained that the purchase was approved and offered to further verify it, the customer made accusatory remarks and yelled at her angrily, saying at one point, "Either you think I'm stupid or you're stupid. You're trying to rip me off." At that point, Chris Zane, the store's owner, walked up to the customer and said, "I'm Chris Zane; get out of my store and tell all your friends!" After the customer wordlessly slapped $40 on the counter and stormed out, the besieged employee looked at Zane and asked "'. . . and tell all your friends'?"

Zane explained to her, and other employees who had gravitated to the front of the store, that he wanted it to be clear that he valued his employee infinitely more than a rude, belligerent customer. "I also explained that this was the first time I had ever thrown a customer out of the store and that I would not tolerate my employees being mistreated by anyone. . . . I believe that my employees need to know that I respect them and expect them to respect our customers. Simply, if I am willing to fire an employee for mistreating a customer (and I have), then I must also be willing to fire a customer for mistreating an employee."

Verbal abusers can also have a profound effect on other customers. This is illustrated by a customer who, during a lunch rush at a very busy restaurant location, insisted that his steak be prepared rare. Although a manager apologized and explained that each steak is prepared uniformly in order to maintain the best quality (and said there would be no charge for the lunch), the customer continued to voice his disapproval to the staff, creating a disturbance that distracted them and degraded the overall experience of the surrounding customers.

In another incident, two customers in a bar loudly criticized the bartender for assisting other patrons before them and then rebuked the restaurant manager who intervened to try to calm them down. The manager then went to the kitchen to check on the progress of their food; when he returned, the two customers were leaving and shouting obscenities as they walked out. A common device of the verbal abuser is the threat to report employees and/or their facility 'to corporate,' a way to prolong employee unease after the offensive incident is over.

3.2. Blamers

Whereas verbal abusers bring misery primarily to customer contact employees, blamers will indict a company's products, policies, and people at all levels for any perceived shortfall. With blamers, 'the company is always wrong.'

Because customers play a co-producer role in many services, they affect the service quality and final outcome. Blamers, however, never see themselves in any way responsible for the outcome, regardless of the scenario. Causal inferences or attributions individuals use to assess the failure of a product or service performance are based on the locus of blame and whether or not the incident could have been controlled

(Sheppard, Lewicki, & Minton, 1992). From the blamer's perspective, not only is the company always at fault, but the perceived problem is always controllable.

Blamers are not discriminate about where they voice discord, and every service provider is familiar with this type of customer. A tennis coach had been working with an adult student for about six months when the student learned that an opponent in an upcoming match had worked briefly with the same coach in the past. The student asked for and received specific advice from the coach on how to win the match by attacking the opponent's greatest weaknesses. However, the opponent had corrected these weaknesses and much to the student's chagrin, she could find no way to beat her. In the clubhouse immediately after the match, she raged at her coach for not preparing her well, giving her poor information and lousy lessons, and causing her to lose the match.

In another example, a customer called the headquarters of a national casual dining chain to complain about the price of its cocktails. It seems the gentleman had spent $86 in the bar of this restaurant having drinks and appetizers after work the previous evening. He wanted to talk to someone about what he considered the excessive price of the drinks and how unfair he thought the cost. The switchboard operator noted the caller's angry tone and put him through to the president of the company.

The man re-explained to the president and said he could not believe the restaurant had charged him $7.50 for each of the beverages that he ordered. When asked how many he had consumed, the man said that was beside the point. The president asked the number in the man's party, and the man said only two. The president asked the man when he learned that the drinks were $7.50, which he said was after he paid the bill. The president then asked what the company might do to make it right. The customer replied that he wanted all of his money back; the president responded that this was unfair, as the customer and his guest had consumed enough appetizers and drinks to total $86. A full refund would not be equitable.

The customer became extremely angry, threatening to go online and destroy the company, report it to the Better Business Bureau, and picket in front of its restaurants for the next month. He raised his voice and asserted, "You will feel the effects of my negative PR efforts for a long time to come." Frustrated at the angry customer's threats, the president asked the customer how he could resolve this negative situation without giving the customer his money back for the food and drinks he consumed. The customer calmed down, thought about it, and told the president that if the company donated double the amount of the bill to the customer's favorite charity, he would consider the situation resolved. The president agreed to do so in order to move past the situation and end the disagreement.

The blamer is a particularly difficult type of customer for the healthcare industry. Patients who fail to take responsibility for their own health status often are blamers. Many such patients believe that a treatment cure exists for every condition and thus see no need to take measures to improve their own health. In one case, a patient was referred to a hospital's patient relations department after lodging serious complaints with the president's office. The patient claimed that his wound from surgery failed to heal because the staff ignored his complaints. In reality, the patient was non-compliant with recommended diet and wound care, refused to follow his doctor's recommendations for exercise and physical therapy, and failed to return for a follow-up appointment. At each point of contact, the patient threatened to hire a malpractice attorney.

This example may sound extreme, but in fact we heard a number of such stories. One healthcare professional noted, "I have been in patient relations for more than ten years now, and I can attest to the fact that these patients are a huge burden on the healthcare system. They tie up resources that could be used to improve services for all of our patients." An executive from a different healthcare institution expressed a similar view: "I hear from the same patients over and over again, and once a resolution is offered, many times it's a prolonged argument because it's their way or no way. Unfortunately, these cases are no longer rare."

3.3. Rule Breakers

Rule breakers readily ignore policies and procedures when they find them to be inconvenient or at odds with their own goals. Rule breakers generally ignore the honor code by which other customers abide. In chronic cases, a rule breaker may be a mild version of a con artist. Rule breakers are not concerned with equity, which is the first principle of distributive justice. Equity exists in an exchange when participants' rewards equal their contributions; rule breakers seek to optimize their rewards at the expense of the company. This not only harms the company, but also puts company employees in a tenuous and uncomfortable situation as they attempt to protect their employer from customer wrongdoing.

The damage done by rule breakers varies, of course, based on the nature of the rules and polices that are being broken. A restaurant that offers "all you can eat" shrimp entrees encounters some patrons who share with their tablemates, even though the menu clearly states that the price is per person. Managers are not quick to put servers in the awkward position of having to remind guests they are breaking the rule, but will do so if the 'sharing' gets out of hand.

A retailer with a catalog operation is subject to 'customers who bend the facts' (in the words of one executive) when post-delivery complainers assert that a telephone sales associate told them that shipping was free. When this happens, a company representative will listen to a tape of the original call and will usually hear the shipping charges discussed. For smaller transactions with first-time customers, the retailer apologizes, deducts the shipping charge, and restates the shipping fee policy for future transactions. For larger transactions, the customer is told that the call was reviewed and the company is not sure why there was confusion. Once customers realize that a company representative has reviewed the call and knows what actually was said, they rarely demand a shipping refund. "It's a nice way of saying we know what happened without becoming confrontational," explains a company manager.

One type of rule breaker can be termed a *rule maker*. Rule makers expect to be exempted from the rules and demand special

treatment because of perceived superior status. Both rule breakers and rule makers demonstrate unfairness to other customers who are behaving according to norms and convention. When certain customers are allowed to break the rules because of their social or financial status, the equality principle of distributive justice is defied (Grover, 1991). A hospital executive describes the rule maker in this way:

"We have had patients who believe that there is some special level of care that we are constantly holding back, and if we knew how special they were that they would get this special executive level care. This is common in the family of trustees and board members. These are families that expect to be cared for only by departmental chairmen. We have coined the concept *chairman syndrome.*"

Often, it is the family-member-turned-advocate who demands to make the rules. For example, a patient's daughter insisted, "I want all of the labs printed out each day and handed to me when I walk in in the morning." A patient's son threatened, "I am an attorney and I demand to know what is going on with my mother!" A corporate chairman transferred his child by private jet to a hospital in another city when his company's physicians (non-pediatric, without privileges to practice in the hospital) were not allowed to direct the team of hospital physicians who were treating the child. These scenarios seem almost amusing until one considers the extent to which medical staff members and other hospital patients may be adversely affected by this disregard for the rules.

3.4. Opportunists

Opportunists have their antennae up for easy paths to personal financial gain. This customer's modus operandi can be demanding compensation by fabricating or exaggerating problems or flaws in a product or service. While this type of opportunist stiffs the company, there is a second type that stiffs 'the little guy.' These penny-ante opportunists, for example, don't tip (or don't adequately tip) service employees because they don't have to; that is, they can get away with it. This behavior is distasteful because, like many cases of verbal abuse, it hurts front-line employees whose tips often represent a significant percentage of their pay.

Opportunists frequently use gamesmanship to optimize their gain. A customer observed a plumbing problem in a restaurant restroom and complained to the manager, who called a plumbing service for the repair, and sent an employee to clean up. The customer contacted the company's customer relations office, complained about the state of the restroom, and requested a refund for his party's $80 meal. In response, the company sent $30 in gift certificates, in addition to an $80 check and an apology. The customer called the company again, stating that $30 was not enough to cause him to return to the restaurant because it would not cover the cost of his dining companions' meals. He was persistent, calling several times to express his displeasure in the amount of the gift certificates. In turn, the company sent an additional $50 in gift certificates, bringing the total compensation to $160, a nice return for encountering a plumbing problem.

The opportunist may not be a chronic gold digger, but rather just someone who recognizes an opportunity to take financial advantage of a company's service failure and recovery efforts. For example, when an ambulatory surgery patient complained to her hospital that her lingerie had been lost, she was offered reimbursement. She claimed that the cost was $400 and, because this was an unusually high amount, the hospital inquired about the value of the items. The patient said she had not kept the receipts. To maintain good will, the hospital paid the $400 and apologized.

The opportunist doesn't require a service failure to take action. Some users of professional services, for example, maneuver to gain pro bono consultation from a prior provider. A communications coach periodically receives 'pick your brain' phone calls from former clients. Because these customers don't intend to pay for this 'informal' advice, the consultant is forced into an awkward position by clients attempting to exploit the relationship.

3.5. Returnaholics

This customer is a hybrid, with traits common to rule breakers and opportunists but engaged in a specific type of activity: returning products to stores. Returnaholics are rule breakers in that they don't adhere to the spirit of the company's return policies, whereby returns are accepted for defective products, a post-purchase change of mind, and gift exchange. In many cases, the returnaholic never intends to keep the product to begin with. Returnaholics are opportunists because they exploit retailer return policies for their own benefit. There are two types of returnaholics: situational and chronic.

Situational returnaholics become active under certain conditions. For example, one retailer's sales of equipment such as snow blowers, generators, and chainsaws would spike just before a major weather event but then fall precipitously shortly thereafter when many customers returned new *and* used equipment, and even products such as ice melt and flashlights, demanding refunds. It was not unusual for a store to see more than half the generators sold the week before a storm returned within two weeks after the storm. This phenomenon was a painful and expensive exercise for the retailer and its vendors. Reluctantly, the company adopted a stricter return policy covering specific items to better manage after-the-storm return rates.

Some situational returners use an item until it is damaged or worn out and then return it for a full refund or new item, claiming it is defective because it 'should have held up better.' They expect the refund to be 100% of purchase price because they believe that retailers carry a manufacturer's warranty for all items indefinitely.

Chronic, or serial, returnaholics are referred to by some store operators as "rental" customers. One customer of a men's shoe and accessories chain started shopping at two of the company's stores in 2001. The customer would often buy a product in store A and return it (after wearing it) to store B, using a different name for the return transaction. He also would complain to upper management about quality or the service he received in hopes of getting discounts on future purchases. The company realized this pattern of behavior spanned six years, once it figured out that all of this activity involved one customer rather than two. In that period, the customer had purchased 23 pairs of shoes and returned 17 for net sales of $381 (which obviously did not come close to covering the cost of 17 pairs of worn and returned shoes). When the customer was contacted about his serial returning behavior, he became angry; he was told it was obvious the company could not please him and that it could no longer afford to do business with him.

Chronic returnaholics can be very crafty. Some purchase expensive items with credit cards to earn rewards or airline points and then return the merchandise during certain periods of the billing cycle when the points will not be removed from their account. Some purchase large quantities of items, try to sell them on the Internet or in private shops, and then return them for a refund if they don't sell. Some interior designers will purchase items for a specific event, such as an open house or a staged model home, and then return the items for a refund. These are but a few examples of how chronic returnaholics operate.

4. What Managers Can Do

Unfair customers need to be dealt with effectively. They can be a big problem for poorly managed companies with customer unfriendly policies and practices that provoke retaliatory customer behavior. Unfair customers also can bedevil well-managed companies that devote considerable energy and investment to serving customers superbly. After all, these companies build their culture on delivering an excellent experience and value to customers. As a long-time operations executive of one of America's most admired supermarket chains told us:

"I think companies that are truly committed to customer service have a difficult time dealing with unfair customers. We always [tell] our store managers that we will give the unfair customer the benefit of the doubt one or two times. The third time, we [will] fire them as a customer."

So, what should managers do about unfair customers?

4.1. Manage Customers to a Standard of Behavior

Companies cannot build a reputation for service excellence unless, in addition to serving customers competently, they treat them with respect and commitment. Treating customers with respect and commitment requires an organizational culture in which employees, themselves, are treated with respect and commitment. Managers that allow customers to behave badly (e.g., to verbally abuse employees, to create a disturbance, to rip off the company) in the name of "customer service" undermine the organizational culture upon which excellent service depends. Appeasing a customer who doesn't deserve appeasement does not go unnoticed within the organization. The bicycle shop owner who ordered an abusive customer out of the store strengthened his culture that day, rather than weakened it.

Just as managers need to manage employees, they should also "manage" customers when the situation warrants. A good manager certainly would intervene if made aware of an employee who treated customers rudely or broke important company policies. Likewise, a manager should be ready to intervene when made aware of customer misbehavior. Effective "customer management," as illustrated by the manager's intervention in the bar ruckus, demonstrated to employees and nearby customers that the disruptive party's behavior was unacceptable and would not be allowed to continue. If the customers did quiet down, the bartender could more easily interact with them because the manager, and not he, addressed their misbehavior.

4.2. Don't Penalize Fair Customers

Companies should design their business operations for the vast majority of their customers who are fair and responsible, rather than for the unfair minority. Firms should not allow unfair customer behavior to instigate needlessly restrictive policies that disrespect the good intentions of most customers. The better approach, for the business culture and reputation, is to deal fairly but firmly with unfair customers specifically.

The retailer experiencing heavy returns of outdoor power equipment following a major storm illustrates this guideline. The retailer could have done nothing, in effect enabling unreasonable customer behavior. Alternatively, the company could have installed a more restrictive return policy for all merchandise, which would have affected all customers, not just returnaholics, and likely hurt the company's reputation for customer service. The company's implementation of a more restrictive return policy for specific products with high afterstorm return rates made returns more difficult for situational returnaholics. The new policy was designed specifically to deal with opportunistic customers.

The goodwill created by *not* treating all customers as untrustworthy is an investment worth making. A supermarket operations executive illustrates this lesson with the following story:

"When I was at [Company X], we had a policy that if customers forgot their checkbook, we would let them leave with their groceries after filling out a simple IOU. The great majority of customers would immediately return to pay the amount. This policy created a great deal of positive goodwill. However, every year we had to write off a significant amount of loss because some customers would not come back to pay off the IOU. I remember one year it was in excess of $30,000. We would make attempts to recover the money, but I don't recall trying to prosecute anyone for it. Our CFO wanted to stop giving the IOUs, but I would not let him. I treated it as a marketing expense because it created so much goodwill. Interestingly, when we started accepting credit, I thought that the loss number would plunge, assuming customers would carry their credit card and use that instead of a check. However, the loss number remained the same. I believe there will always be customers who will take advantage of you. They are very intentional about their unfairness. The loss incurred by them has to be built into your financial model because you should not penalize the great customers for the deeds of a few bad customers."

4.3. Prepare for Customer Unfairness

Companies should strive to both reduce the frequency of unfair customer episodes and effectively manage specific incidents. This requires advance planning. Managers need to determine the kinds of situations that are most likely to produce unfair customer behavior, given the nature of the company's business. Managers can determine at-risk situations for unfairness by: (1) using past experiences to identify conditions in which customer and company goals might conflict; (2) soliciting employee input on causes of customer unfairness; and (3) surveying customers previously involved in unfairness incidents to gain their perspective on what happened and why. Once at-risk exchanges are identified, managers can evaluate the firm's existing practices to consider needed changes. Employee and customer input can again be helpful at this stage (Seiders & Berry, 1998).

Preparing for customer unfairness also involves investing in education and training of front-line employees and managers on how to prevent and manage the most likely types of incidents. Particular emphasis should be placed on the rationale for company policies that respond to customer misbehavior, or that may encourage it. Employees who intervene need to be able to explain the company's position effectively, which makes communications training for dealing with problem customers a priority. Contact personnel (and their managers) would benefit from focused training on the best ways to interact with verbal abusers, rule breakers, returnaholics, and other problem customers. Organizational justice researchers recommend the use of explanation as an impression management strategy (Sitkin & Bies, 1993). Explanations have been found to diffuse negative reactions and convey respect, among other positive outcomes (Seiders & Berry, 1998), although they will not always be effective with unfair customers.

Collecting pertinent information is another way to prepare for customer unfairness. Information can clarify the appropriate company response to a customer incident. The catalog retailer which captures information on every shipping transaction is better prepared to assess post-transaction claims. Has the customer complained about this issue before? If so, did the company explain its policy? What is the customer's purchase history? "Research is a great way to keep things on the up and up," explains a company executive. "It's on a case-by-case basis."

4.4. Don't Reward Misbehavior

As mentioned, companies that take pride in the quality of their service often struggle to satisfactorily resolve acts of customer opportunism. Such companies are so culturally focused on serving customers well and giving them the benefit of the doubt when problems arise that they may offer more than they should to reach resolution. Doing more than should be done for an unfair customer rewards misbehavior and encourages future incidents.

Companies need to respond to customer unfairness with fairness—and firmness. They should respond to unreasonableness with reason. It isn't easy. The case of the restaurant bathroom plumbing problem is instructive. The customer had a legitimate complaint about the state of the restroom, but then used the incident opportunistically to extract as much as possible from the restaurant. The company's first response of a full refund for the party's meal, a small gift certificate, and an apology was fair. The additional gift certificates went beyond fair. The second helping of gift certificates was excessive, reinforcing customer opportunism. Companies need to be willing to cut the cord with unfair customers.

Sometimes unfair customers recant when dealt with appropriately, as shown by a postscript to the bicycle story. The abusive customer phoned the owner to apologize three hours after being told to leave the store, explaining that he had argued with his wife prior to visiting the store. Once he returned home and verified the accuracy of the store employee's explanation, he realized he had been unreasonable. He asked that the store not blame the daughter for his actions and that he be allowed to shop in the store again. He also commented that he respected the owner for supporting his employee, even if it might mean losing a customer. The owner thanked him for the call, welcomed him back to the store, and indicated that the apology would be conveyed to the employee.

5. Rethinking Old Wisdom

Following the old wisdom—the customer is always right—has operated as the basic rule in business for so long that it has become entrenched as an "absolute truth." The practical reality, however, is that sometimes the customer is wrong by behaving unfairly.

Customer unfairness can exact a heavy cost. Company goodwill, employee relations, financial position, and service to responsible customers can deteriorate when customers engage in unfair tactics such as verbal abuse, blaming, rule breaking, opportunism, and "returnaholism."

Companies must acknowledge the unfair behavior of certain customers and manage them effectively. Some customers may need to be fired. Denying the existence and impact of unfair customers erodes the ethics of fairness upon which great service companies thrive.

References

Fullerton, R. A., & Punj, G. (2004). Repercussions of promoting an ideology of consumption: Consumer misbehavior. *Journal of Business Research, 57*(11), 1239–1249.

Grandey, A. A., Dickter, D. N., & Sin, H. P. (2004). The customer is not always right: Customer aggression and emotion regulation of service employees. *Journal of Organizational Behavior, 25*(3), 397–418.

Grover, S. L. (1991). Predicting the perceived fairness of parental leave policies. *Journal of Applied Psychology, 76*(2), 247–255.

Lind, E. A., & Tyler, T. R. (1988). *The social psychology of procedural justice.* New York: Plenum Press.

Rupp, D. E., & Spencer, S. (2006). When customers lash out: The effects of customers' interactional injustice on emotional labor and the mediating role of discrete emotions. *Journal of Applied Psychology, 91*(4), 971–978.

Rupp, D. E., Holub, A. S., & Grandey, A. A. (2007). A cognitive-emotional theory of customer injustice and emotional labor. In D. De Cremer (Ed.), *Advances in the psychology of justice and affect* (pp. 199–226). Charlotte, NC: Information Age Publishing.

Seiders, K., & Berry, L. L. (1998). Service fairness: What it is and why it matters. *Academy of Management Executive, 12*(2), 8–21.

Sheppard, B. H., Lewicki, R. J., & Minton, J. W. (1992). *Organizational justice: The search for fairness in the workplace.* New York: Lexington Books.

Sitkin, S. B., & Bies, R. J. (1993). Social accounts in conflict situations: Using explanations to manage conflict. *Human Relations, 46*(3), 349–370.

Tyler, T. R., & Bies, R. J. (1990). Beyond formal procedures: The interpersonal context of procedural justice. In J. Carroll (Ed.), *Advances in applied social psychology: Business settings* (pp. 77–98). Hillsdale, NJ: Lawrence Erlbaum Associates.

Critical Thinking

1. Which ethical philosophy or perspective underlies the insistence on fairness?

2. Which party has more "right" to fair treatment—the customer or the employee? Under what circumstances would you fire a customer?

First, Make Money. Also, Do Good

STEVE LOHR

Corporate social responsibility efforts have always struck me as the modern equivalent of John D. Rockefeller handing out dimes to the common folk. They may be well-intentioned, but they often seem like small gestures at the margins of what companies are really trying to do: make money.

As well they should, an argument most famously made by the Nobel laureate Milton Friedman decades ago. He called social responsibility programs "hypocritical window-dressing" in an article he wrote for The New York Times Magazine in 1970, titled "The Social Responsibility of Business Is to Increase Its Profits."

But Michael E. Porter, a Harvard Business School professor, may have an answer to the Friedman principle. Mr. Porter is best-known for his original ideas about corporate strategy and the economic competition among nations and regions. Recently, however, he has been promoting a concept he calls "shared value."

Earlier this year, Mr. Porter and Mark R. Kramer, a consultant and a senior fellow in the corporate social responsibility program at the Kennedy School of Government at Harvard, laid out their case in a lengthy article in the Harvard Business Review, "Creating Shared Value: How to Reinvent Capitalism—and Unleash a Wave of Innovation and Growth." Since then, Mr. Porter and Mr. Kramer have been championing the shared-value thesis in conferences, meetings with corporate leaders, and even a conversation with White House advisers.

Shared value is an elaboration of the notion of corporate self-interest—greed, if you will. The idea that companies can do well by doing good is certainly not new. It is an appealing proposition that over the years has been called "triple bottom line" (people, planet, profit), "impact investing" and "sustainability"—all describing corporate initiatives that address social concerns including environmental pollution, natural-resource depletion, public health and the needs of the poor.

The shared-value concept builds on those ideas, but it emphasizes profit-making not just as a possibility but as a priority. Shared value, Mr. Porter says, points toward "a more sophisticated form of capitalism," in which "the ability to address societal issues is integral to profit maximization instead of treated as outside the profit model."

Social problems are looming market opportunities, according to Mr. Porter and Mr. Kramer. They note that while government

programs and philanthropy have a place—beyond dimes, Mr. Rockefeller created a path-breaking foundation—so, increasingly, does capitalism.

The shared-value concept is not a moral stance, they add, and companies will still behave in their self-interest in ways that draw criticism, like aggressive tax avoidance and lobbying for less regulation. "This is not about companies being good or bad," Mr. Kramer says. "It's about galvanizing companies to exploit the market in addressing social problems."

The pair point to promising signs that more and more companies are pursuing market strategies that fit the shared-value model.

Several years ago, executives at General Electric began looking across its portfolio of industrial and consumer businesses, eyeing ways to apply new technology to reduce energy consumption. They were prompted by corporate customers voicing concerns about rising electrical and fuel costs, and by governments pushing for curbs on carbon emissions.

The result was G.E.'s "ecomagination" program, a business plan as well as a marketing campaign. In recent years, the company has invested heavily in technology to lower its products' energy consumption, and the use of water and other resources in manufacturing.

To count in the program, a product must deliver a significant energy savings or environmental benefit over previous designs. G.E. hired an outside environmental consulting firm, GreenOrder, to help in measuring performance. To date, more than 100 G.E. products have qualified, from jet engines to water filtration equipment to light bulbs. In 2010, such products generated sales of $18 billion, up from $10 billion in 2005, when the program began.

"We did it from a business standpoint from Day 1," says Jeffrey R. Immelt, G.E.'s chief executive. "It was never about corporate social responsibility."

Technology has opened the door to markets that have shared-value characteristics. For decades, I.B.M. sold its computers, software and services to city governments around the world, though mainly for back-office chores like managing payrolls. But the Internet, the Web, electronic sensors and steady advances in computing have helped transform I.B.M.'s role, as it now helps cities track and analyze all kinds of data to improve services.

"We've moved from the back office to the core mission of cities—managing traffic, monitoring public health, optimizing water use and crime-fighting," says Jon C. Iwata, a senior vice president.

I.B.M. is now working with about 2,000 cities worldwide as part of its "Smarter Cities" business, which began three years ago. One advanced project is in the sprawling city of Rio de Janeiro, where I.B.M. is designing a computerized command center. It is intended to pull data from dozens of city agencies, as well as weather stations and webcams. One assignment is to closely track heavy rainfall and to predict its impact—where flooding might occur, how traffic should be rerouted, and what neighborhoods may need to be evacuated. The goal is to predict and prepare for the kind of mudslides and floods that killed hundreds of people in April 2010 and left 15,000 homeless.

THE evolution of low-cost Internet and mobile phone technology has also let Intuit pursue opportunities with shared-value attributes. The company offers free online income-tax preparation software and filing services for lower-income households (now earning $31,000 or less). Since 1999, nearly 13 million people have taken advantage of the service.

The cost is relatively inexpensive for Intuit, as the service exploits the efficiency of online distribution; the charge for paying customers is $20 to $50. And the program blurs the line between charity and marketing, because millions of people who are sampling the company's product, may well become paying customers as their incomes rise.

In India, Intuit has begun offering a free information service for farmers that can be accessed on any cellphone. Part-time workers check crop prices at local markets and send the information to Intuit. The company then relays the latest, local price quotations in text messages to subscribing farmers. As a result, the farmers can make smarter decisions about when and where to sell their produce.

The service in India began last year, and 300,000 farmers now use it. In follow-up surveys, farmers report that their earnings are up 25 percent, says Scott Cook, the founder of Intuit and chairman of the executive committee. The company, he adds, is testing ways to make money off the service, perhaps with text ads for simple tractors and fertilizers.

Mr. Cook points to other new business forays that are part of the same strategy. One is an Intuit health debit card for American small businesses that want to pay for some of their employees' medical care but cannot afford conventional health insurance.

"We look for places we can use our strengths as a company to help solve big problems," he says. "You can call that shared value if you like. But I look at it as the business we're in."

Critical Thinking

1. Explain the concept of making money first while doing good along the way.
2. What is Friedman's "shared value" concept?
3. How is the shared value concept an elaboration of corporate self-interest?

Doing Good to Do Well

Corporate Employees Help and Scope Out Opportunities in Developing Countries

ANNE TERGESEN

Last fall, Laura Benetti spent four weeks in rural India, helping women examine stitchery and figure out prices for garments to be sold in local markets.

After working nine-hour days, she and nine colleagues would sleep in a lodge frequented by locals that had spotty access to hot water and electricity. Ms. Benetti, a 27-year-old customs and international trade coordinator for Dow Corning Corp., considered it a plum assignment.

Dow Corning is among a growing number of large corporations—including PepsiCo Inc., FedEx Corp., Intel Corp. and Pfizer Inc.—that are sending small teams of employees to developing countries such as India, Ghana, Brazil and Nigeria to provide free consulting services to nonprofits and other organizations. A major goal: to scope out business opportunities in hot emerging markets.

Despite the promise of long workdays in less-than-cushy surroundings, many employees consider the stints prize postings. There are usually many more applicants than spaces: Intel, for example, says about 5 percent of its applicants win spots in its Education Service Corps.

Though referred to as "volunteer" posts, employees usually continue to receive their regular salaries during the stints, which typically last two to four weeks. They appeal to employees looking to develop new skills and donate time and expertise to those in need—or simply take a break from their routines.

"It gives more meaning to your career," Ms. Benetti says.

At least 27 Fortune 500 companies currently operate such programs, up from 21 in April and six in 2006, according to a survey by CDC Development Solutions, a Washington, D.C., nonprofit that designs and manages these programs.

At a cost of $5,000 to over $20,000 per employee, the programs require a significant investment. It costs International Business Machines Corp., which has the largest such corporate volunteer operation, roughly $5 million a year.

IBM has sent 1,400 employees abroad with its Corporate Service Corps since 2008. Its projects have produced plans to reform Kenya's postal system and develop an eco-tourism industry in Tanzania.

IBM credits its program with generating about $5 million in new business so far, including a contract, awarded in April 2010, to manage two public service programs for Nigeria's Cross River State, says Stan Litow, vice president for corporate citizenship.

Silicone supplier Dow Corning plans to evaluate 15 new business-related ideas generated by the 20 employees it has sent to India since September 2010, says Laura Asiala, director of corporate citizenship. Ms. Asiala declined to discuss specifics, but says the company has "identified opportunities" in affordable housing, energy and other sectors, thanks to volunteers' observations.

The programs drum up good public relations, both internally and externally, via positive media coverage and blogs many participants write from the field.

Companies "gain local name recognition" in the markets they wish to break into, says Deirdre White, president and CEO of CDC Development Solutions.

Company officials also say the popular programs can help them recruit in-demand talent and retain valued employees.

Dow Corning accepted about 10% of the approximately 200 prospective volunteers who applied online for the trips it sponsored in 2010 and 2011. The company says it selects those with strong performance evaluations, and seeks a diverse mix of participants with varying tenure.

The overseas assignments can act as a training ground for future leaders. Caroline Roan, vice president of corporate responsibility and president of the Pfizer Foundation, says some of the 270 people the pharmaceutical giant has sent abroad describe the experience "as a mini-M.B.A."

"They build skills, in part because they are sometimes thrust into situations outside of their comfort zone, which tends to make people more creative," she says.

Chris Marquis, an associate professor at Harvard Business School, was hired by IBM in 2009 to survey its volunteers. His subsequent research shows that alumni of the program remain on the job longer than peers with similar performance and tenure.

"These are the stars at IBM," he says. "If by offering something like this they can retain these people for longer, it is a very smart investment."

Critical Thinking

1. Develop a brief report about the good-works projects of one of the companies named in the article. How do the good-works projects help the company to do well in the marketplace?

2. The article mentions that a major goal of sending employees abroad on good-works projects is "to scope out business opportunities in hot emerging markets." What do you think of this goal? Develop arguments defending the goal as well as denouncing the goal. Bring your arguments to class for class discussion.

3. Beyond the example given in the article of the various good-works projects, can you think of other good things companies might do in order to do well in the marketplace? Make a list of the other good things and bring your list to class discussion.

UNIT 5

Developing the Future Ethos and Social Responsibility of Business

Unit Selections

Learning Outcomes

After reading this Unit, you will be able to:

- Based upon your study of *Annual Editions: Business Ethics,* what are your recommendations for management for developing an ethical culture in a business firm? What steps specifically do you recommend management take to develop and nurture a culture of ethics? Make a list of the steps for management and write a brief explanation of and justification of each step.

- In what areas should organizations become more ethically sensitive and socially responsible over the next five years? Be specific and explain your choices.

- Obtain codes of ethics or codes of conduct from several different professional associations (for example, doctors, lawyers, CPAs). What are the similarities and differences between them? Based upon your analysis of the codes, what specific statements should be included in a code of ethics?

- How useful do you feel codes of ethics are to organizations? Defend your answer.

- What is ethical self-assessment? How might an ethical self-assessment be administered to employees in a business firm?

Student Website
www.mhhe.com/cls

© ColorBlind Images/Blend Images LLC

Business ethics should not be viewed as a short-term "kneejerk reaction" to recently revealed scandals and corruption. Instead, it should be viewed as a thread woven through the fabric of the entire business culture, one that ought to be integral to its design as well as ingrained in its employees. Businesses are built on the foundation of trust in our free-enterprise system. When there are violations of this trust between competitors, between employer and employees, or between businesses and consumers, the entire system of the enterprise ceases to run smoothly.

From a pragmatic viewpoint, the alternative to self-regulated and voluntary ethical behavior and social responsibility on the part of business may be governmental and legislative intervention. From a moral viewpoint, ethical behavior should not exist because of economic pragmatism, governmental edict, or to be in vogue, rather it should exist because it is morally appropriate and right.

This last unit is composed of articles that provide concepts, guidelines, ideas, and principles for developing the future ethos and social responsibility of business. The first article, "Creating an Ethical Culture," discloses how values-based programs can help employees of an organization judge right from wrong. This article offers a framework of seven levels of an ethical organization. The second article, "Outside-the-Box Ethics," discusses five characteristics of an ethical culture. The five characteristics arguably set companies with an ethical culture apart from those companies lacking such an ethical culture. The third article "Hiring Character," presents a look at business leader Warren Buffett's practice of hiring people based on their integrity. The remaining articles discuss the concept of a theoretical basis for diversity, fiduciary principles in shaping ethical and moral duties of managers, and the importance of an ethical self-assessment, what Peter Drucker called the mirror test or the ethics of prudence.

As you conclude this edition of *Annual Edition: Business Ethics* 13/14, please take time to complete Peter Drucker's mirror test and adopt and practice the ethics of prudence. As we examine ourselves ethically, we are strengthened, ethics are renewed, and the profession of business is enhanced.

Internet References

Code of Ethics or Conduct—Key Elements
www.ehow.com/info_8168270_key-elements-code-ethics-conduct.html

Code of Ethics for International Business
www.ehow.com/about_6724519_international-business-code-ethics.html

Code of Ethics—Clashing with Organizational Policies
www.ehow.com/info_8488823_organizational-policies-clashcode-ethics.html

Code of Ethics—What Is a Code of Ethics?
www.wisegeek.com/what-is-a-code-of-ethics.htm

Code of Ethics—Why Writing One Is Not Enough
www.poynter.org/uncategorized/1854/codes-of-ethics-whywriting-one-is-not-enough.html

Ethical Self-Assessment—A Time for Ethical Self-Assessment
www.businessweek.com/managing/content/dec2008/ca20081223_535152.htm

Ethical Self-Assessment—Example of Survey Instrument for Ethical Self-assessment
www.ache.org/newclub/career/ethself.cfm

Importance of Ethics in New Millennium
www.ehow.com/info_8456277_importance-ethics-businessesnew-millennium.html

International Business Ethics Institute (IBEI)
http://business-ethics.org

Institute for Global Ethics
www.globalethics.org

UNU/IAS Project on Global Ethos
www.ias.unu.edu/research/globalethos.cfm

Creating an Ethical Culture

Values-based ethics programs can help employees judge right from wrong.

DAVID GEBLER, JD

While the fate of former Enron leaders Kenneth Lay and Jeffrey Skilling is being determined in what has been labeled the "Trial of the Century," former WorldCom managers are in jail for pulling off one of the largest frauds in history.

Yes, criminal activity definitely took place in these companies and in dozens more that have been in the news in recent years, but what's really important is to take stock of the nature of many of the perpetrators.

Some quotes from former WorldCom executives paint a different picture of corporate criminals than we came to know in other eras:

> "I'm sorry for the hurt that has been caused by my cowardly behavior."
> —*Scott Sullivan, CFO*

> "Faced with a decision that required strong moral courage, I took the easy way out. . . . There are no words to describe my shame."
> —*Buford Yates, director of general accounting*

> "At the time I consider the single most critical character-defining moment of my life, I failed. It's something I'll take with me the rest of my life."
> —*David Myers, controller*

These are the statements of good people gone bad. But probably most disturbing was the conviction of Betty Vinson, the senior manager in the accounting department who booked billions of dollars in false expenses. At her sentencing, U.S. District Judge Barbara Jones noted that Vinson was among the lowest-ranking members of the conspiracy that led to the $11 billion fraud that sank the telecommunications company in 2002. Still, she said, "Had Ms. Vinson refused to do what she was asked, it's possible this conspiracy might have been nipped in the bud."

Judge Jones added that although Ms. Vinson "was among the least culpable members of the conspiracy" and acted under extreme pressure, "that does not excuse what she did."

Vinson said she improperly covered up expenses by drawing down reserve accounts—some completely unrelated to the expenses—and by moving expenses off income statements and listing them as assets on the balance sheet.

Also the company's former director of corporate reporting, Vinson testified at Bernie Ebbers's trial that, in choosing which accounts to alter, "I just really pulled some out of the air. I used some spreadsheets." She said she repeatedly brought her concerns to colleagues and supervisors, once describing the entries to a coworker as "just crazy." In spring 2002, she noted, she told one boss she would no longer make the entries. "I said that I thought the entries were just being made to make the income statement look like Scott wanted it to look."

Standing before the judge at her sentencing, Vinson said: "I never expected to be here, and I certainly won't do anything like this again." She was sentenced to five months in prison and five months of house arrest.

Pressure Reigns

While the judge correctly said that her lack of culpability didn't excuse her actions, we must carefully note that Betty Vinson, as well as many of her codefendants, didn't start out as criminals seeking to defraud the organization. Under typical antifraud screening tools, she and others like her wouldn't have raised any red flags as being potential committers of corporate fraud.

Scott Sullivan was a powerful leader with a well-known reputation for integrity. If any of us were in Betty Vinson's shoes, could we say with 100% confidence that we would say "no" to the CFO if he asked us to do something and promised that he would take full responsibility for any fallout from the actions we were going to take?

Today's white-collar criminals are more likely to be those among us who are unable to withstand the blistering pressures placed on managers to meet higher and tougher goals. In this environment, companies looking to protect themselves from corporate fraud must take a hard look at their own culture. Does it promote ethical behavior, or does it emphasize something else?

In most companies, "ethics" programs are really no more than compliance programs with a veneer of "do the right thing" messaging to create an apparent link to the company's values. To be effective, they have to go deeper than outlining steps to take to report misconduct. Organizations must understand what causes misconduct in the first place.

We can't forget that Enron had a Code of Ethics. And it wasn't as if WorldCom lacked extensive internal controls. But both had cultures where engaging in unethical conduct was tacitly condoned, if not encouraged.

Building the Right Culture

Now the focus has shifted toward looking at what is going on inside organizations that's either keeping people from doing the right thing or, just as importantly, keeping people from doing something about misconduct they observe. If an organization wants to reduce the risk of unethical conduct, it must focus more effort on building the right culture than on building a compliance infrastructure.

The Ethics Resource Center's 2005 National Business Ethics Survey (NBES) clearly confirms this trend toward recognizing the role of corporate culture. Based on interviews with more than 3,000 employees and managers in the U.S., the survey disclosed that, despite the increase in the number of ethics and compliance program elements being implemented, desired outcomes, such as reduced levels of observed misconduct, haven't changed since 1994. Even more striking is the revelation that, although formal ethics and compliance programs have some impact, organizational culture has the greatest influence in determining program outcomes.

Leadership must know how the myriad human behaviors and interactions fit together like puzzle pieces to create a whole picture. An organization moves toward an ethical culture only if it understands the full range of values and behaviors needed to meet its ethical goals.

The Securities & Exchange Commission (SEC) and the Department of Justice have also been watching these trends. Stephen Cutler, the recently retired SEC director of the Division of Enforcement, was matter of fact about the importance of looking at culture when it came to decisions of whether or not to bring an action. "We're trying to induce companies to address matters of tone and culture. . . . What we're asking of that CEO, CFO, or General Counsel goes beyond what a perp walk or an enforcement action against another company executive might impel her to do. We're hoping that if she sees that a failure of corporate culture can result in a fine that significantly exceeds the proverbial 'cost of doing business,' and reflects a failure on her watch—and a failure on terms that everyone can understand: the company's bottom line—she may have a little more incentive to pay attention to the environment in which her company's employees do their jobs."

Measuring Success

Only lagging companies still measure the success of their ethics and compliance programs just by tallying the percentage of employees who have certified that they read the Code of Conduct and attended ethics and compliance training. The true indicator of success is whether the company has made significant progress in achieving key program outcomes. The National Business Ethics Survey listed four key outcomes that help determine the success of a program:

- Reduced misconduct observed by employees,
- Reduced pressure to engage in unethical conduct,
- Increased willingness of employees to report misconduct, and
- Greater satisfaction with organizational response to reports of misconduct.

What's going to move these outcomes in the right direction? Establishing the right culture.

Most compliance programs are generated from "corporate" and disseminated down through the organization. As such, measurement of the success of the program is often based on criteria important to the corporate office: how many employees certified the Code of Conduct, how many employees went through the training, or how many calls the hotline received.

Culture is different—and is measured differently. An organization's culture isn't something that's created by senior leadership and then rolled out. A culture is an objective picture of the organization, for better or worse. It's the sum total of all the collective values and behaviors of all employees, managers, and leaders. By definition, it can only be measured by criteria that reflect the individual values of all employees, so understanding cultural vulnerabilities that can lead to ethics issues requires knowledge of what motivates employees in the organization. Leadership must know how the myriad human behaviors and interactions fit together like puzzle pieces to create a whole picture. An organization moves toward an ethical culture only if it understands the full range of values and behaviors needed to meet its ethical goals. The "full-spectrum" organization is one that creates a positive sense of engagement and purpose that drives ethical behavior.

Why is understanding the culture so important in determining the success of a compliance program? Here's an example: Most organizations have a policy that prohibits retaliation against those who bring forward concerns or claims. But creating a culture where employees feel safe enough to admit mistakes and to raise uncomfortable issues requires more than a policy and "Code training." To truly develop an ethical culture, the organization must be aware of how its managers deal with these issues up and down the line and how the values they demonstrate impact desired behaviors. The organization must understand the pressures its people are under and how they react to those pressures. And it must know how its managers communicate and whether employees have a sense of accountability and purpose.

Categorizing Values

Determining whether an organization has the capabilities to put such a culture in place requires careful examination. Do employees and managers demonstrate values such as respect? Do employees feel accountable for their actions and feel that they have a stake in the success of the organization?

How does an organization make such a determination? One approach is to categorize different types of values in a way that lends itself to determining specific strengths and weaknesses that can be assessed and then corrected or enhanced.

The Culture Risk Assessment model presented in Figure 1 has been adapted from the Cultural Transformation Tools® developed by Richard Barrett & Associates. Such tools provide a comprehensive framework for measuring cultures by mapping values. More than 1,000 organizations in 24 countries have used this technique in the past six years. In fact, the international management consulting firm McKinsey & Co. has adopted it as its method of

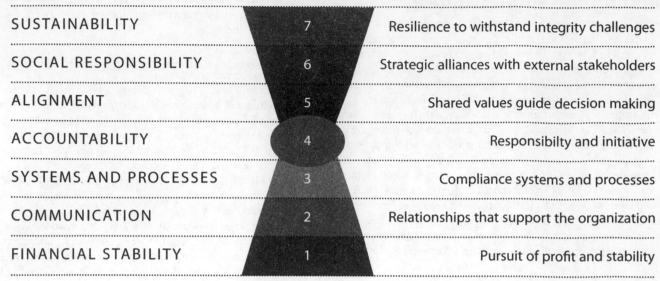

SUSTAINABILITY	7	Resilience to withstand integrity challenges
SOCIAL RESPONSIBILITY	6	Strategic alliances with external stakeholders
ALIGNMENT	5	Shared values guide decision making
ACCOUNTABILITY	4	Responsibilty and initiative
SYSTEMS AND PROCESSES	3	Compliance systems and processes
COMMUNICATION	2	Relationships that support the organization
FINANCIAL STABILITY	1	Pursuit of profit and stability

Based on Cultural Transformation Tools Seven Levels of Consciousness Model, Copyright Barrett Values Centre

Figure 1 Seven levels of an ethical organization.

choice for mapping corporate cultures and measuring progress toward achieving culture change.

The model is based on the principle, substantiated through practice, that all values can be assigned to one of seven categories:

Levels 1, 2, and 3—The Organization's Basic Needs

Does the organization support values that enable it to run smoothly and effectively? From an ethics perspective, is the environment one in which employees feel physically and emotionally safe to report unethical behavior and to do the right thing?

Level 1—Financial Stability. Every organization needs to make financial stability a primary concern. Companies that are consumed with just surviving struggle to focus enough attention on how they conduct themselves. This may, in fact, create a negative cycle that makes survival much more difficult. Managers may exercise excessive control, so employees may be working in an environment of fear.

In these circumstances, unethical or even illegal conduct can be rationalized. When asked to conform to regulations, organizations do the minimum with an attitude of begrudging compliance.

Organizations with challenges at this level need to be confident that managers know and stand within clear ethical boundaries.

Level 2—Communication. Without good relationships with employees, customers, and suppliers, integrity is compromised. The critical issue at this level is to create a sense of loyalty and belonging among employees and a sense of caring and connection between the organization and its customers.

The most critical link in the chain is between employees and their direct supervisors. If direct supervisors can't effectively reinforce messages coming from senior leadership, those messages might be diluted and confused by the time they reach line employees. When faced with conflicting messages, employees will usually choose to follow the lead of their direct supervisor over the words of the CEO that have been conveyed through an impersonal communication channel. Disconnects in how local managers "manage"

these messages often mean that employees can face tremendous pressure in following the lead established by leadership.

Fears about belonging and lack of respect lead to fragmentation, dissension, and disloyalty. When leaders meet behind closed doors or fail to communicate openly, employees suspect the worst. Cliques form, and gossip becomes rife. When leaders are more focused on their own success, rather than the success of the organization, they begin to compete with each other.

Level 3—Systems and Processes. At this level, the organization is focused on becoming the best it can be through the adoption of best practices and a focus on quality, productivity, and efficiency.

Level 3 organizations have succeeded in implementing strong internal controls and have enacted clear standards of conduct. Those that succeed at this level are the ones that see internal controls as an opportunity to create better, more efficient processes. But even those that have successfully deployed business processes and practices need to be alert to potentially limiting aspects of being too focused on processes. All organizations need to be alert to resorting to a "check-the-box" attitude that assumes compliance comes naturally from just implementing standards and procedures. Being efficient all too often leads to bureaucracy and inconsistent application of the rules. When this goes badly, employees lose respect for the system and resort to self-help to get things done. This can lead to shortcuts and, in the worst case, engaging in unethical conduct under the guise of doing what it takes to succeed.

Level 4—Accountability

The focus of the fourth level is on creating an environment in which employees and managers begin to take responsibility for their own actions. They want to be held accountable, not micromanaged and supervised every moment of every day. For an ethics and compliance program to be successful, all employees must feel that they have a personal responsibility for the integrity of the organization. Everyone must feel that his or her voice is being heard. This requires managers and leaders to admit that they don't have all the answers and invite employee participation.

Levels 5, 6, and 7—Common Good

Does the organization support values that create a collective sense of belonging where employees feel that they have a stake in the success of the ethics program?

Level 5—Alignment. The critical issue at this level is developing a shared vision of the future and a shared set of values. The shared vision clarifies the intentions of the organization and gives employees a unifying purpose and direction. The shared values provide guidance for making decisions.

The organization develops the ability to align decision making around a set of shared values. The values and behaviors must be reflected in all of the organization's processes and systems, with appropriate consequences for those who aren't willing to walk the talk. A precondition for success at this level is building a climate of trust.

Level 6—Social Responsibility. At this level, the organization is able to use its relationships with stakeholders to sustain itself through crises and change. Employees and customers see that the organization is making a difference in the world through its products and services, its involvement in the local community, or its willingness to fight for causes that improve humanity. They must feel that the company cares about them and their future. Companies operating at this level go the extra mile to make sure they are being responsible citizens. They support and encourage employees' activities in the community by providing time off for volunteer work and/or making a financial contribution to the charities that employees are involved in.

Level 7—Sustainability. To be successful at Level 7, organizations must embrace the highest ethical standards in all their interactions with employees, suppliers, customers, shareholders, and the community. They must always consider the long-term impact of their decisions and actions.

Employee values are distributed across all seven levels. Through surveys, organizations learn which values employees bring to the workplace and which values are missing. Organizations don't operate from any one level of values: They tend to be clustered around three or four levels. Most are focused on the first three: profit and growth (Level 1), customer satisfaction (Level 2), and productivity, efficiency, and quality (Level 3). The most successful organizations operate across the full spectrum with particular focus in the upper levels of consciousness—the common good—accountability, leading to learning and innovation (Level 4), alignment (Level 5), social responsibility (Level 6), and sustainability (Level 7).

Some organizations have fully developed values around Levels 1, 2, and 3 but are lacking in Levels 5, 6, and 7. They may have a complete infrastructure of controls and procedures but may lack the accountability and commitment of employees and leaders to go further than what is required.

Similarly, some organizations have fully developed values around Levels 5, 6, and 7 but are deficient in Levels 1, 2, and 3. These organizations may have visionary leaders and externally focused social responsibility programs, but they may be lacking in core systems that will ensure that the higher-level commitments are embedded into day-to-day processes.

Once an organization understands its values' strengths and weaknesses, it can take specific steps to correct deficient behavior.

Starting the Process

Could a deeper understanding of values have saved WorldCom? We will never know, but if the culture had encouraged open communication and fostered trust, people like Betty Vinson might have been more willing to confront orders that they knew were wrong. Moreover, if the culture had embodied values that encouraged transparency, mid-level managers wouldn't have been asked to engage in such activity in the first place.

The significance of culture issues such as these is also being reflected in major employee surveys that highlight what causes unethical behavior. According to the NBES, "Where top management displays certain ethics-related actions, employees are 50 percentage points less likely to observe misconduct." No other factor in any ethics survey can demonstrate such a drastic influence.

So how do compliance leaders move their organizations to these new directions?

1. **The criteria for success of an ethics program must be outcomes based.** Merely checking off program elements isn't enough to change behavior.
2. **Each organization must identify the key indicators of its culture.** Only by assessing its own ethical culture can a company know what behaviors are the most influential in effecting change.
3. **The organization must gauge how all levels of employees perceive adherence to values by others within the company.** One of the surprising findings of the NBES was that managers, especially senior managers, were out of touch with how nonmanagement employees perceived their adherence to ethical behaviors. Nonmanagers are 27 percentage points less likely than senior managers to indicate that executives engage in all of the ethics-related actions outlined in the survey.
4. **Formal programs are guides to shape the culture, not vice versa.** People who are inclined to follow the rules appreciate the rules as a guide to behavior. Formal program elements need to reflect the culture in which they are deployed if they are going to be most effective in driving the company to the desired outcomes.

Culture may be new on the radar screen, but it isn't outside the scope or skills of forward-thinking finance managers and compliance professionals. Culture can be measured, and finance managers can play a leadership role in developing systematic approaches to move companies in the right direction.

Critical Thinking

1. Whose values should guide an organization? Senior management? Middle management? "Workers"? Investors?
2. What might happen in an organization that switched "resilience to withstand integrity challenges" and "pursuit of profit and stability" on the right hand side of the seven levels of an ethical organization, while leaving the left hand side as is?

DAVID GEBLER, JD, is president of Working Values, Ltd., a business ethics training and consulting firm specializing in developing behavior-based change to support compliance objectives. You can reach him at dgebler@workingvalues.com.

From *Strategic Finance*, May 2006, pp. 29–34. Copyright © 2006 by Institute of Management Accountants-IMA. Reprinted by permission via Copyright Clearance Center.

Outside-the-Box Ethics

Take "boring" out of ethics training.

Luis Ramos

In the quest for an ethical culture, leaders are finding that one-size-fits-all ethics training doesn't work. *Right-sizing* behavior starts with messaging that speaks directly to employees about specific ethical issues they are likely to encounter on the job. And it delivers the resources and tools they need to do the right thing when it comes to their own actions and to speak out against unethical activity by others when they see it.

Companies that consistently rank high on the lists of *best corporate citizens* tend to make ethics training part of a company-wide initiative to promote integrity. They look for ways to tackle tough subjects and benchmark results to ensure that people don't just get the message, but understand and apply it. These companies see that an investment in an ethical workplace delivers dividends—including a more unified workforce and stock growth.

Cisco does ethics right. With more than 65,000 employees worldwide, building and sustaining an ethical culture is complicated, but the commitment the company has made to an ethical workplace has earned it the status of "repeat performer" on the *Corporate Responsibility Officer's* (CRO's) 100 Best Corporate Citizens.

Five Key Characteristics

Five key characteristics set apart companies with an ethical culture:

1. Leaders Encourage a Two-Way Dialogue about Business Conduct

The message about ethics starts at the top with support from executives and top management who show their commitment to an ethical workplace by modeling behaviors they want to instill in employees. Words like *trust, honesty, values* are part of the vernacular in an ethical company. Internal and external communications reflect the behavioral expectations for every stakeholder.

2. The Company's Code of Ethics Is a Living Document

A code that's built to satisfy curious investors or to fill newhire packets underserves the company. A code should represent the centerpiece of an ethical culture and serve as a ready resource. It should also reflect the look, tone, and voice of the company. Although crafters should work with the legal department to review and approve policies, the code should reflect an easy-to-read style that reinforces the company's core values, and guides ethical decision-making.

When Cisco rewrote its *Code of Conduct,* active voice and user-friendly language drove the process. Once topics were defined, each section began with an affirmative statement written in an employee voice—"I Respect Others," "I Protect What Is Ours," "I Follow the Law." The language was conversational in tone, suggestive of one Cisco employee speaking to another. The design was crafted to complement the user-friendly style, with quick-read call-out boxes that helped employees to "Connect with the Code," "Learn More" links that provided more detailed policy and "What If" scenarios that customized the Code to address Cisco-specific issues.

Although Cisco's Code won awards, the real winners were Cisco employees: 95 percent of them agreed that the new Code was easy to read and comprehend. And a code that's easy to read is also likely to be easy to follow.

3. Ethics Isn't a "Program" but a Way of Doing Business

The word *program* suggests a starting and stopping point—not a defining feature of an ethical culture. In its Code, Cisco emphasizes "doing the right thing is part of our DNA." An ethical culture is the result of a continuous, dynamic process that engages every employee; keeping the ethics *message* visible through media keeps ethical *behavior* at the forefront.

Branding enhances visibility—a name makes an ethics initiative recognizable. Then promote it using media that "fit" your workplace and employee demographics. Monthly manager meetings provide great forums for discussing conflicts of interest, proprietary information, or corporate gift policy. A mix of traditional communication vehicles and customized interactive components—translated into every language that employees speak—helps to disperse and reinforce the message about ethics.

4. Training about Ethics Is Relevant, Maybe Even Fun

If the people depicted in an ethics training don't look or sound like its employees or face ethical situations that employees face, the message won't resonate with them. If the messaging is one-way, they will tune out. If the training is long and boring, they will multitask until it's over.

Cisco knew that ethics initiatives needed to appeal to a global workforce that was highly technical. They wanted something dynamic and interactive, easily accessible from desktops and relevant to the Cisco experience.

The result was "Ethics Idol" a series of four, fun modules, each of which introduced an animated "contestant" who told the story of his or her ethical dilemma using action-packed visuals and witty song parody. Once each episode played out, three quirky judges offered their opinion and employees voted on which judge provided the most ethical answer.

The parody of *American Idol* created a buzz about ethics, winning awards and showing that learning about ethics didn't have to be rote, boring, or easy. Scenarios were designed so that the proper course of action wasn't obvious.

5. Employees Are Actively Engaged as Corporate Citizens, Aligned with the Company's Values

A poster on the wall tells employees that ethical behavior is important. A certification program tells employees that ethical behavior is mandatory. Thanks to an effective launch and a multilingual format, Cisco's annual *Code of Business Conduct* certification process was seamless; within the four-week period of the certification campaign, 98 percent of employees certified that they had received and read the *Code* and, within 10 weeks, 99.6 percent of employees certified.

Companies with an ethical culture ensure employees have the resources they need to promote ethics. Leaders have the power to shape and sustain an ethical culture and inspire people to do the right thing.

Critical Thinking

1. How does Cisco's overall approach to ethical business behavior compare with the approach held by your academic institution toward ethical behavior?

2. Describe a situation in own job (or in a job that you have held in the past) that could illustrate how *ethics is a way of doing business*.

LUIS RAMOS is CEO of The Network, providing ethics and compliance services. Visit www.towinc.com.

Hiring Character

In their new book, *Integrity Works,* authors Dana Telford and Adrian Gostick outline the strategies neces- sary for becoming a respected and admired leader. In the edited excerpt that follows, the authors present a look at business leader Warren Buffett's practice of hiring people based on their integrity. For sales and marketing executives, it's a practice worth considering, especially when your company's reputation with customers—built through your salespeople—is so critical.

DANA TELFORD AND ADRIAN GOSTICK

This chapter was the hardest for us to write. The problem was, we couldn't agree on whom to write about. We had a number of great options we were mulling over. Herb Brooks of the Miracle on Ice 1980 U.S. hockey team certainly put together a collection of players whose character outshined their talent. And the results were extraordinary. We decided to leave him out because we had enough sports figures in the book already. No, we wanted a business leader. So we asked, "Who hires integrity over ability?"

The person suggested to us over and over as we bandied this idea among our colleagues was Warren Buffett, chairman of Berkshire Hathaway Inc.

Sure enough, as we began our research we found we had not even begun to tell Buffett's story. But we were reluctant to repeat his story. Buffett had played an important part in our first book. And yet, his name kept coming up. So often, in fact, that we finally decided to not ignore the obvious.

Perhaps more than anyone in business today, Warren Buffett hires people based on their integrity. Buffett commented, "Berk- shire's collection of managers is unusual in several ways. As one example, a very high percentage of these men and women are independently wealthy, having made fortunes in the businesses that they run. They work neither because they need the money nor because they are contractually obligated to—we have no contracts at Berkshire. Rather, they work long and hard because they love their businesses."

The unusual thing about Warren Buffett is that he and his longtime partner, Charlie Munger, hire people they trust—and then treat them as they would wish to be treated if their positions were reversed. Buffett says the one reason he has kept working so long is that he loves the opportunity to interact with people he likes and, most importantly, trusts.

Buffett loves the opportunity to interact daily with people he likes and, most importantly, trusts.

Consider the following remarkable story from a few years ago at Berkshire Hathaway. It's about R.C. Willey, the domi- nant home furnishings business in Utah. Berkshire purchased the company from Bill Child and his family in 1995. Child and most of his managers are members of the Church of Jesus Christ of Latter-day Saints, also called Mormons, and for this reason R.C. Willey's stores have never been open on Sunday.

Now, anyone who has worked in retail realizes the seeming folly of this notion: Sunday is the favorite shopping day for many customers—even in Utah. Over the years, though, Child had stuck to his principle—and wasn't ready to rejigger the for- mula just because Warren Buffett came along. And the formula was working. R.C.'s sales were $250,000 in 1954 when Child took over. By 1999, they had grown to $342 million. Child's determination to stick to his convictions was what attracted Buffett to him and his management team. This was a group with values and a successful brand.

Arnie Ferrin, longtime friend of Child, said, "I believe that [Child] is a man of extreme integrity, and I believe that Warren Buffett was looking to buy his business because he likes to do business with people like that, that don't have any shadows in their lives, and they're straightforward and deal above-board."

This isn't to say Child and Buffett have always agreed on the direction of the furniture store.

"I was highly skeptical about taking a no-Sunday policy into a new territory, where we would be up against entrenched rivals open seven days a week," Buffett said. "Nevertheless, this was Bill's business to run. So, despite my reservations, I told him to follow both his business judgment and his religious convictions."

Proving once again that he believed in his convictions, Child insisted on a truly extraordinary proposition: He would person- ally buy the land and build the store in Boise, Idaho—for about

$11 million as it turned out—and would sell it to Berkshire at his cost if—and only if—the store proved to be successful. On the other hand, if sales fell short of his expectations, Berkshire could exit the business without paying Child a cent. This, of course, would leave him with a huge investment in an empty building.

You're probably guessing there's a happy ending to the story. And there is. The store opened in August of 1998 and immediately became a huge success, making Berkshire a considerable margin. Today, the store is the largest home furnishings store in Idaho.

Child, good to his word, turned the property over to Berkshire—including some extra land that had appreciated significantly. And he wanted nothing more than the original cost of his investment. In response, Buffett said, "And get this: Bill refused to take a dime of interest on the capital he had tied up over the two years."

And there's more. Shortly after the Boise opening, Child went back to Buffett, suggesting they try Las Vegas next. This time, Buffett was even more skeptical. How could they do business in a metropolis of that size and remain closed on Sundays, a day that all of their competitors would be exploiting?

But Buffett trusts his managers because he knows their character. So he gave it a shot. The store was built in Henderson, a mushrooming city adjacent to Las Vegas. The result? This store outsells all others in the R.C. Willey chain, doing a volume of business that far exceeds any competitor in the area. The revenue is twice what Buffett had anticipated.

As this book went to print, R.C. Willey was preparing to open its third store in the Las Vegas area, as well as stores in Reno, Nevada, and Sacramento, California. Sales have grown to more than $600 million, and the target is $1 billion in coming years. "You can understand why the opportunity to partner with people like Bill Child causes me to tap dance to work every morning," Buffett said.

H ere's another example of Buffett's adeptness at hiring character. He agreed to purchase Ben Bridge Jeweler over the phone, prior to any face-to-face meeting with the management.

Ed Bridge manages this 65-store West Coast retailer with his cousin, Jon. Both are fourth-generation owner-managers of a business started 89 years ago in Seattle. And over the years, the business and the family have enjoyed extraordinary character reputations.

Buffett knows that he must give complete autonomy to his managers. "I told Ed and Jon that they would be in charge, and they knew I could be believed: After all, it's obvious that [I] would be a disaster at actually running a store or selling jewelry, though there are members of [my] family who have earned black brits as purchasers."

Talk about hiring integrity! Without any provocation from Buffett, the Bridges allocated a substantial portion of the proceeds from their sale to the hundreds of coworkers who had helped the company achieve its success.

Overall, Berkshire has made many such acquisitions—hiring for character first, and talent second—and then asking these CEOs to manage for maximum long-term value, rather than for next quarter's earnings. While they certainly don't ignore the current profitability of their business, Buffett never wants profits to be achieved at the expense of developing ever-greater competitive strengths, including integrity.

It's an approach he learned early in his career.

W arren Edward Buffett was born on August 30, 1930. His father, Howard, was a stockbroker-turned-congressman. The only boy, Warren was the second of three children. He displayed an amazing aptitude for both money and business at a very early age. Acquaintances recount his uncanny ability to calculate columns of numbers off the top of his head—a feat Buffett still amazes business colleagues with today.

At only six years old, Buffett purchased six-packs of Coca-Cola from his grandfather's grocery store for twenty-five cents and resold each of the bottles for a nickel—making a nice five-cent profit. While other children his age were playing hopscotch and jacks, Buffett was already generating cash flow.

Buffett stayed just two years in the undergraduate program at Wharton Business School at the University of Pennsylvania. He left disappointed, complaining that he knew more than his professors. Eventually, he transferred to the University of Nebraska–Lincoln. He managed to graduate in only three years despite working full time.

Then he finally applied to Harvard Business School. In what was undoubtedly one of the worst admission decisions in history, the school rejected him as "too young." Slighted, Buffett applied to Columbia where famed investment professor Ben Graham taught.

Professor Graham shaped young Buffett's opinions on investing. And the student influenced his mentor as well. Graham bestowed on Buffett the only A+ he ever awarded in decades of teaching.

While Buffett tried working for Graham for a while, he finally struck out on his own with a revolutionary philosophy: He would research the internal workings of extraordinary companies. He could discover what really made them tick and why they held a competitive edge in their markets. And then he would invest in great companies that were trading at substantially less than their market values.

Ten years after its founding, the Buffett Partnership assets were up more than 1,156 percent [compared to the Dow's 122.9 percent], and Buffett was firmly on his way to becoming an investing legend.

In 2004, Warren Buffett was listed by Forbes as the world's second-richest person (right behind Bill Gates), with $42.9 billion in personal wealth. Despite starting with just $300,000 in holdings, Berkshire's holdings now exceed $116 billion. And Buffett and his employees can confidently say they have made thousands of people wealthy.

We often ask business leaders one simple question: Which is more dangerous to your firm—the incompetent new hire or the dishonest new hire? It's the part of our presentation where attendees sit up straight and start thinking.

We always follow the question with an exercise on identifying and hiring integrity. Though it becomes obvious that many of the executives and managers haven't given employee integrity much thought, most of the CEOs in the audiences are increasingly concerned about hiring employees with character.

So, how do you hire workers with integrity? It's possible, but not easy. It is important to spend more time choosing a new employee than you do picking out a new coffee machine. Here are a few simple areas to focus on:

First, ensure educational credentials match the resume. Education is the most misrepresented area on a resume. Notre Dame football coach George O'Leary was fired because the master's degree he said he had earned did not exist, the CEO of software giant Lotus exaggerated his education and military service, and the CEO of Bausch & Lomb forfeited a bonus of more than $1 million because he claimed a fictional MBA.

It is important to spend more time choosing a new employee than you do picking out a new coffee machine.

Job candidates also often claim credit for responsibilities that they never had. Here's a typical scenario:

Job candidate: "I led that project. Saved the company $10 million." Through diligent fact checking, you find an employee at a previous employer who can give you information about the candidate:

Coworker: "Hmm. Actually, Steve was a member of the team, but not the lead. And while it was a great project, we still haven't taken a tally of the cost savings. But $10 million seems really high."

How do you find those things out? Confer with companies where the applicant has worked—especially those firms the person isn't listing as a reference. Talk to people inside the organization, going at least two levels deep (which means you ask each reference for a couple more references). Talk to the nonprofit organizations where the person volunteers. Tap into alumni networks and professional associations. Get on the phone with others in the industry to learn about the person's reputation. Check public records for bankruptcy, civil, and criminal litigation (with the candidate's knowledge). In other words, check candidates' backgrounds carefully (but legally, of course).

We find that most hiring managers spend 90 percent of their time on capability-related questions, and next to no time on character-based questions. In your rush to get someone in the chair, don't forget to check backgrounds and be rigorous in your interviewing for character. Hiring the wrong person can destroy two careers: your employee's—and your own.

Ask ethics-based questions to get to the character issue. We asked a group of executives at a storage company to brainstorm a list of questions they might ask candidates to learn more about their character. Their list included the following questions:

- Who has had the greatest influence on you and why?
- Who is the best CEO you've worked for and why?
- Tell me about your worst boss.
- Who are your role models and why?
- How do you feel about your last manager?
- Tell me about a time you had to explain bad news to your manager.
- What would you do if your best friend did something illegal?
- What would your past manager say about you?
- What does integrity mean to you?
- If you were the CEO of your previous company, what would you change?
- What values did your parents teach you?
- Tell me a few of your faults.
- Why should I trust you?
- How have you dealt with adversity in the past?
- What are your three core values?
- Tell me about a time when you let someone down.
- What is your greatest accomplishment, personal or professional?
- What are your goals and why?
- Tell me about a mistake you made in business and what you learned from it.
- Tell me about a time when you were asked to compromise your integrity.

It's relatively easy to teach a candidate your business. The harder task is trying to instill integrity in someone who doesn't already have it.

Of course, we don't want to imply that it's impossible. Sometimes people will adapt to a positive environment and shine. Men's Wearhouse has certainly had tremendous success hiring former prison inmates, demonstrating everyone should have a second chance.

But integrity is a journey that is very personal, very individual. An outside force, such as an employer, typically can't prescribe it. It's certainly not something that happens overnight. That's one reason many of the CEOs we have talked with prefer promoting people from inside their organizations when possible.

Don Graham, chairman and CEO of the Washington Post Company, said, "There's a very good reason for concentrating your hires and promotions on people who already work in your organization. The best way to predict what someone's going to do in the future is to know what they've done in the past—watch how people address difficult business issues, how they deal with the people who work for them, how they deal with the people for whom they work. You may be able to put on a certain face for a day or even a week, but you're not going to be able to hide the person you are for five or ten years."

Graham tells a story about Frank Batten, who for years ran Landmark Communications and founded The Weather Channel. "Frank is a person of total integrity," Graham says. "Frank once said, 'When you go outside for hire you always get a surprise. Sometimes it's a good surprise. But you never hire quite the person you thought you were hiring.' "

What do you look for in a job applicant? Years of experience? College degree? Specific skill sets? Or do you look for character? If so, you're in good company.

Years ago, Warren Buffett was asked to help choose the next CEO for Salomon Brothers. "What do you think [Warren] was looking for?" Graham asks. "Character and integrity—more than even a particular background. When the reputation of the firm is on the line every day, character counts."

Don't like surprises? Then hire people who have integrity. Want to ensure a good fit with the people you hire? Then hire people who have integrity. Want to ensure your reputation with customers? Then hire people who have integrity.

Are we saying that nothing else matters? No. But we are saying that nothing matters more.

Critical Thinking

1. Describe Warren Buffett's hiring practices that assure he is hiring integrity.

2. What are the top three characteristics that an ethical leader must exhibit (from your perspective)?

From *Integrity Works: Strategies for Becoming a Trusted, Respected and Admired Leader* by **DANA TELFORD** and **ADRIAN GOSTICK**.

Strategic Organizational Diversity: A Model?

FREDERICK TESCH AND FREDERICK MAIDMENT

Using resources, especially human ones, effectively is a key issue facing organizations and their managers, especially the human resource management staffs. Diversity is about the human resources available to an organization, about recognizing and using the breadth and depth of differences in its employees' experiences, backgrounds, and capabilities, and about viewing these differences as assets to the organization (Watson & Kumar, 1992). A key assumption is that diversity in a population should produce a similar diversity in our labor markets and in turn in the workforces derived from those labor markets.

Organizations that pursue workforce diversity are more likely to be successful than ones that do not (Cox & Blake, 1991; Marquez, 2005). Human diversity can actually drive business growth (Robinson & Dechant, 1997). An organization that manages diversity well can, for example, understand its markets better, increase its creativity and innovation, and improve its problem solving, thereby reducing its exposure to risk and increasing its chances of higher returns on investment. Clearly, these effects make workforce diversity a goal worth pursuing.

The major problem encountered in pursuing diversity is the lack of agreement on a definition. A recent study by the Society for Human Resource Management found that "Almost three-quarters of the HR professionals who responded said their organizations had no official definition of diversity. Those who had a definition said it was very broad and included an extensive set of differences and similarities among individuals, such as race, gender, age, etc." (Hastings, 2008, 34). How are we to manage what we have yet to define conceptually or operationally?

Given the potential benefits of workforce diversity, discussion of possible theoretical linkages between diversity and organizational goals has been minimal. What paradigm could account for the range of positive effects? What ideas move diversity from a practical concept to a management principle? Most discussion has focused on the practical matters and applications. Pragmatically, diversity works. Research (Parkhe, 1999) shows that managing diversity well

gives organizations a competitive edge and reduces business risk. Given these robust, positive effects, we need not examine nor debate the mechanisms producing them. Do it; don't analyze it!

Unguided diversity, however, might lead an organization to a state of confusion and to actions not consistent with its strategic goals. Much diversity training appears to promote diversity for diversity's sake, often as a moral or ethical imperative. A stance of maximizing all types of human diversity as an end in itself might lead an organization to some dysfunctional thinking and actions. For example, would having recently hired someone from University X with a degree in Discipline Y prohibit hiring another such applicant? Hiring the second, similar applicant could be seen as promoting intellectual and academic homogeneity. Should an applicant be hired because her constellation of skills, knowledge, abilities, and background is unlike that of any other employee, even if her attributes have no relevance to the organization's goals?

Developing a Model for Diversity

Our thesis is that an organization's quest for diversity should be guided by the organization's goals and needs, not by a diffuse concept of diversity as the means to social responsibility or good citizenship.

There are two paths to building a theory. The first path is developing a model to explain the observed events, just as scientists build constructs to explain the phenomena they study (Kuhn, 1970). The second path, typically used by business disciplines, is borrowing a model or paradigm from another discipline and modifying it to the new phenomena. Ideas from economics, psychology, engineering, and mathematics abound in finance, marketing, and management. For example, in finance, portfolio analysis is a tool for managing stock purchases and sales, but marketing borrowed it to use in managing a portfolio of products (Hedley, 1977). Borrowing and using what works is characteristic of the business disciplines and of business people.

Following the second path, there is a theory of diversity in investments that can be applied to diversity in human resources. This application becomes especially clear when organizations view their employees not as an expense but rather as an asset—a view fundamental to human resources, as opposed to personnel, management. Employees, when viewed as an asset, are the equivalent of stocks in a portfolio.

Modigliani's Theory of Diversity in Investments

Franco Modigliani won the Nobel Prize in Economics for this theory of diversity in investments. He began by distinguishing between systematic and unsystematic risks. Systematic risk, also called market risk, is the risk that affects all securities. "Unsystematic risk is the risk that is unique to a company. It can be eliminated by diversifying the portfolio. Thus, systematic risk and unsystematic risk are referred to as non-diversifiable and diversifiable risk, respectively" (Fabozzi & Modigliani, 1992, pp. 154–55).

Building on this difference, he discusses how risk can be reduced or removed. "[U]nsystematic" risk . . . can be washed away by mixing the security with other securities in a diversified portfolio . . . Increasing diversification gradually tends to eliminate the unsystematic risk, leaving only systematic, i.e., market related risk. The remaining variability results from the fact that the return on every security depends to some degree on the overall performance of the market" (Fabozzi & Modigliani, 1992, p. 135).

There will always be some market (systematic) risk: such is the nature of capitalism where organizations compete with one another in the marketplace. Eliminating these risks requires a centrally planned or monopolistic economy.

The case of unsystematic risk is different since it is unique to a company and can be eliminated by diversifying the portfolio. Modigliani's point is that people can control the amount of risk they accept and that the risk can be eliminated if there is enough diversity. The goal is to maximize the long-term results while minimizing, if not eliminating, unsystematic risk. Individually risky stocks remain in the portfolio, but holding a variety of stocks in a variety of industries minimizes risk. Simply stated, "Don't put all your eggs in one basket."

Joe Watson, a diversity expert, captured the argument when he said "Think about diversity in terms of your stock portfolio. If someone came to you and said they were going to put everything you own in Southeast Asian bonds, that's probably not what you would want to do. People want a balanced portfolio with 10% in this and 20% in that because it's understood in business that over time that is what will give you the best possible outcome. Well, how is the workforce any different? It also needs to be diverse to give companies the best possible outcome" (Harris et al., 2008). The organization's goals and strategy should determine the specific securities/people (i.e., differences) in which it needs to invest and which it should ignore.

Human Resources a La Modigliani

Building a parallel from how investors view their stocks in a portfolio, managers should view employees as assets to be managed, not a cost to minimize. With this perspective, Modigliani's concept of diversity for investments becomes a model for human resources diversity. Diversifying an organization's workforce should reduce the unsystematic (non-market) risk unique to the organization's human resources. The greater the diversity, the lower the organization's controllable risk, and the greater the likelihood of higher financial return as a result of the efforts of the employees.

Diversity in an organization's human resources can, for example, reduce the possibility of groupthink (Janis, 1982), "A mode of thinking that people engage in when they are deeply involved in a cohesive [perhaps homogenous] group, when the members, striving for unanimity, override their motivation to realistically appraise alternative courses of action." Groupthink diminishes the group's capabilities to consider, thoroughly, all realistic courses of action. Groups of people with similar backgrounds, experiences, and educations are more likely to fall prey to groupthink than groups having diversity of those factors. Diversity, when properly managed, brings a richer, stronger set of individuals who should be more resistant to the groupthink trap when dealing with organizational issues.

A classic example of the lack of diversity as a tactical organizational weakness is the famous incident of General Motors introducing their "Chevrolet Nova" into the Latin American market (Schnitzier, 2005). In Spanish the phrase "No va!" translates to "No go!," a costly blunder in marketing to the Spanish speaking countries of Latin America. Had the groups involved in this decision at GM contained diversity that was representative of Latin America the episode could have been avoided.

Strategic diversity is not diversity for diversity's sake (i.e., simply maximizing all differences randomly), but is rather diversity aligned to the organization's goals, strategies, mission, and vision (Bonn, 2005). Strategic diversity encourages developing a pool of relevant diversity and not developing differences that are not strategically relevant. For example, an organization doing business in China should probably not hire people from Argentina to conduct its business in Hong Kong. Diversity makes business sense when it is done strategically, not when it is done simply for the sake of diversity or in the name of moral or philosophical agendas. Doing business in the United State of America requires a diverse workforce because it is such a diverse country. To operate in any other way would not only be illegal (e.g., EEO) but also illogical and detrimental to its long-term success.

Similarly, doing business in Norway requires a workforce reflecting the Norwegian stakeholders and having an understanding of Norwegian markets, practices, and laws.

The only sustainable competitive edge that can be unique to an organization is its workforce (Pfeffer, 1995). Most organizations have access to the same technology, transportation and communication systems, and financial markets. Managers exert little influence on their organization's external environments, but do have some control over internal ones. Diversifying the organization's human resources promotes controlling, minimizing, and perhaps even eliminating unsystematic (non-market) risk. This is the theoretical base for workforce diversity.

A strong corporate culture, one that embraces diversity, is one approach to reducing risks. When an organization's operations are scattered across distances, time zones, and cultures, a strong corporate culture is a significant element of the glue holding the pieces together. But no glue can overcome missing pieces. All the cultural variables surrounding the organization must be adequately represented within that organization. Recruiting, selecting, hiring, promoting, training, and compensating must all reflect the drive for diversity. Not doing so would leave the organization vulnerable in an increasingly competitive marketplace and subject to unsystematic risk. Managing diversity well brings the advantage of reduced unsystematic risk in a factor that is controllable and has the most potential for competitive advantage, that is, its human resources.

Human Resources Implications

The HR diversity model based on Modigliani's thinking supplies an additional base, a business justification, to the case for workforce diversity. Arguing for diversity based on legal compliance, ethical posture, or simple cost reduction cannot carry the day. HR executives and managers need the stronger theoretical position this model provides by eliminating or at least reducing unsystematic or non-market risk to the organization in the area of human resources. Let's look at some typical applications.

As organizations go global, those drawing only on their home countries to staff senior positions practice a form of discrimination that severely limits their long-term capabilities. As corporations, for example, become more globalized, their management staff must do the same in order to reduce the unsystematic risks (Bell & Harrison, 1996). One example would be the few non-USA nationals who lead or have led USA corporations (e.g., Ford Motor Company, NCR).

Diversity as a risk management strategy means that we must go beyond simply having people of diverse backgrounds in our organizations. It argues, as does EEO, that the strategy requires offering everyone the same opportunities for movement and advancement within the organization. No department, division, unit, or level can be permitted to be too homogenous, but its diversity must be structural, not random. And that structural linkage should derive from and reflect the organization's strategic goals.

Workforce diversity promotes the achievement of excellence in human resources and the concurrent reduction of organizational risk leading to enhanced competitiveness and performance. Under these conditions of risk management the cream of the organization's human resources can perform exceptionally. The cream of the workforce that rises to the top is made of richer ingredients and is a better grade of cream (Ng & Tung, 1998).

Diversity's Challenge to Human Resource Management

In today's highly turbulent and hyper-competitive environments, organizations simply cannot afford to allow their competitors the competitive advantage of better workers, managers, and executives, that is, better human resources. To do so is to risk becoming second rate—or even becoming extinct (Collins, 2001; Olson & van Bever, 2008). HR professionals need to develop action plans that are strongly linked to the organization's goals and that guide their recruiting, succession planning, career development, and compensation activities. They must create workforces having diversity that is congruent with the organization's strategic goals and that promotes and ensures equitable treatment and opportunities for all employees.

References

Bell, M. P. & Harrison, D. A. (1996). Using intra-national diversity for international assignments: A model of bicultural competence and expatriate adjustment, *Human Resource Management Review,* Spring, 6(1), 47–74.

Bonn, I. (2005). Improving strategic thinking: A multilevel approach, *Leadership & Organizational Development Journal,* 25(5), 336–354.

Collins, J. (2001). *Good to Great: Why Some Companies Make the Leap—and Others Don't,* New York: Harper Business.

Cox, T. H. & Blake, S. (1991). Managing cultural diversity: Implications for organizational competitiveness, *Academy of Management Executive,* August, 5(3), 45–56.

Fabozzi, F. J., & Modigliani, F. (1992). *Capital Markets: Institutions and instruments,* Englewood Cliffs, NJ: Prentice Hall.

Harris, W., Drakes, S., Lott, A., & Barrett, L. (2008). The 40 best companies for diversity, *Black Enterprise,* 38(12), 94–112.

Hastings, R. (2008). SHRM diversity report a call to action: Majority of companies say they haven't defined diversity, *HRMagazine,* 53(4), April, 34.

Hedley, B. (1977). Strategy and the business portfolio, *Long Range Planning,* February.

Janis, I. (1982). *Groupthink: Psychological studies of policy decisions and fiascos,* Boston: Houghton-Mifflin.

Kuhn, T. (1970). *The structure of scientific revolutions,* Chicago: University of Chicago Press.

Marquez, J. (2005). SHRM survey shows diversity contributes to bottom line (Society for Human Resource Management), *Workforce Management,* 84.12, November 7, 8. Retrieved February 26, 2007, from General Reverence Center Gold database.

Ng, E. S. & Tung, R. L. (1998). Ethno-cultural diversity and organizational effectiveness: A field study, *International Journal of Human Resource Management,* December, 9(6), 980–995.

Olson, M. S. & van Bever, D. (2008). *Stall Points: Most Companies Stop Growing—Yours Doesn't Have To,* New Haven, CT: Yale University Press.

Parkhe, A. (1999). Interfirm diversity, organizational learning, and longevity in global strategic alliances, *Journal of International Business Studies,* Winter, 22(4), 579–601.

Pfeffer, J. (1995). Producing sustainable competitive advantage through the effective management of people, *Academy of Management Executive,* February, 9(1), 55–72.

Robinson, G. & Dechant, K. (1997). Building a business case for diversity, *Academy of Management Executive,* August, 21–31.

Schnitzier, P. (2005). Translating success: Network of language experts key to Pangea Lingua's growth, *Indianapolis Business Journal,* 26(21), August 1, 3.

Watson W. E. & Kumar, K. (1992). Differences in decision-making regarding risk-taking: A comparison of culturally diverse and culturally homogeneous task groups, *Journal of Intercultural Relations,* 16(1), 53–65.

Critical Thinking

1. Explain what you think "strategic organizational diversity" means.

2. Come up with weaknesses of "strategic organizational diversity" and explain how these weaknesses can be ameliorated.

FREDERICK TESCH, Western Connecticut State University, USA.
FREDERICK MAIDMENT, Western Connecticut State University, Connecticut, USA.

Fiduciary Principles: Corporate Responsibilities to Stakeholders

Susan C. Atherton, Mark S. Blodgett, and Charles A. Atherton

Introduction

The lack of trust in American corporations and in corporate management over the recent scandals and financial crisis has increased public and legislative outcry for accountability in business decisions. Frustration is rampant, with "seemingly unending examples of mismanagement, ethical misconduct, and patterned dishonesty of a society dubbed 'the cheating culture'."[1] International competition created tremendous risks and rewards but forced companies to attract investors through creative accounting practices to raise share value. As a result, three decades of corporate greed, inappropriate financial risk-taking and personal misconduct eroded trust in corporate decision-making.[2]

Corporate governance reform initiatives beginning in 2002 were designed to increase financial disclosure and responsibility; however, such legislation is insufficient to rebuild public trust in business. Restoring trust requires that those individuals who manage corporations, i.e., the board of directors and senior officers, comply with requirements for greater accountability and transparency, *and* abide by the legal norms to which boards of directors and management are already subject, as directors and officers are legally bound as fiduciaries owing duties of care and loyalty to the corporation.[3] However, centuries of legal and religious formalization and codification have diminished the actual meaning and purpose of fiduciaries, with the result that modern corporate fiduciaries have limited responsibility toward stakeholders and the greater society. Restoring the original definitions and roles of fiduciaries may legitimize and guide the corporation in developing new relationships with stakeholders.

This paper does not focus on illegal conduct by corporate individuals, although many criminal violations of fiduciary norms involve intentional assessment of the risk of penalties versus potential profits.[4] Rather, the paper examines the limitations of today's corporate fiduciary duties given the original intent of the fiduciary relationship. In particular, we examine the definitions of fiduciaries and fiduciary responsibilities to determine the extent to which formalization and codification have led to avoidance of corporate responsibility. We then revisit the historical and religious origins of fiduciaries in commercial transactions that defined and shaped the integration of moral and ethical duties in business today yet were so narrowly defined that corporate liability became increasingly limited. We propose a modest but well-defined, consistent and universal definition of "fiduciary duties," that could offer corporate managers guidance in developing new approaches to stakeholder relationships—relationships built on expectations of corporate trust and decision-making that maximize shareholder wealth while protecting stakeholders.

The Modern Fiduciary

Most business students and executives today are introduced to the concept of a "fiduciary" in the context of agency law, where a fiduciary is defined as "one who has a duty to act primarily for another person's benefit," and agency is generally defined as "the fiduciary relation that results from the manifestation of consent by one person (a 'principal') to another (an 'agent') that the agent shall act on the principal's behalf and subject to the principal's control, and the agent manifests or otherwise consents so to act."[5] Restatement (Third) of Agency states that proof of an agency relationship requires the existence of the manifestation by the principal that the agent shall act for him; the agent's acceptance of the undertaking; and, the understanding that the principal is in control of the undertaking. The agency relationship that results is founded on trust, confidence, and good faith by one person in the integrity and fidelity of another, creating certain duties owed by each party established in the agency agreement and implied by law.[6] Within the relationship, fiduciaries have a duty of loyalty—the duty to act primarily for another in matters related to the activity and not for the fiduciary's own personal interest.

Fiduciaries also have a duty of good faith—the duty to act with scrupulous good faith and candor; complete fairness, without influencing or taking advantage of the client. The fiduciary relationship, as defined by history and case law, exists in every business transaction. Moreover, the relationship is defined by the specific role or function of the agent toward the principal, i.e., the relationship of corporate management and boards of directors to shareholders, lawyer to client, or broker to client, and governed by the laws associated with those transactions, including criminal and labor law, securities and corporate law, contracts, partnerships, and trusts.[7] The roles of trustees, administrators, and bailees as fiduciaries were of ancient origin, whereas agents appeared only at the end of the eighteenth century.[8] Partners, corporate boards of directors, and corporate officers held fiduciary duties originating with the formation of modern partnerships and corporations, as did majority shareholders, while union leaders held fiduciary roles only when unions were granted power by statute to represent workers in negotiations with management.[9] While modern definitions of these duties remain intact, the scope of the duties greatly varies based on the fiduciary's role, which increases the complexity of analysis required to understand violations of those duties.

The modern definition of "agent" as a fiduciary was first rationalized and clarified as a legal doctrine in 1933:[10] "When the person acting is to represent the other in contractual negotiations, bargainings or transactions involved in business dealings with third persons, or is to appear for or represent the other in hearings or proceedings in which he may be interested, he is termed an 'agent,' and the person for whom he is to act is termed the 'principal.'" The element of continuous subjection to the will of the principal distinguishes the agent from other fiduciaries and the agency agreement from other agreements.[11] This implies that corporate officers and directors are also agents. However, in law and practice today, the fiduciary roles of corporate officers and directors are not "continuous subjection to the will of the principal (shareholders)" but more flexible as officers and directors make many decisions not approved by shareholders.

Further, the duties of officers and directors are distinct from those of other corporate employees. Corporate officers and directors owe fiduciary duties to shareholders (as defined by state case law and Delaware corporate law) while employees as agents owe duties to employers, suppliers, vendors, or customers in a wide variety of relationships involving trust.[12] This distinction has created a two-tiered definition of fiduciaries, each with different duties, and varying liabilities for breaches of those duties, and is supported by economic theory. Such differentiation in fiduciary roles does not appear to be the intention, either historically or in modern corporate law. In 1928, Judge Benjamin Cardozo, then Chief Judge of the New York Court of Appeals, eloquently recognized the significance and sanctity of fiduciary principles in *Meinhard v. Salmon:*[13]

> [J]oint adventurers, like copartners, owe to one another . . . the duty of the finest loyalty . . . and the level of conduct for fiduciaries has been kept at a higher level than that trodden by the crowd. It will not consciously be lowered by any judgment of this court.

Cardozo's opinion reflects three important principles that reinforce a long line of precedent in defining a *special level of fidelity for all fiduciaries:* 1) fiduciary matters demand a higher standard than normal marketplace transactions; 2) exceptions to the fiduciary standard undermine the duty of loyalty; and 3) neither courts nor regulators who interpret, enforce or modify the fiduciary standard should consciously weaken it.[14] Supreme Court Justice Brandeis later noted that a fiduciary "is an occupation which is pursued largely for others and not merely for oneself . . . in which the amount of financial return is not the accepted measure of success."[15]

Fiduciary Duties: The Required Triad

The Delaware Supreme Court, renowned for its corporate governance decisions and the source of the primary legal standards for the duties and liabilities of corporate officers, ruled in 1993, re-affirmed in 2006, and again in 2010, that the "triad" of duties includes the duty of loyalty, due care and good faith, where "good faith" and "full and fair disclosure" are considered to be the essential elements of, or prerequisites for proper conduct, by a director.[16] Violation of the duty of good faith could remove directors' protections from liability. The Delaware Court also ruled that corporate officers owe the same fiduciary duties as corporate directors, noting that it is not possible to discharge properly either the duty of care or the duty of loyalty without acting in good faith with respect to the interests of the companies' constituents.[17] Major legislation such as The Sarbanes-Oxley Act of 2002[18], or The Dodd–Frank Act[19] of 2010 support these legal standards *and* require that directors and their corporations return to these fundamental principles to which they were formally subject already: individual integrity and responsibility in corporate governance; and, accountable and transparent disclosure of important financial and other information on which investors and the stability of the capital markets depend.[20]

The Court has long held that the board of directors is ultimately responsible for the management of the corporation,[21] although boards often delegate major decisions to corporate officers with more expertise and information on a particular subject. Under Delaware corporate law, officers are granted titles and duties through the corporation's bylaws or the board's resolutions and employees who are not granted this power are deemed agents.[22] Additionally, Delaware law dictates that the terms "officers" or "agents" are by no means interchangeable: officers are the corporation, but an agent is an employee and does not have the equivalent status of an officer.[23] Agents' specific duties include loyalty, performance, obedience, notification, and accounting.

Again, we see this distinction between officers as managers of the corporation and agents as employees as contrary to the historical and case law definitions espoused by two leading Chief Justices. It is noteworthy that agents as employees (and fiduciaries) are not required to act in a manner that ensures that organizational activities are conducted in good faith and with care for stakeholder's interests. Also noteworthy is the omission in corporate law of the duty of obedience (to obey the law), which appeared to occupy a recognized place in corporations through 1946 but eventually was eliminated. As recent courts have made clear that corporate actors cannot consciously violate, or permit the corporation to violate, corporate and non-corporate norms, even when it may be profitable for the corporation, this duty may be resurfacing.[24] The recent *Disney* decision specifically defines the current required triad of fiduciary duties.[25]

The Duty of Loyalty

"[T]he duty of loyalty mandates that the best interests of the corporation and its shareholders takes precedence over any interest possessed by a director, officer or controlling shareholder and . . . is not limited to cases involving a financial or other cognizable fiduciary conflict of interest. It also encompasses cases where the fiduciary fails to act in good faith."[26] The duty of loyalty is often described as a obligation of directors to protect the interests of the company and its stockholders, to refrain from decisions that would injure the company or deprive the company of profit or an advantage that might properly be brought to the company for it to pursue, and to act in a manner that he or she believes is in good faith to be in the best interests of the company and its stockholders.[27] Recent case law also adds that the duty of loyalty requires boards to act *affirmatively and in good faith.*[28]

The Duty of Care

The duty of care is defined as " . . . that amount of care which ordinarily careful and prudent men would use in similar circumstances."[29] Courts review the standard of care in directors' decision-making *process,* not the substance of decisions thus limiting director liability for failure in risky decisions. A breach of the duty of care may be found when a director is grossly negligent if the substance of the board's informed decision cannot be "attributed to any rational business purpose."[30] In response to the financial crisis, legislation has specifically addressed the need for increased risk assessment in our financial institutions, requiring increased disclosure to ensure that effective reporting systems are in place and that all relevant information has been evaluated to ensure financial and economic stability. The duty of care is often perceived as a minimal standard, but addressing the impact of risk could increase the importance of this standard.

The Duty to Act in Good Faith

In the *Disney* case, the court stated that "Good faith has been said to require an "honesty of purpose," and a genuine care for the fiduciary's constituents. . ."[31] A director acts in "subjective bad faith" when his actions are "motivated by an actual intent to do harm" to the corporation, and bad faith can take different forms with varying degrees of culpability.[32] The court clearly ruled that the duty of good faith cannot be satisfied if directors act in subjective bad faith, consciously disregard their duties, actually intend to harm the corporation, or cause the corporation to knowingly violated the law.[33]

Most legal scholars disagree as to the practical importance of the duty of good faith, but proponents of managerial accountability in corporate governance look to the doctrine of good faith because the traditional duties of care and loyalty do very little to discipline boards, even if allegations of self-dealing were made (i.e., violations of duty of loyalty).[34] The Disney decision was critical for corporate governance since the court recognized that conduct that benefits the corporation must be done with proper motives in order to satisfy the duty of good faith, thus making boards and senior managers more

accountable for their decisions. Implicit in these recent cases is the assumption that new rules of "conduct" may be useful in restoring trust to a doubting public. To more fully understand these new rules of ethical conduct we must turn to the historical origins of fiduciary principles.

Origins of Fiduciary Principles
Biblical and Early History

If you would understand anything, observe its beginning and its development.

Aristotle, 4th Century BCE [35]

The historical definition of a "fiduciary" was stated in terms of "an essential code of conduct for those who have been entrusted to care for other peoples' property," carry out transactions, work for another, or aid persons who were vulnerable and dependent upon others.[36] The breadth and complexity of early trust relationships is implicit in today's corporate organizational structure and business relationships. As early as 1790 B.C., the Code of Hammurabi (a Babylonian code of laws) established rules of law governing business conduct, or fiduciary considerations, for the behavior of agents (employees) entrusted with property.[37] For example, a merchant's agent was required to keep receipts and to pay triple damages for failing to provide promised goods, although an exception was allowed if losses were due to enemy attack during a journey.[38] The insightful research of several scholars traces the religious roots of the fiduciary principle to the Old and New Testaments.[39] For example, the Lord told Moses that it is a sin not to restore that which is delivered unto a man to keep safely, and penalties must be paid for the violation,[40] (i.e., duties of loyalty and due care); the right to fair treatment in the marketplace,[41] implying a responsibility to conduct transactions in good faith; and the unjust steward who, expecting to be fired, curries favor with his master's debtors by allowing them to repay less than their full debts, illustrating the precept that one cannot serve two masters.[42] Additionally, the law on pledges obligates everyone to establish his own trustworthiness by carrying out the agreements he has made and by being sensitive to the needs of those who depend on him to meet their needs (i.e., loyalty of master to servant, employer to employee, seller to buyer, powerful to vulnerable).[43]

Fiduciary roles were likened to the roles of stewards in early religious and business history as well as in later corporate development. In this context, "Fiduciary law secularized a particular religious tradition and applied it to commercial pursuits," where the shepherd tending his flocks may be likened to a fiduciary (steward or employer) or an agent (servant or employee) tending the sheep for the owner of the flock.[44] The 'steward,' may be described as a moral agent or representative of "God," a corporate partner or stakeholder whose profits could be distributed by the steward to the poor at year's end.[45] Also, the King (as steward) was described as God's representative responsible for administering the covenant (agreements) for the people, and who must avoid preoccupation with the trappings of office while observing the law.[46] Thus, the king may be described as a model of godliness to the people by governing in a way that conforms to the requirements of the covenant.[47]

The increasing complexity in fiduciary relationships over time is equated to the increasing complexity in the relationship between man and God (as owner) in early biblical history. The relationships change as a function of the increase in the complexity of the duties demanded of the steward (manager of covenants). Similarly, the steward is the precursor to the modern professional fiduciary as well as to those corporate directors or officers who owe a duty of care to the owners (shareholders) of the corporation as well as a duty of loyalty to all stakeholders and to the larger society. Stewards, or fiduciaries, "hold offices with authority, power and privileges set by law or custom, separate from individual personalities, and such office demands moral duties in private conduct, requiring new decision-making habits and reflective capacities that transcend selfishness."[48] Similar to the descriptions of fiduciaries by Justices Cardozo and Brandeis, the description of stewards implies an inherent willingness to serve others (a moral duty), and a willingness to subordinate one's interests to that of others by acceptance of the duty to serve. Both in early law and today, the fiduciary, or steward, is evaluated and compensated for his performance and understands that failure to fulfill his duties will result in penalties. While today's corporations seldom attribute morality to a deity in fiduciary law, acceptance of fiduciary duties does require selflessness and a willingness to subordinate the fiduciary's interests to that of another. Aristotle, who lived from 384 B.C. to 322 B.C., influenced the development of fiduciary principles, recognizing that in economics and business, people must be bound by high obligations of loyalty, honesty and fairness, and that when such obligations aren't required or followed, society suffers.[49]

Fiduciaries in Ancient Law

Modern fiduciary law is traceable to developments in Ancient Roman law and early English law. Ancient Roman law defined fiduciary relationships as both moral and legal relationships of trust. For centuries until the end of the 18th Century, Roman law refined and formalized fiduciary law, recognizing various "trust" (*fiducia*) contracts in which a person held property in safekeeping or otherwise acted on another's behalf (the core duties of loyalty and due care), and acted in good "faith" (*fides*) (core duties of honesty, full disclosure and applied diligence). Failure to uphold such trust could result in monetary penalties as well as a formal "infamy" (*infamia*), in which one lost rights to hold public office or to be a witness in a legal case.[50] These fiduciary relationships in early Roman law were later incorporated into British courts of equity and then into Anglo-American law, providing standards for modern corporate law.[51]

Early English law established the role of steward or agent with the granting of the Magna Carta, an English legal charter issued in 1215 which allowed the King to grant charters (companies) yet retain sovereignty (ownership) in the charter while recognizing the recipient's limited rights.[52] The King served as steward, with fiduciary rights (ownership) in the management of his property but was required to place the interests of his subjects (inferior rights) above his own—a fiduciary relationship. Increasing population growth caused the King to transfer his role as steward to town leaders, creating an early form of agency (master to servant). Scholars describe the king's stewardship duties as similar to the legal or fiduciary duties ascribed primarily to boards of directors and senior officers.[53] Town leaders were similar to "agents" or employees who owed duties to their "stewards" or employers (managers). The continued development of Charter companies and later private companies, during the era of industrialization and specialization in business of the 1700–1800s, formalized the role of fiduciaries and their specific duties.

Early common law separated management from ownership (investors), creating the office of "manager" to protect the interests of investors and to prevent corporate self-dealing.[54] Subsequently, fiduciary duties were attached to such office, and stewardship duties were borrowed from early law and applied to positions of responsibility to promote financial goals. Thus, although a "fiduciary" is a term described by legal statute, case law or professional codes of conduct, this term also describes ethical obligations and duties in a wide variety of business and personal activities and encompasses a "legal or moral recognition of trust, reliance, or dependence and of responsibility often ignored."[55]

A Modest Proposal: New Rules of Fiduciary Conduct

Legal standards for management behavior can be traced to "deeply rooted moral standards" that shaped the "fiduciary principle, a principle of natural law incorporated into the Anglo-American legal tradition underlying the duties of good faith, loyalty and care that apply to corporate directors and officers."[56] Scholars examined early fiduciary history as a potential solution to understanding corporate misconduct, suggesting that revisiting those early fiduciary principles might answer the questions: To what standards should managers be held?; and What are the historical and conceptual bases for these standards?[57] Alternatively, if one assumes that fiduciaries are responsible to the company's shareholders as well as to a wider set of constituents, one might ask questions such as: In whose interests does the company presently function?; and, In whose interests should it function in the future?[58] The latter set of questions not only asks who is served by the company, but also suggests that stakeholders bear some general rights as citizens, and should be protected against an abuse of power or violation that causes injury, as citizens.

If the role of a fiduciary is ascribed only to corporate boards and officers or to licensed professionals, corporate misconduct at other levels may go undetected. Despite this, corporate management argues that directors and officers are responsible only to shareholders, and that corporate management cannot serve two masters, i.e., multiple groups of stakeholders. To the contrary, history has demonstrated that fiduciary duties have been and can be the responsibility of all corporate members, and these duties may be extended to all stakeholders and the larger society. Research supports the theory that the corporation should have one set of duties for multiple stakeholders, an argument made by managers in the 1990s that managers had the skills and independence to mediate fairly among the firm's stakeholders, and could assemble innovative teams capable of expanding wealth and economic opportunity.[59] Managers sustained this claim well into the 1990s, both within their firms and within their major business associations but by 1997 pressure from the global commodity and national financial markets persuaded managers to revise their stakeholder standard. The perception is that managers moved from a focus on a single duty of loyalty to shareholders, to a narrower focus on making their principals (shareholders) and themselves rich, while disassociating themselves from the ideal of widening economic opportunity and improving living standards for the many.[60] The Clarkson Principles, a set of principles for stakeholder management, are considered to be a critical academic effort to revive the idea that managers should be obligated to expand material opportunities for the many through economic growth.[61] Additionally, compliance with fiduciary duties can reduce the principal's costs of monitoring and disciplining agents and lessens the need for government regulation.[62]

Today, although most major corporations support the idea of corporate social responsibility (CSR), and believe that CSR and profit maximization work together, they continue to support the Freidman view that "The social responsibility of business is to increase its profits."[63] A top executive of a major oil company illustrates this view in the comment that "a socially responsible way or working is not . . . a distraction from our core business. Nor does it in any way conflict with our promise and our duty to deliver value to our shareholders."[64]

We propose that adherence to a *new understanding and rule* of fiduciary principles goes hand in hand with CSR and profit maximization and is perhaps the missing link in today's corporate governance. The essential definition of a fiduciary does not change—a fiduciary is a person who has a duty to act primarily for the benefit of another. However, the role of the fiduciary should extend to all corporate members, and the duties of the fiduciary should not differ regardless of the specific function or distinction in roles. The primary focus of all corporate members continues to be to the shareholders (owners of the corporation), but duties toward other stakeholders should be consistent with those duties to shareholders. Any differentiation lowers the high standard of fidelity required of fiduciaries. Thus, the duties of loyalty, good faith, due care and obedience to the law should be incorporated fully into all fiduciary relationships, regardless of role or function within the corporation.

governance "without proper attention to ethical obligations will likely prove ineffectual."[66] Schwartz et al. found that board and officer leadership by example and action are roles central to the overall ethical and governance environment of their firms, a leadership role that is reinforced by board members' legal responsibilities to provide oversight of the financial performance of their firms—based on the assumption that ethical corporate leadership results in the best long-term interests of the firm.

Thus, Schwartz et al.'s study of corporate boards of directors demonstrated that boards have a professional duty expressed as a fiduciary duty to make ethics based decisions. We contend that ethics and morals in line with fiduciary principles *must* permeate the entire corporate culture, if corporate governance reform is to succeed. A return to those central values inherent in ethical and fiduciary duties extended to the greater community as well as to shareholders may provide more socially responsible guidelines for corporations in this period of stakeholder demand for increased government regulation. Defining and providing examples of fiduciary values of honesty, loyalty, integrity responsibility, fairness and citizenship can provide guidance for corporate fiduciary relationships with all stakeholders, and provide a more efficient voluntary control mechanism. Thus, we contend that consistent fiduciary principles should be implemented throughout the firm, regardless of the corporate member's function or role.[67] This view is consistent with Friedman's view, that a corporate executive is an employee of the owners of the business, owes responsibility to his employers to conduct the business in accordance with their desires, which generally will be to make as much money as possible while conforming to the basic rules of society, embodied both in law and ethical custom.[68]

Our review of the historical and religious origins of fiduciary relationships demonstrates that the concept of fiduciary was intended to be both a societal and a legal principle, and this is consistent with Friedman's view of obeying the law and social custom. The leaders of organizations, as stewards, were responsible to the whole organization, and to society, not just to themselves or shareholders. Perhaps a revitalization of the stewardship principle is part of the new perspective required to create sustainable competitive advantage in today's economy. We believe that there is room for stakeholder-focused management that does no harm to shareholder interests while also benefiting a larger constituency, *and* that fiduciary duties require the exercise of care, loyalty, obedience and good faith with regard to shareholders as well as to all stakeholders and the larger community.[69]

Concluding Thoughts

"Many of the most shocking examples of corporate misbehaviors involve conduct that violates existing law."[65] This result occurs when most cost-benefit analysis weighs the potential harm and subsequent penalties against the potential profits, resulting in an ethical question often ignored because of the focus on maximizing shareholder profitability. Therefore, reform initiatives for boards of directors and corporate

References

1. See David Callahan, *The Cheating Culture: Why More Americans are Doing Wrong to Get Ahead* (Florida: Harcourt, Inc., 2004), 12.
2. See LaRue Tone Hosmer, *The Ethics of Management, 6th Ed.* (New York: McGraw-Hill, 2008).
3. Peter C. Kostant, *Meaningful Good Faith: Managerial Motives and the Duty to Obey the Law,* 55 N.Y.L.S.L. Rev., 421 (2010).

4. Alan R. Palmiter, *Duty of Obedience: The Forgotten Duty,* 55 N.Y.L.S.L. Rev., 457 (2010).

5. Restatement (Third) of Agency, 3rd Ed. §1(1). (2006), Restatement Third of Agency is a set of principles issues by the American Law Institute, frequently cited by judges as well as attorneys and scholars in making legal arguments.

6. Nancy Kubasek et al., *Dynamic Business Law* (New York: McGraw-Hill/Irwin, 2009), 856,857.

7. Tamar Frankel, *Fiduciary Law,* 71 Cal. L. Rev. 795, 797–802 (1983).

8. See Tamar Frankel, *Fiduciary Law,* 71 Cal. L. Rev., 801–802.

9. See Tamar Frankel, *Fiduciary Law,* 71 Cal. L. Rev., 801–802.

10. Deborah A. DeMott, "The First Restatement of Agency: What Was the Agenda?," 32 *S. Ill. U.L.J.,* (2007). Restatement (Second) of Agency, 1958, the American Law Institute, is now out of print and has been completely superseded and replaced by Restatement of the Law Third, Agency, 2006. However, some courts will continue to cite to The Restatement of the Law Second, Agency.

11. Deborah A. DeMott, "The First Restatement of Agency: What Was the Agenda?," 31.

12. Kenneth M. Rosen, *Meador Lecture Series 2005–2006: Fiduciaries,* 58 Ala. L. Rev., 1041 (2007).

13. Kenneth M. Rosen, *Meador Lecture Series 2005–2006: Fiduciaries,* citing *Meinhard v. Salmon,* 164 N.E. 545 (N.Y. 1928).

14. Kenneth M. Rosen, *Meador Lecture Series 2005–2006: Fiduciaries,* 1041.

15. See Kenneth M. Rosen, *"Meador Lecture Series 2005–2006: Fiduciaries."*

16. *See In re* Walt Disney Co. Deriv. Litig., 907 A.2d 693, 753–57 (Del. Ch. 2005) (identifying possible duty of good faith), *aff'd,* 906 A.2d 693 (Del. 2006) (affirming the decision of the Chancellor).

17. Michael Follett, "Note: *Gantler V. Stephens:* Big Epiphany or Big Failure? A look at the current state of officers' fiduciary duties and advice for potential protection," *35 Del. J. Corp. L.,* 563 (2010).

18. Sarbanes-Oxley Act of 2002, PL 107–204, 116 Stat 745. Sarbanes-Oxley requires corporate officers to be responsible for earnings reports, prohibits accounting firms from acting as consultants to accounting clients (a conflict of interest) and increases penalties for fraud.

19. The Dodd-Frank Wall Street Reform and Consumer Protection Act, Pub.L. 111–203, H.R. 4173, (2010).

20. Kilpatrick Stockton LLP, *Directors Fiduciary Duties After Sarbanes-Oxley* (Atlanta: Kilpatrick Stockton LLP), 2003.

21. Delaware General Corporation Law section 141(a) provides that "[t]he business and affairs of every corporation organized under this chapter shall be managed by or under the direction of a board of directors, except as may be otherwise provided in this chapter or in its certificate of incorporation." DEL. CODE ANN. Tit. 8, § 141(a)(2006).

22. See Michael Follett, note 57.

23. Michael Follett, note 57.

24. Alan R. Palmiter, citing *Stone v. Ritter,* 911 A.2d 362, 364–65 (Del. 2006), *Graham V. Allis-Chalmers Mfg. Co.,* 188 A.2d 125, 130 (Del. 1963), and *Caremark Int'l Inc. Deriv. Litig.,* 698 A.2d 959, 971 (Del. Ch. 1996), where directors breached the duty of care for 'sustained or systematic failure' to assure existence of reporting systems that identify illegal corporate conduct, e.g., medical referral kickbacks, 459.

25. *In re* Walt Disney Co. Deriv. Litig., 907 A.2d 693, 753 (Del. Ch. 2005), aff'd. 906 A.2d 27 (Del. 2006).

26. Thomas A. Uebler, "Shareholder Police Power: Shareholders' Ability to Hold Directors Accountable for Intentional Violations of Law," 33 Del. J. Corp. L., 199 (2008).

27. Thomas A. Uebler, "Shareholder Police Power: Shareholders' Ability to Hold Directors Accountable for Intentional Violations of Law," 201.

28. See Thomas A. Uebler.

29. *In re* Walt Disney Co. Deriv. Litig., 907 A.2d 693, 753–57 (Del. Ch. 2005), *aff'd,* 906 A.2d 693 (Del. 2006) .

30. *In re* Walt Disney Co. Deriv. Litig., 907 A.2d 693, 753 (Del. Ch. 2005), aff'd. 906 A.2d 27 (Del. 2006)), quoting *Sinclair Oil Corp. v. Levien,* 280 A.2d 717, 720 (Del. 1971), and *Smith v. Van Gorkom,* 488 A.2d 858, 873 (Del. 1985),

31. *In re* Walt Disney.

32. *In re* Walt Disney, at 55.

33. Peter C. Kostant , *"Meaningful Good Faith: Managerial Motives and the Duty to Obey the Law,"* 424,426.

34. See Peter C. Kostant , 426–427.

35. Amanda H. Podany, 'Why Study History? A View from the Past," Presented at The History Summit I, California State University Dominguez Hills, May 29, 2008.

36. See Kenneth Silber, "Fiduciary Matters," www.AdvisorOne .com/article/fiduciarymatters, June 28, 2011.

37. Joseph F. Johnston, Jr., "Natural Law and the Fiduciary Duties of Managers," *Journal of Markets & Morality* (2005), 8:27–51.

38. Kenneth Silber, "Fiduciary Matters."

39. See Brian P. Schaefer, "Shareholders Social Responsibility," *Journal of Business Ethics* (2008), 81:297–312; and Stephen B. Young, "Fiduciary Duties as a Helpful Guide to Ethical Decision-Making in Business, *Journal of Business Ethics* (2007), 74:1–15.

40. John H. Walton, Deuteronomy: An Exposition of the Spirit of the Law, *Grace Theological Journal* 8, 2(1987), 213–25, quoting Leviticus 6:2–5.

41. See John H. Walton, quoting Deuteronomy 25:13–16.

42. John H. Walton notes that the precept that one cannot serve two masters in Luke 16:1–13 was later cited by scholar Austin Scott in an influential 1949 paper "The Fiduciary Principle," which describes boards' and officers' responsibility to shareholders and not to other constituents.

43. John H. Walton, "Deuteronomy: An Exposition of the Spirit of the Law," quoting Deuteronomy 24:14–15.

44. See Stephen B. Young, "Fiduciary Duties as a Helpful Guide to Ethical Decision-Making in Business."

45. Sarah Key, "Toward a New Theory of the Firm: A Critique of Stakeholder 'Theory'," *Management Decision* (1999), 37:317–328.

46. John H. Walton, quoting Deuteronomy 17:14–20, 216.

47. Stephen B. Young details the link between fiduciary and ethical duties in the four covenants, or agreements, between God and man in the Old Testament that establishes and expands man's duties of care. These covenants allow stewards to impose ethical duties on those who obey them (i.e., agents or employees) and reflect the core of modern agency and fiduciary relationships: 1) The first covenant establishes Noah as steward of God's will to care for creation, and if Noah and his descendents take good care of creation it would not be destroyed (duty of care for the owner's property); 2) The second covenant requires Abraham to accept the duty to behave according to a code of holy behavior in return for protection (protection from liability for accepting the responsibilities of duty of loyalty and care); 3) The third covenant requires the children of Israel to behave morally with religious devotion in return for protection of all of society (extending fiduciary duties of loyalty and care from an individual to society, i.e., to all stakeholders); The fourth covenant expanded these promises–if the conduct of all mankind is ethical and moral and not based on material temptations, Jesus will protect them on earth and grant them entry into heaven (fiduciary duties are deeply rooted in moral principles).

48. See Stephen B. Young and Joseph F. Johnston, Jr.

49. John H. Walton, "Deuteronomy: An Exposition of the Spirit of the Law,"

50. See Kenneth Silber, "Fiduciary Matters."

51. See Kenneth M. Rosen, *Meador Lecture Series 2005–2006: Fiduciaries.*

52. See Stephen B. Young, "Fiduciary Duties as a Helpful Guide to Ethical Decision-Making in Business."

53. See Kenneth M. Rosen, "Meador Lecture Series 2005–2006: Fiduciaries."

54. Richard Marens and Andrew Wicks, "Getting Real: Stakeholder Theory, Managerial Practice, and the General Irrelevance of Fiduciary Duties Owed to Shareholders," *Business Ethics Quarterly* (1999), 273–293.

55. Sarah W. Holtman, "Fiduciary Relationships," in The Encyclopedia of Ethics, 2nd Ed, eds. Lawrence C. Becker and Charlotte B. Becker (NY: Routledge, 2001), 545–49.

56. See Joseph F. Johnston, Jr., "Natural Law and the Fiduciary Duties of Business Managers."

57. See Joseph F. Johnston, Jr. "Natural Law and the Fiduciary Duties of Business Managers."

58. Sheldon Leader, "Participation and Property Rights," *Journal of Business Ethics* 21:97–109, (1999), 98–99.

59. Allan Kaufman, "Managers' Double Fiduciary Duty," *Business Ethics Quarterly* 12:189–214 (2002), 189.

60. Allan Kaufman, "Managers' Double Fiduciary Duty," 190.

61. Allan Kaufman, "Managers' Double Fiduciary Duty," 190–193.

62. Kaufman, "Managers' Double Fiduciary Duty."

63. See Peter C. Kolstad, 137–138, citing Milton Friedman, "The Social Responsibility of Business is to Increase Its Profits," The New York Times Magazine (New York: 1970).

64. See Allan Kaufman, 192.

65. See David Callahan, "The Cheating Culture: Why More Americans are Doing Wrong to Get Ahead."

66. Mark S. Schwartz et al., Tone at the Top: An Ethics Code for Directors?," *Journal of Business Ethics* (2005), 58:79–100.

67. R. Edward Freeman, in "The Politics of Stakeholder Theory: Some Future Directors," *Business Ethics Quarterly* (1994) 4:409–421, suggested that "multi-fiduciary stakeholder analysis is simply incompatible with widely-held moral convictions about the special fiduciary obligations owed by management to stockholders. At the center of the objections is the belief that the obligations of agents to principals are stronger or different in kind from those of agents to third parties." This view is not supported by historical development of the fiduciary principle, and may be perceived more as a function of corporate management choosing those functions that support personal, not fiduciary, goals.

68. See Milton Friedman, 51.

69. Bradley R. Agle and Ronald K. Mitchell, "Introduction: Recent Research and New Questions," in Agle et al., "Dialogue: Toward Superior Stakeholder Theory," *Business Ethics Quarterly* (2008), 18:153–190.

Critical Thinking

1. What is a fiduciary?

2. What are the duties of a fiduciary?

3. Pick one of the duties of a fiduciary identified in the article and write a statement incorporating that duty into a code of ethics.

4. Explain the new rules of fiduciary conduct proposed in the article.

5. What are arguments in support as well as against use of the proposed new rules?

United Technologies' $1 Billion Employee College Plan

Looking for a corporate feel-good story? UTC's Employee Scholar Program just hit a major milestone.

ALLAN SLOAN AND STANLEY BING

Sometimes big companies do good things for their employees during bad times. And keep on doing it, quietly, without making a fuss. That's the thought that crossed my mind when I heard that United Technologies Corp., a hard-nosed industrial conglomerate that makes things like aircraft engines and elevators and helicopters and is No. 48 on our new Fortune 500 list, had hit an unusual milestone: spending $1 billion on a program to send its employees to college.

The most interesting part? UTC (UTX) is preparing its employees not just for their UTC future, but for the next job they may take with another employer, or even for their post-employment lives. What's this program all about? More in a bit, but first a little background.

I discovered UTC's Employee Scholar Program 16 years ago while doing research on a Newsweek cover story called "Corporate Killers," about the nasty way companies were firing employees en masse during hard times as Wall Street stood on the sidelines cheering. (Sound familiar?) Yes, I knew (and wrote) that firings are a fact of economic life; sometimes you have to sacrifice a part to save the whole. But I was looking for a big company that was a little different, that recognized that its employees were human beings, something more than just bodies that could be sacrificed to Mammon, the god of Wall Street, to gain a higher stock price.

So I was thrilled to discover that United Technologies, which had cut 33,000 jobs in the previous five years, had just started an ultra-generous Employee Scholar Program. The company would pay for any college or graduate school degree any employee wanted to pursue, regardless of whether it had any connection to a UTC job. The company not only paid for tuition, books, and fees but would also give employees $5,000 worth of stock when they got a degree.

George David, then the company's chief executive, explained that the point was for employees to be able to upgrade their skills either to advance within UTC or to be able to find another job if UTC had to fire them to cut costs. "We're not soft-hearted," said David, whose face turned red when I suggested he sympathized with downsized workers. "It's in our interest to have an educated workforce."

I wrote the story, including one paragraph about the program that got David lauded as a statesman. I never had occasion to talk to him again. Years went by. Memory faded, except for the framed copy of the cover, featuring four mug shot–like photos of job-cutting CEOs, which hangs on my office wall. Then my *Fortune* editor—who was my *Newsweek* editor and my partner in conceiving "Corporate Killers"—came back recently from a lunch with UTC people who told him about the $1 billion milestone.

We realized we had something very rare: a chance for me, a congenital corporate critic, to praise a Fortune 500 company for acting well during hard times. (Alas, I couldn't get David, who left United Technologies in 2008, to talk to me. Try to be nice—see what happens?)

I'm frankly amazed that this program, which has helped UTC employees get 32,000 degrees (some 75 percent of them in the United States) and currently has 10,000 people enrolled, still exists. "This program is a big differentiator for us," says Tom Bowler Jr., head of UTC's human resources department.

The National Association of Independent Colleges and Universities gave the company its advocacy award earlier this year, the first time the award has gone to a company rather than a person. "It's the open-ended nature of the program that's so unusual," said association president David Warren.

Alas, even this benefit isn't what it once was. The company trimmed it as of 2010 to get the cost down to $50 million a year from $60 million-plus. It eliminated the stock bonus for degree completion, capped the benefit at $40,000 ($60,000 for a graduate degree), and required employees to have a year of service before joining. But it's still a great program. So take a bow, UTC. You've earned it.

Critical Thinking

1. Does a company have an obligation to do good during difficult economic times? Develop pro and con answers and be prepared to defend your answers during class discussion.

2. What are advantages and disadvantages to a business firm of instituting an Employee Scholar Program?

3. Should an employee be obligated ethically to refund the company for monies paid to receive a degree if the employee leaves the company within one year of receiving the degree? Also consider within three years, within five years, within ten years of receiving a degree. Explain why and/or why not a repayment should be made upon leaving the company.

A Time for Ethical Self-Assessment

Peter Drucker's literature on business scruples and the Ethics of Prudence is newly timely, and not just because of the holidays.

RICK WARTZMAN

This may be the season of giving, but it sure feels like everybody is suddenly on the take.

Siemens (SI), the German engineering giant, agreed this month to pay a record $1.6 billion to U.S. and European authorities to settle charges that it routinely used bribes and kickbacks to secure public works contracts across the globe. Prominent New York attorney Marc Dreier—called by one U.S. prosecutor a "Houdini of impersonation and false documents"—has been accused by the feds of defrauding hedge funds and other investors out of $380 million.

And then, of course, there's financier Bernard L. Madoff, who is said to have confessed to a Ponzi scheme of truly epic proportions: a swindle of $50 billion, an amount roughly equal to the GPD of Luxembourg.

All told, it begs the question that Peter Drucker first raised in a provocative 1981 essay in the journal *The Public Interest* and that later became the title of a chapter in his book *The Ecological Vision*: "Can there be 'business ethics'?"

Drucker didn't pose this to suggest that business was inherently incapable of demonstrating ethical behavior. Nor was he positing that the workplace should somehow be exempt from moral concerns. Rather, his worry was that to speak of "business ethics" as a distinct concept was to twist it into something that "is not compatible with what ethics always was supposed to be."

What Drucker feared, specifically, was that executives could say they were meeting their social responsibilities as business leaders—protecting jobs and generating wealth—while engaging in practices that were plainly abhorrent. "Ethics for them," Drucker wrote, "is a cost-benefit calculation . . . and that means that the rulers are exempt from the demands of ethics, if only their behavior can be argued to confer benefits on other people."

It's hard to imagine that a Madoff or a Dreier would even attempt to get away with such tortured logic: an ends-justify-the-means attitude that Drucker labeled "casuistry." But we all know managers who've tried to rationalize an unscrupulous act by claiming that it served some greater good.

The Mirror Test

In his book *Resisting Corporate Corruption*, Stephen Arbogast notes that when Enron higher-ups sought an exemption from the company's ethics policy so that they could move forward with certain dubious financial dealings, the arrangement was made to "seem a sacrifice for the benefit of Enron." Reinhard Siekaczek, a former Siemens executive, told *The New York Times* (NYT) that the company's showering of foreign officials with bribes "was about keeping the business unit alive and not jeopardizing thousands of jobs overnight."

For Drucker, the best way for a business—indeed, for any organization—to create an ethical environment is for its people to partake in what he came to call in a 1999 article "the mirror test." In his 1981 piece, Drucker had a fancier name for this idea: He termed it "The Ethics of Prudence." But either way, it boils down to the same thing: When you look in the mirror in the morning, what kind of person do you want to see?

The Ethics of Prudence, Drucker wrote, "does not spell out what 'right' behavior is." It assumes, instead, "that what is wrong behavior is clear enough—and if there is any doubt, it is "questionable" and to be avoided." Drucker added that "by following prudence, everyone regardless of status becomes a leader" and remains so by "avoiding any act which would make one the kind of person one does not want to be, does not respect."

Drucker went on: "If you don't want to see a pimp when you look in the shaving mirror in the morning, don't hire call girls the night before to entertain congressmen, customers, or salesmen. On any other basis, hiring call girls may be condemned as vulgar and tasteless, and may be shunned as something fastidious people do not do. It may be frowned upon as uncouth. It may even be illegal. But only in prudence is it ethically relevant. This is what Kierkegaard, the sternest moralist of the 19th century, meant when he said that aesthetics is the true ethics."

Time to Reflect

Drucker cautioned that the Ethics of Prudence "can easily degenerate" into hollow appearances and "the hypocrisy of public relations." Yet despite this danger, Drucker believed that "the Ethics of Prudence is surely appropriate to a society of organizations" in which "an extraordinarily large number of people are in positions of high visibility, if only within one organization. They enjoy this visibility not, like the Christian Prince, by virtue of birth, nor by virtue of wealth—that is, not because they are personages. They are functionaries and important only through their responsibility to take right action. But this is exactly what the Ethics of Prudence is all about."

Now is the time of year when many of us find ourselves sitting in church or in synagogue, or, if we're not religious, simply taking stock of who we are and where we want to be as the calendar turns. But what's even more critical is that we continue this sort of honest self-assessment when we return to our jobs in early 2009.

"I have learned more theology as a practicing management consultant than when I taught religion," Drucker once said. This, he explained, is because "management always deals with the nature of Man and (as all of us with any practical experience have learned), with Good and Evil as well."

So take the mirror test now—and then keep taking it well after the Christmas ornaments have been packed away and the Hanukkah candles have burned down to the nub. In the meantime, happy holidays to all.

Critical Thinking

1. Explain the meaning of Drucker's question "can there be business ethics?"
2. Defend the position that there can be business ethics.
3. What is the mirror test?
4. What is the ethics of prudence?
5. What is meant by "aesthetics is the true ethics"?

RICK WARTZMAN is the director of the Drucker Institute at Claremont Graduate University.

Test-Your-Knowledge Form

We encourage you to photocopy and use this page as a tool to assess how the articles in *Annual Editions* expand on the information in your textbook. By reflecting on the articles you will gain enhanced text information. You can also access this useful form on a product's book support website at www.mhhe.com/cls

NAME: DATE:

_____

TITLE AND NUMBER OF ARTICLE:

_____

BRIEFLY STATE THE MAIN IDEA OF THIS ARTICLE:

_____

LIST THREE IMPORTANT FACTS THAT THE AUTHOR USES TO SUPPORT THE MAIN IDEA:

_____

WHAT INFORMATION OR IDEAS DISCUSSED IN THIS ARTICLE ARE ALSO DISCUSSED IN YOUR TEXTBOOK OR OTHER READINGS THAT YOU HAVE DONE? LIST THE TEXTBOOK CHAPTERS AND PAGE NUMBERS:

_____

LIST ANY EXAMPLES OF BIAS OR FAULTY REASONING THAT YOU FOUND IN THE ARTICLE:

_____

LIST ANY NEW TERMS/CONCEPTS THAT WERE DISCUSSED IN THE ARTICLE, AND WRITE A SHORT DEFINITION:

NOTES

NOTES

NOTES

NOTES

NOTES